Geor

(153

James

(1544)

Alexander

(1560)

Alexander

(1586)

Alexander, The Old Laird

(1594)

James of Birkenbog

(1615)

Alexander, The Grand Falconer

(1666)

Sir Alexander, The Main Covenanter
First Baronet of Birkenbog

(1686)

Sir James, Second Baronet

(1735)

Sir Robert, Third Baronet

(1715–1797)

Sir George, Fourth Baronet

(1750–1831)

Sir Robert, Fifth Baronet

(1784–1855)

Sir George Samuel, Sixth Baronet

(1824–1872)

Sir Robert John, Seventh Baronet

(1850–1895)

Sir George William, Eighth Baronet

(1886–1964)

Sir Robert Alexander, Ninth Baronet

(1895–1972)

Sir Ian George, Tenth Baronet

(1925–   )

Mr. Jim

The Biography of James Smither Abercrombie

Gulf Publishing Company
Book Division
Houston, London, Paris, Tokyo

Mr. Jim

The Biography of James Smither Abercrombie

Patrick J. Nicholson

To the memory of Mr. Jim and Miss Lillie

Mr. Jim

The Biography of James Smither Abercrombie

Copyright © 1983 by Patrick J. Nicholson. All rights reserved. Printed in the United States of America. This book, or parts thereof, may not be reproduced in any form without permission of the publisher.

Library of Congress Cataloging in Publication Data

Nicholson, Patrick James, 1921–
Mr. Jim: the biography of James Smither Abercrombie.

Includes index.
1. Abercrombie, James Smither.
2. Abercrombie family.
3. Businessmen—United States—Biography.
4. Oil field equipment and supplies industry—United States—History.
I. Title.
HD9565.N52 1983 338.7'68176 [B] 83-12608
ISBN 0-87201-404-5

And what he greatly thought, he nobly dared
Homer: *Odyssey II*

Great and good are so seldom the same man
Thomas Fuller

Acknowledgments

My grateful acknowledgment is due:

To my beloved wife Barbara, and son Michael, both for their patience and understanding during the many months of research and writing which went into this book, and for the valuable assistance they both provided in research—Barbara in London and environs, Michael at the Clayton Genealogical Library.

To my editor, Scott Becken of Gulf Publishing, and his colleague Terry Moore, the highly talented artist and designer for *Mr. Jim*.

To Josephine Abercrombie and to Freda Bowen of the Abercrombie organization, for their invaluable help at every stage from preliminary research to final editing.

To Lord Trend, chairman of the board of the British Museum and its superb library, for the many courtesies of the library staff.

To Lord Perry, founder of the Open University, for guiding me to records in Aberdeen and Edinburgh.

To Robert Ahola, who conducted and transcribed a series of interviews with friends and close associates of James S. Abercrombie.

To Charles Dwyer and Eloise Powell of Sam Houston State University, for research material and photographs of old Huntsville.

To Jean Bradley Anderson, genealogist and expert on Orange County, North Carolina for very helpful research on Robert Abercromby, Sr. and his children and the Piedmont of the eighteenth century.

To the staff of the Clayton Library, that excellent repository of genealogical information.

To Sir Ian George, tenth baronet Abercromby, who provided extremely useful materials and photographs from family records.

And to the many, many other persons who made information available, granted interviews or loaned photographs, correspondence, or other material.

Memorial Day
1 9 8 3

Patrick J. Nicholson
Houston, Texas

Contents

Chapter 1

1457–1741

Scotland

Robert Abercromby is born in a year he and Scotland will remember . . . Malcolm III awards valor after the battle of Hastings . . . The terrible murder of the Old Laird on the moor . . . Charles I is taught to hawk by his future Grand Falconer and creates the baronets Abercromby . . . James Abercromby, S.J., carries out a mission for Pope Paul IV . . . Witches are burned on Castle Hill . . . Lightning strikes warring sisters . . . The Wall of the Skulls . . . Sir Alexander Abercromby, the Main Covenanter, must oppose his king on a matter of principle . . . Birkenbog is laid waste by Montrose . . . Opportunity beckons in the New World, and Robert Abercromby establishes an American branch of the clan in North Carolina

Robert Abercromby would never find it difficult, throughout a long, venturesome, and meaningful life, to remember the year of his birth.

He was born in 1715, the year of The Fifteen—the first of two emotionally-charged, ill-starred rebellions that would greatly diminish the entrenched power of the clans, strike down the Jacobite cause, and rechannel the course of Scottish history forever. Three centuries will soon have passed since The Fifteen, but the revolt and its leaders, with the quixotic appeal that Bonnie Prince Charlie typified even more strongly a generation later in the rebellion of 1745, are still fresh in the memory of Scots today.[1]

Robert bore a proud name, favorably known throughout Aberdeenshire and the surrounding counties of Fife, Clackmannan, Banff and Perth. The name had originally been Abircrumbyn, from the Gaelic *crom adhuinn,* "the crook (or bend) of the stream." Aberdeen itself has a similar etymology, meaning simply, "(at) the bend of the river Dee."

Especially in Aberdeenshire, with its uniquely-accented speech patterns and ancient traditions of loyalty to king and church, lively commerce and emphasis upon higher education; in Fife; and in tiny

Clackmannan; Abercrombys had been leaders for generations as the pivotal eighteenth century began to unfold more rapidly. Charles I had raised Sir Alexander Abercromby to the baronetage (as first baronet of Birkenbog) on February 20,1636, a distinction that has now been passed on within the Abercromby family for almost three hundred and fifty years.[2]

Members of the family, traditionally blessed with numerous progeny, became widely scattered between principal holdings such as Pitmedden, Birkenbog, Tullibody and Forglen, and between other properties (the seats of cadet families) at Glassaugh, Fetterneir, Banff, Dundee and nearby; but the Abercrombys were distinctly of northeast Scotland—Lowlanders of the separate coastal plain that combines urban centers such as Aberdeen and Dundee with good, arable land well-suited to wheat and barley, plus the dry cold in winter and early spring that makes these hardy crops prosper.

The first Abercrombys came to Scotland in the reign of Malcolm III (called Canmore), an able, armipotent monarch known for having fulfilled a solemn oath to kill the regicide Macbeth, murderer of his father, King Duncan, in the real-life version of Shakespeare's timeless historical drama.

Originally from Ireland, the Abercrombys emigrated north after the battle of Hastings. They came under the protection of Malcolm III, who gave refuge to many battle-seasoned Anglo-Saxons fleeing the victorious Normans, and then led them back southward on frequent raids into the border lands. On one of these forays, in 1093, Malcolm was killed by the English William II's pikemen.[3] Before his death, however, King Malcolm had granted the Abercrombys lands on the east coast of Fife, in the last decade of the eleventh century. From this harsh yet promising holding along the North Sea, the family began to put down deep, lasting and widely dispersed roots, almost nine hundred years ago.

Members of the clan Abercromby were at the royal Scottish court from an early age. John de Abercrombie was authorized to use the designation "Cocus" (or "Coquess"), meaning master of the royal household, in 1205. He was apparently a founder of the town of Abercrombie, in the ancient parish of St. Andrews, in the first decades of the thirteenth century. (Even in these times, there were variant spellings of Abercromby, most often as Abercrombie, which became the more usual form in the late seventeenth and the eighteenth centuries.) Cavendish Douglas Abercromby, who wrote the authoritative *Family of Abercromby* (published in 1927 in Aberdeen, but long out of print and very difficult to find), points out that the final "y" and final "ie" have always been interchangeable in Scotland, as Ogilvy/Ogilvie or Leslie/Lesly. His view is that Abercromby or Abercrombie (or simply Cromby, as sometimes misspelled by a hurrying clerk or registrar), they are "all of one ilk (or family)."

The line can be traced directly from Humphrey de Abercromby, of Pettmathen in the Oyne parish of Aberdeenshire. He was given the charter (deed) of Harthill by Robert the Bruce in 1315, *pro homagio et servitio suo* at the climactic battle of Bannockburn the preceding year.[3] The original charter was confirmed to another Humphrey de Abercromby (a great-grandson) on June 4, 1457, by James II of Scotland. This grant is probably the origin of Pitmedden (a variant spelling of both Pettmathen and Pitmachie), which became the principal holding of the clan Abercromby until it was lost in the tumult surrounding almost incessant struggle and strife.

In 1593, the family moved its seat to Birkenbog, a secondary property first acquired from the bishop of Aberdeen by deed of April 11, 1362. Near a fine old forest adjoining the village of Cullen, Birkenbog may have derived its unusual name from the Gaelic *beorc wudu,* or birch wood, which is rendered *birket* in Anglo-Saxon. In the parish of Fordyce, in the northernmost reaches of Aberdeenshire, Birkenbog was a splendid property. It had an imposing tower, fortalice (a small, thickly-walled fortification for withstanding a siege until reinforcements could arrive) and a large manor house. The surrounding land lacked the fertility of acreage to the south, but was reasonably suitable for raising oats and well adapted to running sheep.

The Abercrombys were hardly strangers in the Birkenbog neighborhood. Three miles away, at the little church of Fordyce, the armed knight on their family tomb was a sculpture of Sir James, who would have inherited Pitmedden but died at Flodden on September 9, 1513, with his king, James IV of Scotland. Hundreds of Scottish knights, noblemen and high officials perished with them.

Thomas Howard, earl of Surrey, had challenged King James to battle when he saw his supplies, including fodder for his own mount, running drastically low after a long march into Northumberland. Under the traditions of chivalry, the Scottish king accepted the challenge, although he must have known the advantages of delay. The battle was joined in the late afternoon; by nightfall the English, with superior archers and spearmen, routed their opponents although outnumbered by some ten thousand.

Birkenbog, by then the traditional and principal holding of the main branch of the family Abercromby, would be sacked by the vengeful James Graham, earl and marquess of Montrose, in 1645. In decline for a generation, and much reduced by the sale of land between 1712 and 1732, the property was largely restored by Sir Robert, third baronet. This able, determined and resourceful Abercromby, as we will see, returned from India in 1734 to succeed his father. He began at once, as his younger brother George expressed it in a letter of December 11, 1738 from Campeche, Mexico, "to extricate (himself) from the labyrinth (our) father left his affairs in."

Birkenbog was virtually destroyed by a calamitous fire in 1790, mercifully after the death of Sir Robert, who was spared the tragedy of watching his many years of rehabilitation go up in flames. Lost forever were irreplaceable family records, paintings and heirlooms; fortunately, Sir Henry Raeburn's portraits of Sir George and Sir Robert, the fourth and fifth baronets Abercromby and their respective wives, Jean Ogilvy and Elizabeth Douglas, were saved.

After the fire, little remained except stone walls and the coat of arms of the clan, encised in stone over the front door. The Abercrombys of Birkenbog moved to Forglen, some twenty miles to the south.

Robert Abercromby had heard from early childhood the chronicles and legends that emerge and persist within and around a highly visible, sometimes contentious clan, especially one with the initiative and leadership so characteristic of the Abercrombys. Nurtured on the strong meat of the attainments of intrepid, larger-than-life men of high accomplishment, rather than on the pap of television "sitcoms" and mindless movies, he was told of the Old Laird and the Grand Falconer, and of Robert Scotus—of the witches of Castle Hill, the Wall of the Skulls, and the two jealous sisters, finally reconciled, who were struck down by lightning at the Old Church of Abercrombie. He learned of the Main Covenanter, he with the courage to turn against the king, a boyhood friend, who had raised him to the peerage, on a question of deep principle; and of other Abercrombys over the centuries who had served as Members of Parliament, in other key offices of the northeast shires, or as high dignitaries of the clergy, military or courts of justice.

The Old Laird was Alexander Abercromby of Pitmedden, the fifth to bear the name (a favorite within the family because it was that of Malcolm III's son, who ruled Scotland from 1107 to 1124 as King Alexander I). Beloved throughout the northeast for a long life of good deeds and notable accomplishments, the Old Laird was a man quick to assert and defend his rights and those of his clan. In the spring of 1593, he became embroiled in a bitter quarrel that resulted in his murder, in one of the most heinous crimes imaginable. The quarrel was with the powerful Gordons of Donemad and Leichistoun, even though the Old Laird's daughter and "oy" (grandson) were of that ilk by marriage and descent.

The disagreement was of the most crucial and potentially deadly nature in Scotland: It turned upon the grandson, young John Gordon of Muirake, having been awarded the manor house and lands of Donemad, and taking possession through a Decree of Removal issued by the Lords of the Council and executed by the chief deputy of the sheriff of Banff, one William Duncan. Members of the Gordon clan soon attempted to shoot their cousin John, but "being defrauded of their purpose," decided to turn their wrath against the Old Laird himself. They first "did cruellie sett upoun (his) servants, hurte and woundit them in divers parts of their bodies and left them almaist for deid." Next, they began to seek an opportunity to do away with the aged Alexander, who continued to lead his normal life in spite of continual threats from the Leichistoun Gordons.

On March 12, 1594, the Old Laird was hawking (hunting with falcons) in the near vicinity of Leichistoun. Word of his presence, without weapons and accompanied only by his falconers, was brought to James Gordon. The actual language of the indictment tells what happened next, on the moss (moor) of Cokstoun, after 17 men, fully armed, surrounded their helpless quarry:

The Laird of Birkenbog was hawking, the document recounts,

> . . . (and lacking) anie companie except his falconnirs in sober and quyet manner, dreidant na evill, harme, injurie, persute of anie persone . . . (when the assailants) dischargit twenty shot of hagbuts (harquebuses) and

> pistolets at him, whairby they shot diverse and sundrie bullets in divers parts of his bodie . . . (and next) having circuit him about that he was not abill to escape, they thairafter put violent handis on his persone, tuik from him his owne horse, and cuist him upoun ane bachillane naig. Whairupon they conveyit him as a prisoner the space of ane myle fra the said Moss toward the Place of Leichistoun, and being the lenth of ane half myle to the said Place, ane of the personis that was of thair companie having ane hagbut in his hand charget with thrie bullets preparit for the purpose at thair especiall command and direction behind the said umquhile (deceased) Alexander's back, shot him with thrie bullets through the bodie and thairafter maist barbouslie and crewellie with thair drawn swords cuttit him all in peces and as monsteris in nature left nocht sax inche of his bodie, armis, legis, and heid undevydit and cut asunder, and so was maist monstrouslie and crewellie slane and murtherit by the personis foresaids.

Even in an era of violence and sudden death, all Scotland was shocked by this reprehensible crime. The Gordons themselves denounced the murderers, who apparently fled the country and were never brought to trial. The real pity is that the Old Laird of Pitmedden, one of the finest men of his age, is remembered more for the lurid and detestable manner of his death than for his laudable contributions to family, king, and country.

The story of the Grand Falconer was a far happier account that Robert Abercromby had also heard on countless occasions. The Alexander Abercromby given this title by Charles I was the grandson of the Old Laird. Born 1584 at Birkenbog, he was only a lad of ten when his grandfather was murdered, but he had shown an interest in the Old Laird's falcons while little more than a toddler, watching handlers feed the fierce hawks in their cages, or ready them for the field. Soon he was being taken out onto the windswept moors with the falconry party, first holding on to the pommel of his father's saddle, then riding his own pony until the darkling of light signaled the end of the hunt.

His father Sir James, the Old Laird's heir, was pleased with Alexander's growing preoccupation with falconry, which had become almost an obsession with the nobles and landed gentry in Scotland, England, and much of continental Europe as early as the mid-fifteenth century. No less a personage than Frederick II, the Holy Roman Emperor, had written a Latin treatise on the subject *(De arte venandi avibus)*, and the sport had its intricate customs and traditions. Among these, it had become almost obligatory for noblemen and gentry to take winged fowl only with falcons, leaving snaring, netting, and shooting with the long, relatively awkward matchlock musket to servants and professional hunters. Not that the Old Laird or Sir James, both excellent marksmen,[4] might not go out early or late with the smaller muskets that were coming into use, to bag a brace of grouse or a toothsome autumn hare for the table.

Charles Stuart, king of Great Britain and Ireland from 1625 to 1649 and second son of James VI of Scotland,[5] would have a telling impact upon the future of the Abercrombys, both in the Old World and in the New. He was born at Dunfermline Palace in Fifeshire, barely twenty-five miles southwest of the ancient family holding surrounding the early thirteenth century town of Abercrombie, in east Fife in the parish of St. Andrews, on November 19, 1600.

A shy, introverted lad with a pronounced stammer, Charles was barely five feet, six inches in stature when mature. As a young child, he was so puny that his father left him behind with his nurses when summoned to Westminster Abbey to be crowned James I of England in March of 1603. It was feared that the frail two-year-old might not survive the difficult four-hundred-mile journey to London.

As were all the Stuarts, the future Charles I was almost addicted to hunting and to riding fine-blooded horses. He had his own special reasons to pursue these traditional family interests. A splendid mount (and many of his thoroughbreds were an extra hand or two high) compensated for his own lack of stature, while shyness in company was no real handicap in the field. And he must have noted that horses ignore stuttering. Of far more consequence, long hours in the saddle, in the bracing weather of Fife and surrounding counties, definitely improved his fragile health.

Remaining in Scotland for long periods before his succession to the throne, it was almost inevitable that the future monarch would ride and hunt at Birkenbog. This Abercromby property in northern Aberdeenshire had become more and more a center for falconry, both before and after Alexander succeeded his father Sir James as laird of the manor.

When Charles Stuart did visit Birkenbog, he found an ideal setting among other dedicated horsemen and hunters close to his own age who spoke the Scottish dialect of the northeast with his own accents, and also loved the outdoors. Alexander Abercromby, only sixteen years older than his royal guest, had devoted much of his life to hawking and to riding over the family properties. Married when barely eighteen, he had three sons, all skilled falconers and horsemen, who were about the same age as their king-to-be. They were the younger Alexander, heir to Birkenbog, and his brothers John and Walter, who were to establish cadet branches of the Abercromby line at Glassaugh and Brakenbills, respectively.

All these Abercrombys came to know the future monarch when Charles was a shy, lonely, and insecure adolescent particularly in need of friends. He had just lost the two persons closest to him: his elder brother Henry, the heir apparent, had died in 1612; his only sister (Elizabeth, namesake and cousin of the Virgin Queen) was packed off a year later to Germany to marry Frederick V, elector of the Rhine Palatinate, in one of the frequent maneuvers aimed at adding to the political or military power, or economic bargaining position, of a royal family.

So it was that the king of Great Britain and Ireland remembered the Abercrombys of Birkenbog when he came to power. Soon after his accession in 1625, Charles I named Alexander, Sr. his Grand Falconer in Scotland; eleven years later, he created the younger Alexander first baronet of Birkenbog, the title that has come down through the family for almost three hundred and fifty years, and appointed the new baronet Member of Parliament for Banffshire.

It was fitting that when experts in heraldry designed a coat of arms for Sir Alexander, the most prominent element was a fierce, rising falcon at the crest, just under the motto "Petit Alta" ("He Seeks the Heights"). It was a striking and unusual coat-of-arms, embodying also three boars' heads, supporting greyhounds, and another motto in the more customary position at the bottom: "Mercie Is My Desire." The latter had been encised in stone over the main door at Glassaugh and later incorporated into the entrance to the manor house of Birkenbog.

Alexander of Birkenbog had his baronetage and a coat-of-arms particularly befitting his lifelong interest in falconry, in the tradition of his grandfather, the Grand Falconer. But neither he nor his monarch knew of the painful choice that his new honors would soon force upon Sir Alexander, for he was to become the Main Covenanter.

The story of Robert (or Robertus) Scotus was another captivating tale that Robert Abercromby would remember all his life. It revealed not only the early and persistently deep bonds between the clan Abercromby (and many another eminent Scottish family) and Roman Catholicism, but also how politics and religion became intermingled with intricate, high-level intrigue in sixteenth- and seventeenth-century Scotland.

Robertus Scotus was the alias used by Father James Abercromby, S.J., a priest forever according to the rite of Melchizedek and a member of that great Catholic order, the godly and formidable Society of Jesus founded by a former Spanish soldier, St. Ignatius Loyola, in 1537.

Born in 1533, James matriculated at the University of St. Andrews in 1551, with his brother Andrew. Just as the scions of many other prominent Scottish families, they had been prepared at the Carthusian monastery school in Douai (where the English version of the Old Testament approved by the Church of Rome would be published in 1610). James studied theology at St. Andrews; ironically, so did John Knox,[6] the one-time Catholic priest who became the fiery leader of the Protestant Reformation in Scotland. Father Abercromby would oppose John Knox's trenchantly anti-Catholic disputations all his life, and would become a secret envoy of Pope Paul IV, on a mission to discover new Roman Catholic leadership to offset the massive gains of Knox and Presbyterianism.

James Abercromby's mother was a Murthley. He was thereby a member of the family of the last abbot of Inchcolm, a saintly Catholic monk and scholar who had headed an ancient monastery. James grew up near the castle of his grandfather Andrew Murthley, where priests were always welcome, even as the followers of John Knox began to storm the Catholic monasteries, and raw courage was required to appear in a Roman cassock.

Soon after his ordination, by William Chisolm, bishop of the pristine diocese of Dunblane and Vaison and primate of Scotland, Father Abercromby was presented at court in the first months of the return of Mary Queen of Scots to Edinburgh, in 1561. Before the queen was forced to abdicate (on a long and wretched procession into tragedy that would lead to the executioner's axe at Fotheringhay in 1587), she had the young priest "presented (with the) benefice of Lesser Dunkeld," a handsome living for a young pastor so recently admitted to holy orders.

Father James stayed less than a year at his first parish. He and Edmund Hay, a relative by marriage, left Scotland March 9, 1562 for the Continent. The Church of Rome had apparently decided that the young priest, who had shown unusual promise as a scholar, should be removed from his native land and the furious religious controversies raging there in the early 1560s. These had intensified steadily since the murder of David Cardinal Beaton at St. Andrews in 1546, and markedly since John Knox's return from six years of exile, in 1559.

Father Abercromby remained abroad almost twenty-five years, as a graduate student of theology at Louvain, Belgium's famed medieval university; in the Polish center of Cracow, then as now a great hub of Catholicism; in Danzig; and principally at the English College in Rome with the noted Jesuit William Good. The parishioners of Dunkeld, incidentally, were most patient in his absence. Only in 1573 did they petition for a replacement, citing that the long-absent incumbent was "ane Jesuit beyondit tha say."

John Knox had died at Edinburgh on November 24, 1572, but he left a strongly Presbyterian Scotland engaged in the relentless persecution of Catholic priests, monks and bishops as his monument. The Church of Rome found in the next decade that it was fighting for its very existence. Slowly, a plan of retaliation was devised; it turned upon a long-range counteroffensive looking to the many noble families, especially in the northeast shires, who had traditionally espoused and supported Catholicism.

The first concrete step, just as in a military operation, was setting up a reliable, first-hand source of intelligence. Who better than a highly-trained priest, a native of Fifeshire and descendant of the Scottish nobility? Thus Father James Abercromby became Robertus Scotus, and went to Danzig, an ancient Baltic nexus of intrigue, politics and shipping, to seek a captain willing to take an anonymous passenger to an undisclosed destination in Scotland.

Robertus Scotus was put ashore surreptitiously on the lonely, windswept coast of Fife, in the estuary of the river Tay, early in 1587. He knew that he would be welcome at Megginch, the nearby seat of his brother-in-law Peter Hay. A renowned Catholic leader, Hay was the bailie (chief magistrate) of Errol and a cousin of Edmund Hay, with whom Father Abercromby had originally left Scotland in 1562.

The priest-secret agent carried impressive documents, written in elegantly classical Latin. These included papal greetings to be given at his discretion "to the earls and (other) chief men of Scotland." The documents were signed by Pope Paul IV, with the notation "given at Rome at St. Peter's under the sign of the Fisherman."

Robertus had been given a lengthy and detailed assignment. Among other matters, he was to determine the present state of the remaining Catholic priests and bishops in Scotland; how the leading nobles felt about the principal officers of state; which of the nobles were either overt or covert Catholics, and how their allegiance might be fostered; what could be done to help the Scottish king James VI, then twenty-one and unmarried; and how best to restore the Church of Rome's diminished power and influence among the leaders of Scotland. There were also very detailed questions to be resolved: how best to enter and leave Scotland without detection, or to ship in books and tracts for distribution; which of the monasteries, if any, were still in operation; was the Mass being celebrated, and the sacraments administered.

Father Abercromby's report, also in classical Latin, was probably brought to Rome by his fellow Jesuit, William Good. It has comprehensive answers to the questions Robertus had been asked and provides a unique insight into what Scotland was like in the late sixteenth century.

The priests and bishops of his native land, Father Abercromby made known to the Vatican, were in an appalling state. Only one bishop remained; he was Robert Crichton of Dunkeld, a member of a leading northeast family living in extreme poverty in Edinburgh while attempting to regain confiscated diocesan properties through the courts. Few priests could be found, and some described as "married heretics" had gone over to the theology and church of John Calvin and John Knox; at the traditional Catholic center of Dunfermline, monks and priests had been reduced to begging in the streets.

"The status of the Ministers (of state)" according to Robertus, was that "everybody hates them heartily. (They are of) immense pride and intolerable haughtiness." It was difficult to identify the pro-Catholic nobles, since men of prominence kept their own counsel; but they were thought to be numerous, and would hopefully make themselves known to a fellow man of Fife bearing such high credentials. A sound means of fostering their allegiance would be to provide funds and opportunity for their sons to be educated abroad in Catholic universities.

Most upper-echelon Scottish families had many children, Father Abercromby pointed out, one prepotent laird having thirty-one sons and daughters. Since the eldest son almost invariably inherited the entire immovable (income-producing) estate, there was often little to pass on to anyone else. And consequently, an even more compelling reason to educate the other sons, enabling them to make their own way when they left hearth and home. We will see later many an Abercromby striking out on his own.

"Next to the help of God," Robertus reported, "I think that the most effective way to help King James VI (of Scotland) would be to get him married to Catherine,[7] daughter of the King of Navarre and sister of the heir to that throne." This turned out to be political advice of the highest quality. Navarre, a tiny Basque kingdom astride the principal Pyrennes pass between Spanish Aragon and French Gascony, had been controlled by the French for centuries. Royal marriages with the reigning Bourbon dynasty in Paris followed. In 1589, Catherine of Navarre's brother became Henry IV, king of France and Navarre and a prized ally to have on your side during Europe's constant struggles for power.

Although Father Abercromby struck out as a matchmaker in this particular instance, his advice, ironically, was followed in the next generation. James VI, before he became James I of England, married Princess Anne of Denmark; but James' son married Henrietta Maria, daughter of Henry IV and niece of Catherine of Navarre, in 1625, when he became King Charles I.

Robertus was unable to give a direct answer to the fundamental question of how best to recover Catholic power and influence in his native land. In his report to Rome, he emphasized the gravity of such problems as the persecution of his brother clergymen (as well as laymen), and the degree to which "powerful men have seized Catholic lands and properties." But no quick remedy was prescribed; Father Abercromby was a realist.

He warned against entering Scotland through ports or border towns, and recommended that carefully-selected books and religious tracts be supplied. They should be shipped, he specified, from Scandinavian countries, rather than from France or Poland, to ensure safe arrival. (Why would the Protestants of the lands of the northern lights send pro-Rome material to John Knox's land?) Priests should be given considered yet wide dispensations allowing them to wear mufti instead of clerical garb, and to celebrate the Mass whenever and however they could. The Countess of Atholl, he had determined, was still supporting three chaplains, but they found it more and more difficult to appear even on her estates in priestly attire. This was increasingly the case since the fearful day when "the Earl (of Atholl, his high title descending from the twelfth century), chancellor of Scotland, was poisoned by heretics."

Father Abercromby's report was in summary a realistic and invaluable document, compiled at great personal risk and with marvelous acumen and presence. From later records, it was studied in minute detail by the Vatican's skilled diplomats and analysts, aided by Father William Good's long friendship with Robertus Scotus and knowledge of what his fellow Jesuit was attempting to accomplish.

The report concluded reluctantly that there was no quick solution for the Church of Rome in Scotland; rather, generations, or certainly decades, would pass before the status quo could be reestablished. The long and patient campaign that Scotus envisioned was based on restoring priests and bishops to their normal functions and activities while regaining the active support of the peerage, as civil polity emerged again. This was in effect a blueprint for Rome's policies in Scotland for the ensuing century; and it must have been a factor in bringing about the watershed legislation of 1689, when religious toleration, if not political equality, was reaffirmed in Great Britain.

Neither Robert Abercromby, half-dozing beside the fire as his father or grandfather recounted again the story of Robertus Scotus, nor Father James Abercromby, S.J. could foresee that centuries later, in Rosenberg, Texas in 1983, there would be another Father James (Jamie) Abercrombie, a Roman Catholic priest named for his uncle James S. (Mr. Jim) Abercrombie.

Just as the adolescents of today, young Robert Abercromby must have been fascinated by tales involving violence, or the macabre. Three such stories within the clan were those of the Witches of Castle Hill, the Wall of the Skulls and the Two Warring Sisters.

The grisly incident of the Witches of Castle Hill is documented in Scottish court records. Late in 1586, Alexander Abercromby, recently given charter as the new laird of Pitmedden, fell mysteriously ill. This occasioned great concern, for he was both the Abercromby heir and the favorite son of Elizabeth, eldest daughter of the puissant Leslie clan of Pitcaple. When Alexander died on December 9, 1586 (to be succeeded by the Grand Falconer), witnesses came forward to blame a Janet Clark and a Janet Grant, suspected of being witches, of having cast a spell on him; moreover, it was alleged, they had maliciously brought about the death of sixteen cattle by various incantations and other practice of black magic. The unfortunate Misses Janet were found guilty after long imprisonment. The sentence was that ". . . tha sorceres both be worreit (strangled)" by the official executioner, and that their bodies then be burned to ashes on Castle Hill in Edinburgh. The sentence was carried out before an immense audience, on August 26, 1590.

The story of the Wall of Skulls is an entrancing, if macabre, tale that is claimed to substantiate other indications that the Abercrombys were originally Irish. When a recess within the interior walls of the Church of Abercrombie, in the parish of St. Andrews[8] near the Fifeshire village of Abercrombie, was opened in 1769, nineteen human skulls were discovered. Virtually all of them could be identified by names and dates cut into the individual niches of stone in which the skulls were found.

The explanation is that the Abercrombys were following an Irish custom dating back to primeval days, before the aboriginal Scots left Eire for what came to be known as Scotland (land of the Scots). When the chief of a clan died, the skull of his predecessor was removed from the skeleton, and placed with the skulls of his ancestors in a secret place known only to the Druids (thereby safe from conqueror and marauder).

The skulls of St. Andrews were thus identified, with at least an approximate date of death in most cases: (1) John, mid-twelfth century; (2) Thomas, circa 1198; (3) John de Coccus (our master of the royal household), early thirteenth century; (4) Richard, 1270; (5) William, soon after he signed the Ragman Roll of 1296 (a primitive census and pledge of loyalty to the warrior king Edward I, known as the Hammer of the Scots); (6) John, son and heir of William; (7) an early Alexander, 1375; (8) David, his son; (9) John, circa 1444; (10) Thomas, described as a "baron of Parliament"; (11) Sir Robert, circa 1490; (12) Alexander, grandson of Humphrey, circa 1505; (13) Thomas, thought to be a younger son who predeceased, 1513; (14) Alexander, the Old Laird, 1594;

(15) Thomas, an heir apparent who died before succeeding as head of the clan; and (16) Alexander, the Grand Falconer. Three other skulls were not identified.

The story of the Two Warring Sisters was a melancholy tale of unrequited love ending in sudden violence. Daughters of a Humphrey de Abercromby who headed the clan in the early twelfth century, the sisters fell in love with the same knight, who ignored them both. They vented their anger not on their gallant paladin, but on one another, in a bitter family feud. When the knight was killed in one of the endless wars of the clans, the sisters became reconciled in their common grief, and decided to build the Church of Abercrombie as a memorial to their fallen warrior. The bishop of St. Andrews was asked to dedicate the new place of worship before the assembled gentry of Fife, and the dedicatory rites began with the two sisters kneeling for the episcopal blessing outside the imposing front doors. Just as the bishop raised hand and crozier to recite the familiar *Benedicite in nomine Patris et Filii et Spiritus Sancti* of the Roman Catholic benediction, there was a tremendous crash of thunder and brilliant flash of lightning from the darkling, threatening skies. The two sisters, hit point blank by the lightning bolt, fell dead at the bishop's feet.

There was nothing of the macabre, but violence aplenty, in the story of the Main Covenanter (Sir Alexander Abercromby, first baronet of Birkenbog), and his intriguing life during the chaotic years of the mid-seventeenth century in Scotland. It is probable that his chronicle will be remembered by historians long after other captivating accounts of the Abercromby family in centuries gone by have dimmed in memory, primarily because of his personal impact upon those in high station, and his unflinching decisions under telling stress.

Sir Alexander had been a baronet less than a year when his friend, fellow falconer and monarch Charles I made a major move in the field of religion—a dangerous gambit in Scotland, where issues touching upon the ecclesiastical had so often become surcharged with emotion. This came in 1637, when King Charles found his realm at peace, without the usual treasury-depleting necessity to raise and maintain a large standing army and/or comparable naval forces. Moreover, economic conditions had been improving steadily, and there seemed to be at least a temporary standoff in his ongoing struggles with Parliament.

The time had come, Charles Stuart decided, to bring the Church of England (increasingly pro-Rome at the time in its liturgy and leadership), and the Presbyterian Kirk of Scotland much closer together. The principal vehicle (probably at the urging of William Laud, the Archbishop of Canterbury and nominal head of the Anglican denomination) was to be a new prayer book doctrinally rooted in Church of England theology and liturgy.

The moment that the prayer book was promulgated in Edinburgh, the fat was in the fire. The Scottish people, not forgetting John Knox for a moment (although the fiery old preacher and reformer had been in his grave sixty-five years), rioted in the streets. From Old Town to New, and up and down the Royal Mile as well as the tenements of the original city, the burghers made it known that they fervidly preferred Old John's Book of Common Order to the new liturgy and dogma now proposed. Charles I had a tiger by the tail, amid cries of "Popery" and "Leave the Kirk be."

The counteroffensive was based upon a so-called National Covenant, in which Scottish leaders formally pledged themselves to "resist innovative worship (in the Kirk) by any means possible." This was adopted and signed (in blood, some claimed) at Greyfriars[9] Kirk in Edinburgh on February 28, 1638. The General Assembly of the Presbyterian Church had in the meantime overwhelmingly rejected the new book of prayer, and the Scottish bishops who had helped to write it.

Charles I felt that these actions were a direct and dangerous challenge to his most fundamental tenet: the divine right of kings. Once accurately described as stubborn beyond either common sense or obstinacy, he decided to invade Scotland in order to enforce his religious views by force of arms. He crossed the border in 1639 with an ill-equipped, unpaid, ragtag army and was forced to sue for peace in a matter of weeks.

When the king renewed the attack in the summer of 1640, a formidable Covenanter force marched into northern England, triggering a chain of events that brought deepening disaster to King Charles. He could neither have foreseen, nor believed, what would happen within less than a decade: the transfer of traditionally sovereign powers to Parliament, bitter civil war, basic changes in the very structure of government in Great Britain, and his own execution at Whitehall, on January 30, 1649. It was as if the classic Greek tragedies of Aeschylus were being rewritten, two millenia later.

Sir Alexander Abercromby was in a quandary from the moment the National Covenant was proposed. He had known his monarch for many years, and had hunted and ridden over the moors with him countless times; both he and his father, the Grand Falconer, had been signally honored by their king. Yet as a Scot of many generations, he could understand the reaction of his fellow peers and countrymen who were so highly incensed at Charles' maladroit attempt to regiment their religious beliefs and practices.

A further complication was the fact that many Abercrombys had been strongly identified with Catholicism for generations and were reluctant to support either the Anglican Charles I or the Covenanters, direct descendants of Presbyterians who had so ruthlessly persecuted Roman Catholics less than a century before.

Sir Alexander's own great-great-grandfather (Alexander of Pitmedden) was a kinsman and contemporary of Father James Abercromby, S. J. (Robert Scotus). One generation before, in the first quarter of the sixteenth century, James Abercromby of Pitmedden had married Marjory Hay, eldest daughter of a prominent Catholic family. Sir Alexander's grandfather, the Old Laird, was described as late as 1567 as a "strong adherent of Mary Queen of Scots," the Roman Catholic ruler who had been forced to abdicate in 1561. The charge was regarded so seriously that the Old Laird sought and was given a pardon for his support of Queen Mary, by regents for the boy king, James VI, in 1581.

In the end, Alexander Abercromby, first baronet of Birkenbog, not only signed the National Covenant in the crescent agitation against Charles I, but was so active against the Stuart king that he was always described later as a Main Covenanter. Charles took full and costly retaliation against the Abercrombys, not directly but through one of the most unusual men in Scottish history. This was the singular James Graham, fifth earl and first marquess of Montrose.

Montrose was also a Main Covenanter in the beginning, but primarily because he resented English interference with the Kirk. He was essentially a royalist; and as such gained the enmity of Archibald Campbell, leader of the anti-royalists, earl of Argyll, Marquess of Argyll, prominent Catholic leader and one of the most powerful, resourceful and mysterious men in Scottish history.

The earl of Montrose was with the victorious Covenanter army that invaded northern England briefly in the summer of 1640. Argyll, informed of his adversary's presence, offered a handsome reward for Montrose's capture, took him prisoner and carted him away for six months of incarceration in Edinburgh.

Once released, the earl of Montrose began to restudy his situation, which he had probably been examining in some depth while in prison. He resolved to abandon the Covenanter cause and to regain the confidence of Charles I, did so and offered to raise and train a new army for the king. Charles, hard-pressed by a new alliance between Covenanters and Oliver Cromwell's Parliament army, accepted the offer. He named Montrose a marquess of the realm and lieutenant governor for Scotland. The new marquess somehow brought together a Highlander army in the space of a few weeks late in the summer of 1644, and won a series of major battles including Auldearn, Tippermuir and an attack on the outskirts of Aberdeen itself by sound strategy and the effective use of limited supplies and equipment. He was then named captain-general of King Charles' forces.

Montrose's fortunes spun rapidly into reverse, however. Within a year, he had lost crucial battles at Naseby and at Philiphaugh. He then escaped to France, where other adherents brought him news of the execution of their monarch, Charles I, and his last, brave, defiant words: "(when) Power without Lawe may make Lawes . . . (who) . . . can be sure of his Life or any thing Hee call his own."

Ill-advisedly, Montrose returned to Scotland in the spring of 1650 with about fifteen hundred men, hoping to find support among the royalists dismayed by the execution of Charles I and loyal to his son and heir Charles II (denied the throne because of the abolition of the monarchy by the Rump Parliament). Montrose was soundly defeated at Carbisdale on April 27, 1650. Fleeing after the loss, he asked Neil McLeod, chief of a Highland clan but no friend of a royalist, for refuge.

McLeod turned James Graham, marquess of Montrose, over to Oliver Cromwell's forces, and he was hanged in the marketplace of Edinburgh on May 21, 1650, with a copy of the writings of George Wishart, a condemned heretic burned at the stake a century earlier, tied around his neck. He was then drawn and quartered.

Montrose had a fearful and appalling end, but he wreaked a special vengeance on the Main Covenanter after learning that Sir Alexander had been a long-time friend of King Charles before joining the anti-royalists. Then serving as high sheriff of Banffshire, Sir Alexander fought with distinction under Major Sir John Urry at Auldearn on May 4, 1645, but Montrose carried the day. The Main

Covenanter helped to salvage a portion of Major Urry's forces and was leading them toward Birkenbog when he learned that the victorious Montrose had sent an advance party to the estate to devastate it.

As soon as the marquess of Montrose could oversee the difficult crossing of the river Spey by his supply trains, he hastened to Birkenbog to relish the extent of the damage. Next, he quartered his troops in every part of the Abercromby lands, levying upon cattle, crops or anything at hand for provisions. Raiding parties were sent out regularly to scourge the countryside, while on the constant lookout for booty. The nearby town of Cullen was burned to the ground, the inhabitants scattering to the four winds.

It was a severe blow to Sir Alexander and his neighbors, and especially trying to the Abercrombys because it would be (as we saw earlier) two generations before Birkenbog was even partially restored by the third baronet. Montrose had his revenge, and in full.

The Main Covenanter reacted in typical fashion. He was never heard to complain about Montrose, or to question his own decision in 1638 to side with those defending religious liberty. Instead, he accepted an even more active role in raising troops to oppose a new threat to Scotland: Oliver Cromwell. (Cromwell invaded western Scotland late in the summer of 1650 to counter rising sentiment for Charles II, the deposed son and heir of Charles I. Charles II, crowned king of Scotland at Scone by the marquess of Argyll, had landed at Leith with a considerable force on June 16, 1650.)

Once again, Sir Alexander acted on principle. He could not continue to support a man who had deposed a legitimate king and ruled outside the established framework of the law. Even though he, and many another Covenanter, had fought side by side with the forces of Parliament against Charles I, they now heeded their former monarch's words from the executioner's platform, and broke with Parliament's dictatorial leader General Cromwell.

A letter of August 23, 1650 from Sir Alexander's cousin Lady Glencairn is revealing. "For my honorable and loveing cusine . . . Knight Barronet," she begins. "Honored Cusine: I have this Fryday receaved . . . (a note from Lord Glencairn)." Her husband wants Sir Alexander to be instantly ready for military counsel and action, since " . . . Cromwell is in Glasgow himselfe with all his foote (infantry) and his hoarse (cavalry) is all a long the Water of Clyde."

The Main Covenanter and high sheriff was available, and took a leading role in alerting the men of Aberdeenshire to the potentially deadly danger of an invading force armed both with fanaticism and more tangible weaponry. Sir Alexander had taken a new oath of allegiance, this time to Charles II, the son of his hunting companion of long ago.[10] He and Charles II were united against a pernicious common foe: Parliament and Oliver Cromwell, Lord Protector-to-be.

Nor do the English forget quickly; here is an item from the ''Personal'' column of the *Times* commemorating the 370th anniversary of the Lord Protector's birth on April 25, 1599: ''CROMWELL: To the eternal condemnation of Oliver. Seditionist, traitor, regicide, racialist, proto-fascist and blasphemous bigot. God save England from his like.''

Now it was 1735, in the eighth year of the reign of George III, the stolid German great-great-grandson of James I of England. Robert Abercromby of The Fifteen was leaving adolescence for full manhood, armed with a proud name and tradition, plus a sound Scottish grammar school education well grounded in the fundamental three R's—and a lean purse.

Just as the sons of so many other Scottish families, Robert knew from an early age that he would have to make his own way. He was even more aware of this as the male offspring of a cadet branch of the clan Abercromby. If it was of any comfort, the younger brothers of another Robert Abercromby (his contemporary, the third baronet) would also have to seek their own fortunes.

A country still recovering from a century of political, economic and religious turmoil, Scotland had suffered from a succession of maladies since the 1630s, among them such major ailments as civil war, riots, rebellion, invasion and the shock of transforming in large part from agriculture to the raising of sheep. The economy was on the upswing in 1735, however, due to an underlying factor that many Scots still bitterly opposed: the 1707 Act of Union. This fundamental statute, widely misunderstood and often interpreted as nothing more than a final blow to the centuries-old dream of an independent Scotland, was actually an economic boon of first significance.

The Act of 1707 provided not only for a constitutional and governmental union joining England and Scotland in the entity of Great Britain, but for an economic union as well. This immediately abolished the most negative effects of the Navigation Acts upon Scottish commerce; these discriminatory acts, aimed primarily at restricting the water transportation of English agricultural products and other goods to English ships, had treated Scottish ships as foreign vessels, severely limiting their use.

Suddenly, there were vast new opportunities for Scots, and their traditionally able, hard-working entrepreneurs, in textiles, cotton, rice, tobacco, indigo and sugar. An early shipbuilding industry boomed along the Clyde, and the numerous Scottish ports began to hum with activity. Glasgow took leadership in the lucrative tobacco trade away from Bristol and Liverpool and grew six-fold from barely twelve thousand five hundred inhabitants in 1710 to almost seventy-five thousand in 1800.

There were other effects of the Act of Union, none of them lost upon Robert Abercromby and his contemporaries, searching as they were for a career that would hopefully bring them a comfortable and interesting livelihood, if not riches. One outcome was a burgeoning interest in the new English colonies, especially the "sugar islands" of Barbados and Jamaica, and in the vast new territory of the Carolinas which stretched from Virginia to Spanish Florida.

The spellbinding Quaker evangelist and preacher, George Fox, had aroused particular interest in what he described as the "soft, black, fertile land of Carolana" after skirting the province while floundering his way through the Great Dismal Swamp. The huge new colony had been named for Charles II by the eight noblemen he gave it to, in gratitude for their support during some especially trying years of his troubled reign. (Seven of the eight gave the gift back, but that is a later story.)

Robert Abercromby must have chewed on the sweet sugar cane that was unloaded in such great quantities at the old port of Glasgow, or at Aberdeen's wharves. He certainly knew that almost forty thousand colonists, many of them Scots, were on Barbados, the tiny (twenty-one by fourteen miles) colony with a fertile mountainous area called the Scotland District, before 1725. Abercromby (and Abercrombie) cousins had settled there (principally in the parishes of Christ Church and St. Michael) by 1700. They wrote home of wondrous things: extremely fertile land; temperatures in the narrow range of 70–90°F throughout the year; gorgeous trees and shrubs such as poinciana ("show-off"), brilliant bougainvillea, bottlebush ("rooster foot") and the fragrant frangipani; huge doves resembling dull-colored grouse, exquisite hummingbirds, tiny monkeys and a tree frog that whistled in tune with a sailor's hornpipe. And these expatriates wrote as well of dictating and witnessing last wills and testaments that told of substantial fortunes quickly garnered, as well as of extraordinary provisions and codicils.[11]

Robert, or any young Scots coming to manhood in the 1730s, would have been quite aware of the quickening interest in the New World, both generally and within the clan Abercromby, especially among the maturing male members of the several "junior" families at Banff, Dundee, Fetterneir, Glassaugh and adjoining areas. The situation in their native land was definitely on the upswing, after decades in the economic doldrums, yet there was added fascination, along with the hope of far greater reward and accomplishment, in lands thousands of miles away to the west.

Perhaps the first recorded emigrant to the New World colonies bearing the family name was David Abercromby, who left for "Carolana" from Glasgow in 1671. He was granted one hundred acres plus a ten-acre town lot in Charles Town (Charleston) on May 26, 1672.

James Abercromby, younger brother of Professor David Abercromby, who gave lectures in Publick Law and the Laws of Nature both at the University of Edinburgh and at his home in Peterson Court, was attorney-general of South Carolina[12] from 1733 to 1742. He took office only four years after the Carolinas were separated into two colonies, in 1729. After almost a decade, he returned to England to recruit experienced troops for the defense of the colony. James was the first Abercromby philanthropist in America; he gave £10 toward the establishment of Charles Town, on a donor list dated April 11, 1734. Named to the staff of the judge advocate general after returning home, he was given a lucrative appointment as agent for Virginia by the great prime minister, William Pitt.

James Abercromby was of the prominent collateral line of the Abercrombys of Tullibody. His father Alexander, second son of the first baronet of Birkenbog, had married Mary Duff of Braco. James' sister Helen would marry their first cousin Sir Robert, the third baronet. On May 11, 1741, Mary Duff Abercromby (Lady

Tullibody) wrote with pathos of the death of a younger son William who had gone to South Carolina with his brother James. Leaving Charles Town "with discouragement at being separate from James," he had gone to a new plantation at George Town on the coast sixty miles north of Charles Town on the Waccamaw River. There "Prettey William . . . but newly arrived . . . took ill and although tended by Mistress Fleming and Cleland's lady as if ther owen cheild died before James could come to him . . . your father and I heavey afflickted and poore James so heavey upon him . . ."

William Abercromby was only eighteen when he died, the promise of the New World dimmed forever for him.

The Abercrombys also sent a foremost religious leader to America in the early years of the eighteenth century. This was the Reverend Robert Abercromby, a graduate of the University of Edinburgh in theology who landed at the foot of State Street in Boston on August 4, 1718, with twenty Presbyterian families from Ulster. These were descendants of Protestant sheep raisers and farmers sent to northern Ireland as part of an overall plan to break the entrenched power of the Roman Catholic Church, and of the Irish ruling class, by seizure and redistribution of much of Ireland's arable land.

Originally put into motion by Henry VIII, the scheme was expanded by Queen Elizabeth I in the late sixteenth century. The Reverend Mr. Abercromby's group, many of them in Ulster for generations, left in protest of sharply increased rents and other direct and indirect persecution, reportedly ordered by ministers of both Queen Anne and George I who did not relish how well the frugal, hardworking new Ulstermen, most of them Scots Lowlanders, were succeeding in northern Ireland, or the fierce tenacity with which they held to the Calvinistic Presbyterianism of John Knox.

The Reverend Mr. Abercromby married Margaret Stevenson. They had eight sons including the traditionally-named Robert, James and John, and a daughter (Sarah) who lived to age ninety-three in Pelham, where her father founded one of the first Presbyterian churches in the New World.

A descendant of these pioneer Massachusetts Presbyterians, Reverend James Abercromby, went to Philadelphia with the many other Ulstermen who settled in Quaker-dominated Pennsylvania in the next generation. His granddaughter, Mary Josephine Abercrombie (daughter of Charles Steadman Abercrombie, M.D. of Roseland, Tennessee), established an interesting link with one of the most ancient of Scots families when she married Clifford Stanley Sims at Memphis, Tennessee on August 2, 1865. Sims, a Union officer once captured by the Confederates, was a direct descendant of Sym, a chieftain on the border lands of the River Tweed, who married Ada, granddaughter of Oswulfe, the earl of Northumberland; and Buethsym, thane of Gillesland in Cumberland. Buethsym fell at Hastings, along with some of the Irish progenitors of the clan Abercromby. Sims was later a prosperous cotton planter, and United States marshal, in eastern Arkansas. He and Mary Josephine appropriately named three of their sons Charles, James and Ralph, the latter for General Sir Ralph Abercromby.

Among the first planters to emigrate from Scotland to North Carolina was John Joseph Abercromby, identified only as "son of Alexander" (a favorite Christian name among the Abercrombys of long ago). This man, who arrived in the Piedmont in 1741, forty-eight years before statehood, was not the son of Alexander, laird of Tullibody, whose own son John (a captain in the First Royal Regiment of Foot) died unmarried in Halifax, Nova Scotia in 1759.[13]

We do know that John Joseph Abercromby married Sarah de Normandie, and was the father of General John Joseph Abercromby (1798–1844), one of the many illustrious military leaders within the clan whose careers we will examine briefly in following chapters.

The inclination among younger sons of prominent Scots families to emigrate in search of career and fortune was even more pronounced at Birkenbog and among certain cadet families of the clan Abercromby. There were many sons, but only one heir, with frequent loss of property and income over the generations. The losses could often be traced directly to costly political opposition to Charles I or (ironically) his nemesis, Oliver Cromwell; to long-established ties to Catholicism; or to support of "The Fifteen."

Sir Robert, the third baronet, was a unique example. Although he was to be the heir of Sir James, he could see even in childhood that Birkenbog was reaping the bitter harvest of earlier generations, and of what his grandfather and great-grandfather, the Main Covenanter and the Grand Falconer, had found to be honorable and necessary courses of action.

The Grand Falconer, for instance, could neither escape, nor would he have wanted to avoid, the continuing identification of the family with the Church of Rome in the seventeenth and earlier centuries. One of his favorite grandsons, Thomas Nicolson (brother of another favorite, the eminent jurist Sir George, Lord Kemnay) was consecrated in 1692 as the first Catholic bishop in Scotland since 1560. This development plus other ties political, emotional and personal (his daughters and nieces had almost without exception married into prominent Jacobite families) made it natural for Sir James to take an active role against George I in the rebellion of 1715. As a result, he was declared guilty of high treason and imprisoned in 1716, although soon free through the intervention of the powerful duke of Argyll. This all came at a most unfortunate time when the full effect of Montrose's sacking of Birkenbog, in retaliation for the Main Covenanter's opposition, and the dreaded Cromwell's later raids in the county, were being felt increasingly in cumulative loss of income and the need to continue selling off portions of the principal Abercrombie property.

The future Sir Robert, still second in line of succession, decided to make his own way in India, while his younger brother George, after military service in Holland, the West Indies and what was then the Spanish province of Mexico, settled in Mexico City and founded another branch of the clan there. A rich merchant and importer, he had a son with the traditional family name of Alexander who became a monk.

Other brothers and cousins took commissions in the armies of Holland, Germany, Denmark and Russia, leading to the establishment of the Von Abercorn line in Germany and Scandinavia after 1715. But of Sir James' eight sons, only Robert, George and Arthur lived to full maturity. Alexander died in adolescence soon after The Fifteen, Ludovic (William) was lost at sea and three others perished in Europe's perennial wars of the mid-eighteenth century.

Upon the death of Sir James in 1734, Sir Robert returned to Scotland as head of the family. In 1739, after the five years mentioned earlier in which he partially recouped the family fortunes, he married his first cousin Helen, only daughter of Alexander, laird of Tullibody. They lived not at diminished Birkenbog, but at Skeith, a beautifully-situated castle which the Abercrombys of Tullibody had inherited in 1699. Skeith, late seventeenth century accounts tell us, was a mile south of Deskford Church, "delightfully situated upon an eminence rising from the burn (smallish stream) having a peep of the sea. On each side are waterfalls, descending between rocks and fertile fields, beautifully interspersed with natural wood."

A strong-willed yet sensitive man beloved by his wife, six children, surviving brothers and indeed by the entire family, Sir Robert had resolved to follow at least for a few years the Abercromby tradition of military service. When war flared up again between England and Spain, he obtained the promise of a commission from Lord Cathcart, a long-time family friend named by George II to command the expeditionary force being raised to attack the Spanish colonies in the West Indies. Lord Cathcart then unfortunately fell ill and died; the promise was honored, however, by his successor, Brigadier-General Thomas Wentworth. General Wentworth signed Sir Robert's commission as a captain in Colonel Robert Fraser's marine regiment while on board HMS *Grafton* in the old harbor of Port Royal on June 14, 1741, and Captain Abercromby was soon off to war.

Helen Lady Abercromby was "filled with the strongest anxiety" as English losses mounted in the West Indies, but the third baronet remained on active duty for years between leaves to return to Scotland. One of these was of a strongly political nature. Henry Fox (Baron Holland), a conservative leader in Parliament, was much concerned at the possibility of Sir Robert's cousin James Abercromby losing his key seat from Banffshire. He obtained a leave of six months (signed by George II himself) for the very popular Sir Robert to return home to campaign for his cousin. James won reelection with little difficulty.

There are unfortunately no written records of how our own Robert Abercromby, progenitor of the Abercromby/Abercrombie line in America, left Scotland for the New World; or of his precise ancestry. He always reported his birthplace as "Scotland," with no additional data, and further details are unavailable in the Scottish Records Office in Edinburgh, in Aberdeen, or in the few remaining parishes or towns where they might be expected to be found. (Centralized records were not kept in Scotland before 1855.)

A further complication lies in the fact that Robert, just as James, John, Charles and (in an earlier era) Alexander, was extremely popular in a family almost addicted to the same repetitious forenames. No less than seven Robert Abercrombys, all contemporaries of the man who founded the American branch, have been identified. It seems reasonable to conclude, however, that "our" Robert was a member of one of the numerous cadet families of the name, most probably of the branch at Fetterneir, Dundee, Glassaugh or one of the smaller towns near Tullibody in Clackmannanshire which sent James, the attorney-general of South Carolina, and other Abercrombys to the colonies.

It is interesting that the lineage of John Joseph Abercromby, who arrived in North Carolina-to-be at about the same time as Robert Abercromby, has also been very difficult to substantiate. Perhaps they were close relatives—uncle and nephew, brothers, or even father and son. Among the eight sons of the Reverend Robert Abercrombie who came to Boston in 1718 as a graduate in theology of the University of Edinburgh was a Robert, Jr., thought to have come to the Carolinas as a young man.

There are custom house invoices indicating that a Robert Abercromby was importing horn buttons and other merchandise into the West Indies as early as the mid-1730s, and possibly exporting sugar from Barbados. George Abercromby, Sir Robert's brother who lived in Mexico from 1740 until his death in 1777, had a brisk trade going between the West Indies and Hernan Cortes' old port of La Villa Rica de Vera Cruz (Vera Cruz, founded in 1519 as "the rich town of the True Cross"), the key Spanish port on the sultry Mexican coast.

A Robert Abercromby wrote from the colonies[14] on July 21, 1745, a letter now in the muniments (official archives) of Forglen that concerns information he had from a "Colonel Abercromby" about a Spanish attack on the French at Ghent. George Abercromby was in the Low Countries before he went to Mexico, following a brief career as a professional soldier. Was Robert Abercromby somehow in contact with George, and passing on information to Forglen too difficult to transmit directly through the chancy postal system of eighteenth-century Mexico?

The present head of the Abercromby family, Sir Ian George, tenth baronet, has not specifically identified the progenitor of the American line, although he has been especially cooperative and most helpful in searching family records in Scotland and in Spain. He wrote to the author on March 3, 1983 his conclusion that "Josephine Abercrombie (and thereby her father Mr. Jim, and her own sons Jamie and George) are of the main branch of the family, descended from my great-great-great-great grandfather Sir James Abercromby, second baronet." (Sir James was the son of the Main Covenanter, and grandson of the Grand Falconer.)

In any event, we have voluminous records of Robert Abercromby's life in North Carolina, where he apparently married Jane Gresham (or Grisham) in 1741 and set down the birth of their first-born, Charles, the following year. These range from his appointment as a justice of the peace and frequent other political and civic assignments to his will, filed for probate August 31, 1779; but all that we really know of his origins in Scotland is that he listed his birthplace as "Scotland, 1715," and spoke often of Abercromby "cousins" for whom he named his sons and grandsons.

There was lively traffic between the principal Scots ports of Edinburgh and Glasgow, as well as nearby Liverpool; and New England, the Carolinas and the West Indies in the first half of the eighteenth century. One can imagine young Robert, determined to make his mark, and hearing constantly of opportunities in the New World, reading the notice in the Edinburgh *Evening-Courant* (conservative, founded in 1689) of January 10, 1735:

> The *St. Andrew* of Glasgow, John Brown, Master; burden 180 tons, now lying in harbour; will sail thence for (the colonies), wind and weather permitting, against the first day of February next. Gentmn inclining to transport themselves, goods or passengers may apply Messrs Thos Clarke or Lawrence Dinwiddie, Merchants, Glasgow who will agree with them on terms.

Similar notices would have been found in the other Edinburgh newspapers of the day: the *Caledonian-Mercury* (liberal, 1660) or the government *Gazette* (assumedly neutral, and dating from 1600). Here you had many other choices in a given month. You could select, for example, the *Diligence*, a one hundred and twenty-ton bark under Captain Hugh Crawford and Agent James Jamieson which specialized in swapping highly-trained artisans such as joiners (finish-work carpenters), millwrights, coopers (makers of barrels and staves), masons and blacksmiths "having a mind to indenture for four years," ship's passage for servitude and later opportunity; the *Dove*, on a regular run between Boston, Santa Lucia (the island source of tropical fruit, which fetched tremendous prices back home, and sweet wines), and Glasgow; or the *Elizabeth and Anne*, which plied regularly between Liverpool; Bridgetown, the capital of Barbados; and Charlestown, in the southern reaches of the Carolinas.

Sailing registers and lists of passengers for the period between 1735 and 1738 are very sketchy (or simply non-existent), but it is quite possible that Robert Abercromby left his native land on one of the vessels above. He was never to return to Scotland and would soon establish his American branch of the clan Abercromby, in what was to become Orange County, in the Piedmont of North Carolina.

Notes

[1] The Scots began to fight the English as soon as Kenneth I (The McAlpin) could unify them enough to be offered the throne of what was then called Caledonia, in 844. The battle was usually waged to establish or to defend self-determination in such vital matters as personal freedom, form of government, religion and economic well-being. Robert I (The Bruce) won a decisive victory over Edward II at Bannockburn in 1314, regaining independence for Scotland after centuries of struggle. Typically, he outmaneuvered a much larger English force after suffering through six earlier defeats and bitter criticism within his own ranks.

The beginnings of both The Fifteen rebellion and the revolt of 1745 are rooted deep in history, then, but heavy new emphasis on self-determination was added in 1513. In that fateful year, Scotland was ruled by the highly capable James IV, husband of Margaret Tudor and brother-in-law of Henry VIII of England. King James, always in support of the traditions of chivalry, was drawn up in battle array against Thomas Howard, earl of Surrey, at a tiny hamlet called Flodden in Northumberland. When Howard, short of supplies, proposed that the opposing armies decide the issue the next day, the Scots monarch accepted the challenge, although it was clearly to his disadvantage to do so. As a result, James IV and ten thousand of his men, among them the acknowledged leaders of the land, died. From this defeat came generations of repression and difficulty, but also, stubborn admiration for tradition, gentlemanly conduct and the underdog.

Fuel was added to the fire when Mary, Queen of Scots, unpopular though she had become with many of her countrymen, was executed by her cousin, Queen Elizabeth, in 1587. And Scots who had fought Charles I tooth and nail were appalled when he too was beheaded, in 1649.

Motivation for The Fifteen increased with the deposition forty years later of James II, younger brother of Charles II and the obvious heir to the English throne. Even though his ardent Roman Catholicism was anathema to Scots Presbyterians, many members of the Kirk joined the substantial Catholic population in expressing their opposition to William and Mary, who succeeded James II in 1689. Then the popular Old Pretender, the son of James II who would have been James III, was denied the throne (in spite of strong support from the ruling Tory party) after his sister Queen Anne (the last of the Stuarts) died in 1714.

When the German elector of Hanover (the great-grandson of James I of England, who was also James VI of Scotland) became George I, the Tories lost power almost completely to the Whigs. Henry St. John (Viscount Bolingbroke) and a few other Tory leaders then fled England for France, there to set up a government-in-exile for the Old Pretender. Working toward political ends, and some strictly non-violent means of regaining power, they were increasingly dismayed to discover the counter plans of some Scots led by John Erskine, the earl of Mar. They were far along with a scheme to launch the Jacobite (from Jacobus, the Latin for James) rebellion in the late fall. And they seemed to have a considerable amount of support, especially in the old Catholic strongholds of the Highlands and the northeast coast of Scotland.

Viscount Bolingbroke enlisted the services of the illegitimate half-brother of James III, James Fitzjames, the duke of Berwick. The son of James II and his mistress Arabella

Churchill, Fitzjames was a lieutenant-general in the French army, and both an able field commander and military analyst. Duke Berwick made a hurried and secretive trip to Scotland, and returned with an alarming report in the fall of 1715: The earl of Mar had recruited an enthusiastic and loyal Jacobite force, with minimal training, mediocre officers and little equipment or supplies. The matter was so far along, and morale so high, that little could be done to deter them.

The earl of Mar began the rebellion of 1715 with a premature uprising and demonstrations near the border, and then marched boldly into English territory. He was soon met by well-trained, adequately-supplied forces sent by the Whig ministers of state, and had to disband his own overmatched battalions in full retreat. The Old Pretender himself landed in Scotland soon thereafter, and aroused much sympathy and support; but he was forced to escape to France, and then to Italy, after a few clandestine meetings with his supporters.

So, The Fifteen was over, in realistic terms; but just as many another lost cause, it was fiercely alive in the emotions and memory of the Jacobites, and especially among the still-powerful Catholic clans of the Highlands and northeast shires.

George I, wisely counseled by his principal ministers, Charles (Viscount) Townshend and James, the earl of Stanhope, was reasonably lenient with the rebels. There was persecution at the leadership level, however, and some Jacobite prisoners, common soldiers fighting for what they felt was a just cause, were transported to the colonies for life.

A writ of attainder was issued against John Erskine, earl of Mar, and his vast estates in Aberdeenshire, dating back to the twelfth century, were forfeit. Mar himself was a controversial figure, but his great-grandfather had been the regent for, and protector of, the extremely popular James VI of Scotland (James I of England), and the family had held the highest posts for centuries. Further, Mar had caught the imagination of the Scots by boldly proclaiming the Old Pretender to be king of Great Britain before the earl's defeat by the Whig general John Campbell in Perthshire on November 13, 1715. There were also enough families bereft of a transported father, brother or cousin to cause deep, smouldering resentment. When John Abercromby of Dunfermline was sent from Liverpool to New England in chains on the ship *Elizabeth and Anne* on June 29, 1716 with other rebels, there was a rumor that the ship would be deliberately scuttled, and all Jacobite prisoners left to drown. In a tragic incident in 1679, 175 of 200 political prisoners being sent to Virginia perished when their ship went down off the Orkneys.

The rebellion of 1745 was fed by the still-flickering flames of The Fifteen, and by the romantic vision of Bonnie Prince Charlie, the handsome Young Pretender and son of the exiled James III, coming back to lead Scotland to final ascendancy over England. Reared a staunch Roman Catholic abroad, and ever hopeful of discovering enough French, Scots and dissident English support to regain the throne, Charles Edward Stuart was enroute to England with a powerful French invasion fleet in 1744. This came to nothing; the Dover-bound ships were decimated by a furious storm. One year later, buoyed up by reports that the Highland clans were readying potent support, and some indications that both French and English help would be forthcoming, the Bonnie Prince landed on the desolate coast of Inverness with seven followers on August 19, 1745. He was met (and blessed) by Bishop Hugh MacDonald, vicar apostolic to the persecuted Catholics of Scotland.

Prince Charles raised his standard at Glenfinnan, and the clan bagpipes wailed the most warlike of the traditional *pibrochs*, or martial airs played before battle. Within weeks, he had not only the Highlands, but much of Scotland in tumult. His countrymen seemed more and more of the opinion that the Young Pretender's cause was not simply Roman Catholic Jacobites versus the Hanoverian intruder George I, but Scots, whether Catholic, Presbyterian or Jacobite, against the ancient enemy, England. Edinburgh fell to his enthusiastic forces on September 17, and he soundly defeated an English force under Sir John Cope at nearby Prestonpans on September 21.

In mid-November, Prince Charles invaded England, although he was still anxiously awaiting help from France and from English dissidents, as well as further reinforcements and supplies from Scotland. At Derby, Charles Stuart came face to face with reality. It was December 4, with the weather deteriorating daily and weeks of bitter cold and punishing sleet in prospect. He had neither the manpower nor the equipment or supplies to push further south without major assistance. The reasonable option seemed to be to retreat north in good order, thereby shortening supply lines and hopefully attracting new Scots recruits. And northward he marched.

After a minor victory over a pursuing Royalist force at Falkirk, the Bonnie Prince watched his troop strength dwindle day by day. He and his commanders decided to plead with the clans for maximum reinforcement, allowing the Jacobite army to risk everything on a decisive engagement in the spring.

The showdown came on April 16, 1746, on the moor of Culloden (in Old Gaelic, *cul lodain*, or "the back of the swamp"). The clans were drawn up in battle array, with the terrible broadswords and dirks at the ready. In the ranks were even a few nine- and ten-year-olds, and a teenaged Malcolm MacLeod, who ran away from school with a purloined pistol and dirk to join the fray. Up front was the beautiful Anne, Lady Mackintosh, on a spirited cavalry charger, her curls covered by a blue tam. Her estranged husband had disgraced the clan by taking an English commission; with much misgiving, she would be allowed to take the field and redeem the family honor.

Across the moor in a strategically superior position were the English, under George I's son (and Charles Stuart's cousin), the pudgy William Augustus, duke of Cumberland. His artillerymen, firing endless rounds of grapeshot, would inflict terrible losses on the clansmen from the very beginning. The Jacobites were to lose the battle soon after it was joined. For the remainder of the spring, Cumberland earned the title "Butcher of Culloden." His execution squads roamed the countryside constantly, seeking out anyone even suspected of having rebel ties. Hundreds, including women and children, were relentlessly hunted down and murdered in cold blood.

The Bonnie Prince Charlie escaped to France after being hidden by the Nicholsons, a sept of the clan MacLeod, on their lands at Scorrybreck. But the rebellion of 1745 was only a bitter memory, the power of the clans was diminished forever, and the Jacobite cause irretrievably lost. Charles Edward, the lost last hope of the Stuarts, would wander over Europe until his death in Rome in 1788, a lonely quixotic whose story still lives in the plaintive, lament-laden ballads of the Highlands.

[2] The baronets Abercromby now stand sixty-fifth in order of precedence on the Official Roll of the United Kingdom.

[3] There is substantial documentation of how Sir Hugh of Padavan, once a knight of Normandy, came along with a detachment of archers and pikeman just in time to save Malcolm III from King William's border guards on an earlier raid. Sir Hugh had been given marginal lands along the River Tyne for his services at Hastings, but a grateful Malcolm now awarded him a far better holding in Renwickshire, and the right to embellish his modest coat-of-arms substantially. A winged hourglass was added above the shield, and surmounting this, the motto, "In Tempore" ("In Time"). Rampant greyhounds were placed left and right, indicating the speed with which Sir Hugh had come to the rescue of the Scots king.

Malcolm's protector called his new estate along the River Clyde "Padavan," but the Lowlands Scots had difficulty pronouncing this, and renamed it "Hughstown," or Houstoun. The variant spelling was Houston.

None other than General Sam Houston learned of the Houstoun/Houston coat-of-arms and claimed it for his own. When President Edison E. Oberholtzer and Chairman Hugh Roy Cullen were searching for a seal for the new University of Houston in 1938, they adopted Sir Hugh of Padavan's insignia. They especially like the motto "In Time," so appropriate for a beginning institution in a city and area of vast potential.

[4] Three centuries and more after the Old Laird and Sir James Abercromby, their kinsman James S. Abercrombie was one of the best shots in Texas, if not in the United States, when it came to hunting quail or dove.

[5] Often slighted by historians, James VI (the great-grandson of Henry VIII's sister, Princess Margaret) was the son of Mary, Queen of Scots. His 22-year reign as King James I of England was a sorely-needed time of peace and the binding up of wounds, after a long period of controversy, war and unrest. The first of the Stuart kings, he became the link to the Hanoverian dynasty through his daughter, Elizabeth of Bohemia. Elizabeth married the Elector Palatine, and was George I's grandmother. At the outbreak of World War II, every ruling monarch in Europe except the King of Albania was descended directly from her, and thereby from James VI.

[6] John Knox became interested in the nascent Protestant Reformation in Scotland soon after being ordained as a Roman Catholic priest at the age of twenty-five in 1539. He was greatly influenced by the writings of George Wishart, who was burned at the stake as a heretic, and became the leader of the Reformation after Wishart's death. Imprisoned in 1647, he was sent to France as a galley slave, but released two years later through the intervention of English Protestants.

After preaching in English reformed churches, and beginning to publish the first of his significant works on the Reformation in Scotland, Knox had to flee London for Geneva when Mary, Queen of Scots came to the throne in 1553. Six years later, he returned to Edinburgh as the stern and powerful leader of the Reformation in the Presbyterian Kirk. By the time of his death, in 1572, he had reshaped Protestantism in Scotland, from its markedly austere tone through all aspects of finance, administration, liturgy and theology. If John Knox could be remembered for only one thing, however, he would want it to be for his fierce, unrelenting opposition to Catholicism.

[7] Catherine of Navarre is sometimes confused with her cousin Catherine of Aragon, Henry VIII's first wife. Pope Clement VII's refusal to annul King Henry's marriage to Catherine of Aragon brought about England's break with Rome and the establishment of the Anglican Church.

[8] For some inscrutable reason, St. Andrew's Parish, named for the apostle and brother of St. Peter who is the patron saint of all Scotland, is now St. Monan's Parish, which makes it even more difficult to discover ancient records from the parish town of Abercrombie. St. Monan was probably Monanus, an archdeacon who was martyred in the year 871; but he could also have been St. Moineen, the celebrated bishop of Clonfert (died 571), or St. Monyn, a friend of St. Patrick who died early in the sixth century.

[9] If the dour John Knox had any sense of humor whatsoever, he must have been at least mildly amused to see Calvinist Presbyterians take over "Greyfriars Kirk." The "grey friars" were the Franciscans, one of the great medieval orders of Catholic monks, founded by St. Francis of Assisi early in the thirteenth century. The Franciscans built Greyfriars Church half a millenium ago, only to see it become a Protestant stronghold during the Reformation.

[10] Charles I fled in disguise to the Isle of Wight in the last days of 1648. There he signed a secret agreement with the New (Scots) Model Army and agreed to at least the temporary establishment of the (Presbyterian) Kirk as the state church of Scotland, in return for military support against Oliver Cromwell and Parliament. The agreement was a prime factor in Charles Stuart's being brought to trial for high treason a month later.

[11] William Lyte of St. George's Parish disposed of a handsome estate under a will of November 27, 1701, witnessed by Alexander Abercrombie. A codicil adds as a beneficiary "that childe in the belly of my wyfe," and makes further grants of "those Cows I did bring from Scotland" and "that certain Negro woman bought of Mrs. Edward Lascelles."

In the first quarter of the eighteenth century, sugar could be produced in Barbados at perhaps a tenth of a cent a pound, by slave labor. Laid down in London (for many exporters, in hogsheads, large casks holding 52.5 Imperial gallons), sugar was priced at about seven pence. It rose to eight pence and then as high as ten pence when there was a drouth throughout the Sugar Islands early in the 1730s. From such profitable trade, Edward Lovell, Gent(leman) of Christ Church Parish, Barbados had enough land and other resources after less than twenty years as a planter to leave separate estates to each of his five sons, his wife Mary Maycove, daughter Sarah, and even to his brother-in-law, Patrick Maycove. Mary Abercrombie witnessed the Lovell will on December 23, 1718.

Even a cordwainer (shoemaker, curiously enough, from the Spanish leather center of Cordoba where cordovan leather originated), one Markham McKale of Bridgetown did well enough on Barbados to point out specifically in his will that "Henry Mullineux has (in safekeeping) 130 pounds sterling of mine."

[12] James Abercrombie, a Latin as well as a legal scholar, is thought to have suggested during colonial days the motto of the state of South Carolina: "Dum spiro, spero," or "Whilst I breathe, I hope." A Houston wag sent George Fuermann, then the Houston *Post*'s highly popular Post Card columnist, a telegram shortly after Richard Nixon had selected the obscure governor of Maryland, Spiro Agnew of later gross culpability, as his vice presidential running mate. "Have identified Spiro Agnew," the telegram read, "he is a Latin epigram, '*dum spiro, spero*'."

[13] Captain Abercromby was stationed near sixteen thousand acres of Nova Scotian land which were at least technically granted to the family in 1636 by Charles I. Actually, formal possession, or the feudal act of *seizin*, was never accomplished by the Abercrombys, since Nova Scotia was ceded to France in 1632. Holders of earlier such grants could go by Whitehall in London for the ceremonial rite of *seizin* in which they scooped up and took with them a small quantity of Nova Scotian dirt, specially imported for the purpose.

[14] The letter unfortunately does not indicate either the state, county or town from which it was written, although the date, contents and signature (Robert Abercromby) are easily decipherable.

Chapter 2

1741–1786

Orange County, North Carolina

Robert Abercromby, Orange County planter, justice of the peace and gentleman . . . Sir Walter Raleigh's Lost Colony . . . Charles II gives away "Carolana" . . . The first of the new American Abercrombies: Charles, Robert, Jr. and Jane (called Jenny) . . . Part of the power structure in a unique society . . . Eastern cliques against western Piedmont "Regulators" at Alamance Creek . . . The Revolution, as Patriots, not Tory-Loyalists . . . Major Charles' muster ground and Moore's Creek . . . The death and legacy of Robert, Sr. . . . Robert, Jr. learns of Georgia's new cotton land . . . Downtown Durham, or fresh opportunity?

Orange County, North Carolina was not organized until 1752, eleven years after we believe Robert Abercromby reached the then almost desolate area of the Piedmont, less than twenty miles south of the Virginia border. To understand what could be one of the most forbidding, and yet challenging and potentially rewarding areas in the New World, we should go back briefly into history: first, a century-and-a-half to one of the most captivating figures of the Elizabethan era, Sir Walter Raleigh; and then to the post-Restoration years of Charles II, whose enormous grants of land to loyal supporters resulted in the establishment of six of the original thirteen American colonies, including North Carolina.

Raleigh's half-brother, Sir Humphrey Gilbert, held charter to a vast tract that encompassed present Virginia plus portions of the Carolinas coast. When Sir Gilbert was lost on the tiny pinnace *Squirrel* on his way home from Newfoundland in 1583, his grant was inherited by Raleigh, a favorite of Queen Elizabeth who would be knighted in 1585, and appointed captain of the royal guard two years later.

Raleigh ordered a reconnaissance of what is now Croatan Sound, North Carolina in 1584. The report emphasized fertile soil, marvelous air and Indians who were said to be, "utterly free of guile, living as in a Golden Age, most gentle, loving and faithful." Accordingingly, Sir Walter sent a party of one hundred colonists the next year to adjoining Roanoke Island. All that saved this group, which included an artist, writer, surveyor and metallurgist—but no one who had ever attempted to wrest a living from a windswept, storm-plagued island next to a swampy wilderness, was the decency of Sir Francis Drake.

The circumnavigator Drake, commanding an ill-provisioned ship with a scurvy-ridden, half-mutinous crew anxious to return home after months at sea and highly successful raids against the Spanish Main, remembered his friend Raleigh's hapless colonists and went by Roanoke Island for a look. He found an ill, half-starved group attempting to live on seafood, short even of drinking water and too weak and inexperienced to construct proper shelter against the fierce storms that battered the nearby Outer Banks, or to clear enough acreage to plant crops.

News of this near-disaster failed to impress Sir Walter Raleigh, or apparently to become widely known after the grateful survivors were taken home to England. Within months, Sir Walter had organized a new venture in partnership with Governor John White of Virginia. This time, one hundred and seventeen men, women and children were taken to a different part of Roanoke Island, in the northern reaches of Pamlico Sound.[1]

History tells us that Raleigh's reconnaissance report was flawed in the extreme. The truth of the matter is that the Indians in the vicinity, reported to be "living as in a Golden Age," were malnourished themselves, in a severely overpopulated area. Food soon became a crucial problem for Sir Walter's tiny outpost, and things went from bad to worse there while he and England's other leaders prepared for a showdown with Spain, averted when the mighty Spanish Armada was destroyed in 1588 by a combination of Elizabeth I's fleet, superior naval strategy and unprecedented storms in the English Channel. Drowned Spanish seamen washed ashore for weeks, from Lyme Bay to Dover.

It was two years before Raleigh got around to inquiring about the second group sent to Roanoke Island. Early in 1590, he arranged for a privateer enroute to the Sugar Islands to bring supplies to the little settlement. The ship finally arrived offshore, fired a six-pounder, and even had the crew sing English folk songs as a further means of identification. When there was no response, a longboat went ashore with an increasingly puzzled party of captain and crewmen.

They found scattered remnants of supplies, rusted weapons and bits of armor, the beginning of a stockade and a few huts covered with quick-growing vines—but no sign of life. On the largest tree in the area, there was carved the word "Croatan," the name of a principal island some hundred miles to the south.

The searching party spent a day or two looking around, without discovering any further clues to one of the mysteries of history: The Lost Colony. They then sailed home, and later investigations of Croatan Island and the entire coast turned up nothing. It was presumed that the unfortunate settlers perished of starvation and disease, probably aggravated by raids from Indians who saw the newcomers as a threat to already minimal food supplies. It has also been surmised that the armor, pikes and harquebuses with which some of the colonists were equipped greatly alarmed the natives, who launched stealthy attacks by night, when the advantage of a harquebus over a knife or club was greatly diminished.[2]

The Indians may have killed and buried surviving adults, taking children with them to be raised by the tribe. The Croatan-Lumbees of southeast North Carolina (now the few remaining Lumbees) have songs and legends that tell of white children raised by them long ago, and absorbed into their gene bank and culture.

The tragedy of The Lost Colony meant that the sixteenth century would end without an English colony on the American mainland, while the intermittent war with Spain flared up again; but Britain's emergence as a world power, through her domination of the seas, meant that the spotlight would return to the New World, rather than to the earlier pattern of costly, bloodletting wars on the Continent.

Charles II has been roundly criticized for everything from his plethora of mistresses to reportedly chasing butterflies for the royal collection while the Dutch, enraged by losing profitable English shipping contracts after promulgation of the protectionist Navigation Acts of 1660–1663, captured and burned most of his naval fleet near the mouth of the Thames[3]; he was an excellent man to have on your side, however, if you were a loyal and ambitious supporter seeking a vast concession of land.

Three such men came to their king in the first months after he had regained the throne following the death of the arch-enemy of the royal Stuarts, Oliver Cromwell. They were Sir Anthony Ashley Cooper, later the powerful earl of Shaftsbury; Sir John Colleton, an enormously wealthy planter seeking new homes for his overcrowded colonists on the Sugar Island of Barbados; and Governor William Berkely of Virginia. A year later, in 1661, the trio added General George Monck (later duke of Albemarle), the one person most responsible for Charles II being restored to the throne; Edward Hyde, earl of Clarendon, who fled to France with the young Charles II-to-be in 1648, and became a leading statesman and the historian of the English Civil War; George Lord Granville, a member of the Privy Council who would one day own half of North Carolina; and two silent partners with little influence but plenty of capital.

These so-called "proprietors" apparently decided early on to ask for a vast territory from which they could carve out huge chunks for resale to various colonizing groups. And a vast territory is exactly what they received from Charles II in 1663: "Carolina" (first called "Carolana"), which grandly included everything from Virginia to some vague borders near Spanish Florida.

Most of the first emphasis was on what is now South Carolina, although it would be 1729 before the Carolinas were made twain, and an early settler, James Abercromby, was sent to Charles Town as first attorney-general of South Carolina. There were enormous difficulties connected with the beginning attempts at colonization: two of the first three ships to depart England with settlers for the new colony were shipwrecked; a third limped into Barbados, finally re-embarked with deep misgivings by the passengers, and reached the original site of Charles Town in the spring of 1670[4]; a highly impractical "constitution of Carolana," drafted, of all people, by the philosopher John Locke, discouraged immigration by requiring approval of all legislation by a clique of the largest landowners, most of them absentee speculators; another settlement, Port Royal, had to be abandoned even by a tough detachment of Highland militiamen, battle-hardened in the endless clashes between the Scots clans, because of continuing skirmishes with the threatening Spanish, who still claimed virtually all of the Carolinas, and operated from an impregnable fort at old St. Augustine, on the northern borders of Florida.

A fundamental problem in the Carolinas was one encountered later in Georgia: the climate was not really suited to, nor did the markets yet exist for, the raising of silkworms, wine grapes, currants and olives in commercial quantities; it would be almost a generation before Henry Woodward, responsible for many things including the relocation of Charles Town, brought in a strain of rice (originally smuggled out of Madagascar by a ship's captain) ideally suited to the soil, climate and increasingly black population of South Carolina. North Carolina was even less adapted to silkworms, currants and olives, although wild grapes did thrive in some areas; but there were never enough slaves, other than in the coastal areas, to support labor-intensive rice growing.

As a result, the early Carolinians simply gave up on the rather exotic crops originally envisioned for them, and existed raising scrawny cattle and half-wild hogs; cutting timber; making barrel staves; distilling crude turpentine, rosin, pitch and tar from the millions of pine trees that covered much of the colony; and tanning deerskins. Most of these products went to Barbados, where the planters were too busy raising sugar to be bothered about the extra cost of imports, especially if they were essentials from such a relatively close source, and not the luxury items—often extremely expensive, obtainable only in England. In time, tobacco (and to a limited extent, cotton) would become important crops in North Carolina, and South Carolina would emerge as a very significant source of rice, along with the Cape Fear region in North Carolina.

Meanwhile, what would become North Carolina was beginning to develop quite differently, although there would be relatively little settlement in the future state until the Carolinas were split in 1729. This was to be particularly true in the gently undulating northwestern paraplain of the Piedmont, separated from eastern North Carolina by swamps and other natural barriers, and far from South Carolina's superior ports and harbors.

We know something of how Orange County appeared a half-century before it was organized in 1752 as a huge political subdivision of some 2.6 million acres, or four thousand square miles. This is through journals kept by a German physician, John Lederer, and by a prospective settler, John Lawson. Dr. Lederer, primarily a man of medicine but evidently a broadly-educated, highly intelligent immigrant who had settled in Virginia, wanted to observe the Indians of the region at first hand. He took the Great Trading Path of the regional tribes (later a part of the Great Wagon Road) from the deep south border of Virginia through present-day Hillsborough and Mebane to the Haw River, enroute to the lands of the Catawba Nation. His first impression was of a beautiful but desolate land, uninhabited as yet by white settlers, where you could travel in pristine silence except for your own footsteps and those of your guide-interpreter and temporary porter, walking almost soundlessly over a thick carpet of pine needles or struggling through underbrush growing undisturbed for months and even years.

A few miles from what would become the colonial capital of Hillsborough (and in the vicinity of Robert Abercromby's first home, near the future settlement of West Point), the German physician came upon a branch of the Eno tribe. These were primitive farmers of Siouxan extraction who lived in small huts of wattle and mud on the edge of clearings where they raised three crops of corn or millet-like grain a year. When he expressed much surprise at this rate of productivity, the Enos explained through Dr. Lederer's interpreter that they were semi-nomadic, moving on as soon as the soil showed any appreciable decrease in output; further, they understood the principles of fertilization and used forest humus to enrich their fields. As proof of their agricultural prowess, they showed the German primitive granaries from which they bartered with their Eno and Shocco cousins, who lived primarily on venison and fish, looked with disdain on farmers, yet still needed corn and millet for Indian bread, a staple of the frontier diet.

Dr. Lederer learned much from the farming Enos; not only concerning their crops, but the secrets of the dense forests and scattered plains, and of the many creeks and rivers of the area. They showed him the more fertile land along the watercourses; the almost countless varieties of game, from the highly prized bronze turkeys to the opossums they trapped along the creeks; fish, also plentifully available; where to find herbs in the forest, and their many uses; delicacies such as the fruits of wild trees and shrubs, and nuts that they parched over a slow fire.

He was much impressed by long and sometimes marginally translatable conversations around a campfire at night, usually inspired by a potent liquor the Enos distilled from grain; in these long discussions, they attempted to spell out their ideas concerning democratic rule within the tribe, great respect for the aged, and other laudable traits described by the German visitor. He left the tribe puzzled as to why some of them, and not others, would hire out by the day as porters, to be paid in trinkets each evening by his interpreter. The porters, he wrote, were usually those of less than average height or strength, possibly held in low regard within the tribe.

Another area of Orange County is described by Lawson, who noted first of all the rich, deep alluvial soil in narrow bands along the Big and Little Alamance Rivers, during a journey from the Virginia border south to the Cape Fear region along the coast, in 1701. Although he had some ability himself in the Indian dialects (which would be corrupted later by the invasion of pidgin English), he took along a skilled interpreter. This was ''Eno Will,'' a member of the island-dwelling Oconeechee tribe; a native of lands well to the west, over the future boundary with Georgia, he had been driven from his home by a series of floods, but had not been too well received by the Eno, Shocco and Adushusheer tribesmen of the Carolinas.

After a none-too-hospitable reception by some Shoccos, Eno Will found that he was looked down upon for associating so closely with a white man. He turned things around by insisting that John Lawson had substantial standing in his own world, knew a number of Indian words and phrases and had come as any man of wisdom, to learn from others. He then won the day by presenting a crude pocket knife to the head Shocco.

This enabled Eno Will to purchase a supply of dried venison and bear meat, not unlike the beef jerky that brought other pioneers through the great transcontinental migrations in later eras. Now, with the fish readily available in the creeks and rivers, and the small animals they trapped at night, he and Lawson would not want for food.

Although there was some lingering of distrust of both Eno Will and John Lawson, the Indians they encountered in the future area of Hillsborough and West Point were soon curious enough to gather around at night with gifts of smoked fish, nuts and the same distilled ''white lightning'' that Dr. Lederer had imbibed. This went well enough, Lawson wrote, until the ever-more-friendly visitors broke out a variety of drums and rattles some time after midnight. The ensuing serenade, apparently an unmatched exercise in atonality and cacophony, went on until dawn. Eno Will explained the next day that this had been a mark of high regard for both John Lawson and himself, amounting almost to honorary initiation into the regional tribes represented.

Just as other observers, John Lawson was struck by the almost total desolation of the future Orange County, but taken with evidence of large regions with fairly fertile soil. He too traveled for hours, even days, without encountering a white man or any evidence of a settlement, in the ongoing expanse of the vacant Piedmont. This was a phenomenon to be experienced by travelers on into the next century, as they sometimes found the larger plantations separated by distances of ten to fifteen miles, and only a sprinkling of smaller towns in some western counties.

Lawson also pointed out the absence of a fine natural harbor such as Charleston or Savannah anywhere in North Carolina, which had only Wilmington in the Cape Fear area, and the nearby river landings at Brunswick on the Waccamaw as anything resembling a major port. New Bern, the future Swiss-German settlement in the eastern part of the colony, would have limited access to the Atlantic Ocean through Ocracoke Inlet, Pamlico Sound and the broad Neuse River; and Edenton, much farther north and east, was on Batchelor Bay at the mouth of the Chowan River, but arrivals and departures via Albemarle Sound and the ocean beyond were quite difficult. Many a skipper making for New Bern or Edenton in the years to come would complain constantly of long delays occasioned by sand bars and treacherous currents; of a lack of warehousing; of being tied up for days in "Okracock" (Ocracoke Inlet) or "Choosey" (the Chowan River). Ocean transportation was not North Carolina's strong suit.

Sales of land in the Carolinas did not go well at all for the eight proprietors, in spite of some heroic efforts by the energetic and optimistic Sir John Colleton. The first group of settlers from overcrowded Barbados he sent to the Cape Fear region in 1665 found poor soil, mosquitoes, illness and antagonistic Indians. Two years later, near desperation, they split into two parties. The first walked two hundred miles somehow to a tiny outpost on Albemarle Sound, where ships that could negotiate the narrow passages and shallow water in the area finally took them on to Virginia, or back to Barbados. The remainder of the unhappy new Carolinians went to Wilmington to await infrequent sailings that finally returned them to England, via Boston, or to Virginia for another try at life in the colonies.

Sir John, little dismayed and handsomely financed out of his own exchequer, next brought French Huguenots to Charles Town in

1680. These religious dissidents, intelligent, hard-working and inured to difficulty by long years of persecution, became in time the nucleus of a highly prosperous and cultivated capital city of South Carolina; but that prosperity was half a century and more down the road, awaiting the full flowering of the rice and indigo industries, and the deliberate development of a gracious and fulfilling way of life that alternated between great coastal plantations and elegant Charleston townhomes of distinctive and felicitous architecture. Prominent Huguenot families from the original settlement of 1680, including such names as Pettigrew (Pettigru), Pingree and Huger, would lead their city, region and state for generations.

Turning next to the northeastern borders of what would be North Carolina, Colleton, with the aid of Lord Granville, sold a huge tract to Swiss and German developers at New Bern (identified earlier at the confluence of the Neuse River and Pamlico Sound).

On balance, however, the Carolinas scheme simply did not seem to be working. The entire white population of North Carolina, for example, was estimated at less than five thousand (virtually all of them concentrated in the Cape Fear and nearby coastal region) in 1700. Charles Town had been moved ten miles downstream to a far better location at the confluence of the Ashley and Cooper Rivers (both named for Anthony Ashley Cooper) and was showing real progress when the Creek and Yamasee Indians revolted, killed four hundred settlers, including some leading merchants and planters, and set the entire colony in reverse. There were difficulties in North Carolina, as well. Highly profitable crops such as rice and the government-subsidized indigo could be grown only in the extreme south around Cape Fear, and even in that favorable environment, required a heavy investment in slaves. Further, North Carolinians had problems with the warlike Tuscaroras in the north, and even with the far-away Cherokees,[5] who had begun to come east and south on raiding parties.

But the central problem remained: not enough sales of land, and not nearly enough settlers, for such a gigantic grant as the Carolinas.

By 1720, seven of the eight proprietors, or their heirs and successors, were ready to throw in the towel, including the highly active Sir John Colleton. Only Lord Granville, whose one-eighth of the 1663 grant encompassed the northern half of North Carolina, decided to stick it out. The seven sellers struck a bargain with the brilliant Robert Walpole, who served under George II as England's first prime minister, in the later sense of the term. This was accomplished very soon after the second Hanoverian king acceded to the throne, in 1727. There had been earlier attempts to deal directly with George I, first of the Hanovers, but the difficulties were several: he spoke German by preference, knew more Latin than English, spent most of his time in northwest Germany and seemed to have no interest whatsoever in the Carolinas.

Charles II's friends the proprietors, or at least seven of the eight, simply gave up too soon. George II quickly split off Georgia in a separate grant to James Oglethorpe and the other trustees of that new colony in 1732, but both South and North Carolina began to move strongly toward prosperity almost before Parliament had ratified their reacquisition by the crown. As the rice plantations in South Carolina began to expand almost geometrically with the importation of thousands of slaves, they initiated an enormously profitable export trade through the booming port of Charleston. North Carolina saw a quite different development, based upon the burgeoning arrival of immigrants from Virginia and Pennsylvania, in the main small farmers or indentured craftsmen; of English and Scots emigrating directly from their homeland; and of colonies such as that established by more than one thousand German and Swiss settlers at New Bern.

The word was finally out, albeit too late for all but Lord Granville, and it was a compelling message: cheap land, low taxes and plenty of work ranging from the constant task of clearing land for planting to coopering to complicated wheelwrighting.

In the period between 1730 and 1750, North Carolina's population doubled; it then almost tripled again between 1750 and 1770. This represented a gain of nearly six hundred percent in little more than a generation. And the increase was heavily concentrated in the underpopulated western Piedmont after 1750. Orange County, for example, had less than nine hundred "white taxables" when organized in 1752. The later figures speak for themselves: 1753, 1108; 1757, 1595; 1761, 2627; and 1767, 3870. Lord Granville made an astounding offer for a brief time to underscore just how cheap land could be if you owned millions of acres and wanted them settled. He actually offered land in less attractive parts of the Piedmont at a section (six hundred forty acres or a square mile) for three silver shillings. There were certain homesteading and land-clearing provisions, but three shillings a section is free land.

The North Carolinians who flocked into the future state were a quite different breed of cat from settlers in the surrounding colonies. These were yeomen, small independent farmers discouraged by the relatively high cost of land in Virginia and Pennsylvania, and by a social structure, especially in Virginia, that militated against upward mobility or the creation of a middle class. They were also Highlanders, Lowlanders and English, often still in their early twenties, seeking a better opportunity in agriculture, commerce or a combination thereof; dour, canny Scotch-Irish who would either stay on small farms or open an ordinary (tavern) at some crossroads; and a much more cosmopolitan category of settlers from continental Europe. To add to this interesting mix, there was a small percentage of the younger sons of well-established Scots and English families; a few attorneys and physicians; merchants; speculators; and a sprinkling of the soldiers of fortune every frontier attracts.

There were very few slaves in North Carolina, especially when compared to South Carolina or Virginia, although concentrations began to develop in the coastal sector of the south and southeast with the introduction of rice as a principal crop; and there was a natural tendency for farmers climbing the economic scale through succeeding rungs of prosperous farmer, planter and rich planter to purchase more and more blacks, even if outside the rice belt.

The unique raw materials available spawned in North Carolina an intriguing new society divided into a singular version of what colonial historians and sociologists termed the categories of Better Sort, Middling and Lower Sort. The categories, however, were without the sharp differentiations and impermeable boundaries that one might expect. The numerous "middling" yeomen were conscious of the fact that a "better sort" existed, saw the clear possibility of moving up one notch by industry and good fortune, and were perfectly willing to allow the "better sort" the prerogatives (and problems) of leadership so long as a "democratick" atmosphere prevailed in which they or their sons and daughters might scale the social and economic ladder if they chose to attempt it.

The "better sort" accepted these unwritten but clearly-understood rules; held their style of living well below the ostentation of their Virginia peers (or of a heavily-mortgaged South Carolina planter they might be able to buy out in any test of liquid assets); ate with their hats on in the presence of similarly-attired yeomen; and were willing to help a deserving "middling" who was clearly on the ascent, even to the occasional extent of marrying a son to a "middling" daughter, if there were enough barrels of pitch or corn-fed cattle in the dowry.

It is interesting to note that the difficult years of the "Regulator War," as we shall see, were caused as much as anything by a violation of the essential understanding that "middlings" had yielded power of their own volition, with an unwritten guarantee that the "better sort" would not usurp "middling" rights, whether respecting tangible property or the intangible, and priceless, prerogative of social mobility and reasonable equality. A few unscrupulous members of the "better sort" abandoned the rules, sparks began to fly, mass meetings were held, and scattered instances of violence flared into armed conflict at the Alamance.

The "lower sort" tended to be heavily outnumbered by "middlings" in North Carolina. They were usually indentured servants or common laborers, rather than trained artisans who had "signed on" for the usual period of four years to obtain passage to the New World, and quickly found employment and their place in "middling" society after completing their term of indenture. The inability to read or write, or to "cypher to the rule of three," also tended to condemn a man to the bottom rung, even though illiterate "middlings" escaped this often by delegating to a literate wife, son or daughter, or through uncommon shrewdness or common sense. There were a small number of transported prisoners, or those totally lacking in ambition or presence (or both) who gravitated naturally to the third level. Many transported for political reasons, including a goodly number of those rebelling in "The Fifteen," were in contrast given special welcome and standing in the Wilmington and Brunswick areas, and in Scotland and Cumberland counties where the Scots were concentrated.[6]

The "lower sort" tended to look to the "middlings" for protection of their rights, as well as for employment. Both were usually provided, and there was no inclination among the middle class (or for that matter, among the "better sort") to hold down a "lower sort" with the ability to ascend the sociological ladder. In a unique case, a man less than a decade out of debtor's prison made a fortune in land speculation, built himself a handsome brick home in New

Bern, and vaulted into the "better sort" category, later marrying into one of the leading families of eastern North Carolina.

This, then, was North Carolina; or more specifically, the northern half of that colony (Lord Granville's "District"), when Robert Abercromby arrived there in 1741, presumably from Barbados: the locus for what would be a very different, essentially egalitarian society, sandwiched between the long-established First Families of Virginia and the beginning elegance of South Carolina. This was a land of dense forests, yet with plains that could be cultivated with minimal effort, while the forests and lesser woods were being cleared; much of the soil a fairly fertile mixture of loam and clay best suited to corn, wheat, oats and legumes (and thereby for raising cattle and hogs as well); areas throughout the colony, extending into the northern boundary with Virginia, where a fine quality of tobacco could be grown. On the negative side, North Carolina had marginal transportation on shallow rivers obstructed from the Atlantic Ocean by wide, deep stretches of swampland and sand barriers; and, as we will see: roads so bad that a colonial governor would label them "wretched," that pungent British descriptive; it was as well a colony handicapped by a clearly inchoate infrastructure, with rudimentary schools, churches and governmental apparatus—yet, overall, a land of energy, promise and opportunity.

In retrospect, much of the energy and promise, and thereby the opportunity, contemporary observers pointed out, may well have come from the difference between the healthy, upland Piedmont and the malarial swamps of eastern and deep southern regions of North Carolina.

By the time Robert Abercromby arrived in what would become Orange County, Henry McCulloh, an English speculator encouraged by the continuing withdrawal of the remaining hostile Indians, Lord Granville's bargain basement prices and the growing influx of settlers, had blocked together holdings totaling 1.2 million acres. He and his son Henry Eustace would offer tracts averaging only three hundred acres, in order to continue stimulating immigration. Although land records prior to 1752 do not exist in Orange County, the McCulloh offerings and Lord Granville's own extremely generous terms would indicate that Robert began to amass land soon after his arrival. As late as 1770, he was purchasing tracts by the section (640 acres), as were his sons Charles (born 1742) and Robert, Jr. (born 1748); the father and sons held individually, jointly among them or with various relatives by marriage, thousands of acres at differing times.

Homes were quite modest in the Piedmont of pre-Revolutionary Orange County, and for that matter over much of the state of North Carolina-to-be. A man wanted what was often described as a "tolerable" dwelling place, not one advertising his material progress. Robert Abercromby and his wife Jane Gresham probably began their married life in a log cabin, since lumber was very difficult to obtain in the western sector of present Orange County before the first sawmills were opened along the Eno River in 1752.[7]

The usual design was a small structure twenty to twenty-four feet square (or rectangular in a somewhat smaller dimension front to back), with a single large room dominated by a huge fireplace of chimney rock, a loft above for sleeping, puncheon (split log) floors and a detached kitchen. Outbuildings, pens and corrals were added in the rear.

In the next stage, and this must have come rather soon for the Robert Abercrombys, a daughter Jane (Jenny) having arrived between her two brothers in 1743, a cottage of pine lumber would replace the log cabin. This might have been delayed until the first mill opened on the Eno in 1752, but it customarily would still have been a relatively small home, with four rooms separated by the traditional "dog run" straight through the downstairs, and the addition of a porch plus an inside stairway to the bedrooms in a half-story above.

As the family increased in size, well-to-do farmers and planters normally built a considerably larger dwelling on a nearby clearing, using the best grade of pine covered with several coats of the expensive yet surprisingly good white paint that area merchants carried at the standard mark-up of two-and-a-half times London retail prices. Some Piedmont residences in this category began to add such attractions as large living and dining rooms, or even a sewing room and library, as the pre-Revolutionary era was drawing to a close; but few homes in North Carolina, even well into the nineteenth century, approached the elegance found in other areas of the colonies.

A notable exception, mentioned in a later chapter, was the residence at the Brick House Farm, a showplace of antique English brick probably brought over as ship's ballast. This had been built by Sheriff Tyree Harris, Robert Abercromby, Jr.'s father-in-law and neighbor; it was said in jest to rival (Governor William) Tryon's "Palace" at New Bern, an expensive and controversial structure designed in the Georgian style by the English architect John Hawks. While the Harris home was not up to the governor's residence, so ornate and costly that it helped bring about the "Regulator War," it was comparable to some of the other handsome homes that would be built in New Bern and in Edenton, another early commercial and political center in North Carolina.

Robert Abercromby, in the pattern of the early settlers of Orange County, would have begun a small output of turpentine soon after his arrival, in order to bring in some cash and barter while clearing more and more land to plant corn and tobacco. Longleaf pine, the source of turpentine, was far more plentiful along the southeast coast, but there were more than enough stands of the trees in the Piedmont to provide a substantial level of production of the valuable oleoresin, as well as other naval stores, in western North Carolina.

There was a limiting factor in the turpentine business, however, and a basic one: manpower. It was generally reckoned that a slave could collect from two thousand five hundred to three thousand five hundred of the receptacles ("boxes") cut into the bark of a pine during the "sap run" of spring, summer and early fall, and thereby produce the raw material for perhaps one hundred to one hundred twenty-five barrels of turpentine. But once you left the Cape Fear region with its rice plantations, even the wealthiest planters might have fifty slaves, or fewer, in contrast to Virginia or South Carolina, where the black population was climbing toward the sixty percent figure by 1750, and some planters owned hundreds of slaves.

Robert Abercromby, Sr. slowly acquired slaves, strong and well-treated from all indications, who would remain with the family for generations and be left with their issue to his sons, but at the time of Orange County's first tax list, in 1755, he either did not own slaves or chose not to report them. The controversial John Frohock, Henry McCulloh's surveyor and finally one of the richest men in North Carolina, owned eight thousand acres of choice land, but

The Bettman Archive, Inc.

Charles I of England, from life by Sir Anthony Van Dyke, "Paynter in ordinary to their Majesties."

The Bettman Archive, Inc.

A witchburning. Sixteenth century engraving.

The Bettman Archive, Inc.

Seventeenth century English gentlemen falconers. Engraving circa 1680.

The Bettman Archive, Inc.

King Charles the Second.

The Bettman Archive, Inc.

James Graham, Marquis of Montrose.

Courtesy Charles Fleetwood and the University of Houston Foundation.

Oliver Cromwell, Lord Protector of England, from life by George Walker.

The Bettman Archive, Inc.

Sir Walter Raleigh.

Courtesy Sir Ian George Abercromby, tenth baronet of Birkenbog.

Sir Alexander Abercromby, Grand Falconer to Charles I of England.

The Bettman Archive, Inc.

General James Edward Oglethorpe.

The Battle of Culloden (from a print published in 1746).

The Bettman Archive, Inc.

Prince Charles Edward Stuart ("Bonnie Prince Charlie").

The Bettman Archive, Inc.

George II of England, from life by Thomas Hudson.

Courtesy Sir Ian George Abercromby.

Sir Robert Abercromby, third baronet of Birkenbog.

Courtesy Sir Ian George Abercromby.

The Abercromby coat of arms encised in stone over the front door to Birkenbog.

Courtesy Sir Ian George Abercromby.

Forglen House, seat of the Abercrombys of Birkenbog after 1790.

Courtesy Sir Ian George Abercromby.

Tullibody House, seat of the line of Tullibody founded by Alexander Abercromby, second son of Sir Alexander, first baronet of Birkenbog.

Courtesy Sir Ian George Abercromby.

Sir George Abercromby, fourth baronet of Birkenbog, from life by Sir Henry Raeburn.

In the name of God Amen. I Robert Abercromby of the County of Orange and State of North Carolina Gent^n being weak in Body, but of perfect mind and memory thanks be given unto God, calling to mind the Mortality of my Body, and knowing that it is appointed for all men once to Die, do make and ordain this my last Will & Testament, that is to say principally & first of all I give and recommend my soul into the Hand of allmighty God that gave it and my body I recommend to the Earth to be buried in decent Christian burial at the discretion of my Executors hereafter named, and as touching such worldly Estate wherewith it has pleased God to bless me in this Life. I give demise and dispose of the same in the following manner & form.

First I give to my loving son Charles Abercromby two Negroes, one named Bello, the other named Rachell to him and his Heirs forever, I also give bequeath & devise all that Tract or parcel of Land on Ellibees Creek where I now dwell to my son Charles Abercromby his Heirs & assigns forever.

Also. I give bequeath and devise to my loving son Robert Abercromby three Negroes named Rodger, Buck & Peter, and my Copper Still & Capp, to him and his Heirs forever.

I give to my daughter Jenny Mcbain, five pounds Current Money of North Carolina State & no more; And the residue of my Estate both real & personal after payment of all my just Debts Viz^t Money Horses, Horn-Cattle, Hoggs, Household Goods with all the Moveables whatsoever. I give and bequeath to my loving sons Charles Abercromby and Robert Abercromby (to be equally divided between them) to them and each of them and their Heirs forever.

Lastly. I nominate constitute & appoint my sons Charles Abercromby & Robert Abercromby Executors of this my last Will and Testament, hereby revoking and disannulling all other Will or Wills by me made either in word or writing, In Witness whereof I the said Robert Abercromby have to this my last Will and Testament set my Hand & affixed my Seal this thirty first day of May in the year of our Lord, one thousand seven hundred & seventy nine

Signed Sealed, published and declared by the said Robert Abercromby the Testator as and for his last Will and Testament in the presence of us

Robert Abercromby (Seal)

William Lason
James his X mark Dixon
Enoch Lewis

Orange County, August Court 1779

The Execution of the above Will was duly proved in open Court by the Oaths of Wm Lason & James Dixon two of the subscribing Witnesses thereto, and Ordered to be Recorded.

Test, N Rochester Clk

The last will and testament of Robert Abercromby, progenitor of the American branch and great-great-great-grandfather of James Smither Abercrombie, was written May 31, 1779 and filed at Hillsborough, North Carolina, the old colonial capital. It was discovered by Jean Bradley Anderson, expert on the history of Orange County and the Piedmont.

Photographs: Eno River Association and Hugh Mangum.

These two grist mills were constructed on the remnants of the original foundation of the mill Charles Abercrombie built along the Eno River in 1780. Top: how the facility long in place on the site at West Point, North Carolina looked in 1900, circus posters and all. Bottom: a recent reconstruction by the Eno River Association, with reinforced foundation of concrete block filled with cement and steel rods, after a disastrous 1942 flood swept the mill at top downstream.

The handsome Hancock County courthouse dominates Courthouse Square in Sparta, Georgia. Charles Abercrombie and his kinsman Anderson Comer donated the Square to Hancock County.

Photographs: W. Elmer Harper.

The Eagle Tavern, across from Courthouse Square, was the scene of the historic 1826 banquet honoring General Lafayette, at which General Anderson Abercrombie was master of ceremonies.

Sparta Cemetery, the burial place of Charles and Edwina Dicey Booth Abercrombie, Mr. Jim's great-great-grandparents.

A map of the new state of Alabama as it appeared shortly after admission to the Union in 1819. Principal Abercrombie settlements were at Brickyard, on the Chattahoochee River just south of Columbus, Georgia in Russell County; and at Cross Keys, halfway between Tuskegee and the state capital of Montgomery in Macon County.

The marquis of Lafayette, who was a guest of members of the Abercrombie family both in Russell County, Alabama and in Hancock County, Georgia, during a triumphant tour of America almost fifty years after his heroic assistance to the colonies during the Revolutionary War.

Andrew Jackson, whose defeat of the Upper Creeks in 1814 at Horseshoe Bend opened up much of Alabama to an increasing flood of immigrants.

A warrior of the Upper Creek nation about 1830. Anderson and Charles Abercrombie bought their first land in Russell County, Alabama from the Upper Creek leader Konoyarhika, in 1834.

Pleasant Gray's Courthouse Square at Huntsville, Texas about the time Jamie Smither Abercrombie was born nearby, in 1891.

Old Main, the original building on the campus of Sam Houston State University, destroyed in a tragic fire in 1981 that left this historic and beloved structure in ruins. Mr. Jim's uncle, Senator (and Colonel) Leonard Anderson Abercrombie, had a key role in establishing what was then Sam Houston Normal Institute at Huntsville in 1879, and in funding the construction of Old Main. *Photographs courtesy of Sam Houston State University and James Lanier Britton.*

A recently-discovered oil portrait of Sam Houston, apparently painted while The Raven was a resident of Huntsville, after serving as president of the Republic of Texas, United States senator and governor of Texas.

Senator (and Colonel) Leonard Anderson Abercrombie.

Houston's Main Street, then much more concentrated to the north, looking south from Franklin Avenue about 1907. Young Jim Abercrombie often delivered milk and cream to Herman Stude's Bakery and Coffee Saloon, which was two blocks from Main and a block to the right on Preston Avenue, opposite old Market Square.

Cotton awaiting shipment through the booming Port of Houston in 1920, a three-million-bale year.

Photographs courtesy of Houston Public Library and Houston Independent School District.

Main Street between Prairie and Texas Avenue, in 1920. The Binz Building, recently remodeled into a twenty-story structure, has leased some valuable advertising space to five-cent Owl cigars. The Rice Hotel is at the right. A much earlier version of Foley's (Foley Bros.) is at left top, with the handsome hitching posts in front. Other recognizable signs of old Houston include Bering Hardware, Leopold and Price, Tuffly and Scoggins, Barringer-Norton and the Isis (Theater). Jim Abercrombie wanted to lease space in the Binz Building, but no leases were available there at the time.

The Charlotte Allen School on Chenevert and Elgin, where six of the Abercrombie children attended with their good friend V. F. (Doc) Neuhaus after the new school opened in 1907.

City of Houston seal.

The imposing Presidential Palace at Havana, a generation before Fidel Castro and the Sierra Maestra, when Mr. Jim and Miss Lillie spent part of their honeymoon there, May 13–17, 1925.

The Myrtle Bank Hotel at Kingston, Jamaica in 1925 when it was the finest hotel in the Caribbean.

An afternoon surrey ride for Miss Lillie through the beautiful gardens at Myrtle Bank, in the fall of 1925.

only thirty-eight blacks. In a typical year, sixty or seventy slaves would be brought into Charleston for every one landed at Brunswick or Wilmington.

Turpentine could also be turned into rosin, a costly ingredient of varnish, by two-step distillation; or made into pitch (and finally, tar) in crude kilns fired to high temperatures. These latter operations were for the winter, utilizing fallen trees and dead limbs from the forests.

Robert Abercromby must also have turned quickly to raising cattle (both for beef and for milk); and "hoggs," the source of the thick-cut bacon that was a staple of the Piedmont diet, along with Indian bread, made from hand-ground cornmeal before numerous grist mills were built alongside the sawmills on the Eno River. Hogs (almost invariably spelled "hoggs" in eighteenth-century North Carolina) roamed freely through the woods, subsisting mainly on acorns and pine seeds, although they and the cattle, which existed largely on prairie grass and moss, were fed corn a few weeks before being put up for sale at crossroads auctions or being sent to the slaughterhouse.

Lumber became an important product in Orange County when the first sawmill was constructed on the Eno shortly after the county was organized in 1752, but there was a far greater, and earlier, output in eastern and southern North Carolina. Here you found not only thicker and more frequent stands of pine, sometimes covering hundreds of acres with hardly a break between the lush, dark green groves; but hardwoods, prized over pine for making shingles, or in the manufacture of barrel staves, as well.

The Abercrombys and their neighbors sold their limited yields of tobacco and, in time, cotton, to Scots factors who shipped to Europe through Virginia. They came to depend to a major degree upon corn as a cash crop, because of the constant demand for it (and for barrel staves) in the West Indies. There was also some experimentation in Orange County with hemp and flax, but neither crop, although subsidized by the colonial government, reached a significant level of production.

By the time Orange County was established, Robert Abercromby had become a member of what came to be known as the "courthouse crowd,'' or to those recalling rather recent English history, a cabal.[8] As in every place and time, a power structure inevitably surfaced, and Robert was a part of it from early on, both because of his marriage to Jane Gresham and as a result of personal attributes that would reinforce his position of leadership. His two sons, Charles and Robert, Jr., as well as the only daughter, Jenny, primarily through her marriage to William Mebane (scion of a family of dominant influence in the area from colonial times until the present), joined the cabal as teenagers.

At a session of the County Council, held May 23, 1757, Robert, Sr. was named a justice of the peace, a title of wide ambit and one especially advantageous to hold in the early days of western North Carolina.[9] From this point on, until his death in 1779, both Robert, Sr. and his sons, as they reached maturity, would serve as justices of the peace, deputy sheriffs, tax assessors, special commissioners, overseers of the public roads and, as the revolt against their British cousins began in earnest, as high-ranking military officers. Their brothers-in-law and fathers-in-law were often being sworn in with them as fellow officials of high rank, all in the developing pattern of the cabal, which worked quite well throughout most of American (or for that matter, world) history.

What was described earlier as a clearly inchoate infrastructure, with rudimentary schools, churches and governmental apparatus in western North Carolina, would stand in contrast to what the Abercrombies were to find as they continued their march ever westward to Georgia, Alabama and Texas in succeeding generations.

There was simply no public education in the Piedmont prior to the Revolutionary War, other than that arising from a seldom-enforced statute of the colonial legislature requiring orphaned apprentices to be taught to ''read and write'' as part of their apprenticeship contract. This was interpreted to mean less than six months of attendance at a part-time school, for a maximum of two years, without any determination of competency during or after the instructional period. Most ''middlings'' and those of the ''better sort'' simply taught their children themselves, from age seven on, banded together to hire a ''master'' for a portion of the year, or helped to finance sectarian grammar schools which included instruction in religion and Protestant editions of the Bible. Most of these modest yet reasonably effective operations had been started up by Scots and Scots-Irish Presbyterians, but the concept expanded to other sects and nationalities.

Educating negroes was simply not addressed in any meaningful manner during the early colonial history of North Carolina, or in the first decades of statehood. While some settlers in the 1740s and 1750s taught selected blacks to read and write at a low level in order to make them more useful, extremists wrongfully blamed a brief 1741 uprising by the Stono tribe on a few Indians educated by well-meaning circuit riders, and prejudiced a laudable effort by a small group of English philanthropists to establish small schools for the children of slaves, as well as white students, in Wilmington, Brunswick and other coastal settlements. One Wilmington man, described later as being filled with "the prejudice of the ignorant, . . ." simply claimed that the townspeople "did not want their children associating with slaves." The wonder is that the English philanthropists involved actually found a member of the Governor's Council who was sympathetic enough to recruit a schoolmaster willing to teach black and white children, side by side, in North Carolina in the early 1760s, even though nothing came of the attempt because of a community boycott.

Thomas Thomlinson, an experienced schoolmaster who had operated his own small institution in England, opened what apparently developed into a fine private academy in New Bern early in 1763. Within five years, this school had an enrollment in excess of seventy-five, but it went into a decline early in the 1770s. Various reasons were given: relatively high costs, especially for boarders; the distance from other parts of the colony; or a requirement that tuition and fees be paid in gold or silver coins rather than in paper currency (itself in short supply). The foremost reason for the eventual collapse of what seems to have been an excellent little institution, however, may have been that Master Thomlinson found it necessary to turn to the birch rod, rather than to further admonishments, in order to discipline two obstreperous students. Both miscreants happened to be the offspring of trustee-contributors.

Master Tomlinson's academy, however, had its beneficial effects. The Englishman's school was recalled in later debates in Assembly, after legislators had become more and more aware of the crying need for public education. This led to the establishment of a Free School at Edenton, plus support for a similar institution in the western counties. The intent was to convert the best of the several private grammar schools in the area (probably the Liberty Hall Academy near Charlotte) to public aegis, and then to add similar institutions. When these schools were found to be Presbyterian, however, the plan was vetoed in order to maintain strict separation of church and state.

A few of the "better sort" sent their sons to boarding schools in Charles Town or "the North" (generally to Philadelphia or Boston); or even to England. Daughters, taught their "three R's" alongside their brothers, either by a parent or a tutor, were sometimes enrolled in "finishing" schools in Charles Town or in northern cities. Here the curriculum featured music, either instrumental, vocal or both, to a level permitting the daughter to shine forth before family friends or serious candidates for her hand; deportment; the English classics; and fine needlework. Both sons and daughters were encouraged to continue their education through reading in the sometimes excellent small libraries maintained by the more prestigious families.

Overall, the level of education in North Carolina prior to 1776 would have to be described as distressing, when measured against a realistic criterion such as the rate of illiteracy. This was at one-third, or above, in most counties; and this high rate would persist, with discouragingly slow improvement, into the first quarter of the nineteenth century, in spite of increasing emphasis on free public education. North Carolinians could take some comfort from similar statistics elsewhere in the South, and for that matter, over the nation. Even today, the relatively steep rate of illiteracy in the United States, as compared say to Japan, western Europe or Scandinavia, is a puzzling phenomenon.

As a crown colony, North Carolina was officially Anglican from its first beginnings, but the Archbishop of Canterbury could not take much consolation from the status of the established church in the colony during the eighteenth century. When the Bishop of London, as the archbishop's surrogate, asked for volunteers for the colonies of North America, almost 750 Anglican priests responded. All were granted the necessary ecclesiastical "exeat" (literally, "(thou mayest) go forth"), but barely six percent chose North Carolina, and only a half-dozen had actually shown up by 1765. One of the six was said to frequent public houses and to spend more time fishing on the Chowan than ministering to his flock.

The situation for Anglicanism did improve considerably under Governor William Tryon, who was able to obtain the immigration of many able Church of England clergymen, but there were major difficulties in the offing. These centered around the close connection that many Patriots would see between the crown and its established church, and the loss of government financial support after the Revolution.

The fundamental problem for any denomination in the early decades of North Carolina, however, was that the colony was essentially a hodgepodge of various ethnic and religious groups, comprising an overall population with large segments best described as "independent as a hog on ice." There were marked differences from South Carolina and Virginia, for example, where a large percentage of settlers had been christened in the Anglican faith and continued to practice it in long-established parishes, under the guidance of rectors and vestries known to the membership for many years.

Presbyterianism had arrived early in the person of Scots Highlanders settling in the southern coastal counties; it expanded solidly into the far western parts of the colony with the advent of Scots-Irish adherents of John Knox. German colonists were either Lutherans, Calvinists or Moravians, and they brought their own ministers with them. The Moravians, a small but influential offshoot of the German Pietists, had the finest, best-tended farms in the whole of North Carolina.

The Quakers of North Carolina, originally settling around Albemarle Sound, came into the Piedmont in substantial numbers from Virginia, as well as from their original settlements in Pennsylvania. Pro-abolition and anti-war, the Friends (as they preferred to be known) were widely admired for their industry, behavior and quiet good works, in spite of the unpopularity of some of their views. Without clergymen, ecclesiastical trappings, or even a formal creed, the Quakers obviously added unique components to the religious array. The Methodists, although destined to be far more numerous and influential in Georgia, where John Wesley himself had preached during an evangelistic tour under the sponsorship of none other than General James Oglethorpe, had several hundred dedicated members scattered over North Carolina. Only the Roman Catholics had little or no representation in the early days of the colony; none of the immigrants were from predominantly Catholic countries, and there were few settlers from Maryland, where the Church of Rome was in the ascendancy.

Into this rich theological mix came the Baptists, afire with the evangelistic fervor of George Whitefield's Great Awakening.[10] They made substantial inroads into Anglican ranks and elsewhere, with such spellbinding preachers as Shuban Stearns, who reportedly converted six hundred in one month during a 1755 revival at Sandy Creek in Orange County.

Some denominations fought fire with fire: they baptized by immersion, after using a font in an elegant baptistry for generations; they spoke of unfamiliar doctrines—of free-flowing grace and a direct, personal relationship with God; they asked George Whitefield himself to address their flock on the Great Awakening. But the Baptists, and their several sects including the New Lights and the Separates, continued to make many conversions among the independent-thinking North Carolinians, who were apparently hungering for more attention to their spiritual needs, and more emphasis on personal relevancy, than other denominations had provided on the frontier of the mid-1700s.

The shaky governmental apparatus in North Carolina had a severe test in the decade from 1761 to 1771, and for the few years thereafter immediately preceding the outbreak of the Revolutionary War. The problem was a fundamental one, leading to an almost inevitable confrontation between western and eastern sectors of the state-to-be, with its major differences in everything from social structure through ethnic background, language, religion, tradition and life style, to perception of the proper role of government and of public officials.

The west, epitomized in Orange County, was essentially ''middling'' country, with a significant overlay of the ''better sort,'' as noted earlier. The dominant racial backgrounds were essentially Scots, Scots-Irish and German, with a few English and some Welsh in tiny pockets. There were relatively few blacks until the last quarter of the eighteenth century. The Highland Scots still spoke Gaelic among themselves; the Germans not only their native tongue, but several dialects thereof; and you could occasionally hear the lilting, difficult, polysyllabic Welsh (little changed from the accents of

Shakespeare's heroic Hotspur, as he plotted the overthrow of Henry IV). These sharply differing attributes, and the rich mix of religions just discussed, meant inevitably divergent traditions and life styles between eastern and western North Carolina.

At the crux of the matter was how the two dissimilar parts of the colony saw government and those who governed. With the rapid influx of settlers into the west, particularly into giant Orange County, this one political subdivision had more "white male taxables," or eligible voters, than five of the old eastern counties of North Carolina combined. Yet the east was alloted five representatives to the colonial Assembly, as compared to the drastically smaller two in the west, per county. This patent imbalance was reflected in the fact that the eastern counties traditionally supplied not only the governor of the colony, but the treasurer and the powerful speaker of the Assembly, who in effect controlled the introduction and eventual passage and signing into law, or failure, of key legislation.

When the new settlers in the west first began to develop their views on political and governmental matters, this obvious imbalance in the new temporary capital at New Bern was not too noticeable; or it was overlooked, in the "middling" philosophy of letting the "better sort" have their way, so long as a reasonably "democratick" atmosphere prevailed. As the basic disparity became more apparent, though, the traditional explanation that "this had always been the situation, from the earliest days of the Assembly," quickly wore thin. This was particularly true after 1755, when taxes were escalated sharply, ostensibly to pay for the French and Indian War, and state and county fees, largely kept by the numerous officials to whom they were paid, also advanced markedly.

Those who inquired found that most fees were set by such key officials as the registrar of deeds, tax assessor and judge of the county court, all appointed by the governor, with one person sometimes holding more than one of these offices. And the governor was named by the proprietor, Lord Granville, or Lord Granville's resident agent. Both governor and agent saw themselves as direct representatives of King George II, with the basic authority to make key appointments perceived as a property right. There was even the inference that this authority proceeded somehow through the king, much as his divine right to rule, until there was a reminder that this view had brought Charles I to the executioner.

The worsening situation regarding taxes and fees was exacerbated by the great scarcity of both gold and silver coins, and paper money, with which to pay them; and especially by heavy penalties, and a few forced sales and dispossessions, for failure to pay on time. Then it was discovered that in the eastern counties, you could meet your tax and fee obligations by pledging tobacco or indigo warehousing receipts until ready money was available, while cash on the barrel head was required in the west.

The only ingredients now lacking for a major public uproar were rumors, a public scandal and maladroit handling of some beginning confrontation on the issues. All three were soon at hand.

The rumor was that Governor Tryon's over-elegant new "palace" at New Bern was costing £15,000 in tax funds; the truth of the matter is that before John Hawks the architect and his marble masons had finished the job, it would run almost twice that sum. The scandal surfaced when Lord Granville's agent, Francis Corbin,[11] was accused of issuing the same land title to more than one person on many occasions, and of downright fraud; his successor, Dr. Thomas Child, then closed the colonial land office late in 1760 and refused to reopen it for months (the second Lord Granville later padlocked the office from 1766 to 1773, creating complex and costly problems for landowners throughout the colony). It was Governor Tryon's chief advisor, however, who may have actually launched what was termed the "Regulator War."

This was Edmund Fanning, a Yale graduate, class of 1757; attorney; judge; registrar of deeds; member of the Assembly; colonel of the militia; and shining example of what the rising opposition termed over-concentration of power in the hands of a few.

Herman Husband, an articulate leader of what was at first called "The Mob" (no relationship to the Rice University band of a much later era!), was the principal author of a series of "advertisements," or political tracts, widely distributed in western North Carolina beginning in late 1767. In the tracts, Husband protested with a rare combination of solid logic and unusually persuasive rhetoric, the evils of unequal taxation and representation, the fee system, the preponderance of "pettifogging lawyers" as opposed to planters in the Assembly, and other grievances. A key tract, appearing in April, 1768, declared that a group now identified as the "Regulators" were determined to adjust grievances and to equalize both the costs and the benefits of government. Their first move would be to stop paying taxes that they regarded as unlawful, until matters could be regulated.

The tract concluded by asking specifically for negotiations leading to a "redress of grievances," which the government at first agreed to schedule. On second thought, Judge-Registrar-Assemblyman-Colonel Fanning simply threw Herman Husband and three colleagues in jail, although he was technically not a Regulator, but a friend of the organization appointed to arbitrate differences with the authorities in power.

In response, hundreds of Regulators marched toward Hillsborough and the Orange County jail to free Husband and three other "rebel insurgents." The men were released by uneasy authorities, but stood trial later in Superior Court. Almost a thousand militiamen, under the direct command of Governor Tryon, stood guard around the courthouse during the trial, but it was noted that hundreds of enlisted militiamen had ignored the call to active duty, their ranks being filled by almost two hundred fifty officers. Herman Husband was found not guilty, and to the delight of the Regulators, Judge Fanning himself was adjudged guilty, in a separate action, of charging illegal fees. He resigned as registrar of deeds immediately after a jury returned the verdict.

Husband, the hero of the hour, was named to succeed the discredited Judge Fanning in the next election for members of the Assembly.

Dissension reached a new and vocal level in the west when the Assembly, unable to reach agreement on a bill for redress of grievances recommended by Governor Tryon himself, was dissolved by Tryon. The frustrated Regulators then marched again on Hillsborough, the first weekend in September, 1770; dragged some particularly obnoxious attorneys out of the courthouse and beat them; threw the remains of an executed felon, still in chains, in Judge Fanning's chair; fired a few musket rounds into the roof of Fanning's home; roughed up Sheriff Tyree Harris; and thoroughly alarmed anyone opposed to the Regulators anywhere in Orange County.

This inexcusable conduct, described by one contemporary newspaper as unworthy even of savage Hottentots, harmed the Regulator cause considerably. Nevertheless, when tempers cooled a bit later in the fall, both Governor Tryon and prominent members of the Assembly expressed concern over, and guarded sympathy with,

Regulator grievances. The January 1771 session of the legislature, however, was of a quite different mind; its members wanted vengeance, not conciliation. They passed a harsh anti-riot bill mandating the death penalty for convicted violators, and made it effective *ex post facto,* thus threatening those involved in the September 1770 fracas at Hillsborough with hanging. The *ex post facto* statute, defying a cardinal point in English jurisprudence, was later declared to be unconstitutional. You cannot hang a man under a law passed months after the offense he committed.

There were attempts at a negotiation of differences. Some fees were lowered substantially, audits were ordered, and new courts as well as substations for the payment of taxes and fees were opened in the west. But these moves, too long delayed, were merely palliative; they were comparable to treating a deep-seated cancer with mustard plasters.

The inevitable showdown came on May 16, 1771, after a series of mass meetings by Regulators and their adherents. Governor Tryon, sensing a crucial test of strength, mustered his militia. Less than four hundred responded from the west, but more than one thousand from eastern units met the roll call.

The Regulators, largely unarmed except for a haphazard collection of weapons including some pitchforks, drew up their ragged ranks of more than two thousand men at Great Alamance Creek near Hillsborough and demanded an audience with Tryon and his commanders. This was refused; instead, the governor gave the Regulators one hour to lay down their arms, such as they were, and surrender.

When the order was ignored, the militiamen fired at the expiration of the deadline, precipitating a two-hour battle in which both sides lost the same number killed in action: nine. More than fifty men from the militia companies were wounded, and there were even heavier casualties among the Regulators. Alamance Creek had gone down in history, with a confrontation sometimes described as the first battle of the Revolutionary War, if you perceive Tryon's men as Tories, and their opponents as Patriots.

Twelve men identified as ringleaders of the "rebels" were brought to trial; six were hanged, and six were pardoned. There was continuing unrest, tempered later by the departure of Governor Tryon, and the installation of his far more conciliatory replacement, Josiah Martin. Tryon's parting shot was an order that anyone who had joined, or given support to, "The Regulation" movement would now have to swear allegiance to the government in order to be considered for a pardon.

When almost seven thousand came forward, government officials were at first gratified by what they perceived as their firm control of the situation; upon reflection, they saw the matter differently, as an indication of widespread, stubborn and continuing sympathy with Regulator demands for equity in government. Pardons were quickly issued, while the taking of additional oaths was quietly suspended. Warehouse receipts were soon being accepted in the west in lieu of cash, at taxpaying time. There were further reductions in fees, and some indictments of corrupt officials.

The later history of the principals in the Regulator troubles is both interesting and revealing. Governor Tryon was out of office within a year after Alamance, his departure speeded by a scathing denunciation from Judge Maurice Moore, leader of one of the old-line North Carolina families. The judge accused Tryon of needlessly precipitating a "civil war," of being a man of "littleness," more vindictive and impulsive than dignified, and more ridiculous than worthy of high office. He then declared the riot act of 1770 unconstitutional.

Tryon took a colonel's commission in the British Army and distinguished himself during the Revolutionary War by leading raids against small towns and farms on the New Jersey and Connecticut shore, burning crops and creating general havoc.

The holder of multiple offices, Edmund Fanning was only thirty-four at Alamance Creek, where he was second in command to Tryon. A native of New York, Fanning returned there in 1774 and was given command of a Tory regiment of infantry. After the Revolution, he remained in the British Army, rising to the rank of major general. Fanning lived on in London until his eighties, probably telling and retelling how the Hottentots of Hillsborough had attacked him so long ago, until the end.

Howard Husband, true to form, surfaced a quarter-century later as a leader of the Whisky Rebellion in deep western Pennsylvania, which had remarkable similarities to the Regulator upheavals.[12] Husband, very old at the time (1794), had President George Washington, Alexander Hamilton and fifteen thousand militiamen pursuing him and his tough mountain protestors through the Alleghenies, in a glorious end to his long and adventure-packed life.

The "War of Regulation" had to be a particularly trying time for the Abercrombies of Orange County. When the conflict broadened and intensified in 1768, Robert, Sr. was fifty-three and growing steadily in prestige and influence within the ruling cabal. While county court records at Hillsborough are unfortunately missing for the period from 1766 to 1777, we know from later deeds and minutes that his sons (Charles was twenty-six in 1768; Robert, Jr., twenty) were also gaining an assured position in the frontier society, along with their twenty-five-year-old sister Jane Abercrombie Mebane,[13] wife of an heir to large holdings of land, cattle, naval stores and political impact.

Members of the family, and their peers, were reasonably sympathetic to the Regulator movement, which included in its ranks a number of their friends and neighbors and was so characteristic of North Carolina's underlying ethos of democratic independence. You could side with the courthouse clique, and be clearly identified with the "better sorts" in Orange County, without in any way being oblivious to the rights of others in the society. Unless you were, as Howard Husband had claimed, a William Tryon or an Edmund Fanning.

The Regulators made things considerably more difficult by having in their midst landowners with holdings in excess of two thousand acres, and comparable other assets. They were not, as members of Assembly had attempted to brand them, "common rebels and insurgents," but often the men with whom the Abercrombies did business, conversed with at the grist mill or at the Cross Creek branch of Hogg & Campbell, Merchants, or sat with on the grand jury. You and your family saw them as well at church, and at the modest gatherings of Orange County's slowly-evolving social life; often, you shared their resentment at some particularly galling action by the eastern establishment, or wanted redress yourself for the grievances that the Regulators put forward and complained about ever more strongly.

Nevertheless, Abercrombies were Harrisses and Booths, Greshams and Mebanes—and a power in their own right, easily singled out as part and parcel of the establishment, or at least of its western affiliate.

The solution to this obvious dilemma of a family within a controversial circle of power and influence, yet abundantly aware of the rights of others, probably lies in the fact that nowhere in the reasonably voluminous accounts of the War of Regulation do you find specific mention of the Abercrombies. They did not draw the ire of the "rebel" leadership, nor did they lose the friendship of the "courthouse crowd." It is reasonable to assume that Robert, Jr., son-in-law of Sheriff Tyree Harris (who was Governor Tryon's second-in-command under Edmund Fanning) and a militia officer, rode with Tryon's men to the showdown at Alamance Creek; and that his father, brother, cousins and brothers-in-law were close at hand. But they probably rode quietly, with misgivings, some of them attempting to the end to arbitrate the matter, as did Judge Maurice Moore and others who could recognize the two sides to a question.

There was a new burst of growth and economic activity in Orange County, together with increasing prosperity, as the after-effects of the battle of Alamance slowly subsided. Farms were producing far more of the basic crops, especially corn, as additional hundreds of acres were cleared. Tobacco, limited primarily to a northern tier of counties (Northhampton, Granville and Halifax) settled by former Virginians, began to be grown elsewhere in the region, particularly in Edgecombe County, after 1770.

Together with corn and tobacco, the colony was exporting more and more lumber and naval stores, and while these products still came in the main from the southeast, Orange County showed an increased output as additional sawmills were put in place and more turpentine "tappers" were put to work. Ships sailing primarily from Wilmington took three-quarters of British imports of tar, and over half of the colonial production of turpentine, back to England; captains scoured the region for good oak barrel staves, which were always in short supply. The Cape Fear mills, manned by well-trained blacks (some of them valued at £1000 each) turned out thousands of board feet of prime lumber every working day; a strong slave experienced in coopering would fetch £500 on the Wilmington auction block, but such men were seldom for sale.

Grist mills blossomed on the rivers and creeks of Orange County to such a degree that fishermen complained about interference with their catches on these inland streams. And the merchants expanded and prospered as never before. Granville County alone had almost fifty mercantile operations, ranging from the large importers such as Hogg & Campbell, or Johnston & Benneken, to an erstwhile peddler opening a tiny shop at some crossroads, although the county had not a single incorporated town. The bills of lading began to include more "fancy items" such as church-going bonnets, in addition to the normal preponderance of salt, molasses, sugar and what the Baptist evangelists denounced as that "deadly, ever-present" rum.

Still, there were few sales for cash; long-term, after-harvest credit or barter was the fashion. One settler brought suit after he discovered that it required twenty-two pounds of pork to pay for a single pair of common thread stockings imported from Lanarkshire.

As the mid-1770s approached, a curious but highly significant development began to manifest itself in North Carolina. The "better sort," under the joint leadership of two aristocrats, Samuel Johnston and John Harvey, found themselves more and more in opposition to England, the distant yet still legal fountainhead of government, and more and more in consonance with the "democratick" ideas of self-rule put forward by the defeated Regulators. The losers at Alamance were winning the new battle of persuasion.

This vital shift was undoubtedly brought about by many factors, among them the Boston Tea Party, the battle of Lexington Green, and the first and second Continental Congresses. The very audacity of Bostonians disguised as Indians pitching three hundred fifty cases of valuable tea into the harbor excited both widespread interest and spreading sympathy for the cause of the fiery revolutionist, Samuel Adams. Old Sam himself scurried away at Lexington before Major John Pitcairn's redcoats could shoot him, but the sudden outburst of violence had already meant the achievement of Adams' goal of bloody, irreversible revolt, and fired both the determination and the emotions of colonial America. The Continental Congresses,[14] beginning on September 5, 1774 and May 10, 1775, then confirmed a course of action that would finally end with British surrender at Yorktown and ratification of the Constitution of the United States of America in 1788.

The turnabout in basic loyalties among North Carolina's leaders, reflecting enormously consequential changes in attitude and outlook throughout the colonies, was of particular significance to the Abercrombies. Scots for centuries, and allied in Orange County both with British officials and many prominent Anglophiles, they might have easily sided with the estimated fifty percent of their fellow colonists who were either Loyalist-Tories, or neutral.

British Army records show that six Abercrombys were ordered overseas to serve as officers in the American colonies between 1755 and 1781, some of them with the famed Royal American (or 60th) Regiment of Foot. James Abercromby, who once commanded the 60th, was promoted to lieutenant-general on March 31, 1759, and named head of all English forces in the French and Indian War. An even better-known officer in a family with a distinguished military tradition was General Sir Ralph Abercromby, born at Tullibody on October 7, 1734. He served almost a half-century in ranks from cornet (the junior commissioned officer in a cavalry troop, who carried the colors into battle) to full general, and is credited with rebuilding the British Army after disastrous losses in the Netherlands campaigns during the last years of the eighteenth century.

Sir Ralph, named Knight of the Bath by George III, fought with distinction in battles as far apart as Seringapatham, in the East Indies; the Sugar Islands of the Caribbean; and Alexandria. While defeating the French as commander of the British Army of the Nile at Alexandria, he was mortally wounded, died on an English flagship enroute home on March 28, 1801, and was buried with great ceremony at Malta, where his monument stands in the harbor.

Instead of joining the Tory cause, Robert, Sr. (still spelling his name Abercromby while most of the family had changed over to Abercrombie) cast his lot with the Patriots, as did his children, grandchildren and virtually all their many relations by marriage. Although Robert, Sr. resigned his commission as a lieutenant-colonel of the Orange County militia early in 1778 because of his age (sixty-three) and increasing illness, he is shown in many records in Hillsborough and the later capital of Raleigh as having been a "most substantial" provider of important assistance to the Patriot cause. He is continually identified as a "Patriot of the Revolutionary Army."

Charles Abercrombie, in a report by Colonel Nathaniel Rochester, was shown as first captain of the same unit his father served in 1778. He would become a major in the 3rd North Carolina Line Regiment in 1781, as we will see, and a participant in the crucial battle at Moore's Creek and other Revolutionary War engagements in North Carolina. Robert, Jr. rose to the rank of first major of the South Regiment of Orange County, under Colonel John Butler, and would also have a distinguished military career.

Abercromby did not meet Abercrombie on the battlefields of the Revolutionary War, even though the clan of Birkenbog, with its proud record of providing military leadership over the centuries, had members in combat against patriot units. Among them was General James Abercromby's son, another James Abercromby. He was a colonel commanding General John Burgoyne's grenadiers when he died of wounds received at Bunker Hill.[15] Some military accounts mention a "Sir Robert Abercromby" who was with British units at the final surrender at Yorktown on October 19, 1781, and "died 1827 near Stirling Castle." This was not Sir Robert, the third baronet Abercromby; Sir Robert served with an English unit in India while barely in his twenties and was with expeditionary forces in the West Indies in the 1740s. He died at Birkenbog on March 11, 1787, in his eighty-third year.

Charles Abercrombie is remembered for many things in the early decades of Orange County, and perhaps best of all for his muster ground. Here, as militia captain for the Hillsborough District, he drilled and trained the men who would help defend their embattled state a few years later. Among them was his own father-in-law John Booth, a very well-to-do planter who owned as many slaves and cattle as anyone in the county, yet enlisted as a private of the line. Private Booth reportedly took great pride in being the best soldier possible, as he learned military fundamentals from his son-in-law on land that Charles Abercrombie had purchased as a farm, not a muster ground.

The muster ground is mentioned several times in the records of both Orange and adjoining Wake counties. It may well have been located in Tract 1324, immediately south and east of today's Duke University campus, near the center of Durham. This tract, a six hundred-acre holding, illustrates how large, widespread and well-located were the properties of the Abercrombies and their relatives. Adjoining 1324 on the north were two pieces totaling about four hundred acres, in the possession of Edward Gresham, an uncle. Charles Abercrombie owned the next two tracts of four hundred forty-seven acres to the east; these sandwiched Robert, Sr.'s original grant of three hundred twenty-four acres along Ellibers Creek. Scattered around this general area (now so vital to the entire southeast because of its heavy concentration of higher education and research facilities) are a dozen other tracts encompassing perhaps another two thousand acres. These belonged variously to Charles; Robert, Jr.; his Mebane brothers-in-law; Davis Gresham (another uncle); or the other members of the extended clan Abercrombie.

Of all the phenomena of the 1980s to be predictably puzzling to Charles and Robert, Jr., nothing would be more mystifying than today's young men who refuse even to register for the draft. To the Abercrombies, the county and the colony provided certain privileges and protections to the citizen; you in turn accepted the basic obligations of citizenship without demanding, or even expecting, anything else in return. Neither of the brothers, then, anticipated the considerable honors that came to them through their leadership roles in the militia.

These honors evolved because Richard Caswell was a colonel in the North Carolina forces, soon to be promoted to command one of the colony's brigades in 1774, as rising controversy with the government of George III began to escalate into open revolt. He came to know Charles and Robert, Jr. well, and to respect their abilities both as officers of the militia and as leading citizens, before he embarked upon a meteoric rise in which Caswell would serve as North Carolina's representative to both Continental Congresses and the Constitutional Convention, and as first governor of the new state, from 1776 to 1780.

Although North Carolina would not be a major battlefield again until 1780 and 1781, Colonel Caswell, together with Colonels James Moore and Alexander Lillington, won a brilliant victory over General Donald McDonald at Moore's Creek, eighteen miles northwest of Wilmington, on February 27, 1776. McDonald headed a brigade which emphasized the sharp and often bewildering divisions within a colonial America erroneously thought to be completely united against the British. The Highland clans of the coastal counties of North Carolina (some of them hardly a generation past the terrible defeat by the English at Culloden) had joined with Loyalists and some disgruntled Regulators still smarting from Alamance to create a formidable striking force of about sixteen hundred men. They were enroute to Wilmington to join a battalion of British regulars reinforced by reserve units from the English garrison at Boston. After regrouping at Wilmington, McDonald was to lead about two thousand men on a quick campaign to capture North Carolina.

The general staff of the militia of the recently-organized provisional government learned of this plan and ordered three regiments commanded by Colonels Caswell, Moore and Lillington into action. They quietly moved into impregnable positions at the bridge over Moore's Creek, in the swamps along the Cape Fear River. McDonald had to cross the bridge to proceed south, and upon reaching it he attacked what appeared to be a small Patriot force. Within minutes, his forward units were being overrun by militiamen appearing from nowhere. McDonald realized too late that he had been lured into a classic trap; in a sharp but brief battle, he lost sixty dead and more than nine hundred wounded and captured, plus large amounts of stores and ammunition and a £15,000 sterling payroll. Patriot losses totaled one killed and two wounded. Moore's Creek would in effect keep English forces out of North Carolina for almost four years, as General McDonald's campaign was abandoned.

Charles and Robert Abercrombie, Jr. were in the midst of the Moore's Creek victory, and William Caswell did not forget them. They were both promoted to major, and named justices of the peace as well as tax recorders and assessors. Other appointments followed, both directly and within the family. When Tyree Harris left the key office of sheriff, Alexander Mebane was appointed in his place, to be succeeded later by Alexander Mebane, Jr. The brothers Abercrombie were their deputies and bondsmen.

Soon after the victory at Moore's Creek, both Charles and Robert, Jr. started to spend far more time with the militia, as the increasing threat of a long, drawn-out war (always predicted by George Washington, Benjamin Franklin and other founding fathers), was acknowledged. In North Carolina, all able-bodied men sixteen to sixty were subject to military service.

Richard Caswell had arrived in Philadelphia on May 10, 1775, for the opening of the Second Continental Congress. He was the first delegate to be instructed by a provisional government "to declare independency," the course of action so strongly urged by Thomas Paine's *Common Sense* after England continued to pass a series of "intolerable" acts aimed at disciplining her restless American colonies. As the Congress continued tortoise-like through its seemingly endless deliberations, Caswell returned home during the winter. He would soon fight at Moore's Creek, and then be named as North Carolina's first governor.

When the Congress went back to work in earnest the following June, North Carolina sent William Hooper, Joseph Hewes and John Penn as its delegates to Philadelphia's Independence Hall. On the morning of July 5, 1776, they could read the first newspaper account of the adoption of the Declaration of Independence, but only if they had a reading knowledge of German. The *Pennsylvanischer Staatsbote,* printed in their native tongue for the numerous German-speaking Philadelphians, carried this epochal story:

> Philadelphia, den 5 Juli—Gestern hat die Achtbare Congress dieses Desten Landes die Vereinigten Colonien freye und unabhangige Staaten erklaret. Die Declaration in English ist jetzt in der Presse; sie is datirt den 4ten Juli, 1776 und wird Heut(e) oder morgen im druck erscheinen.
>
> (Yesterday the Worthy Congress of this Our Land declared the United Colonies to be free and independent States. The Declaration in English is now in Press; it is dated the fourth of July, 1776 and will appear today or tomorrow in print.)

The die was finally cast. The Hillsborough *Recorder,* Cape Fear *Mercury* and North Carolina *Gazette* of Wilmington were not publishing at the time and did not carry the tremendous scoop by the *Pennsylvanischer Staatsbote*. There were no newspapers in North Carolina between 1778 and 1783, because of a dearth of newsprint, but accounts of the adoption of the Declaration of Independence did appear in the *Gazette* of New Bern during the summer of 1776, thus preserving at least a single account of a story to outlast the centuries for archivists in the Tar Heel State.

Meanwhile, the Revolutionary War was entering a crucial phase centering upon Benjamin Franklin's wily campaign to obtain an alliance with Louis XVI of France, whose countrymen were enchanted by the Declaration of Independence and the strong, honest, idealistic image of American leadership it projected. Louis XVI's ministers advised against a formal alliance until General Burgoyne was defeated by Benedict Arnold at Saratoga on October 7, 1777. Then, hearing that Frederick Lord North, George III's vacillating prime minister, was preparing to offer the colonies very conciliatory terms to conclude what had become a quite unpopular war, the French suddenly signed agreements with the United States on February 6, 1778.[17]

The marquis de Lafayette, who would be entertained by another generation of the Abercrombies during a triumphal tour of Georgia a half-century later, would now be coming with vital reinforcements. He had already been in America, where he received an appointment by George Washington as a major-general, and fought with distinction at the September 11, 1777 battle of Brandywine. Now he returned to France; there he persuaded his friend Louis XVI to send six thousand men and experienced, combat-wise officers to help the American cause; perhaps more significantly, Lafayette was also able to obtain the assignment of a powerful fleet under the command of Admiral Francois-Joseph-Paul de Grasse, count of Grasse-Tilly, to counteract the domination of U.S. waters and ports by English naval might. De Grasse, a scintillating tactician on occasion, would be at his best at Yorktown, where his ships were instrumental in bringing about the final capitulation of Charles Lord Cornwallis.

The war was to accelerate again on several fronts, including a major invasion of North Carolina by Lord Cornwallis and the rampaging Colonel Banastre Tarleton's British Legion in 1780 and 1781; but as 1778 lengthened into 1779, the Abercrombies of Orange County were faced with their own crisis: the growing illness of Robert, Sr., now in his mid-sixties.

Robert Abercromby, Sr. was very much a Patriot, just as his sons; he would have gloried in the final victory over England that came on October 19, 1781, where the York River empties into Chespeake Bay, just forty miles north of the Dismal Swamp. Instead, as his illness worsened, he wrote his last will and testament on May 31, 1779, and died six weeks later. The will, probated at the August 1779 term of county court in Hillsborough, was witnessed by William Saxon, James Desern and Enoch Lewis. Desern was a prominent man in Orange County, but an illiterate; he could not sign his name, but made his mark. Nathaniel Rochester, clerk of court and a close friend of the deceased, accepted the will for probate. It was Rochester who had reported Robert, Sr.'s resignation as a lieutenant-colonel of militia to Governor Caswell less than a year before, when the elder Abercromby became too ill to command his regiment.

In deference to the family, no bond was required of the co-executors, Charles and Robert, Jr.; this although a 1779 tax list, one of the first to survive the perils of early-day record keeping, showed that Robert, Sr. had rendered property a few months earlier in the very sizable amount of £12,251 and twelve shillings. Charles, by this time one of the area's prime entrepreneurs[18] and major landowners, admitted to a slightly larger amount of £12,382 and one shilling; Robert to just half that, at £6,180.

Robert, Sr.'s last testament, which somehow did not make the journey to the new capital of Raleigh when other documents were transferred there from Hillsborough, was found minutes away from where it was first filed. The failure to transfer it from the old colonial capital may have preserved the instrument for posterity; Raleigh's first capitol building burned to the ground in 1831 and was replaced nine years later by today's gracious example of Greek Revival architecture, in its spacious setting among other structures of central importance to North Carolina's state government.

Robert Abercromby, Sr.'s will provides valuable insights into his own thoughts and feelings, the details of his holdings and the customs of the times. He begins by stressing that although "weak in body," he is of "perfect mind and memory, thanks be given unto God." Then, after recommending his soul "into the Hand of allmighty God that gave it," he first of all carefully distributes his favorite slaves between his sons. Since Charles, the elder, is to receive the "home place" along Ellibers Creek, Robert, Jr. gets an extra black and that most valuable piece of property in colonial North Carolina, "my Copper Still and Capp," in order to even things up a bit. His daughter, Jenny Meban(e), is left "five pounds current money of north Carolina state, and no more;" the message is that Jenny, married to a Mebane, has no need of bequests. She does not even get her five pounds in sterling, but in depreciated paper money of the struggling new state of North Carolina.

The text of the will, written in the modified "round hand" taught in Scots and English grammar schools of the eighteenth and late seventeenth centuries, follows:

> In the name of God Amen. I Robert Abercromby of the County of Orange and State of North Carolina Gentn being weak in Body, but of perfect mind and memory thanks be given unto God, calling to mind the mortality of my Body, and knowing that it is appointed for all men once to die, do make and ordain this my last Will and Testament, that is to say principally & first of all I give and recommend my soul into the Hand of allmighty

God that gave it and my body I recommend to the Earth to be buried in decent Christian burial at the direction of my Executors hereafter named, and as touching such worldly Estate wherewith it has pleased God to bless me in this Life, I give devise and dispose of the same in the following manner & form,

First I give to my loving son Charles Abercromby two Negroes, one named Billo the other named Rachele to him and his heirs forever. I also give bequeath and devise all that tract or parcel of land on Ellibers Creek where I now dwell to my son Charles Abercromby his heirs and assigns forever.

Also I give bequeath and devise to my loving son Robert Abercromby three Negroes named Rodger, Birk & Peter, and my Copper Still & Capp, to him and his heirs forever. I give to my daughter Jenny Meban, five pounds current money of north Carolina State & no more; and the residue of my Estate both real & personal after payment of all my just Debts viz Money Hors(e)s, Horn-Cattle, Hoggs, Household Goods with all the Moveables whatsoever, I give and bequeath to my loving sons Charles Abercromby and Robert Abercromby (to be equally divided between them) to them and each of them and their heirs forever.

lastly I nominate constitute and appoint my sons Charles Abercromby and Robert Abercromby Executors of this my last Will and Testament, hereby revoking and disannulling* all other will or wills by me made either in word or writing. In Witness whereof I the said Robert Abercromby have to this my last will and Testament set my hand and affixed my seal this thirty first day of May in the year of our Lord, one thousand seven hundred and seventy nine

(Signed) Robert Abercromby

Signed sealed published
and declared by the said
Robert Abercromby the
Testator as and for his
last Will and Testament
in the presence of us

William Saxon
James Desern X his mark
Enoch Lewis

Orange County, August Court 1779

The Execution of the above Will was duly proved in open Court by the oaths of Wm Saxon & James Desern two of the Witnesses thereto, and ordered to be Recorded.

(Signed) N Rochester CC

* The word "disannulling" is probably a mistake for disallowing or for the now archaic legal term, "disaffirming"

Charles and Robert, Jr. and Jenny must have watched with mingled pride and sorrow as their father was buried five thousand miles and more from his native land. He would rest forever beside their mother Jane, near West Point along the Eno.

At sixty-four, Robert, Sr. was a patriarch in terms of the respect and admiration deriving from almost four decades of leadership in the Piedmont, if not for span of life alone. The militia of Orange County he had helped organize must have marched in full strength and regalia, along with representatives of other units from elsewhere in the region, their pennants all at half mast. By tradition, a young cavalryman would lead Lieutenant Colonel Abercromby's riderless horse, the empty stirrups turned backwards. The horse was ahead of the flag-draped coffin[19] on an artillery caisson and held on tight rein while the final musket volleys rang out.

Billo and Peter and the other blacks would be there with their rapidly-increasing families, as well as a few of the peaceful Eno, Shocco and Adushusheer tribesmen who had remained behind while so many Indians joined the earlier migrations to the west; they were indebted to Robert, Sr. for providing protection from the occasional Cherokee raiding parties (looking for slaves to be sold to Sugar Islands traders), or redcoats seeking Indian recruits to serve as scouts. The elder Abercromby had built a secure stockade of stout pine logs along Ellibers Creek; it was primarily for his own family, and for neighbors, but friendly Indians had been welcome also since the day they first appeared to warn that their scouts had spotted Cherokees, still a threat to isolated settlements, in the area. Remembering those earlier days, and the use still made of the stockade from time to time, news of the death of a good white friend had boomed out on the tribal drums, reverberating through the plains and forests during the long twilight of summer.

Orange County and the Piedmont had lost a pioneer leader, but it was a far more personal and telling loss for the Abercrombies. Now they were without the man who had come from afar to found a propitious new branch of an ancient family—one soon to rise to additional prominence in North Carolina before moving on to increasingly significant accomplishments in Georgia, Alabama and then in Texas.

The Abercrombie brothers were never busier than in the next several years. The British, temporarily repulsed at Charleston, were obviously planning a new campaign against both South and North Carolina. As high-ranking militia officers, this threat kept them both occupied almost full-time at Charles' muster ground, or elsewhere in the county, in a continuing progression of military duties. The North Carolina regiments would be tested as never before, and soon.

Meanwhile, the older brother had opened his grist mill in partnership with William Thetford, near Shoemaker's Ford on the Eno River; Robert, Jr. would also become a partner in this major venture, built so well that a mill resting on portions of the original foundation would be grinding corn in 1942 for the descendants of the Abercrombie neighbors. And both Charles and Robert, Jr. were serving in a multiplicity of assignments. They were jurors, foremen of the grand jury, overseers of the various county roads (all of them in virtually constant need of attention, if you can believe the records of the county court), tax assessors, justices of the peace and deputy sheriffs. This in addition to the lengthy, complex business of settling their father's estate, farming, raising and marketing cattle and hog(g)s, producing naval stores, buying and selling land, and sueing and being sued in what had become a quite litigious county and region.

There also had to be time for their key roles as husbands, and as fathers to what would become a total of sixteen children, at a time when North Carolina parents, especially in the Piedmont, had to supplement classroom instruction (such as it was) with a substantial amount of teaching in the home. Providing for the future of these numerous offspring, as we will see, was to become a prime consideration for both Charles and Robert, Jr.

Suddenly, life for the Abercrombies became telescoped almost entirely into military considerations during the years 1780 and 1781. The triggering event was the fall of Charleston, on April 8, 1780. The South Carolina capital, not only the center of regional commerce, but the most important port in the entire southeast, was taken with the loss of almost six thousand Patriot prisoners, after a brilliantly-executed amphibious assault by Lord Cornwallis and Sir Henry Clinton. They landed a force of nine thousand men (three thousand of them Loyalists from the Carolinas) packed like sardines into nearly one hundred small troopships protected by a dozen men-of-war, and had the upper hand over General Benjamin Lincoln's out-maneuvered defenders in a matter of hours.

South Carolina had been overrun by summer, and Cornwallis, reinforced by the bellicose and barbarous Banastre Tarleton, was a constant threat to North Carolina. Hillsborough itself became the center of a new theater of war in late June 1780 when George Washington, knowing full well the crucial importance of the Carolinas, sent two seasoned regiments he really could not spare to their defense. These veteran troops, under the command of the able Major-General Johann DeKalb (a German baron who had fought under both Washington and Lafayette) arrived in Hillsborough half-starved and near exhaustion. They had marched for weeks from New Jersey, attempting to live mainly off an inhospitable countryside.

After stuffing themselves on good Orange County roasting ears, beef and plentiful summer fruit (some of it provided by the Abercrombies and their neighbors), they were ill for days, much as concentration camp prisoners released by American soldiers who gorged themselves on entire cans of Spam, that World War II delicacy. And when DeKalb's Patriots recovered, they had a worse problem: their able, popular general had been replaced by unwarranted meddling on the part of the Continental Congress; the new commandant of the Southern Department was General Horatio Gates, a controversial leader whose adherents were principally politicians. DeKalb was no longer in charge.

The stubborn, inept Gates insisted on marching about one hundred fifty miles south and slightly west to Camden, South Carolina, a strategic crossroads town at the time, after learning from patrols that Cornwallis was headed north and west with a relatively small force of some fifteen hundred, on a line of march that would take him directly through Camden. Gates' route was over difficult terrain and long, uninhabited stretches of scrub pine where quartermasters found few if any supplies. The troops, many of them militia not inured to difficult campaigns and half-rations, were soon in poor condition again, with sinking morale.

Lord Cornwallis, in contrast, had a well-provisioned, tightly-disciplined force of high morale, built around a cadre of English regulars. Although outnumbered three-to-two, he carried the day after a fierce fight on August 16, 1780. DeKalb, mortally wounded, stayed the field with his men; Horatio Gates escaped to what was then called Charlottestown (Charlotte), reportedly riding fifty miles on a fine thoroughbred stallion in record time.

Just when it appeared that the British might overrun both Carolinas at will, they overplayed their hand, and a Scots was at fault. Major-General Patrick Ferguson had recruited hundreds of South Carolina Loyalists into one of his regiments soon after the British installed a new royal governor at Charleston. This enraged the fiercely independent Patriots in the mountainous area on the border dividing North and South Carolina in the west, and in nearby parts of Virginia's Blue Ridge country. Many of these men had fought at Camden, only to find that a large percentage of their opponents were what they termed "turncoat Americans." Now even more Tory/Loyalists were flocking to the seemingly victorious English colors.

Soon there was increasing unrest in the far western stretches of the Carolinas, and a series of raids on small British outposts. New units of tough frontiersmen began forming throughout the region, especially in Watauga County, North Carolina; along the Catawba River in South Carolina; and north into the Blue Ridge. The so-called "Wataugas" vowed to avenge Camden, and to maul the Loyalists severely in the process.

Just as most professional soldiers, Major Ferguson tended to disparage volunteers, unless of course they had been trained under his personal supervision. Following a predictable pattern, he organized a special unit heavily infused with Loyalists prepared for battle by his own Scots instructors and drillmasters. He then sent word to the far west that he was ready to track down what he termed the "Watauga scum and rebels," hang their leaders and burn their small, isolated settlements.

The gauntlet of challenge was clearly on the ground, and the Wataugas had no difficulty in seeing it. Major Ferguson moved first, by leading his regulars and Loyalists to a seemingly impregnable position at Kings Mountain, during the night of October 6–7, 1780. On came the rugged mountaineers, deadly marksmen all; they were armed with the long rifles of the frontier they had used since preadolescence and were accustomed to wasting little or no ammunition.

After an initial and foolhardy charge in which they were repulsed with bayonets, the Patriots simply took up positions behind (or preferably in) trees, killed Patrick Ferguson early in the battle and then carefully picked off hundreds of his Loyalists and Scots until the remainder surrendered without quarter. At the very end, it was a slaughter.

Kings Mountain could not have come at a more opportune time for the Patriot cause: word of a signal victory spread quickly, with a remarkably positive effect upon sinking morale; Lord Cornwallis, deprived of a top commander plus protection for his flank, halted his northward march at Charlotte and moved his troops into winter quarters just west of Camden. Perhaps more important was the breathing space that this gave George Washington to recover from the disastrous choice of Horatio Gates, and sell the Continental Congress on a new commander for the Department of the South. This the commander-in-chief was able to do, sending the brilliant Nathaniel Greene to Charlotte in the last days of 1780. There General Greene found a ragged army of about one thousand ''Continentals,'' and half as many militia. Many of the militiamen were from Charles Abercrombie's North Carolina line regiment, and from the South Regiment, in which Robert, Jr. served as first major.

Greene, an improvisor and master strategist beloved by his men, had a new plan. He would depend upon today's guerilla tactics: small units of well-trained sharpshooters, skilled in scouting, ambush and sudden, unexpected appearances after a quick march over difficult terrain. The old concept of the line regiment, with infantrymen attacking in lines, three deep, was out.

For guerilla warfare, Nathaniel Greene split his main force into two columns. General Daniel Morgan commanded one, and Greene himself the other. They both depended upon lightning-like strikes by Francis Marion, the ''Swamp Fox,'' who had learned how to move swiftly and stealthily through impossible terrain while fighting the Cherokees two decades before; and a superb cavalry unit commanded by Colonel Harry ''Light Horse'' Lee, the latter on detached assignment from George Washington's own special forces. The Abercrombies and their Orange County militia furnished additional scouts with detailed knowledge of surrounding areas while they and their men were taught the new tactics.

General Morgan and his units had the first major test under fire, after harassing Cornwall and Banastre Tarleton (a prime target because his British Legion bayoneted more than one hundred Patriots to death and wounded twice as many under a flag of truce) for months. At Cowpens, less than twenty-five miles from Kings Mountain, Greene took Tarleton by surprise soon after dawn on January 17, 1781, killed or wounded three-quarters of two Tory regiments, and lost only sixty men.

Cornwall, deprived once again of a principal supporting unit, pondered whether to continue his long-delayed invasion of North Carolina, or to retreat with the battered remnants of Tarleton's British Legion. He decided to move on north toward Hillsborough, leaving Colonel Tarleton to lick his wounds alone.

The wily Greene, seeking a showdown with Cornwallis now that the British commander had neither Patrick Ferguson nor Tarleton in reserve, pushed northward himself. Just west of Hillsborough (and within almost shouting distance of the principal Abercrombie farms), he crossed the Dan River in broad daylight, entered Virginia and apparently continued on due east for Petersburg, a Patriot stronghold where he would be expected to rest and be resupplied from quartermaster stores. About the time that Lord Cornwallis' reconnaissance patrols were reporting this, as the British prepared to make camp for the night along the Deep River, Greene was awaiting nightfall. In the dark, his units quietly recrossed the Dan to take up superior positions at Guilford Courthouse, North Carolina, his real objective.

Instead of having North Carolina open before him for a quick takeover, as the ripe plum of South Carolina had been the year before, Cornwallis was soon perplexedly studying an updated scouting report: Nathaniel Greene had not left the area to escape into far friendlier territory in Virginia; to the contrary, he was waiting for the British at Guilford Courthouse, where the Abercrombie brothers had gone so many times on land acquisitions and sales; and within the day, Greene was joined by his other fighting column, under Daniel Morgan. Their combined units totaled four thousand; Cornwallis could put about twenty-five hundred on the field, but most of them were veteran redcoats, from seasoned regiments.

There followed, on March 15, 1781, the type of battle for which General Greene would become famous, as he in effect freed North Carolina from an ever-present threat of invasion and provided a significant turning point in the Revolution. After hours of a fierce and bloody struggle, Lord Cornwallis seemed to have carried the day at Guilford Courthouse, where Patriot sharpshooters were in protected positions but without the usual flexibility provided by guerilla tactics. When the battle was broken off and Cornwallis could analyze the situation, however, three vital things were apparent: British casualties were running about seven hundred, or almost one-third, with all forces committed; English ammunition and provisions were virtually exhausted, and would have to be replenished from as far away as Wilmington; Greene, although also suffering major losses in manpower, had retired in good order to live off the countryside, while his sharpshooters continued to make every bullet count.

For a few days, Cornwallis quartered his unwelcome troops in Hillsborough, where they seem to have behaved themselves reasonably well; the British general then headed back south for Wilmington, to regroup and refit his regiments. Nathaniel Greene (who would settle at Mulberry Grove, fifteen miles north of Savannah in a few years, after accepting Georgia's generous land grants along with his comrade-in-arms, Charles Abercrombie), resumed his guerilla tactics in a new series of battles with the Tories in South Carolina. He soon had British units except those under the direct command of Cornwallis penned up in their main base at Charleston. When Lord Cornwallis' troops had been resupplied by the British fleet lying off both Wilmington and Charleston, he made a most important, and erroneous, decision. He would leave a number of smaller units to garrison Charleston, but head north and east with his main force for a new headquarters out of the Carolinas and away from Nathaniel Greene, Charles Morgan, Harry Lee's tormenting cavalry and the Swamp Fox of large surprises and small disasters.

Charles Lord Cornwallis left Wilmington in the last days of April, 1781. He was enroute to Yorktown, and the final disaster of total surrender to George Washington and Jean-Baptiste Count Rochambeau less than six months later. As governor-general of India and viceroy of Ireland, during later and happier stages of his long career, he must have pondered many times how Patriot generals and the frontiersmen of the Carolinas and Virginia helped bring about siege and capitulation in an isolated Virginia town near Chesapeake Bay.

Life was of course different for Charles and Robert, Jr. after Yorktown; although both retained their commissions, their regiments quickly returned to normal strength, and their daily routine to something approaching equanimity. Charles did accept an important new assignment as auditor for Orange County, as each of the brothers was able, after two years of peril for the Piedmont, their state and their new nation, to concentrate on more normal pursuits.

There had been, however, an overriding development in the lives of the brothers Abercrombie, of their many children, and in the chronicles of their growing American clan. Late in 1781, as North Carolina, always the most independent of the original thirteen colonies, first began to emphasize its strong advocacy of a Bill of Rights as a vital and indelible codicil to the Constitution,[20] Robert, Jr. was asked to attend a meeting in Savannah organized by some of his fellow officers from the South Regiment.

He returned talking enthusiastically for days of two things: first, cotton, he was convinced, was the crop of the future, and Georgia had hundreds of thousands of acres of land in regions ideally suited to cotton, especially in the great alluvial plain between the Oconee and Ogeechee Rivers; second, the provisional government of Georgia was hungry for new settlers who had proved themselves in the crucible of war; grants of valuable land, in generous quantities, might be available even before statehood was achieved, probably with preference to Patriot veterans from any of the colonies.

Charles and Robert, Jr. had deep roots in North Carolina, and particularly in Orange County; a realization of just how strong those ties were must have been their first reaction to the younger brother's report from Savannah. But cotton was becoming a magic word; and new, unbroken land was a powerful attraction if your fields had been under constant cultivation for forty years, with crop yields falling steadily.

Both men decided to keep open minds on the intriguing subject of a possible move; Charles, with five children and another on the way, thought that he might discuss it with General Nathaniel Greene, under whom the brothers had served. The Savannah newspapers were reporting that the hero of Guilford Courthouse (also described, to the modest Greene's discomfort, as the ''savior of the Carolinas'') had turned down an appointment as secretary of war, and would instead move to the Savannah area as the recipient of one of the very first of Georgia's land grants to veterans of the Revolutionary War.

Little did Charles Abercrombie realize that he and his high-ranking comrade-in-arms would indeed be pioneers in Georgia's new program of bounty grants, General Greene settling at Mulberry Grove, and Charles near Sparta in what would become Hancock County (named for John Hancock, the old Massachusetts firehorse and future president of the Constitutional Convention).

The Abercrombies were soon to launch a series of treks to the west, ending in Huntsville, Texas in 1850. There, more than a century after his great-great-grandfather stood with Nathaniel Greene at Guilford Courthouse, James Smither Abercrombie would be born. But that is another story, to be told only after we have recounted three generations of signal accomplishments by Charles and Robert, Jr., and their descendants, in Georgia and Alabama.

Notes

[1] Sir Walter Raleigh's second colony landed less than a dozen miles from Kitty Hawk (then an Indian hamlet called Chickahauk), where Orville Wright would usher in the age of powered flight by keeping the Wright Flyer I he and his brother Wilbur had invented in the air about fifteen seconds on December 17, 1903.

[2] The harquebus, replaced by muskets early in the next century, had been improved since its invention in Spain about 1450. Its range was increased to 600 feet, and it could be fired (with some discomfort because of a tremendous recoil) from the shoulder. The original models were fired by two men using a prop or cradle for support.

[3] Most historians perceive Charles II, who escaped Cromwell only by hiding in an oak tree and then riding to Bristol disguised as a servant, a young girl seated postillion behind him in the manner of the time, in the positive context of his many accomplishments. The Dutch did thoroughly rout the English navy in two climactic battles near London, adding insult to defeat by towing away the *Royal Charles,* Britain's finest ship of the line, and burning four others; but Charles II discovered an obscure bureaucrat (and diarist) named Samuel Pepys who planned and built for him a far better Royal Navy. Charles also saw London destroyed in the Great Fire of 1666, which consumed almost fifteen thousand homes and places of business after starting in a baker's shop on Pudding Lane; but as he walked the streets to commiserate with his people, he was planning a new city of wide streets and stone buildings; and he found the man who could translate ideas into reality, a master builder, Sir Christopher Wren. Wren, a professor of astronomy at Oxford, turned architect to produce the plans for a new London, although his king could not afford his detailed and expensive ideas *in toto*.

What Charles II did not realize was that the Great Fire, by destroying the rat-infested wharves along the Thames that had spawned the Great Plague less than two years earlier, might have prevented a recurrence of bubonic fever, the agonizing and deadly infection caused by a bacterium isolated by Louis Pasteur.

By the time of his death, in 1685, Charles Stuart had given the English twenty-five years of post-Restoration government marked by relative calm after long turmoil. He is remembered in retrospect not only for such vital accomplishments as rebuilding the Royal Navy, and London itself, but for other deeds that loom larger over the centuries: the Habeas Corpus Act, a cornerstone of individual freedom; the reinstitution of religious toleration; and the establishment of The Royal Society. Dog-loving England, where the leading television program is a canine obedience class, remembers him also for developing the King Charles spaniel.

[4] The early history of Charles Town is interwoven with the incredible adventures of one Henry Woodward, who arrived with the immigrants of 1670. Ranging too close to the border of Spanish Florida, he was captured by a patrol checking intruders along St. Mary's River, freed by friendly pirates enroute to San Augustine, shipwrecked, and rescued by Englishmen he had known in Barbados. He then settled a while with the amiable Kiaweh Indians and built up a roaring trade based upon deerskins, furs and slaves. He

next tamed the cannibalistic Westo tribe, but had to leave the area when the Spanish set the Savannahs upon him. Little dismayed, he returned to London, raised fresh capital, and was instrumental in relocating Charles Town ten miles downstream in 1682, at the far more accessible juncture of the Ashley and Cooper Rivers.

[5] The fierce Cherokees, who were raiding frontier settlements, killing an Abercrombie in Alabama and challenging the white man's move to the west as late as the 1830s, terrorized the tribes of the southeast by capturing their young braves and selling them into slavery in the West Indies.

[6] There is no record of any of the numerous Abercrombys involved in The Fifteen and the subsequent revolt of 1745 being transported as punishment for political activity except for the John Abercromby, otherwise unidentified, who sailed from Liverpool in chains on the *Elizabeth and Ann* on June 29, 1716. He is shown as "Jacobite prisoner bound Virginia."

[7] Both grist mills and sawmills finally became so numerous on the Eno that Charles Abercrombie would have to delay what became the best-known grist mill in Orange County until a jury had ascertained that the new venture would not adversely affect existing operations in the area.

[8] The unique word "cabal" has not only strengthened its position in the English language over the past three centuries and more, but may be more in use than when it was coined in 1672. It is simply a combination of the initial letters in the five names of Charles II's Committee for Foreign Affairs, thought by many to have been a forerunner of the English Cabinet: C(lifford), A(rlington), B(uckingham), A(shley) and L(auderdale).

[9] When Robert Abercromby, Sr. first took office as a justice of the peace in the early years of Orange County, its four thousand square miles of territory pretty well encompassed the northwestern part of North Carolina. This gargantuan size of course encouraged the creation of new counties, or portions thereof, until the original area had been shrunk by more than ninety percent.

[10] The Great Awakening, which came to western Europe a generation earlier, was experienced in the American colonies in the second quarter of the eighteenth century. It was essentially an evangelical movement emphasizing a closer personal relationship between God and man. George Wakefield, a former Anglican priest greatly influenced by John Wesley, brought the Great Awakening to the southern colonies with a series of fervent, emotional revival meetings between 1739 and 1741. A virtual cult of "Wakefieldism" arose as the evangelist spoke to thousands in huge outdoor meetings. In the inevitable reaction by ecclesiastical authorities. Wakefield was harshly criticized for his "unorthodox" preaching, and even more for invading established parishes and districts without appropriate permission. He had, however, a potent and lasting effect upon religion in North Carolina and elsewhere in the South, not only advancing in time the strength of principal Protestant sects such as the Baptists, Presbyterians and Methodists, but stimulating the Anglicans to far greater attention to their parishes.

[11] Hillsborough had originally been named Corbin Town, for Francis Corbin, the agent deposed in disgrace. To illustrate how insensitive Lord Granville and his advisors could be to public opinion, they promptly renamed the town Childsburg, for Corbin's successor Dr. Thomas Childs, at a time when land agents were regarded with extreme suspicion. Only later was the county seat and sometime colonial capital permanently named for Lord Hillsborough, first secretary for the colonies because of his appointment to head the new Board of Trade and Plantations.

[12] A 1791 act of Congress establishing a tax on whisky was bitterly opposed by the mountaineers of Washington County in far western Pennsylvania, who had distilled their excess corn for generations both for private use and to raise a little cash. In almost a comic opera showdown, President George Washington called upon Governor Thomas Mifflin to en-

force the law, which he saw as a test of federal powers within the states. As a canny Pennsylvania politician, Mifflin declined; whereupon Washington called out fifteen thousand militia in five states, and marched them over the Alleghenies himself. The rebels fled in all directions as soon as the militiamen crossed the county line; the ringleaders were later brought to trial, and two were convicted of treason. As they awaited execution, they were pardoned by President Washington. He had made his point, with an outing in the bracing climate of western Pennsylvania to boot.

[13] Jane Abercrombie Mebane and the women of colonial North Carolina merit study by today's NOW leaders, and other battlers for female equality. North Carolina provided some important rights as early as 1729 that were not to be allowed by other colonies, and even states, for many years. Among these, women could serve as executors, hold property in their own right and name, and apply for land grants.

[14] North Carolina's delegates to the first and second Continental Congresses reflected the balanced yet essentially conservative views of the colony. By the time of the Constitutional Convention, however, younger leaders such as the patrician radical Willie Jones had supplanted the traditional political chieftain Samuel Johnston. It was the philosophy of maximum freedom for the individual, strongly espoused by Jones and his peers, that caused North Carolina to insist so vehemently upon the adoption of the entire Bill of Rights and to delay joining the Union until November 21, 1789. By that time, there were firm commitments regarding the ratification of Articles I through X as first business for the First Congress. The agreements had been hammered out in a series of meetings, some extending past midnight. The delegates, incidentally, had plenty of nourishing food to sustain them on through the evening. The menu for one 4 p.m. dinner began with clams, oysters and turtle steaks, proceeding through roast beef, a half-dozen vegetables, fruits of the season and those ubiquitous desserts of colonial America, trifle and flummery.

[15] General John Burgoyne mentioned the loss of James Abercromby in a letter dated June 25, 1775 from Boston. A playwright and considerable figure in London society who was devoted to horse racing, Burgoyne sent the letter to "a certain Noble Lord." This was probably Edward Stanley, twelfth earl of Derby and originator of the English Derby, in 1780. Burgoyne tells how Colonel Abercromby advanced up Breed's Hill ("mistakenly called Bunker Hill") as part of a force of two thousand men covered by heavy artillery fire and a cannonade from British ships in the harbor. From the heights, General Burgoyne watched "strait before me a large and noble town in one great blaze, the church steeples . . . as pyramids of fire." The day "ended in glory ," he concluded, but "with an uncommon loss of officers for the total number of troops engaged."

[16] You could also change your allegiance, even after having been on the opposite side in battle. A particular example of this is one of North Carolina's outstanding churchmen during the colonial period: George Micklejohn. The Reverend Dr. Micklejohn, educated at Cambridge, had served as chaplain to Frederick the Great, and to the future duke of Cumberland at Culloden. Possibly because of the latter experience, he "was inclined at first to be Loyalist." When captured at Moore's Creek, however, he was paroled and became a staunch Patriot. Rector of St. Matthew's Episcopal Church in Hillsborough for many years, he was president of the first state-wide conference of Episcopalians when seventy-three, in the year 1790. He was first sent to North Carolina by the Bishop of London and was one of the very few doctors of sacred theology in the colonies.

[17] Some historians maintain that the Revolutionary War might well have been averted, with the colonies accepting a status similar to the present Commonwealth nations, except for the ingrained tradition of long English weekends which took Lord North and his chief lieutenants away from London the first few days of February, 1778.

[18] The loss of many early records makes it very difficult to ascertain the detailed components of Charles Abercrombie's estate, surprisingly large for a man of thirty-seven. Land maps of the area would indicate, however, that much of his net worth was in real estate, and therefore quite conservatively rendered.

[19] The flag of the United Colonies had retained the British Union Jack in its design until 1777, when the new standard of the thirteen original colonies was substituted.

[20] We saw earlier how the liberal Willie Jones would wrest political power from Samuel Johnston's pride of old lions who had controlled the statehouse in North Carolina, and go on to become a prime leader in the last years before statehood and ratification of the Bill of Rights. Yet ironically, the pendulum would swing back once more to conservatism, and Jane Abercrombie Mebane's brother-in-law Alexander, Jr., who had succeeded his own father as sheriff of Orange County, would be elected to the U.S. Congress. The courthouse cabal was back in the saddle, with a direct line to George Washington's new government.

Chapter 3

1786–1832

Hancock County, Georgia

James Edward Oglethorpe, fighting general and visionary, forms a new colony . . . The War of Jenkins' Ear(s) . . . Slave labor opens fertile cotton fields between the Oconee and the Ogeechee . . . Land grants, and Robert, Jr. joins Charles in migrating west to Georgia . . . Life on an ante-bellum plantation, after house-raisings and Savannah tabby . . . A new Abercrombie generation begins to make its mark . . . Expansion to 16,104 acres . . . Death comes to Robert, Jr. and then to Charles, surrounded by eleven children and twenty grandchildren . . . Eight years to settle a "vast" estate . . . Of tariffs, political imbalance and worn-out land . . . General Anderson Abercrombie entertains the Marquis de Lafayette, and he and Charles, Jr. buy land from the Indian Konoyarhika . . . New plantations at Brickyard and Cross Keys, Alabama as Leonard joins the new wave of Abercrombie migration to the west

Georgia could have been much more appropriately named for its founder, James Edward Oglethorpe. George II probably expected the honor, remembering the earlier pattern of Virginia (belauding Elizabeth, the Virgin Queen) and the Carolinas (for Charles II, a generous man with a grant); but George II did little or nothing for the colony after issuing a royal charter for it to Oglethorpe and the other members of the Trustees of Georgia, in 1732.

Oglethorpe, an Etonian who studied briefly at Corpus Christi College, Oxford, was a curious and praiseworthy mixture of soldier, sociologist, reformer and politician. Entering the army at sixteen, he transferred to an Austrian regiment five years later and campaigned against the Turks from 1717 to 1722. Only twenty-six, yet with a full decade of invaluable, ripening experience in the military, he returned home to England and a seat in Parliament in 1722. In the House of Commons, he became interested in prison reform, particularly in the plight of those thrown into debtors' prison for months, even years, unable to help themselves while their families suffered unjust and intolerable hardships.[1]

Named chairman of a parliamentary commission investigating not only the imprisonment of debtors, but prison reform in general, Oglethorpe soon had a unique opportunity to study the problem in depth. More and more concerned with the commission's findings, he brought together a select group of other members of the House—philanthropists, reformers, businessmen and chauvinists concerned with the slowdown in colonization since the glory days of New England, Virginia and the Carolinas. As trustees of the proposed colony of Georgia, they went next to George II's ministers with an idea: Why not provide a refuge in America not only for those in debtors' prison, but for selected other prisoners, persecuted members of dissident religious sects and others seeking a new life far away from England?

George II's close advisors were almost exclusively Whig ministers of state, in full flower for generations after siding with the victorious Hanover succession in the Revolution of 1688. Dedicated to centralizing power even more in their own party, and to projects appealing to, or benefitting the upper class, they liked Oglethorpe's proposal for a number of reasons: He was a gentleman of means and a loyal Whig, only thirty-six years old yet already a seasoned officer with the potential to become a skilled general. Since he had (wisely) agreed to raise a regiment of tough Highlands infantrymen for service in Georgia, why not use his talents and his troops against the troublesome Spanish? Philip V of Spain had vowed to "extirpate" the English settlements in South Carolina and claimed every inch of what the Trustees of Georgia were requesting as their new colony.

The new outpost in America was also the type of proposition which often presented opportunities for profit to the alert entrepreneur, or for that matter, to a government minister. Further, the Whig leaders were distressed at the amount England was spending on silk, indigo, cotton and rare spices brought in at great cost from afar. The Trustees, it was noted, planned to raise silkworms, indigo plants, cotton and some varieties of spices in Georgia's relatively mild climate. And finally, what could be wrong with deporting such troublesome segments of the population as debtors, minor criminals and religious dissidents while gaining points for restimulating colonial expansion?

A twenty-year grant was made by the crown to the Trustees of Georgia in 1732; it encompassed a vast territory extending from the Carolinas to Spanish Florida, and from the Atlantic Ocean to the Gulf of Mexico. Oglethorpe was named governor and general, went himself to found the city of Savannah in 1733, and vigorously pursued both grants from Parliament to underwrite the new colony of Georgia, as well as colonists to settle it.

Meanwhile, a publicity campaign worthy of Florida real estate agents in 1927 was launched in London to attract both qualified indigents as well as settlers able to pay their own way and to buy land from the Trustees of Georgia. After a barrage of articles on the healthy climate, fertile soil and great opportunities for both a good new life and the possibility of amassing a fortune, Oglethorpe returned from his new colony with a seven-foot Indian chief, by name Tomochichi.

Chief Tomochichi was displayed in Parliament, newspaper offices, coffeehouses and even in a few carefully selected drawing rooms, to enormous notice and enthusiasm. In addition to the sugar cane and rice piling up on British docks (and increasing other imports including cotton and sorely-needed naval stores such as North Carolina pitch and turpentine), Londoners could now see and read about a real, live, fascinating giant from over the seas.

General Oglethorpe formed up the Highlands regiment as promised and had its members drilling in kilts at a settlement with the unlikely name of Frederica on the Altamaha River before the first shipload of emigrants arrived. These colonists were the more than one hundred English settlers who sailed from Liverpool to Savannah on the good ship *Ann* in the summer of 1733; meanwhile, there was lively recruiting of Austrian, German and Swiss religious dissidents, among them a Geneva group whose Protestant roots went back to John Knox and his exile in the capital of Switzerland. Almost a third of the passengers on the *Ann* died within a year, many of them children succumbing to the rigors of frontier life and a variety of fevers; but England continued to send colonists.

Things went badly for Georgia in those early years, although General Oglethorpe worked might and main for success and was quite popular with those who had chosen a new life under his disciplined yet benevolent leadership. There were, however, underlying problems that simply proved to be insurmountable:

James Edward Oglethorpe was primarily a military man, in spite of his broad interests and multiple abilities; he located settlements in terms of strategic values, brought in soldiers before colonists and was prone to think first in terms of defense and attack; as a dedicated reformer, he was instrumental in convincing his partners that there should be neither strong drink nor slaves in Georgia; and although a Whig, and a man of inherited wealth and property, he granted indigent settlers only fifty acres of land, while making it difficult for those who paid their own passage and purchased their own holding to amass the acreage needed for large plantations, or even to pass land on to future generations.

The constant emphasis on the military, exacerbated by ongoing threats from both the Spanish forts in Florida and belligerent Indian tribes, drained manpower from agriculture and trade alike and was increasingly costly. Then, just when Georgia's colonists were beginning to show some modest progress, the ludicrously-named War of (Edward) Jenkins' Ear(s) broke out in 1739.[3] After Parliament officially declared war against Spain, the Spanish seized a little fortification on Amelia Island, and Oglethorpe put together in response a force of almost one thousand Highlanders, adventuresome South Carolinians and several hundred Indian recruits, presumably friends of Chief Tomochichi.

This motley crew shaped up into a reasonably good striking force, although they appeared a sorry and undisciplined lot on the drill field. Oglethorpe headed them south, and soon took two Spanish forts east of the Okefenokee Swamp on the St. Mary's River. Next, he marched against ancient, heavily-garrisoned St. Augustine. The Spanish commander, Count Manuel de Montiano, was more appalled at the audacity of the attackers than concerned, but General Oglethorpe did impose a siege of six weeks before quarreling with the feisty South Carolinians under his command and marching back north to his own territory.

The prohibition against rum and other strong drink was a troublesome thing for settlers who liked their grog or, more in point, a little cash or barter from distilling operations; far more significant, however, was the strict interdiction against slavery. A man could hear a dozen stories a month about the enormous income from growing rice in the Carolinas (or sugar cane in the Barbados, only a few days distant from Savannah in a fast schooner) with slave labor; and you listened ever more closely after another failure with raising silkworms or some exotic spices unsuited to the soil and climate of Georgia. As early as 1738, there were some instances of settlers giving up their land in the Oglethorpe colony to move north into the Carolinas. Finally, fifty acres was simply not enough for even subsistence farming, and many colonists had as their first objective putting together large tracts for their heirs, a practice prohibited in early Georgia.

In 1743, James Edward Oglethorpe returned to England and remained there to complete a distinguished career as a member of Parliament and public figure, always concerned with the progress of Georgia and the betterment of the quality of life for the English people overall. Meanwhile, it was more and more obvious in lengthening perspective that the original conditions under which the Trustees of Georgia had attempted to develop and administer their colony were over-authoritarian, and impractical in many respects.

As a dedicated reformer, Oglethorpe could not bring himself to recommend the introduction of slavery into Georgia. He did, however, quietly champion a move to increase local autonomy through some form of an elected body chosen by the settlers themselves.

The Trustees met in London in 1752 as their twenty-year charter was nearing expiration. A summary report showed less than two thousand five hundred persons then resident in Georgia, most of them in a narrow strip just west of the Savannah River. A surprising number were skilled and semi-skilled artisans with little or no experience in farming. This, later historians discovered, was not by accident. General Oglethorpe himself screened all applicants to join his colony, and was quite partial to men skilled in construction—particularly carpenters and stonemasons. They could plan, build and maintain the many forts he envisioned for the protection and defense of Georgia, regardless of their skill as farmers. All applicants, moreover, had to be prepared to bear arms, and to attend regular "musters," or military drills and lectures.

The establishment in 1750 (at Oglethorpe's urging) of a legislative assembly designed to strengthen local government at the expense of the proprietors' authority had not had any particular effect on immigration. This remained disappointingly low, with more applicants from the Continent than from England, and too few good yeomen experienced in how to make a living from the soil.

One encouraging development had been the success of General Oglethorpe's earlier efforts to win the Indian tribes away from the Spanish. The Cherokees, and the smaller tribes to the south, had ceded much of their lands along the coastal rivers to the colony.

The Trustees of Georgia voted in their 1752 meeting to turn the royal charter of 1732 back to the crown. When they came face to face with reality, the population of their colony was only a fraction of what had been expected after two decades; and there was too low a percentage of farmers able to sustain themselves on the land. The raising of silkworms and indigo plants had simply not worked out, and earlier plans for the cultivation of wine grapes and spices had long been forgotten. Oglethorpe himself, the crux of the entire experiment, had devoted a decade to it but showed no inclination to return to America; it was noted by the other Trustees that he might be pretty well irreplaceable.

Another factor was a fundamental shift in English political life. The Trustees, primarily politicians and businessmen, saw with every other intelligent observer the rising influence of William Pitt the Elder, who was opposed to George II and to many of his ministers. It was only a matter of time until he would form a government (1756), and realists felt that they should be carefully seeking a place on the new ship of state instead of concentrating on an apparently worthless royal charter for lands five thousand miles from London.

So, the charter was abandoned, and as England became heavily involved in the Seven Years' War (1756–1763), with its vexing costs in manpower and treasury deficits, relatively little thought was given to any of the American colonies. The scene had shifted dramatically to Europe, even though the Seven Years' War was a natural outgrowth of the French and Indian War in the New World. Great Britain's ability to defeat the combined forces of France, Austria and Russia with formidable help from the superbly trained Prussian armies of Frederick II the Great, however, protected her interests in North America as much as it established the English as a world power.

The Trustees of Georgia could not have foreseen that George II would allow slavery in their former colony soon after they had abandoned it to the crown, or how this plus the Treaty of 1773[4] would open the fertile uplands west of Augusta, Georgia to almost a century of fabulous prosperity based on King Cotton. Among those most affected would be Charles Abercrombie, James S.

Abercrombie's great-great grandfather, of Orange County, North Carolina; first captain of the Hillsborough District; major in the American forces during the Revolutionary War; planter; justice of the peace; and father of a large and growing family who would now become the next member of his clan to respond to the urge to move ever westward in search of new, fertile and available land.

It had been a troublesome decision for Charles Abercrombie, his wife Edwina and their seven children, ranging from the infant John Booth to the fifteen-year-old Abner, to leave Orange County, North Carolina. The family had been in the county since before it was organized as a political entity and were probably as well and as favorably known as anyone in the western part of the state. They would leave behind not only dozens of relatives and friends, but substantial and valuable holdings of land; Charles' significant appointments as a justice of the peace, deputy sheriff and member of key county boards and commissions were also to be abandoned. And there were memories of childhood in early Orange County, of the stirring time of the Regulators and Captain Abercrombie's muster ground and the grist mill—of the hundreds of threads that tie a large family to the place of its members' birth and upbringing.

The die had been cast, however, from the time that his brother Robert, Jr., on a 1781 visit to Georgia, brought back news of the fertile, well-drained loamy soil between the Oconee and Ogeechee Rivers, in a mild climate well suited to growing cotton. There was also the persistent rumor that Georgia, with plenty of land, would offer grants to veterans of the Revolutionary War, including those from other states of the new republic.

Charles Abercrombie, a native of Orange County, had been aware for years that he should seek better land elsewhere, a conclusion that was reinforced regularly as his family grew apace toward the final total of eight sons and three daughters. The county had its enticements, but those who had lived there over the years knew only too well that the quality of the soil was not among them. The Abercrombies and their neighbors for miles about were in the paraplain so typical of the Piedmont of North Carolina. Here you found a loam of little quality, heavily impregnated with clays. Small, sinuous hills aggravated the constant problem of erosion, and kept yields from profitable crops such as cotton and tobacco distressingly low, with a frequent need to rotate (or even abandon) entire fields. The land was really best suited to oats, wheat, various legumes or corn, although the yield per acre from the latter crop tended to be discouraging at times also.

There was another problem for the Abercrombies in Orange County, although this difficulty centered about Robert, Jr. rather than his brother Charles. During the so-called War of Regulation, culminating in the Battle of Alamance on May 16, 1771, the family and their kinsmen had sided with the victorious militiamen of Governor William Tryon and Sheriff Tyree Harris against the Regulators. Almost fifteen years had passed, but few people had forgotten the nine Regulators killed in action, the six later hanged as traitors or the fact that more than six thousand in the county were required to sign a hateful oath of abjuration (similar to that required in Scotland after the rebellion of 1745) in order to receive pardons and restoration of citizenship.

Feeling ran high in the county as late as 1773, after Sheriff Harris was finally ''roughed up'' by the same riotous Regulators who had fired muskets into the home of Edmund Fanning, colonel of militia, judge and spokesman for Governor Tryon. The sheriff moved to Caswell County to tone down the continuing controversy, but he remained high on the ex-Regulator ''hate list'' for years.

When Robert Abercrombie, Jr. married the sheriff's daughter, Nancy Harris Moore, he inherited part of the feud. Indeed, the disgruntled Regulator who took his grievances to the Hillsborough *Recorder*, and then had copies of his ''tract'' reprinted for distribution as a broadside, might have been complaining about the Abercrombies, among others. He railed against '' . . . mercenary, tricking attornies, clarks and other little officers . . . usually American-born adventurers of English descent . . . who have sniffed from afar opportunities for wealth and position.''

These smouldering arguments, best forgotten, tended to resurface with some frequency. They were a factor, as we shall see, in Robert Abercrombie, Jr.'s somewhat unexpected decision to leave Orange County himself in 1788, but must have affected Charles far less. Major Charles Abercrombie was probably far along in his decision to make a new life elsewhere when finally relieved from duty as an officer and veteran of the Revolutionary War late in 1784.[6]

When confirmation came that the Commonwealth of Georgia would indeed provide free land for non-resident soldiers of the Revolution, he was even more determined to seek new and wider opportunities for his large and growing family. Well situated though they were at the time in Orange County, Charles felt that he must look to the future. He would select the best possible five hundred acres of cotton land, and leave Robert, Jr. and his sister Jane (Jenny) Abercrombie Mebane behind to look after affairs in North Carolina.

It was, after all, not such a difficult journey to Greene County, Georgia. He reckoned it at about two hundred fifty miles by horseback, or closer to three hundred by infrequent stagecoaches to the South Carolina border, then southwest to their new home. Nothing you would want to negotiate every month or so, but once the move was made with the big wagons and the slaves, equipment and farm animals, and things had settled down a bit for Edwina and the children who would follow, he and Robert, Jr. and other members of the family could visit back and forth on occasion without any particular difficulties. In the meantime, the U.S. Postal Service would not be established by old Ben Franklin for almost another decade (1794), but there was reasonably reliable dispatching of mail through combinations of stagecoach and packet boats plying the principal rivers.

During the summer of 1785, Charles and Robert, Jr. went together to the Georgia uplands to inspect specific sites for his grant of land at first hand. They decided on an area fifty miles west and a little south of Augusta, James Edward Oglethorpe's old fur trading post that had seen furious battles during the Revolutionary War.

Back in Augusta, the temporary capital of Georgia several times during the Revolution and again from 1786 to 1795, Charles was advised to make his actual application for land in Savannah, where the office specifically concerned with grants to veterans had been moved. He returned to Savannah, completed his application, and learned that a famous comrade-in-arms under whom he had fought in the crucial engagement at Guilford Courthouse four years earlier would be living some one hundred miles east of the uplands area in which he had chosen to settle. This was General Nathaniel Greene,[5] who penned the British up in Charleston just when they were threatening to overrun both South and North Carolina.

General Greene had already moved to an estate he would name Mulberry Grove, some fifteen miles north of Savannah. There had been spirited competition between Georgia and South Carolina to determine who would have the general as an especially honored citizen; he settled the controversy as best he could by accepting a large grant of land on the border of both states; although in Georgia, Mulberry Grove was so close to South Carolina that you could literally throw a rock from one state to the other from some points on the estate.

Major Charles Abercrombie was also soon to become a new citizen of Georgia. Early in 1786, the state surveyors had completed their work, in compliance with the "survey warrant" from the land office in Savannah. When his deed was finally filed with the records clerk in Greene County, he was the owner of two adjoining tracts totaling 517.5 acres some five miles east of present-day Lake Sinclair. This was obviously not enough for the big plantation he had in mind, but it was a fine start. The property was near a point where the Oconee and the Ogeechee were less than six miles apart, with rich, alluvial soil built up over eons of time. There was already talk of carving a new county from Greene and Washington counties, which extended together more than one hundred miles north and south from Oglethorpe and the South Carolina border. If this came to pass, he would probably be in the center of the new political subdivision, with the natural advantages of living near the county seat.

The Charles Abercrombies moved into two log cabins at their new home in the late spring of 1786, after the children had completed the school year back in North Carolina. There were a few families in the area, and the population would increase steadily around what was to be the town of Sparta, under the impetus of land grants, beginning speculation in large tracts and the first indications of what would become an almost feverish boom in cotton. As Charles was to discover, the upland soil was ideal for cotton farming; it was a mixture of sand and very fine particles of clay, with traces of long-decayed vegetable matter and other alluvial humus. The erosion he and other major landowners in the North Carolina Piedmont had battled against constantly was simply not a problem, even when raising a row crop such as cotton.

Life was not easy along Buffalo Creek in the late 1870s, in what came to be known as the Zion District just west of Sparta, Georgia. Major Charles Abercrombie took growing satisfaction, however, in developing the two tracts he had personally selected from a semi-wilderness of pine, hickory and oak to choice farmland. Just as in the pioneering days in North Carolina, neighbors from miles around gave invaluable help in the beginning; the Abercrombies, in turn, would assist many another family of settlers in the years to come.

The word went out first for a ''log-rolling'' at which men and older boys helped to trim, notch and stack the pine logs that slaves had cut under the direction of Billo, the negro overseer given Charles in his father's will. A week or so later, there was a ''house-raising'' at which the big logs were quickly set into place as the walls of the two cabins required by a large family. It was hard work, especially as the walls moved higher, but quickly done in a competitive atmosphere between the good-natured teams of volunteer builders. While the ''raising'' proceeded, an older boy was mixing up the ''Savannah tabby,'' a rough but virtually indestructible concrete made of lime, sand mixed with pea gravel, and oyster shells crushed into tiny pieces. This was spread between the logs, over the fitted notches at the corners and around the crude windows and doors that a neighbor skilled in cutting these apertures was busily fashioning.

After stopping for a plain but hearty lunch packed at the nearby farmhouse where Charles was a temporary boarder, and washed down with cold water from the little spring he had discovered on his property, everyone went back to work. They finished up well before sundown and watched the new owner install the handmade iron hinges and other hardware that he had purchased from a blacksmith in Augusta.

Billo and the other slaves (including Rodger and Peter and some of their youngsters on temporary loan from Robert, Jr.) would put thick cedar shingles on the roofs of the structures the next day, and then move inside to finish up. Next, quarters for Charles' slaves, plus the ones he hoped to acquire at Savannah, were built in a grove of trees near the log cabins. Billo, as overseer, would have his own separate dwelling; this was the custom.

Over the next several years, many of the elements of a small, self-sufficient community grew up around the new Abercrombie home. There were various outbuildings, plus sheds and shanties to protect equipment and tools and harvested crops enroute to market from the weather; a combination smithy and carpentry shop; a smokehouse in which to prepare succulent ham and thick, tasty bacon; chicken yards (near the house for protection from watchful hawks and other predators); stables; barns; a small carriage house; and a tiny dairy in which cows were milked, cream separated and butter and cottage cheese made. Further away were the pig pens and pastures for cows and horses, with a detached enclosure for the big, plodding, hard-working mules. A large vegetable garden was near the kitchen, a separate structure because of the ever-present danger of fire.

Edwina chose the best locations for flower beds, a rose garden and a fruit orchard and grape arbor soon after she and the younger children had arrived in the ''Jersey'' wagon, with its special springs, canvas top and reasonably comfortable seats. They brought with them the frightened daughter of Rachele, the black cook, because the girl was about to deliver her first child and would have been uncomfortable in a provisions or equipment wagon.

Edwina had cuttings or seeds for the fragrant ''pinks'' (which also came in white or crimson); violets; the sweet-smelling, night-blooming cape jasmines (''jessamines''); and spring's bright harbinger, the yellow primrose. She had also selected from their North Carolina home the best specimens of a half-dozen varieties for the rose garden, and small mimosa and ''Pride of India'' chinaberry trees noted for their quick growth and cooling shade in summer.

For the orchard, there were healthy little apple, peach, pear, plum and fig trees; and for the arbor, vines to yield scuppernong grapes. Native to the southern counties of the Carolinas, these muscadine-like grapes were the source of a prized wine, very sweet and light in color. Stores of vegetable seeds and tiny tomato plants were also unloaded from the Jersey wagon, but their planting in a special garden, a vital source of food on the frontier, would be left to Abner and the older Abercrombie boys.

Their mother had carefully brought enough cuttings and seeds, plus fruit trees, to have some for the slave quarters. And Rachele had been given a fine specimen of a young chinaberry tree to plant right in the middle of the quarters area, against the devastating sun and heat of Georgia summers.

Charles Abercrombie could hardly have timed his move to the cotton uplands of middle Georgia in 1786 any better. He needed about five years to sell his extensive holdings back in North Carolina, obtain far more acreage in Georgia, clear his land for planting and purchase enough additional slaves to operate a large plantation property. As it turned out, it would be 1791, or exactly five years, before cotton was produced in significant volume in Georgia. This was largely because of the time required to clear large tracts with what was essentially hand labor, the lack of major marketing centers and the enormous difficulties involved in getting anything transported over a hopeless system of roads. Other negative factors included the need to separate the cotton seeds from the lint by hand, and the primitive state of looms in early textile mills, which greatly curtailed demand for cotton.

Suddenly, there was both a cotton gin to separate seed from lint mechanically, and a crude version of a power loom. Eli Whitney, a 1792 graduate of Yale College, accepted a teaching position in a Savannah academy, stayed a few days at Mulberry Grove as a guest, and immediately became interested in devising a "gin" that would in effect comb out cottonseed. Within a year, he had a patent on a workable machine, and Savannah had lost a good teacher. Earlier, in 1786, an obscure English clergyman named Edmund Cartwright became interested in weaving during a visit to a Derbyshire mill using the slow, cumbersome machinery then available. He invented a crude but usable power loom that came into general acceptance after 1800, when it had been improved many times by Cartwright and his associates.

The effect of the Whitney and Cartwright inventions was spectacular. In England, for example, the value of cotton goods exported annually rose one hundred seventy-five times between 1770 and 1830, from £215,000 to £37.5 million. And there was a corresponding jump in the demand for cotton, not only by the dominant English mills, but increasingly in New England and the older colonies of the United States. Closer to home, Savannah and Charleston grew from little more than handsomely planned towns to significant cotton ports, and small textile mills began to appear along the rivers of both Georgia and South Carolina. From a crop of barely two thousand bales in all of Georgia in 1791, production climbed more than a thousand percent to twenty thousand a decade later, and went skyrocketing upward along with prices for cotton, the new bonanza.

Meanwhile, Charles Abercrombie was making steady progress on several fronts, as he moved on the problems involved in becoming the owner and operator of a major plantation. Using a combination of cash obtained from the sale of land in Orange County[7] and the liberal terms available for purchases on credit, he bought another one thousand two hundred acres adjoining his original grants along Buffalo Creek, plus an additional one thousand two hundred thirty-one acres just over the border into Washington, the next county to the south. Now he had just under three thousand acres of prime middle Georgia land, all of it within a day's ride by horseback. He also acquired smaller tracts in southern Virginia between 1786 and 1789, probably for speculation, as there are no records indicating that this acreage was ever put into production.

As land clearing proceeded more rapidly with the acquisition of more slaves in Savannah and at smaller auctions back in Suffolk, New Bern and Hillsborough, North Carolina, Major Charles began planting test tracts of cotton. He obtained fine yields per acre, with the average staple length at an inch and a half—not the two inches and more of premium Sea Island cotton, but good middling that any buyer would want.

A surprising development within the family also pleased Charles greatly. He and his brother Robert, Jr., with their sister Jenny the only children born to their parents, Robert, Sr. and Jane Gresham Abercrombie, had understandably been very close. While it was comforting to have Robert, Jr. looking after things in Orange County, where he still had substantial holdings, he missed the younger brother constantly. On one of a number of trips back to North Carolina, Charles noted that Robert was in the process of selling both some of his own land and that held in partnership with his first cousin, Robert Gresham. He also seemed anxious to sell a grist mill and surrounding acreage that belonged jointly to him and to Charles.[8]

The answer was that Robert, Jr., possibly influenced by the lingering feud between his father-in-law (ex-Sheriff Tyree Harris) and the Regulators, had decided to join the trek to the west. Also a major in the Revolutionary War, Robert, Jr. was eligible for grants from the state of Georgia. He acquired 202.5 acres of good land in the Flournoy District near Warrenton in Warren County, less than a dozen miles east of Charles' new home, in 1788. He was to add another 202.5 acres in District 12 of Baldwin County (ten miles to the west) in 1807, and an additional tract of five hundred forty acres in Warren County that same year.

It would be years, if ever, before Robert Abercrombie, Jr. and his wife Nancy Harris would have a home in Georgia comparable to that in which she grew up, and there must have been some misgivings on her last visit to the Brick House Farm. Sheriff Tyree Harris had built the family residence there years before the Piedmont began to fill up with settlers, probably of brick brought to Savannah from England as ship ballast. There were few, if any, brick homes in those earliest days of Orange County, and Tyree Harris had built well, on a beautiful site at the confluence of the Eno and Flat Rivers. Her father had died in 1787; how surprised the former sheriff would have been to know that the Brick House would still be on its original site as late as 1975.

Soon everything was in readiness for the momentous move of the Robert Abercrombies to Georgia's Warren County; this was accomplished with much assistance from Charles and Edwina, and the growing number of their slaves, in May of 1788. Robert and Nancy's four daughters (Elizabeth, Bersheba, Polly and Retinca, ranging in age from fifteen to eight) and Charles, the ten-year-old named for his uncle, would miss their friends in Orange County, and especially the good school there (substantially improved since the 1763 arrival at New Bern, the colonial capital, of the English schoolmaster Thomas Thomlinson, who visited Hillsborough with some regularity after opening his academy at New Bern, one hundred miles to the east near Pamlico Sound.) The parents pointed out the counterbalancing advantages of having nine first cousins, including the new baby Nancy, only ten miles from the new family home in Georgia.

As production that would in time exceed ten thousand bales per year on his total acreage began in earnest in the mid-1790s, Charles Abercrombie realized how fortunate he was to be almost within the city limits of Sparta, county seat of the new Hancock County organized in 1793, and barely fifty miles from the new cotton docks on the Savannah River at Augusta.

Sparta soon had an early model of the new Eli Whitney gin, and a few cotton merchants (although higher prices were almost always available in Augusta, or from the Scots in Savannah, one hundred miles to the southeast).[9] A heavy wagon hitched to a double team of mules could make it from the Abercrombie cotton yard to Augusta in a long dawn-to-dusk summer day. The cotton bales were then shipped to Savannah on barges that had replaced the pole(d) boats of an earlier era and sent on to mills in the East or abroad.

The backwoods farmers or "crackers" scratching out a living from the thin soils of south Georgia, and even fairly affluent tobacco and cotton growers of the north central and northern parts of the state, had a constant problem with ground transportation over wretched, miserably maintained roads that simply ended at the numerous creeks and small rivers and continued on the other side. Some crackers resorted to "hogsheading" tobacco, or to using oxen to pull cumbersome wagons to distant markets.[10] The latter could be downright dangerous to driver, wagon and cargo if the thirsty oxen smelled water at a ford and started galloping downhill toward it.

The Abercrombies of Georgia, more and more resembling their Scots kinsmen of long ago in the size and cohesiveness of the family, and its impact on the area and region, were gathered together at the home of the Charles Abercrombies on the outskirts of Sparta. It was the last day of 1799, and an excellent day on which to look, as did the Roman god Janus for whom the month January was named, both backward and forward in time.

It had been a memorable ten years, that last decade of the eighteenth century, for Charles and Robert, Jr. alike. They had healthy, well-liked children; new homes; good, productive land in growing quantity; increasing income; and excellent standing among the planters, businessmen, and political, military, civic and social leaders of middle Georgia.

Their sister Jane (Jenny) had also prospered. Married originally to James Wade, a well-regarded but impoverished farmer, she was left a debt-ridden young widow in May, 1760 when her husband died suddenly. Within the year, she had married William Mebane, whose father Alexander, Sr., a wealthy landowner and justice of the peace, would succeed Tyree Harris as sheriff.[11] The Mebanes, principal growers of corn, oats and tobacco, were close friends of the Abercrombies. Their holdings centered upon the present-day town of Mebane, ten miles west of Hillsborough on the far western border of Orange County. As noted earlier, Robert Abercromby, Sr. left Jane only £5 in his will (and North Carolina specie, at that), the reasoning being that as a Mebane, she was well provided for otherwise.

In a time of high infant mortality rates, the Abercrombies had certainly been blessed with both numerous and sturdy offspring. They had their playmates, and later their sweethearts, from all over

Hancock County. There were no grandchildren yet, but Charles' middle daughter Jane, born on Christmas Day of 1781, had married Bolling Hall when not yet seventeen, and was carrying their first baby, Polly. (Bolling Hall would serve three terms in the U.S. Congress and become a leading public figure as well as the best-known layman among the Methodists of Georgia.) And three of Robert's daughters, Elizabeth, Bersheba and Retinca, would marry during 1800. One of the purposes of the New Year's Eve gathering of the clan was to announce Elizabeth's engagement to Aaron Smith, whom she would marry in Warrenton on January 21, 1800.

Both of the Abercrombie brothers had replaced their original log cabin homes with the two-story frame residences of ripsawed pine, painted white with green shutters, that were seen on most plantations at the time. These houses, set well back from the road with an approach of pine trees and native shrubs giving way to flower beds and an occasional strolling peacock as you neared the residence itself, had a long hallway running from front to back. Downstairs, you found a sitting room, dining room and two or three bedrooms. There was a wide veranda in front, and a big porch in the back overlooking a lawn, more flower beds and the orchard and arbor.

Upstairs were additional bedrooms, a sewing room for the mistress and the slave she had trained as a seamstress, and a spacious attic. The furnishings were rather Spartan throughout, although fine pieces were gradually added in the dining room and in the guest bedroom. The rosewood piano on which Robert's daughters had been learning to play back in Orange County had been left temporarily with Jane and William Mebane. It was brought overland as soon as the "big house" was occupied, and installed proudly in the sitting room.

There were fireplaces everywhere, and young blacks assigned to keep plenty of firewood nearby, fires laid and ashes removed, all during the months of fall, winter and early spring. And throughout the Abercrombie homes, as in similar residences in Georgia and North Carolina, there was an ample supply of sand boxes—not for the family cats, but for the high percentage of tobacco "chawers." There aim was often none too accurate.

The Abercrombies would never lack for servants; although both Charles and Robert needed all the field hands they could muster, particularly as they cleared, planted, cultivated and harvested more and more acres, they also knew that their wives required a great deal of help to run large households. Edwina had something of a special claim on the blacks trained for work as maids, serving women, cooks and housemen (including one majordomo). Her father John Booth had died since the move to Georgia, leaving her a number of his seventeen slaves, including several trained for the inside duties prized both for status and for relief from the more physically-demanding jobs assigned to field hands on the plantation.

There was much comfort in one aspect of the spiralling income accruing to the Abercrombie brothers from productive land and escalating prices for cotton. There was of course no income tax, state or federal, and the annual levy on land in Hancock County in the late 1700s was twenty-five cents per *one hundred* acres. The county court had also set a rate for the ''idle and unemployed,'' presumably on the theory that there was plenty of work available, and the shiftless could not be coddled. This tax was $2 per year, payable in cash.

There had been a heavy trail of citizen involvement for both Charles and for Robert, Jr. in the old record books of Orange County. These detailed their appointments as justices of the peace; deputy sheriffs; jurors, grand jurors and foremen of juries; bondsmen for the sheriff, or even for a friend renewing his license for an ordinary (tavern); witnesses to important documents, administrators and executors; delegates to official meetings; or overseers for county roads. As former Revolutionary War officers of high rank, they were even more involved in the ongoing operations of the county militia.

This continued in Georgia, with ever more responsible appointments, and especially as population continued to soar in the new state. The gain from 1790 to 1800 alone was from 82,548 to 162,626, and ninety percent of this phenomenal growth was in the land-grant counties such as Hancock. Both Charles and Robert took roles in assuring that their county would be created from portions of Greene and Washington in 1793, and that Sparta would be selected as the ''seat of justice'' (temporary jail and all) in 1795, and as the county seat after formal incorporation of the town in 1805.

Charles Abercrombie and Anderson Comer, an emigrant from Maryland, were among Georgia's earliest philanthropists. They gave valuable town lots in Sparta as sites for Hancock County's first courthouse and a handsome park. Charles' son Leonard married Sarah Comer, Anderson Comer's niece and his ward after the death of her father John Comer, in 1804. Leonard and Sarah were the great-grandparents of James Smither Abercrombie, and the source of names such as Charles Anderson, Leonard Anderson, Sarah Comer and John Comer Abercrombie in future generations.

More significantly for the history books, Charles Abercrombie was a delegate from Hancock County to the memorable convention at Louisville, then the seat of government, which adopted the constitution of the state of Georgia on May 30, 1798.

Both Robert and Charles would have described themselves as "getting a bit long in the tooth" as the year 1800 dawned. They were fifty-two and fifty-eight, respectively, when those were fairly senior ages for military men. They therefore took more of an advisory, than an active, role in the formation of the militia of Hancock County, although Robert was named colonel of the county regiment and served for several years before passing the oriflamme on to his nephews and to his own son Charles.[12]

Schools for the Charles Abercrombie children remained a considerable problem in 1800, although not the dilemma that primary and secondary education had represented for both Abercrombie families during the first years in Georgia. In 1786, the oldest child of Charles and Edwina (Abner) was barely fifteen, and he and all of his siblings of "schoolable" age. All of Robert and Nancy's children were under fifteen when the family moved to Warren County in 1788. At the turn of the century, Robert's children ranged in age from twenty-five to nineteen; but Charles' youngsters, the last four born in Georgia, included John Booth, fourteen; Anderson, thirteen; Nancy, eleven; Charles, nine; and James, seven; all were still in school.

Georgia had an early tradition of education, especially in Savannah and Augusta; this emphasized, however, private institutions, some without boarding facilities for students from outlying towns and counties. A feeble attempt at public education was undertaken in Savannah in 1743, but little came of it, just as from a little school for Indian youngsters that existed as early as 1730 at Irene, a hamlet near Savannah. And when the colonial Commons (House of Assembly) expanded and improved the concept of free schools in 1755, and again in 1758 and 1764, the effort was marred by a troublesome requirement that parents apply under conditions considered to be demeaning. It was, one citizen protested, "like signing a pauper's oath."

The brothers Abercrombie sent some of their children to the private academies in Savannah, in Augusta, and in Richmond, Wilkes and Burke counties; later, they would enroll them in two excellent such institutions right in Hancock County. They also depended heavily upon their own teaching, instruction by the older children and the "old field schools."

These were one-room operations housed in a log cabin, usually "on the edge of a wood or a worn-out or poor field." There was a fireplace against the heavy frost of winter mornings, a gourd beside a wooden bucket of water fetched by the older boys from the spring or creek nearest by, hard benches around the walls, and some well-worn hickory switches conveniently at hand.

The teacher was usually a bachelor from outside the county who came around in August or September with "school articles." Subscribing parents signed up for $10–$15 for a five- or six-month term in most schools (although some tuition ran as low as $7.50–$10). Fifteen pupils was the minimum, but more often twenty to thirty youngsters ranging in age from six to twenty-one were in the schools. "Master" knew readin', writin' and "cyphering to the rule of three," but little else. Study consisted of repeating the lessons over and over, aloud, with all grades often going at once; the teacher watched for those whose lips did not move, or for half-dozing miscreants nodding off; these were for him the non-learners in the Babel-like cacophony that droned on most of an eight-hour day.

Nevertheless, learning did take place, with the aid of such peerless works as Webster's *Blue-Backed Speller*, Murray's *English Reader* (and *Grammar*) and the *Federal Calculator*. Cruel, almost barbarous, discipline was the rule, at least for the more obstreperous boys. At the weekend on Friday, the older girls labored over compositions, and the boys who already "had their three R's" declaimed. Any master from outside Savannah, Charleston or adjoining coastal areas would have to adjust to one of the most pleasing, and yet unique accents he would ever hear as the declamation sessions proceeded. Some students had been raised as infants or small children by Negro women of the Gullah tribe, prized for their skill as nursemaids. The Gullahs (Geechees) spoke a combination of seventeenth-century colonial English and key West African words and phrases. And their lilting, distinctive and pleasant dialect, without any Southern drawl, was almost invariably stamped indelibly upon the speech of their young charges, in word patterning and accent.

When school became too tiresome, the more senior boys arrived at sun-up (usually barefooted even in the coldest weather, after a walk of several miles) and stoutly barricaded the door. If "master" could loosen it without damage to door and sills, classes were held. If not, there was a holiday. Some masters were accused by parents of connivance in these episodes, which were more prevalent at the end of term, in early spring.

In sharp contrast to the "old field schools," some of the academies in early Georgia sent a number of their graduates on to colleges or universities, and not merely to the fledgling University of Georgia, which would in time mature into one of the finest institutions of higher learning in the southeast. (Chartered by the colonial government in 1785, it had been founded just as the new century opened, in 1801 at Easley's Mill on a high hill overlooking the Oconee and the future city of Athens.)

The academies often demanded a curriculum that would send today's high school senior reeling: Latin and Greek literature and grammar (including usually Caesar's *Commentaries,* Pliny, Homer and Aeschylus), astronomy, philosophy, logic, rhetoric, etymology, geography, algebra, beginning calculus and that forgotten art, penmanship. Among the best of these institutions, supported by the Abercrombies and attended by some of their children, were Duncan McLean's Mount Zion Academy and the Powel(l)ton Academy, both in Hancock County.

The broad, illuminating classical education offered by the academies, and the mental discipline plus lifelong habits of reading and further study they instilled, must have been factors in the growing number of Abercrombie children, grandchildren and cousins who would enter high public office and the professions in the nineteenth century, both in Georgia and in Alabama. Nor did a good education emphasizing the classic disciplines of knowledge handicap anyone running a plantation, or going into business.

Charles Abercrombie reached the Biblical allotment of three score and ten years on March 4, 1812. He was sound in mind and body, riding for hours each day (except on Sundays)[13] to watch over various plantation operations after an early-morning conference with Billo's son, who had succeeded his father as principal overseer.

The children were all grown now. The youngest, James, born February 18, 1792, had just celebrated his twentieth birthday. There were twenty grandchildren, with more than thirty still to follow.[14]

Abner, Leonard, Charles and John Booth had chosen to help operate the primary family plantation at Sparta, along with nearby holdings. James was also working with his father, but he spoke increasingly of the opportunities represented by new land to the west, just north of Mobile along the Alabama River in Monroe County, Alabama Territory.

Leonard, as noted earlier, was the great-grandfather of James Smither Abercrombie, and the grandfather of Abercrombie children whose names we will encounter again and again down the generations to come: Leonard Anderson; John Comer, II; Robert Haden; Milo Bolling, Jr.; Annie; James; and Sarah Comer, II. Leonard was also the father of Milo Bolling, Sr., and John Comer, Sr., the former being Jim Abercrombie's grandfather.

Sarah Comer Abercrombie, II married Dr. W. H. Crawford, the son and namesake of William Harris Crawford of Oglethorpe County, Georgia on February 4, 1864. The elder Crawford, once rector of the famed Richmond Academy at Augusta, served as United States senator from 1807 to 1813, and received forty-one electoral votes in the presidential election of 1824 to run third against the most redoubtable opposition in history: John Quincy Adams, Henry Clay and Andrew Jackson. No one gained a majority, and the choice was up to the House of Representatives, which chose Adams, even though he had trailed General Jackson ninety-nine votes to eighty-four. A staunch friend and political ally of President James Monroe, Senator Crawford had previously served as minister to France, secretary of war and secretary of the treasury under Monroe.

Sarah Comer Abercrombie Crawford died in childbirth on November 22, 1866. She was buried at the new Abercrombie plantation headquarters at Cross Keys, Alabama, in the first somber days of Reconstruction.

Edmund had distinguished himself in the Indian Wars of the late 1790s and had been given his own grant of land in the northeast reaches of Hancock County along the Ogeechee, the "river of rippling water." He would later represent the county in the state legislature, amass a fortune, and see one of his grandchildren, Judge H. Warner Hill, named to the Supreme Court of Georgia.

Wylie (often Wiley or even Willie in the record books) was the seventh son of Charles and Edwina Abercrombie. He had been elected lieutenant in the Hancock County Militia in 1796, carrying on a strong family tradition, and lived for many years at Fort Creek. His home was near an old block house where he and his comrades-in-arms had often been on patrol during the final skirmishes with the Upper Creeks (known for some reason as the Red Sticks). Always one of the most popular men in the county, he signed the charter for the incorporation of Sparta in 1805, but had recently purchased land in Putnam County near the county seat of Eatonton, some fifteen miles northwest of Sparta. He was almost immediately appointed justice of the peace and would represent Putnam County later in the Georgia legislature.

The eighth son, Anderson, enlisted as a private in the War of 1812 and rose to the rank of adjutant general after being wounded while fighting the Creeks at the battle of Calabee in eastern Alabama. He met both General Andrew Jackson and the fabled Davy Crockett while both were enroute to the decisive victory Jackson won over the Creek Nations at Horseshoe Bend on March 27, 1814.[15] Back in Sparta, Anderson obtained land on the edge of the town and became a leading citizen of the area. He would be appointed brigadier general of the Second Division, Second Brigade of the Georgia state militia, in 1825. We will see much more of General Anderson and of his children in the next chapter of this book.

One of Anderson Abercrombie's daughters, Florida, was to become the wife of Governor James M. Smith of Georgia; another, Mary, married General S. C. French, CSA; his son James Jackson, an honor graduate of Emory College and the Harvard Law School, had a distinguished career as an attorney, judge and state senator before enlisting as a private in Ross' Battalion (Company G, the Minute Men) in 1862 at the age of thirty-seven. He rose to the rank of major. Judge of the Superior Court of Muscogee County, Georgia on the Alabama border at an early age, he returned to the practice of law after the War Between the States and was a prominent member of the Georgia bar during the remainder of a long life that ended in 1901.

One of Charles Abercrombie's daughters, Sallie, had married at eighteen the son of a prominent Hancock County family. Her husband was Thomas Raines, captain of the county militia and an elder in the newly-organized Universalist Church of Sparta. Nancy married William Barnes, son of an Orange County family which had helped to establish early Baptist churches in North Carolina. (As indicated before, Jane, the eldest daughter, had married Bolling Hall, a future United States congressman, in 1798.)

Ann, the daughter of William and Nancy Abercrombie Barnes, would marry Green Wood; and a niece, Polly Hall (first-born of Charles Abercrombie's many grandchildren), would later marry Green Wood, Jr. This connection would become quite significant to the Abercrombies of Texas almost a century later.

Ann Barnes Wood, Charles Abercrombie's granddaughter, and Green Wood, Sr. had a son, William B. Wood, who emigrated to Texas in 1850 and settled in Huntsville. His wife, Josephine Mitchell, was a remarkable woman and the maternal grandmother of James Smither Abercrombie. Less than five feet tall, she came to be known as the "Little Grandmother," and would exert a strong, positive influence not only on her grandson Jim, but on the entire Abercrombie family, especially as its members adjusted to life in Houston after 1905.

Josephine and William B. Wood were the parents of Evelina Wood, born in Huntsville in 1855, on October 23. Evelina would marry James Buford Abercrombie on November 27, 1879, signing the register with the name she used throughout her life: Lina. The officiating minister's church at the time was Grace Episcopal in Galveston, but the Reverend Jeremiah Ward had known J.B. and Lina for many years and was delighted to be asked to come back to his former parish in Huntsville for the ceremony.

Apparently, James Smither Abercrombie's parents were distant cousins. His great-aunt Nancy Abercrombie Barnes was his mother Evelina Wood Abercrombie's great-grandmother.

In the quarter-century since leaving North Carolina, Charles Abercrombie had become a very wealthy man. An 1812 tax list shows the following property in his name in Hancock County: forty-seven slaves (many of them well-trained and highly valuable artisans including blacksmiths, wheelwrights and farriers), two thousand seventy-one acres of land and long inventories of movable as well as immovable possessions. He also owned two hundred eighty acres in Jones County, eighty acres in Wilkinson County, two hundred sixty-eight acres in Twiggs County, 202.5 acres in Morgan County, 202.5 acres in Putnam County and a huge tract of thirteen thousand acres in Glynn County, in extreme southeastern Georgia near Sea Island. There the two-inch cotton was grown, and the field hands gathering the silky lint spoke pure Gullah. His total holdings, then, were sixteen thousand one hundred four acres plus slaves owned outside Hancock County and other real and personal property elsewhere.

Charles Abercrombie and his peers also had intangible possessions of great consequence and value. Theirs was a relatively simple life, and certainly so in terms of the comforts, medical and scientific technology, sophisticated gadgetry, conveniences and amusements available today. There were corn-shuckings, cane-grindings and Independence Day gatherings instead of cocktail parties; and a three-day ride in a stagecoach to visit Orange County at Christmastide instead of a two-hour flight to the ski slopes at Aspen. But the planters of Georgia's golden years had an existence with a deeper tone, rich in the satisfactions of inner confidence and psychological strength; in such a simple yet priceless thing as the ability to have time to read of, think about and discuss matters of lasting significance to a man.

In sum, Charles Abercrombie was blessed with a life of hard work and constant challenge, but a life that fed the inner man with tranquillity—with a sense of accepted identity and role in his world, and a feeling of well-being and accomplishment.

Charles also had his problems in 1812, chief among them the grave illness of his brother, who would die on May 12, 1812 in the spring of his sixty-fifth year. Robert Abercrombie's will, probated July 6 at Warrenton, listed his wife Nancy and two of his sons-in-law, William Jones and Aaron Smith, as executors. They were required to post bond of $50,000, indicating the value of his nine hundred forty-five acres of prime land, slaves and other properties. All militia units in Hancock and Putnam counties were mustered for Robert's funeral, and a special guard of honor attended from his Revolutionary War unit, the South Regiment of Orange County in which he had served as first major under Colonel John Butler.

Two weeks after Robert Abercrombie's last rites, on June 18, 1812, the United States declared war on Great Britain, citing illegal seizure of American seamen, violation of the principle of free trade for neutral vessels on the high seas, invasion of our territorial waters, and the constant threat of blockade.

It was a curious war, beginning with the fact that the peacemaker Robert Stewart (Viscount Castlereagh) had just come to power in England and had ordered attempts at conciliation two days before the declaration of hostilities in Washington. There was neither transatlantic cable nor satellite, however, and the war was on.[16] The southern states and their war hawks were at first solidly behind the conflict, under the leadership of South Carolina's John C. Calhoun; New England, New Jersey and New York were as solidly opposed. The English were far more concerned with Napoleon, who would abdicate in 1814 but return for The 100 Days and his final defeat at Waterloo in 1815. The ground war was fought to major extent in Canada, after sporadic attempts by the British to stir up the legendary Shawnee Chief Tecumseh and his blind twin brother Tenskwatawa, the medicine man and mystic, against the western territories. U.S. naval forces, thought to be completely outclassed by a Royal Navy still basking in the glorious triumph at Trafalgar, won stirring victories with "Old Ironsides" (the USS *Constitution*) and Captain Stephen Decatur's tiny fleet.

Then suddenly, in the same baffling and unpredictable pattern, the war was over. General Andrew Jackson's sharpshooters and artillerymen, superbly protected behind massed rows of thick bales of cotton, had killed General Edward Packenham and two of his brigadiers, plus almost three hundred British redcoats, while inflicting more than two thousand casualties in the battle of New Orleans. The remaining English forces sailed back to Portsmouth without knowing that the Treaty of Ghent had been signed fifteen days earlier, on Christmas Eve. Their grievous losses on January 8, 1815, and seventy-one United States casualties, were totally unnecessary.

The articulate Billo, Jr. was soon telling the slaves at Sparta (gathered at sundown as usual under Rachele's chinaberry tree, now a gigantic dark green umbrella of shade and shadow) how Old Hickory had "whupped the Brits," firing from behind massed bales of Abercrombie cotton. He knew as well as Master Charles that the Abercrombies always shipped via Savannah, and never through New Orleans; but it made a good story, nevertheless.

The War of 1812 itself had little lasting effect upon the Abercrombies, or upon Georgia for that matter, aside from the temporary loss of British markets for cotton after the Glasgow factors simply disappeared from their closed office in Savannah for several years. Even this was made up in large extent by increased orders by United States textile mills fulfilling war contracts and expanding to meet an unexpected jump in national population of thirty-two percent (from 7.3 to 9.6 million) between 1810 and 1820. Indirectly, however, the conflict with England began to uncover fundamental circumstances that would tear at the fabric of the nation, and eventually change a way of life forever in Georgia, and throughout the South.

These were a deepening conflict over the old question of tariffs versus free trade; a beginning imbalance of population (and thereby of political strength and impact) between North and South that would exacerbate sectional rivalries and differences, with accelerating divisions between "free" states and "slave" states; and the first indications of exhausting the deep, fertile but overworked soils of middle Georgia, in the Kingdom of Cotton.

John C. Calhoun, a dominant voice in the United States Senate moving toward eight years in which he would preside over that august yet disputatious body as vice-president under John Quincy Adams, and then under Andrew Jackson, had at first clamored for tariffs. He wanted them to protect small textile mills in his home state of South Carolina. Later, after slashing and cogent attacks on these imposts in the British House of Commons (reported by our embassy in London), and sharp domestic competition from the huge mills in New England, he and his constituents began to restudy their situation. They decided that tariffs were strongly tilted toward benefitting the North, and were on balance quite damaging to states in the South. The South stood both to lose cotton sales and to end up paying more for the increasing volume of manufactured goods they bought in England. The British were waving a double-edged sword: they threatened not only to step up purchases of West Indies cotton, but to raise the prices of their manufactures to make up for any losses in sales volume caused by tariffs.

Until 1820, the "free" or non-slavery states of the North had been in virtually complete balance with the South in terms of population. The 1820 census, however, saw the states above Mason and Dixon's line move ahead at 5.2 million versus 4.5 million in the slave states. Even though the Senate remained equally divided at eleven all, the House of Representatives consisted of one hundred five members in the more populous Northern tier of states, with only eighty-one in the South. This imbalance had great potential dangers to the republic as the slavery question loomed ever larger.

The loss of soil fertility was not something that developed overnight, and indeed, it was delayed for years by the innate strength of the humus-suffused loams, with a small but invaluable admixture of microscopic clay, that are found in middle Georgia. The breakdown, however gradual, was still inevitable in an era before the emergence of formal agricultural research, or the use of chemical fertilizers.

During the first decades in Georgia, the Abercrombies countered lower yields by clearing new fields, rotating fields with less-demanding or restorative crops, or simply allowing a field to remain fallow. By 1815, however, Charles Abercrombie and his New World clan were running out of new acreage to clear, except for the tremendous new holdings recently acquired in distant Glynn County. At the same time, the large Abercrombie family was increasing substantially; and among the slaves, so much a part of the family that one of the traditional and cherished duties of Edwina Abercrombie (or of the mistress of any large plantation in the early nineteeth century) was to care for them personally in times of severe illness, the birth rate was escalating almost geometrically.

The day was approaching when a new generation of Abercrombies, spearheaded by some of Charles' eight sons, would start the new migration in search of new land and broader opportunities. Predictably, the move would once again be toward the west.

March 4, 1817 was a festive day in Sparta, Georgia. It was Charles Abercrombie's seventy-fifth birthday, and the proliferating clan Abercrombie, with their friends from counties around, had gathered to do him honor. Grandfather Charles rode out early with some of the grandsons, taking along his best hounds from the plantation pack in the hope of their picking up the scent of one of the fewer and fewer foxes in the area. They raised a fox, but he was a shrewd old customer who escaped into a thick stand of loblolly pine after making sport of the hounds for a time. He accomplished this by cannily running along the shallow edge of a tributary of Buffalo Creek for a while and then emerging, scentless, well downstream. It was an instinctive stratagem that had worked for centuries on end, and it worked again.

The hunters gave up on their original quarry, tethered their horses, and went looking for game birds. They soon found coveys of fat quail, feeding on the remnants of winter grain fields, to add to the grouse and northward-migrating ducks and geese Charles and his sons had bagged the previous day for his birthday dinner. Game was still plentiful in Hancock County, but not in the tremendous quantities of a generation before. And black bears had been seen as far north as the upper reaches of the Altamaha River, deserting the Okefenokee Swamp in search of the fish they no longer found in small creeks feeding into the swamp.

During and after the seventy-fifth birthday celebration, a chief topic of conversation was young James Abercrombie's rather abrupt move to the Alabama Territory, which had already launched the next wave of migration to the west. James, the youngest son, was a precocious lad, always bright in school, who had discussed the new opportunities in the Territory with his father while still a teenager. He purchased land in what would become Monroe County, north of Mobile, late in 1812. It would still be five years before Alabama was formally organized even as a territory, but James told his father and brothers that he wanted to participate in the early history of what he felt would become a key state in the developing southeast. After marrying Elizabeth Evelyna Ross, daughter of one of the prominent families in the area, on July 27, 1816, he and his bride moved to the future Montgomery County. He had picked his location carefully; it was almost in the exact middle of Alabama-to-be, in the heart of the fertile Black Belt and only a few miles from the future state capital. The Territory would be formally organized (on March 3, 1817) as the young Abercrombies were settling down in their new home, and statehood was only two years away, in 1819. James was positioning himself.

Well educated in the Georgia academies, James Abercrombie had been quite interested in government, and in politics, from boyhood. He would become extremely active in Whig politics, embracing the party and the moderately conservative principles of his father and grandfather, who used the term "Whig" interchangably with "Patriot."

James would serve as a representative and as a state senator in the Alabama legislature before moving on to the United States Congress. His standing in central and eastern Georgia, extraordinary for a man of his relative youth, would become a major factor in the decision of his older brothers, Milo, Charles and Anderson, to leave Sparta and Hancock County for new homes in Russell and Montgomery counties in Alabama.

Charles Abercrombie must have sensed, at three-quarters of a century, that his birthday celebration might well be a final opportunity to see his big family together. That it was, for he died in the summer of 1819, full of honors, accomplishment and memories, leaving what regional historians in the southeast have described as a "vast" or "immense" fortune. It was indeed a huge estate, and it would not be until May 5, 1827 that the Inferior Court of Hancock County, Sitting for Ordinary Purposes, would finally discharge Anderson Abercrombie, sixth son and executor, of his long and successful administration of his father's complex holdings.

Again, the militiamen gathered, to slow-march a comrade of old to his last resting place with muffled drum. But those who had actually served with Major Charles Abercrombie, late of the Third North Carolina Regiment of the Patriot Army, were a small and ghostly rank, for it was nigh on forty years since Lord Cornwallis' defeat at Yorktown, and a half century since the Hancock County militia stood against the Regulators at Alamance.

They buried the major in a small, private graveyard at Sparta, surrounded by a brick wall now carefully reconstructed and marked with historic plaques. There he lies beside Edwina Dicey Booth Abercrombie, mother of their eleven children, and Jim Abercrombie's great-great grandmother. Many of the eleven children, and the fifty grandchildren, would leave their mark on future generations, just as Charles, Robert, Jr. and Jane, with their father Robert, Sr., left their positive and lasting imprints on North Carolina and Georgia in the meaningful hundred years that spanned the mid-eighteenth and mid-nineteenth centuries.

Bolling Hall, husband of the younger Jane Abercrombie and a former congressman from Milledgeville, Georgia, also had a profound influence in bringing about the deepening conviction among three of Charles Abercrombie, Sr.'s surviving sons that they should follow young James and the family tradition of moving on west for new land and fresh opportunities.

Hall, scion of a distinguished line that went back to seventeenth century Virginia, was a veteran of the Revolutionary War who enlisted at sixteen. His Christian name, still used today by the Abercrombies of Texas, came from his great-grandfather, Robert Bolling. Hall's abandonment of a seat in Congress won in 1812, to move on to the fertile lands on the Georgia-Alabama border with sister Jane, ten daughters and the son and heir, Bolling, Jr., must have been a powerful incentive to his brothers-in-law, all of whom respected his judgment and were themselves politically knowledgeable and ambitious.

Soon after arriving at his new Georgia headquarters just over the Alabama border in Harris County, Bolling Hall built in 1824 the first house in Georgia with glass windows, where he and Jane received Paul Yves Roch Gilbert du Motier. Better known as the marquis de Lafayette, this was George Washington's close friend, the legendary general who persuaded Louis XVI to order a well-equipped French expeditionary force of more than five thousand men to Virginia in the spring of 1780. Later, Lafayette outmaneuvered Charles Lord Cornwallis in a series of engagements that reinforced General Nathaniel Greene's successful strategy of pinning the British down in a narrowing area. This forced Cornwallis' retreat to the bottleneck that meant final surrender at Yorktown.

It was Bolling Hall who wrote the proclamation making the marquis de Lafayette an honorary citizen of Georgia, which he read at the public ceremony honoring the French general in 1824, to tumultuous applause for the man who had helped the Patriot cause so tremendously.

And it was Hall who first showed Anderson and Charles Abercrombie, Jr. prime land in Russell County less than ten miles from his own properties. He had told his brothers-in-law that a fine tract just west of the Chattahoochee River might be available from some friendly Indians he had once represented in the territorial courts. The Abercrombie brothers rode over the land, liked it, and saw that it might become the nucleus for a big cotton plantation. Then they went home to Sparta to think about it. For good reason, it would be several years before they could make up their minds about a matter that would affect the Abercrombies down all the years.

Anderson Abercrombie had the most difficult decision to make regarding a move from Hancock County. A wounded veteran of the War of 1812, in which he had reached the rank of adjutant general, he had a good farm almost within the Sparta township, plus the lands inherited from his father. He had married Sydney Grimes, of a leading Greene County family in 1819. They soon had three sons (John, Charles and James Jackson) and two daughters (Elizabeth and Sarah), and were as popular as any family in the area. A natural leader, Anderson had been given a very signal honor in 1825, when he was named brigadier general of the Second Brigade, Second Division of the Georgia state militia. A year later, he was elected to the state legislature. Another high point in 1826 was when he, just as his brother-in-law Bolling Hall, had the historic distinction of serving as host to General Lafayette.

The formal dinner honoring the marquis de Lafayette was at the Eagle Tavern in Sparta, without the beneficence of French cuisine. Prices were kept at the usual level to attract a large audience, which happily showed up. Dinner without spirits was at the teetotaler rate of thirty-seven and one half cents; the price with spirits was fifty cents. Those staying overnight were charged twelve and one half cents for bed and lodging, or just half what it cost to stable a horse and feed him corn plus fodder (corn alone: eighteen and one fourth cents). The Eagle attempted to catch up on after-dinner spirits, which went at twenty-five cents for the best Jamaican rum, as opposed to a dime for white lightning (corn squeezings).

Reports were that the evening went off with reasonable elegance and aplomb, despite the marked differences between the marquis de Lafayette's more usual haunts in Paris and Versailles, and the Eagle Tavern. General Abercrombie served admirably as chairman and toastmaster, and there was fortunately no direct comparison with an earlier July 4 dinner honoring Parson Weems, the noted biographer of George Washington. Among the seventeen toasts called and downed at that event, which concluded after midnight, were those to King Ferdinand and Queen Isabella and to The Moral Law.

By 1830, cotton yields per acre were substantially lower in Hancock County, and the price of new land (after a temporary drop following the Panic of 1819), higher. Anderson knew that he must come to some decision regarding a possible move to Alabama, although he had understandably delayed making it. Bolling Hall had told him and Charles at a recent family gathering that the land they had liked along the broad Chattahoochee might still be available. As he finally confronted his dilemma, General Abercrombie recognized that there were powerful, almost irresistible forces involving prestige, financial stability, sentiment and tradition telling him to remain in Sparta, his birthplace and emotional home. On the other hand, there were clear indications that the economic future for him and his family might be increasingly less promising in Hancock County. In the end, Anderson came to a decision similar to that reached four decades earlier by Charles Abercrombie, Sr. His family, already including nine children, would be better off in a fresh setting of rich, unplowed land and broader opportunity.

Charles was quick to decide to join his brother in the new venture in Alabama. Seeking someone to look out for their remaining interests in Hancock County, they decided upon John Booth, who had been serving as speaker of the state House of Representatives but had spent his entire life on the family plantations. Of the remaining brothers, Wylie had decided to make his career in adjoining Putnam County as a landowner and justice of the peace; Edmund was increasingly busy with his large holdings in northern Hancock County, and as a legislator; Abner was discussing the possibility of moving near the youngest brother, James, in Montgomery County, Alabama; and Leonard, to their vast surprise, was negotiating for a large plantation, also near James, at Cross Keys in Macon County, Alabama.

Early in 1832, Anderson and Charles Abercrombie made the first recorded purchase of land in recently-organized Russell County, Georgia. Bolling Hall had been correct; the land just west of the Chattahoochee, at a little hamlet they would name Brickyard, was still available. For the sum of $1590 in cash, Anderson and Charles obtained the conveyance of the east half of Section II, Township 16, Range 30 from the Indian Konoyarhika. In the tradition of his father, who had built and maintained a fort to encourage and maintain peace with the Indians, General Anderson had always got on with them well, even during the campaigns of the War of 1812. He insisted, and Charles agreed, that they pay a fair price, in cash, for what was obviously good land.

Konoyarhika understood and appreciated this. When there was a drouth in the first years after the Abercrombies were in their new Russell County home, his braves brought gifts of grain for the Abercrombie farm animals. In return, the Indians were later given seed corn of the best quality to replant parched fields.

Within a year, Anderson had been named to a committee to select a location for the courthouse of Russell County; next, he was elected to the Alabama legislature and appointed "foreman of the court" in the first case ever heard in Russell County (both attorneys had to take an oath against dueling, an aftermath of Alabama's earliest days as a state). General Anderson had clearly reestablished the tradition of leadership he brought with him from Georgia.

In 1834, Leonard Abercrombie completed the acquisition of his own new properties, at Cross Keys, Alabama in Macon County. He was less than thirty miles from his brothers at Brickyard, and he had brought with him his son Milo Bolling (the grandfather of James Smither Abercrombie). Milo had married Sarah Lee Haden, daughter of pioneer settlers from Clark County, Alabama, on December 15,1829. They would have eleven children, the last of them James B. (J. B.) Abercrombie, James Smither Abercrombie's father.

The Abercrombies of Scotland, North Carolina and Georgia had completed another journey to the west. They would soon be one of the dominant families in central and eastern Alabama, in the fertile Black Belt of the newest principality of the Kingdom of Cotton.

Notes

[1] Charles Dickens' father, a real life Mr. Micawber, was apprehended one morning at his desk, even though he was a Royal Navy paymaster, and literally flung into prison with other debtors for some pecuniary misadventure. Young Charles had to leave school and accept an exhausting, demeaning job in a factory to help support his mother and the younger children. Fortunately for the Dickens family (and for world literature), this bitter experience was a relatively brief one for the future novelist, and gave him priceless insights into both the life of the working class and the injustices of English penal and correctional institutions.

[2] The Whigs were so entrenched that they survived an extremely unpopular attempt by Robert Walpole, the able but ill-advised prime minister, to impose taxes on wine and tobacco in 1733.

[3] The War of Jenkins' Ear(s) would be best forgotten by both sides. The South Sea Company had arranged for a treaty with Spain permitting one English ship per year to unload slaves at Porto Bello, on the Caribbean coast of Panama. Porto Bello was a key center for the transshipment of cargoes between Spain, the New World and England, and a notorious nexus of the slave trade. The English, tempted by the unconscionable profits involved, sent in a fleet packed to the gunwales with captured Africans instead of the single vessel permitted by treaty. The Spanish were furious when prices collapsed on the oversold Porto Bello slave market, but even more disturbed by the callous disregard of their one-ship agreement with London. A fleet was hardly a single ship.

A sea blockade was organized, and another English slave ship, captained by the unfortunate Edward Jenkins, was soon intercepted. Jenkins' ears were sliced off and tossed into the Caribbean.

When the disfigured Captain Jenkins returned to London, he was exhibited before Commons in his earless condition. Derisively howling Whigs, seeking just such an opportunity, had war declared against Spain within the hour. A month later, on November 20, 1739, Admiral Edward Vernon and an English fleet captured and burned Porto Bello.

[4] The Treaty of 1773 was signed at Augusta fifteen years before Georgia became the thirteenth state, and last of the original colonies, to join the Union. It opened two million acres of Cherokee and Creek lands to colonization, including the lush areas of middle Georgia so well suited to cotton, and paid questionable debts run up by Indians dealing with white traders looking to future land speculation.

The path of history for the Cherokees was accelerating after 1773 toward the dreadful "Trail of Tears" (1838 to 1840). In this sad hegira, the tribe, once a proud nation of some twenty-five thousand, lost almost a third of its members during a forced march of more than a thousand miles to the northern reaches of the Oklahoma Territory. During the intervening sixty-five years, the Cherokees (often joined by the Choctaws and Creeks) suffered a series of devastating defeats and reprisals by U.S. militia responding to raids on white settlements, primarily in Georgia and the Carolinas. The Indians then agreed to further treaties which in time broke the power of the tribes completely and led to the "Trail of Tears."

[5] A native of Rhode Island, Greene had distinguished himself in campaigns with George Washington at Boston, Trenton and Brandywine. Washington named him commander-in-chief of the new republic's Army of the South in the fall of 1778, and he immediately divided his relatively small forces into two striking groups to harass the much larger army of Charles Lord Cornwallis. As a result, Cornwallis was compelled to split his own troops, and Greene's subordinate, General Daniel Morgan, soundly defeated units under Colonel James Stuart at Eutaw Springs.

Cornwallis himself, who had won a resounding victory over General Horatio Gates at Camden, South Carolina, faced Greene at Guilford Courthouse in North Carolina on January 17, 1781, when Major Charles Abercrombie commanded the Third North Carolina Regiment. Although Lord Cornwallis carried the day, his casualties were so high, and his supply and ammunition trains so damaged, that he had to return to the safe haven of Charleston, under the protection of a British fleet, and abandon a plan to conquer the Carolinas. Six months later, Cornwallis marched his rested and re-supplied forces east to Yorktown, Virginia. Here, trapped by George Washington and his French naval and ground force allies, the English general was forced to surrender, thus giving victory and independence to the Americans.

[6] The Revolutionary War did not officially end until April 3, 1783. It was almost eighteen months later that Charles Abercrombie, who had apparently served in Virginia and South Carolina in addition to North Carolina, was finally placed back on inactive duty. He was paid eight pounds, eighteen shillings and a penny on May 14, 1784 for "sundries furnished and cash paid (to) the militia of North and South Carolina and Virginia."

[7] Some of the Orange County tracts that Major Charles Abercrombie disposed of almost two hundred years ago are now part of downtown Durham, North Carolina.

[8] This was the water-powered mill which Charles Abercrombie and William Thetford built on the Eno River in 1780, two years after petitioning the county court to locate the mill on property they owned at West Point (western terminus of the mail route from Raleigh to Roxboro). A mill utilizing parts of the original foundation was actually in operation until 1942; it was destroyed and washed downstream in a storm a decade ago, but has now fortunately been rebuilt as a joint project of the Eno River Association, other donors and the City of Durham.

[9] Originally cotton factors in Glasgow, buying on commission for Scots and English mills from arriving ships, these men had come to the colonies a generation before, as the tobacco trade in Virginia and the Carolinas expanded greatly in volume and in the opportunity for profits. Just as others of their countrymen in the New World's growing commerce with England and Scotland, the energetic and astute Glaswegians came quickly to dominate their specialty. Out of favor during and after the Revolutionary War because of their Loyalist sentiments, they departed the tobacco trade and reverted to factoring cotton in Savannah and Charleston.

[10] If they had neither wagon nor oxen, some ingenious "crackers" would fill a hogshead (a barrel containing 52.5 Imperial gallons) with cured tobacco leaves, and then literally roll it to the nearest market town between shafts connected by a rolling axle.

[11] Jane could not have known that a fifteenth-century kinswoman, Alicia de Abercromby, widow of Alexander, the high sheriff of Perth, was fined the very substantial sum of twenty gold merks (marks), or almost three hundred shillings, by the high sheriff of Banff for remarrying too soon after the death of her husband.

[12] The militia continued to play a central role in Georgia, and for that matter throughout the South, for another century, both as a military and as a social force. In Georgia, as in the Carolinas, there was generally a company in each district or town, and one or more regiments in a county, depending upon its size. Several regiments made up a brigade, and there were finally two brigades per division (and three divisions in all of Georgia in 1800).

It was the militiamen of Georgia who put down General Elijah Clarke (who had a considerable amount of popular support, as did the anti-militia Regulators of Orange County in 1771) when he attempted to set up his Trans-Oconee Republic in 1794; and it was the militia who later had to fight the same Indians Clarke had challenged. The general was alarmed lest a treaty with the Indians of the Upper Creek Nation stop white settlements at the Oconee River. The Creeks were increasingly distressed that the Oconee had become too much for them "the river of muddy waters," due to heavy land-clearing along its eastern shores. And were determined that the white man would stay across the Oconee, as decided in a little-known agreement (the 1786 Treaty of Shoulderbare Creek) which their chieftain Cusa Mico and his brother Nunnechowata had signed for the tribes.

The Creeks, egged on by their embittered advisor Alexander McGillivray, the son of a Scots trader and a half-French, half-Indian beauty who hated all encroaching settlers, finally raided the northern reaches of Hancock County near the old federal Fort Fidius. They were then successfully repulsed by one hundred fifty militiamen led by Major David Adams and a handful of other officers including Robert Abercrombie, Jr., on May 10, 1793.

One great attraction of the militia was the resplendent uniforms worn by officers: colorful tunic and striped trousers worn with a wide silken sash, epaulets fringed with gold braid, a cocked hat (often with plumes), and a heavy saber. Enlisted men, however, drilled, paraded, socialized and fought in the ordinary drab homespun of the frontier.

[13] Sundays were strictly observed as days of rest and relaxation on the Georgia plantations of long ago. The only work was necessary care for animals, and the preparation of the traditional "Sunday dinner" by the household staff. This was done in the separate kitchen, well supplied with three or four ovens and huge, wood-fired stoves (ranges), plus a collection of copper pans and pots acquired from travelling tinkers. The menu centered around wild game, ham, and beef or pork roasts, plus a vast variety of vegetables (but always baked yams) in season. In winter, there was a hearty soup as a first course; and always, a heavy pudding or array of pies for dessert. There were no salads, as we know them today, except for cut fruits from the orchard, and "cold slaw" (cole slaw), finely-chopped and covered with a vinegary mayonnaise.

In the early days of Hancock County, there was a monthly church service by a circuit-riding preacher, usually a Protestant interdenominational ceremony with plenty of vigorous hymn-singing and a long homily on a Biblical theme, followed by a hearty meal served on the church grounds by the women of the congregation. (The Abercrombies, apparently Roman Catholics for centuries in Scotland although experiencing continuing losses to the Presbyterian Kirk, found virtually no Catholic churches or priests in western North Carolina in the mid-eighteenth century, and even fewer in the first days of Georgia. They tended in America to follow the Baptist or Presbyterian faith, or even more, the church of their spouses.) For many years, the blacks from the plantations sat in a gallery above the white congregation, participating vigorously in the singing, and supporting the preacher with loud or even shouted agreement as the sermon became forceful.

As time went on, the Presbyterians (on a three-acre tract sold them for the price of one peppercorn), Baptists, Methodists and Episcopalians built churches in Sparta, and regular services were held in them as well as in the old (Mount) Horeb, or Fundamentalist, church at Folsom Creek, which dated from 1792. The slaves had their own Baptist congregation in Sparta as early as the first decade of the nineteenth century, but many plantations continued to hold their own services, conducted by blacks well-versed in Scripture, as late as 1860.

[14] In 1812, marriage and baptismal records showed the following for the eleven children of Charles and Edwina Abercrombie: Abner, married Mary Patterson, children: Charles, John, Alfred, William and Mary; Edmund, married Mary Pollard, children: Sarah, Malinda, Robert and Mary; Sallie, married Thomas Raines, no children; Wylie, married first to Jane Simmons, child: Rebecca; Leonard, married to Sarah Comer, children: John Comer and Charles; Jane, married Bolling Hall, children: Polly, Ann, Martha, Eliza, Jane and Emma; John Booth, married Elizabeth Martin, children: Martha and Sarah; and Nancy, married William Barnes, no children as yet. Anderson, Charles and James had not yet married in 1812.

[15] Andrew Jackson cornered the Upper Creeks at Tohopeka, the so-called Horseshoe Bend of the Tallapoosa River. His tough militiamen, force-marched down from Tennessee and reinforced by Indian allies, killed almost six hundred Upper Creeks and allowed peaceful settlement of most of present day Alabama, including the rich cotton lands of the Black Belt.

[16] Castlereagh, one of the most overlooked figures in English history, later negotiated the alliance with Austria and the Prussian generals which toppled Napoleon and personally drafted key provisions of the Treaty of Paris. He then attempted to obtain acceptance of a far-sighted plan for the peaceful realignment of spheres of influence in Europe that was widely endorsed, failed and committed suicide after becoming *persona non grata* with the dissolute King George IV. George IV had distinguished himself by very questionable treatment of his insane father George III, and of the woman he had secretly married, loved all his life, and abandoned.

Chapter 4

1832–1850

Alabama

In the Black Belt, at Brickyard and Cross Keys . . . Shipping cotton on the Tallapoosa . . . The Central of Georgia runs right through the plantation . . . Slave markets and abolitionist lectures in early Montgomery . . . A billion-pound cotton crop . . . James Abercrombie in the United States Senate . . . A banquet for the Marquis de Lafayette . . . King Cotton's days of glory end . . . The War Between the States and its bitter consequences . . . Colonel John Comer Abercrombie rides west to Texas

The new Abercrombie outposts in Alabama prospered, after two beginning years of drouth and adjustment that included many months of moving and building, this time for three separate families. Both principal holdings, at Brickyard and at Cross Keys,[1] were in what was coming to be known as the true Black Belt, with thick, fertile, humus-laden limestone soils recommended so highly by Bolling Hall, and reminiscent of the early days of virgin land in Georgia. Russell and Macon counties were safely distant from the far less productive red clay and occasional dark loams in some of the northern reaches of the state, and from the increasingly sandy stretches to the south.

The Alabama climate was even more temperate than that of Georgia, reflecting more southerly locations and nearness to the warm waters of the Gulf of Mexico (which sometimes could spawn destructive hurricanes). There were as many as three hundred growing days and, ordinarily, quite adequate rainfall triggered by cloud structures drifting in from the Gulf.

Aside from the decided advantages of soil and climate that it provided, far eastern Alabama was simply beautiful country. Here you found not only the dense pines and oaks of Georgia, but stands of thick, slow-growing walnut, hickory and beech (some of the latter three to four hundred years old), undisturbed over the generations.

The Indians had little need for wood, other than for young saplings; the few trees carefully selected for canoes and rafts; and strong, supple branches to be shaped into bows and arrows, or into fire-hardened handles for axes and tomahawks. The saplings were planted firmly in the ground in a small rectangular pattern, and then bent over to join in the middle as the framework of the wigwams preferred by the forest tribes. (Tepees, of buffalo hides tightly stretched over supporting poles, were used by the nomadic Plains tribes, who could haul them from place to place behind a pony.) The Upper Creeks along the Chattahoochee so respected nature, and feared the gods of the forest, that they had the squaws gather fallen limbs for firewood, rather than chopping down small trees.

Along the many creeks, rivers and watercourses of the area the Abercrombies had chosen for their new home, you found dense stands of cypress and maple, near flat, fertile terraces of land that could be cultivated almost to the water's edge. Hardy cedar, so useful for fence posts and railing, grew well away from the watercourses in barren areas of mediocre soil; and all through the small hummocks in the scattered marshlands were clumps of flowering dogwood, gorgeous in springtime bursts of white, pink and shades of red.

At Brickyard,[2] Anderson and Charles found an ancient Indian burial mound in the midst of one of the fields near the Chattahoochee River. It was carefully fenced and preserved after neighbors had called attention to the curious structure, and would be professionally explored by historians and archeologists in years to come. Konoyarhika was called in to consult and identified the mounds as probably belonging to the earliest progenitors of his own tribe, the Upper Creeks (Muskogees). After some difficulty in locating one of the few remaining tribal shamans, Konoyarhika brought him to the site. He and the shaman later pronounced the spirits of their ancestors of long ago appeased after appropriate ceremonies. They warned the Abercrombies, however, never to disturb the mound, after expressing appreciation for the care and protection provided for it.[3]

Anderson always felt that the fields surrounding the burial site were extraordinarily productive, as if some long-forgotten Indian god of the harvests was also showing his appreciation.

At Cross Keys, a little community halfway between Montgomery and Tuskegee, Leonard Abercrombie also found excellent land and growing conditions, plus the advantage of having his brothers close by for counsel, assistance and comfort during a difficult time of transition from the life they had all known since childhood back in Hancock County, Georgia.

James, who had led the migration to Alabama as early as 1812, was especially helpful. He was a real pioneer in a state where he had taken up residence seven years before statehood, and was exceptionally well connected in politics and in business. James had represented Montgomery County for three terms in the Alabama House of Representatives before moving up to the state Senate from 1825 to 1831. He had decided to take up residence in Russell County soon after the Brickyard property was acquired, and was asked to stand for the legislature as soon as he was eligible. Additional terms in both the House of Representatives and in the upper chamber followed.

James Abercrombie would win a seat in the United States Senate in 1851, be re-elected in 1853, and serve until 1859, during the crucial struggles over states' rights and slavery that would in time destroy the Kingdom of Cotton.

Leonard, fifty-five and ailing when he decided to move to Cross Keys, also leaned heavily upon Milo Bolling, his favorite among three sons. Although younger than either John Comer or Charles, Milo had matured at an early age, and married years before the first-born John, at twenty-three. By the time of his move to Alabama, Milo and his wife Sarah Lee Haden had already been blessed with three children in less than three years of marriage, although a little girl (Alabama) lived only a single day. There would be eight more living children before Sarah died on August 4, 1850, one week after giving birth to her sixth son, James Buford (father of James Smither Abercrombie).

Leonard's dependence upon his youngest son (although all three sons got on well together), and Milo and Sarah's many children in contradistinction to John and Charles,[4] made Milo the natural heir to a large percentage of the Cross Keys property. This may have heavily influenced John Comer's decision to move on to Texas in 1850, and Charles' determination to follow him there.

After Leonard died suddenly in 1837, Milo operated Cross Keys until his own death on August 22, 1860. Just as many of his peers among the major plantation owners, he and Sarah and the younger children had visited resorts in the East and Northeast during the summers, traveling to Boston or New York on new connections provided by the Central of Georgia railroad, or on the more frequent sailings between Mobile, New Orleans or Charleston and the Yankee ports. In 1853, three years after Sarah's death, Milo Bolling married a Boston widow, Sarah G. Greenleaf. They had four children: Daniel Webster, Bolling, Winona and Talulah, between 1855 and 1858.

Sarah Greenleaf Abercrombie and the children lived on at Cross Keys after Milo's death. Following the War Between the States, they all removed to Massachusetts, and lived out their lives in the East. Daniel Webster Abercrombie, a Phi Beta Kappa graduate of Harvard College, served thirty-six years as principal of the Worcester Academy (1882–1918). He named one of his two sons Ralph, after the famed General Sir Ralph Abercrombie.

The Abercrombies had timed their move to Alabama well, in terms of overall growth and improving conditions within the newborn state, and especially in relation to the increasingly vigorous health of the cotton industry.

The population when Alabama went from territory to state in 1819 was about one hundred and twenty thousand. A decade later, the total was slightly over three hundred thousand, for an increase of one hundred and fifty percent in only ten years. The three hundred thousand residents in 1830 included one hundred and twenty thousand slaves, or a number equal to the entire population a decade earlier. This reflected the constant influx of wealthy, slave-owning planters, primarily from South Carolina and Georgia, selling less productive land to establish themselves in the lush new acreage of the Black Belt. And it underscored again the significance of Andrew Jackson's victory over the Upper Creeks at Horseshoe Bend, which was followed by the ceding of much of Alabama, including the very heart of the cotton country, to the United States.

The strapping growth in Alabama's population was to continue undiminished until 1860, when it crossed the one million mark for an increase in excess of eight hundred percent in forty years. Just under one-half of those million inhabitants in 1860 were black.

As the boom in population picked up steam in the 1830s and 1840s, it was helped considerably by the final resolution of the Indian problem, and by considerable progress in the development of schools, churches and a reasonably stable state government. There were also some badly-needed improvements in what had been a miserably inadequate transportation system, if one utilized the rivers and that new medium of transport, the railroad.

The Abercrombies made their usual consequential contributions in all these areas, one at great cost. Young Robert Abercrombie Jones, the namesake and grandson of Robert, Jr., was killed in a skirmish with the Upper Creeks in 1830, as one of the last casualties of the long-continued disturbances with the Indians that had plagued Alabamans. He was hit by a poisoned arrow during the brief battle on the outskirts of Tuskegee, not five miles from the future plantation of his great-uncle Leonard, while serving with the Alabama militia.[5]

Anderson and Charles, Jr. were active in the early development of what came to be an excellent public school system in Russell County (one of its products being Anderson's son James Jackson, honor graduate of Emory College and of the Harvard Law School). The two brothers also contributed toward the establishment and operation of private schools in eastern and central Alabama, remembering the excellent academies of western Georgia. As early as 1831, the Englishman James Lyon launched his grammar school, with much of the classic British curriculum, in Montgomery. Two years later, Andrew S. Vigus, a Harvard graduate with special knowledge of the expanding discipline of chemistry, established the Franklin Institute, one of the first schools in the South to emphasize science. About the same time, Peter Maher, who had been operating the Valley Creek Academy in Macon County's future boundaries, moved his little institution to Montgomery, where it soon earned a sound and deserved reputation. His wife then opened a Female High School, which was also a success.[6]

The Alabama churches of the first decades of statehood, just as in earlier eras in Scotland, North Carolina and Georgia, were a vital and essential part of the developing social (and political) infrastructure, apart from their fundamental religious and moral missions and goals. As indicated earlier, the Abercrombies had moved from their ancient and often intense affinity with the Church of Rome, to a considerable degree because there were so few Catholic priests and churches in early North Carolina or Georgia. The same situation obtained in Alabama, even though the very few Catholics in the Montgomery area managed to build a tiny church named for the first Bishop of Rome (St. Peter), which Bishop John Porter of Mobile consecrated on April 25, 1834.[7]

Four Protestant churches had been established a few years earlier in Montgomery: the Methodist, with pledges of $800, in 1827; and the Episcopalian (September 15); Presbyterian (November 12); and Baptist (November 24), just as soon as the 1829 cotton crop had been paid for in hard money. These were significant beginnings, yet infinitesimal in the number of charter members involved. The Episcopalians registered ten; the Presbyterians, eight; and the Baptists, four, although they reorganized a few years later with a dozen members. The seeds had been sown in seasonable ground, however, and ecclesiastical harvest, however delayed, would be forthcoming. Still, the spirit of ecumenism was faltering in those early days: the Montgomery *Advertiser* reported October 7, 1839 that the "first of Joe Smith's fanatics (Mormons) had spoke last night at the old Court House."

Of the clan Abercrombie, Bolling Hall was by far the best known person within religious circles. He was the foremost Methodist layman in Georgia, a distinction he had inherited in part from his father. The elder Hall had met John Wesley, the founder of Methodism, while the noted English clergyman and evangelist was on a trip to Georgia during the colonial era, and had maintained a correspondence with Wesley.

Bolling Hall had lived for a number of years at Coosada, Alabama, near Governor William Wyatt Bibb and General John A. Elmore. This trio, with the prominent planter Abner McGehee and his sons-in-law, formed a powerful corps of Methodist leaders who served the Alabama District of their church as officers and key committeemen for a generation.

Hall could not sway his brothers-in-law from the Presbyterian faith (hearkening back to the Scots Kirk) that Anderson and Charles had adopted. He had better luck with their nephew, the laird of Cross Keys, however; Milo Bolling was a prominent Methodist all of his adult life. Also an officer and committeeman of the Alabama

District, he saw it grow from a tiny nucleus to three thousand, three hundred and ninety-eight white and one thousand and sixty-six colored members in the census of 1850. The Montgomery Circuit had comparable figures of two hundred and forty-nine and two hundred and fifteen, plus forty-five white and sixty-five colored members in the town of Montgomery itself.

Bolling Hall, Jr., the son Jane Abercrombie had presented her husband in the midst of ten daughters, maintained the family tradition as an active Methodist and perennial District Officer and committeeman. He tried for years to establish a Methodist high school at Robinson Springs, Alabama, but could never find the necessary financing.

The Abercrombies, with a long record of service in the Georgia legislature that had included multiple terms and key appointments for Edmund, Wylie, John Booth and Anderson, continued this practice of providing political experience and stability, especially through James and Bolling Hall. James Abercrombie, a member of the first Alabama legislature, in time became the obvious candidate for a United States Senate seat, which he won handily. Hall had served as a United States congressman during the War of 1812, and maintained close political ties not only throughout Georgia and Alabama, but in Washington, D.C., for the remaining twenty-five years of his life. The ranking state officials of Alabama learned from the earliest beginnings of statehood to prize the advice and counsel not only of James and Bolling Hall (frequent visitors to Brickyard), but of Anderson as well.

The Alabama legislators turned to Anderson Abercrombie when confronted with one of their most significant assignments: naming commissioners who would choose a "seat of justice" for the respective counties, and provide for the construction of those two fundamental facilities, a courthouse and a jail. General Anderson served as commissioner for Russell County, along with two other leading citizens, Hardeman Owens and Thomas M. Martin. Fort Mitchell was the first county seat, winning the honor hands down because it was the only settlement at the time within the statutory requirement that the "seat of justice" be "within six miles of the center of the Chattahoochee River." Fort Bainbridge, the only other "town" in Russell County in 1834, was a good ten miles west and south, near the border with Barbour County.

Anderson and Charles were acutely aware of the problems involved in a poor system of road transportation for agricultural products and supplies, and of how this could handicap the proper development of a state with an almost completely rural population. For this reason, they were quite concerned with Alabama's roads as they began to assume broad responsibilities in their region, and in the state overall. Except for a few main routes used by the stagecoaches, but of minimal use for farm-to-market traffic, the roads were either terrible or non-existent.

The Abercrombies in Georgia had all been reasonably close to the broad and deep Savannah River, with its expanding fleet of flatboats and barges able to negotiate the hundred miles or so downstream to Savannah's docks and warehouses with a cargo of cotton in a day or two. (Upstream was entirely a different matter; a pole(d) boat or barge could average only two or three miles a day against the current.)

Similarly, although Alabama's Chattahoochee (so near that its banks bordered parts of the Brickyard property) ended at Lake Seminole instead of at Savannah, both Cross Keys and Brickyard cotton could be loaded on big forty- or fifty-foot keelboats on the nearby Tallapoosa and transshipped with little difficulty to Mobile via the connecting Alabama River. (Mobile and New Orleans were to surpass Savannah and Charleston in cotton tonnage by the late 1830s, because of burgeoning new shipments from expanding plantation acreage in Alabama, Mississippi and Louisiana and declining plantings in Georgia and South Carolina.)

Regardless of the Abercrombies' own good fortune in being able to depend upon water transportation, Anderson in particular remembered Georgia's long-continued problems with roads from his service as a legislator, and as a brigadier-general of militia required to travel widely over the state. He wanted something to be done in Alabama as soon as possible, and especially after he had reviewed Georgia's lamentable record.

There had been a hopeful breakthrough near Hancock County as early as 1805, when a new road was built to connect the cotton country of middle Georgia with central Tennessee. This allowed Georgians access to markets in Tennessee for their tobacco, corn and grain, which could be sold or bartered for the cattle, horses and mules of the southern reaches of the Cumberland Plateau. The road also stimulated the development of Memphis (established by General Andrew Jackson and others in 1819) as an important new marketing and shipping center for cotton.

But after 1805, the only other road of immediate consequence built in early nineteenth century Georgia was a crude, barely passable one constructed by the federal government, and primarily for military purposes. This ran directly west for about one hundred and fifty miles, from Putnam County to the Alabama border. Property owners along the route (in lieu of being paid for right-of-way) were given franchises to operate toll ferries and bridges across the many creeks and small rivers intersecting the road.[8]

One reason for the poor system of roads in east and central Alabama, and generally over the state, was over-optimism concerning the development of railroads, which many felt would be far along by 1840, greatly lessening the need for farm-to-market roads. Investors and promoters had almost taken the headlines away from the pioneer, highly-publicized Baltimore & Ohio in the East by constructing the remarkable Charleston & Hamburg (South Carolina) Railway from Charleston to the east bank of the Savannah River at Augusta, Georgia in little more than a year.

Soon after the new line was completed in 1830, there were mass meetings in Alabama, followed by the organization of railroad companies and stock issues. Anderson Abercrombie was not particularly impressed. He could recall how he and his brother John Booth, while legislators back in Georgia, had met with their Sparta neighbor and fellow plantation operator Governor William Rabun, and with his successor in the state house. They had urged sound, longer-range studies on the new-fangled railroad, but immediate action toward a timelier objective: the expansion of a system of good roads in Georgia. Unfortunately, nothing was accomplished other than the delivery of some high-flown rhetoric in the legislature about the need for improved transportation.

Anderson was reminded however, to have General Lafayette, who would soon be his guest in Sparta, come north from Savannah by steamboat, rather than by stagecoach. Upstream steamboating was a little slow in 1826, but it was far more comfortable and convenient to be met in Augusta for the final forty miles west to Sparta in a sulky, than to attempt the rugged one-hundred-twenty mile journey from Savannah to Sparta by road.

Now the same pattern was being repeated in Alabama: over-emphasis on railroads at the expense of a balanced system of overall transportation, in the mistaken idea that railroads could quickly solve virtually all transportation problems. The Montgomery & West Point Railroad was chartered January 30, 1832, after the initial offering of stock was quickly oversubscribed. An engineering study was rushed through to completion, with preliminary plans to build seventy-six miles of track to West Point, Georgia on the Chattahoochee at a cost of $8,000 per mile. Difficulties arose, primarily concerning lack of capital and underestimation of costs. The company was then reorganized January 15, 1834, as the Montgomery & Western, but the Panic of 1837 intervened. It was June 6, 1840, before the first twelve miles of track were laid, and final completion was delayed to 1851.

These long delays became a blessing in disguise for James and Anderson Abercrombie. They joined another group which organized the Mobile & Girard Railroad. Strongly financed and soundly planned, this enterprise became in time the Central of Georgia, running right through the heart of the best cotton country (and the middle of the Abercrombie plantation at Brickyard), with connections in all directions including daily trains to and from Columbus, just five miles from Brickyard.

General Anderson Abercrombie was a realist. In time, he simply accepted the truth about transportation in Alabama during the first half of the nineteenth century. His state had a surprisingly good system of transportation by water, steadily improving as more efficient steamboats of lesser draft plied further and further reaches of the Savannah, Alabama and Chattahoochee and their major tributaries. The epochal invention of a Quaker artist[9] was also being used sparingly for the vital task of pulling small supplies-laden barges upstream. Railroads, although understandably delayed by the hard truth of building costs and economic cycles, would soon provide a reasonably diffuse network serving the major cities and towns, with increasing connections north, east, south and west. The third element, surface roads, would simply require a longer time to develop.

In the interim, Anderson persuaded the local officials in Russell, Macon and Montgomery counties to adopt variations of the system his Abercrombie grandfather and father had helped to establish and operate long ago in Orange County, North Carolina. Each Alabama county and district involved would continue to press for state financing of roads, but would at the same time build and maintain their own through modest levies of taxes and manpower. As in North Carolina, overseers appointed by the county court would be the administrators. And slowly but steadily, in spite of complaints and frustrations, the roads began to improve in central and in far eastern Alabama.

Curiously enough, with all the political and business acumen of James in particular, and of Anderson, Charles and Milo Bolling, none of the Abercrombies or the other major plantation owners ever took effective action toward resolving one of the Cotton Kingdom's fundamental problems: finance.

For a full generation between 1830 and 1860, even the most affluent planters in Alabama and adjoining states depended upon interim financing between crops, often because they were plowing handsome, even phenomenal, earnings back into more land and more slaves. It had become an established custom to negotiate short-term loans, usually of one hundred and eighty days, each spring. It would be six months between initial planting (after the danger of frost was past), and final settlement for cotton delivered in the fall.

A branch of the State Bank of Alabama had been opened July 1, 1832 in Montgomery, to serve the eastern and central counties. This was authorized by the Banking Act of January 21, 1832, a statute unique in banking history. Financed by the sale of $500,000 in State of Alabama bonds in Europe, and designed to keep sales of public land as well as immigration at high tide, the Bank of Alabama immediately encouraged what contemporary journalists described as "wild speculation," with a sense of (false) prosperity. The speculation was fired by notes and paper money, as opposed to specie (silver or gold coins, or bullion). Land could be purchased with as little as five percent down, and rocketed up in price; there were "chimerical" schemes, promising astronomical profit; merchants offered any terms desired. As one editorial warned, there was deepening danger when the cry was, "buy now, and pay when you will; but buy."

The Bank of the United States was able to restrain the speculative tendencies of state banks and their branches to some degree by insisting that their obligations to the federal system be paid when due, without automatic renewals or extensions under differing terms; but President Andrew Jackson, feuding with Nicholas Biddle and the money magnates of the East, nullified this powerful and effective means of controlling speculation before he was reelected in 1836 by refusing to continue channeling federal deposits to the Bank. He then became a fiscal conservative, oddly enough, after sentencing the Bank of the United States, the paladin of conservatism in banking, to death.

Jackson precipitated the Panic of 1837 by shifting his financial policies sharply to the right. He ordered the Treasury to accept payment for public lands in nothing but specie after changing the coinage ratio between gold and silver from the fifteen-to-one in effect since 1792, to sixteen-to-one. The so-called "specie order" of 1836 caused immediate distress, and then spreading bankruptcies in the southern and western states, where enormous sums were owed for public land. Particularly in Alabama, where the fever of speculation had been raging for almost four years, there was little of the "hard money" the banks now demanded, but promissory notes and paper money aplenty. It is possible that Anderson and Charles, counseled by James, had seen the inevitable storm clouds gathering as early as 1832, when they paid the Indian Konoyarhika in cash for their prime land along the Chattahoochee, rather than buying on credit.

Jackson's 1834 order changing the gold-silver ratio also had an unsettling effect on monetary policy. It made millionaires out of some foreign exchange specialists, who simply bought sixteen ounces of silver for an ounce of gold here, sold fifteen ounces of the silver in London or elsewhere in Europe for an ounce of gold, and then repeated the process. President Jackson was receiving a costly lesson on the inexorability of Gresham's Law.[10]

The Montgomery *Advertiser,* which had succeeded the *Planter's Gazette* four years earlier, reported in the spring of 1837 that "universal ruin" was facing central Alabama, "when all are drawn into the maelstrom of speculation, (with) specie payments (suddenly demanded) and the discount of paper suddenly suspended." By the midst of the cotton harvest of 1837, the situation had eased somewhat; Hugh McGuire, the editor of the *Advertiser,* reported that the local branch of the state banking system had "begun to afford relief," probably by extending the due date of notes or by allowing some limited discounting of paper; but by 1840, as we shall see, there were new banking crises in the area.

Little wonder, then, that even the most financially prosperous and stable planters, such as the Abercrombies, Judge B.S. Bibb, Abner McGehee and his sons-in-law, William Taylor and Thomas

Jarrett, were distressed at the lack of a dependable banking system in their region, or for that matter in all of Alabama. This became more and more serious with President Jackson's specie order and the inevitable aftermath of speculation.

Meanwhile the cotton industry, as we shall see, was experiencing constant increases in demand and an excellent price structure through all these difficulties, except for temporary downturns during 1837 and 1838, and again from 1845 to 1848. The major growers needed, more than ever, planting-to-harvest loans to support their expanding operations.

The obvious solution seemed to be to turn from the State Bank of Alabama in search of a stable and reliable source of banking service. On March 7, 1836, at a meeting in Montgomery, area planters subscribed for what were reported as ''large'' amounts of stock in a new bank, the Merchants & Planters of Mobile. This had been organized by a combination of cotton factors, shippers, merchants and leading planters in the south Alabama and western Mississippi region.

There were still serious problems for planters attempting to confine their banking to Alabama, however, and these seemed to increase as cotton production entered another phase of expansion in 1840. Some of the principal growers turned to institutions in Charleston, Savannah and New Orleans, in addition to the Merchants & Planters of Mobile. Others obtained temporary financing from a few extremely wealthy individuals over the South who had discovered the comfortable rate of return available to astute private bankers able to operate outside governmental restrictions with their own capital. And a few planters, including Milo Bolling Abercrombie, banked with large institutions in the East. These institutions had traditional ties to some plantations, but remarkably little knowledge of the detailed operations of the cotton industry.[11]

Turning to banks other than the state branch at Montgomery seemed amply justified again when that institution, even after the Panic of 1837 had almost totally subsided, made a disturbing announcement on February 27, 1840: it would no longer pay depositors in gold or silver coinage or bullion. As late as 1852, the new Bank of Montgomery was organized to serve Alabama's state capital and surrounding area, but it was noted that virtually all of the resources of this institution had been furnished by the Bank of Augusta, Georgia, which controlled its shares of stock. Earlier in the same year, there had been a run on the bank at St. Mary's on the Georgia border.

The Abercrombies were experts in growing cotton, and well they might be; when the family planted the 1836 crop in Russell, Macon and Montgomery counties of Alabama, it had been just a half-century since Charles, Sr. began operating the original plantation at his new home in Hancock County, Georgia. They knew that high yields of good-quality lint and cottonseed depended upon obvious factors: soil fertility, the weather and skill in planting, cultivation and harvesting.

The soil was quite fertile at Brickyard and at Cross Keys, although somewhat inferior in smaller Abercrombie properties to the west, over into Montgomery County; the weather, problem-laden though it might be in any given season, was generally very conducive to a good crop; and if not, what could you do about the weather, anyhow?

Anderson, Charles and Milo Bolling recognized more and more, however, that the principal variable relating to success or failure in raising cotton might be how the crop was put in the ground, brought to maturity, and then picked and transported to market. If so, the quality of slave labor, and of supervision, could be the difference between minimal yields of marginal cotton, and maximum yields of better grades.

The Abercrombies had helped to organize a small agricultural society in Montgomery in 1839; this met in various locations within the immediate three-county region during the year. Even though most of the reports and discussions turned upon the problems of the smaller planters, and sometimes those of tenant farmers working tracts of only ten acres, some member of the Abercrombie family usually attended meetings of the society.

It must have been disconcerting to hear a report presented at the September 28, 1840 session of the agricultural organization. This showed that forty growers in Montgomery County had raised only six thousand, one hundred and ninety-two bales on ten thousand, eight hundred and one acres the previous season (.573 bales, or two hundred and twenty-nine pounds of cotton per acre in the four hundred pound bales of those days), and expected just three thousand, six hundred and thirty-five bales on eleven thousand, five hundred and thirty-five acres for the 1840 crop (.315 bales or one hundred and twenty-six pounds per acre).

There had been a troublesome drouth in the late spring and early summer of 1840, but the yields for both 1839 and 1840 were far enough below the average of a bale per acre usually produced on Abercrombie land that a quiet study was made of just what was going on in Montgomery, an adjoining county with somewhat inferior, but reasonably comparable soil to that found in Cross Keys and at Brickyard.

The study revealed what common sense would have told the Abercrombies anyhow: much of the secret of high yields and better quality lay in the quality of the work force, and of the supervision provided, once soil fertility, weather conditions and other obvious factors such as quality of seed were equated. The best field hands, strong, well fed, provided with good mules and the best tools well maintained, and given proper housing for their families in a positive atmosphere, could look after about ten acres per man. The average field hand, in contrast, could tend only five acres, and the poorer hands, three acres.

This confirmed an Abercrombie tradition going back to the first days in America, in Orange County, North Carolina. The family had always had the best slaves, who were never subjected to the ultimate terror of having their own families broken up by private sale or on the auction block. Abercrombie slaves were never sold except in the rare instances when one wanted to marry a black on another plantation, and the transaction was mutually agreeable to all concerned. They were well housed in adequately-maintained quarters, and given basic food such as meat, flour, cornmeal, beans, rice and sugar plus the opportunity to raise extras such as additional chickens and pigs, vegetables, fruits and walnuts, pecans and hickory nuts on their own. There were always flower beds, carefully tended, in Abercrombie slave quarters.

There was a resident blacksmith, farrier and carpenter, plus necessary assistants, on Abercrombie properties. All these black artisans were well trained and among the most valuable of slaves. They were instructed to keep tools, horses, mules, houses, barns and outbuildings in the best of condition. Chopping cotton is hard enough work, without attempting it with a dull hoe; and you cannot plow a straight furrow with a poorly shod horse, or work a ten-hour day when a leaking roof keeps you up half the night.

Negro overseers were selected and trained with special care, and given incentives such as separate housing, garden and orchard. They were charged with maintaining discipline, but only with the knowledge and agreement of the Abercrombie owner if punishment were involved. The public floggers hired by some counties to whip slaves were anathema to an Abercrombie.

The lady of the plantation by tradition looked after seriously ill slaves in cooperation with their immediate family, but did not hesitate to bring in a physician when necessary. Midwives were provided for slave quarter confinements, at the expense of the owner. Abercrombie wives trained the household staff from seamstress to majordomo, and they relied heavily upon the ability and loyalty of these servants. Among many duties requiring tact and judgment, a top-flight majordomo was expected to assess quietly the appropriateness of major suitors for the young ladies of the ante-bellum Abercrombie families and to report in confidence to the master. Many majordomos were said to have an uncanny knack for spotting ne'er-do-wells.

The entire atmosphere surrounding the blacks on Abercrombie plantations, then, was as positive as any you would find at the time. And from this developed a sense of loyalty on the part of the slaves, plus real pride in "their family." Many blacks adopted the surname of their masters after it became more common for them to have this further identification; there would be black Abercrombies, descendants of former slaves who came from Alabama in the 1850s, living in Huntsville, Texas and in Houston well into the present century.

Loyalty and pride on the part of slaves was balanced by the care and concern for the blacks on their properties that the Alabama generations of Abercrombies manifested, just as their predecessors in Georgia and in North Carolina.

There is evidence in old Russell County records that General Anderson Abercrombie once interceded with his friend Chief Konoyarhika on behalf of the slaves owned by the more prosperous Creek Indians, urging a better diet and improved housing for the slaves. These unfortunate blacks lived in wretched small wigwams on the edge of the forests, tilling tiny fields of corn and carrying out endless tasks for their Indian masters, who fed them the least choice cuts of venison and small portions of *msiquatash* (succotash, a mixture of corn and beans cooked with bits of pork) doled out grudgingly by the squaws in charge of the tribal cooking pots.[12]

Both Brickyard and Cross Keys, Alabama were vital to the ongoing history of the Abercrombie family, and Brickyard would assume a key role in the industrial development of Alabama, Georgia and the southeast, as the founding headquarters for Bickerstaff Clay Products[13]; but neither of these communities grew past the size of small towns, because they became respectively satellites of Brownsville (now Phenix City, the county seat of Russell County) and nearby Columbus, Georgia; and of Montgomery, Alabama.

Brickyard still exists as a separate community within the combined two-state metropolitan area of Columbus and Phenix City, although Bickerstaff Products employees are by far the most numerous inhabitants within Brickyard itself. The Macon County Cross Keys of Leonard and Milo Bolling Abercrombie no longer exists. There is a locality of the same name in DeKalb County, dating from the first years of Alabama's statehood; but this was only a tiny farming community when the post office was closed early in 1907.

The Abercrombies at Cross Keys in Macon County naturally tended to look upon themselves almost as citizens of Montgomery, less than fifteen miles to the east. As for the Brickyard Abercrombies, Phenix City did not exist in their day; Brownsville, Alabama was quite small; and Columbus, Georgia, although it expanded greatly as a cotton port and textile center after 1840, did not have the appeal then of Montgomery, Alabama, a small but vibrant city with the myriad attractions of a state capital.

For these reasons, Charles, General Anderson and James, as well as the members of their families, often made the sixty-mile trip from Brickyard to Montgomery, breaking the journey midway at Cross Keys as guests of Milo Bolling. In Montgomery, they stayed in a second home that James and his wife Evalina Elizabeth Ross had maintained during his long service in the Alabama state legislature. Stagecoaches were available as early as 1821 from Montgomery eastward to Columbus, and return, although at the not inconsiderable fare of twelve-and-a-half cents per mile. The railroads gradually supplanted this mode of travel, with a direct connection between the state capital and Columbus and friendly conductors who would make a stop at Brickyard (right on the Central of Georgia main line east).

Montgomery was known for many disparate things, almost from the time of its founding, in 1818, by Andrew Dexter. Judge Dexter, late of Massachusetts, bought a three-hundred-and-twenty acre townsite from the territorial government for seven dollars an acre. Of the total purchase price of $2240, he had to pay exactly five percent, or $ll2, down; the balance was due in four installments over the next five years. Dexter's town was first called New Philadelphia; then it was merged with an adjoining area called East Alabama, as Montgomery. James Abercrombie had moved to Monroe County, Alabama (half-way between Mobile and Montgomery) as a young man of twenty, in 1812. He came on north to Montgomery a few months after Alabama was granted statehood, sensing the opportunities in what would become Alabama's capital. He was a state representative as early as 1820.

Here are some of the incongruous attributes and happenings that made Montgomery, Alabama such an interesting town in its earlier decades, most of them well known to James Abercrombie, his older brothers Charles and Anderson, and their nephew, Milo Bolling: visits by eminent figures of the time and epidemics; lawlessness and scandal balanced by civic indignation and corrective action; slave auctions and abolitionist lectures; a commendable emphasis upon public buildings, schools and churches along with disastrous fires; patriotism and the massive deportation of Indians; thespian societies and lynchings; and early, crusading newspapers unafraid to expose questionable banking practices.

Montgomery was blessed with a central location halfway between Mobile, on the Gulf of Mexico, and Huntsville, the prosperous town on the northern border with Tennessee that would soon attract members of the clan Abercrombie. Steamboats began to call at Montgomery, on the deep reaches of the Alabama River, by 1821; they were seen next on the major tributaries of the Alabama. Because of this accessibility, and the fact that Montgomery was the seat of government, there were visits from the marquis de Lafayette as well as three ex-presidents (Martin Van Buren, James K. Polk and Millard Filmore) in little more than a decade; and formal addresses to the Alabama legislature by two of the most skilled orators of the time: General Sam Houston and Henry Clay.

Among the visitors of less renown, but perhaps of more public interest, were Ching and Chang, P. T. Barnum's famed Siamese twins; Monsieur Paul, the "French prodigy of strength" who lifted four bales of cotton off the ground; the first live giraffe ever brought to the U.S.; and Tom Thumb, another of Barnum's collection of the grotesque.

An epidemic of "bilious fever," blamed by the Montgomery *Advertiser* on huge piles of rotting cottonseed around the river wharves, killed an estimated one-fifth of the town's population in 1825–1826 (reducing the number of residents from about fifteen hundred to twelve hundred). This was followed in early September of 1839 by a severe outbreak of yellow fever, and another serious loss of life before cold weather stopped the chain of infection from mosquitoes.

Murder and attempted murder were both fairly common in early Montgomery, the favorite weapons being pistols and Bowie knives. In 1840, Monsieur Adolphe Adrian, self-described as a juggler and sleight-of-hand artist, moved into town and began giving performances in an office over the livery stable. He was shot and killed by Dr. J. R. McLeod at Huie's Ferry on the Alabama River, while allegedly attempting to abduct Mrs. McLeod in broad daylight. No charges were filed.

All during 1835, public indignation was rising against a group of what were termed "idlers and sporting gentry" who gathered daily at the Montgomery Exchange, later renamed the "Kentucky Whiskey House" and described as a bar room and gambling den. Finally, Colonel John H. Thurington organized a mass meeting in protest, marched at the head of several hundred men to the "Kentucky," and arrested two ringleaders: Isaac Ticknor and John Tittle. Both were placed under peace bond, and Captain Ticknor was persuaded to raise a volunteer company from among his followers, who were then marched off to Texas via New Orleans to answer a call for help against invading Mexican forces.

Slave auctions were held with some regularity in Montgomery, but there was also a different auction, customarily on New Year's Day, during which you could bid for the services of a black for the remainder of the calendar year. In sharp contrast, James G. Birney, later a candidate for president on the Abolitionist Party ticket,[14] urged at a downtown rally in 1832 that slaves be liberated and sent to form their own independent nation in Liberia. The courageous Birney barely made it outside to a waiting sulky when it was revealed that he was the son of a wealthy Kentucky tobacco planter who had purchased his own cotton plantation in Alabama, which he proposed to operate with hired labor.

The positive attitude toward schools and churches has been noted earlier, but these institutions, along with the new state capitol and much of the business district, would suffer from disastrous fires. Brick did not come into general use until almost 1850, and pine from the few small mills in the area was the usual construction material. This burned quickly and fiercely from causes ranging from an untrimmed lamp wick to vandalism. The handsome new capitol, accepted from contractors only two years earlier after the collapse of part of the second floor had killed three men and seriously delayed final completion, burned to the ground on the night of December 14, 1849. Just a decade earlier, what was always termed the "great fire of December 16, 1838" started in the offices of the Alabama *Journal* and raged out of control in the main downtown area, wiping out stores, churches and schools in its wake.

Abner McGehee, the close friend of the Abercrombies and perhaps the wealthiest man in the area, lost his Planters' Hotel, even though it had a brick veneer exterior, in this major conflagration. This was a heavy blow, since the "Planters'" had been the leading hotel of the area since the Indian Queen Tavern burned eight years before.

After raising two volunteer units to assist the Texians in their war for independence, the people of Montgomery watched four thousand Creek Indians sent into exile in the Indian Territory in a series of steamboat departures. There was no particular reaction as the Creeks, almost all from peaceable tribes, were forced into a miserable existence thousands of miles from the lands they had tilled and hunted over for hundreds of years.

There was a thespian society in Montgomery from 1822, and a surprising number of amateur actors belonged to the organization. Nothing less than Shakespeare's *Julius Caesar* was the first offering at the Montgomery Hotel (formerly Bell's Tavern) for the 1822 season, with Benjamin Fitzpatrick, later governor and U.S. senator from Alabama, in the leading role. There was far more interest, however, in what was described as the "first legal execution," following a number of lynchings. One Colman Williams, confronted by Constable Silas Goree (who was attempting to serve a "writ of debt" upon him) stabbed the unfortunate Goree to death. Williams was then subdued, imprisoned, tried, found guilty and hanged in the public square on January 27, 1832.

The early newspapers in Montgomery were of surprising quality, and quite willing to take a hard stance against whatever they felt they should criticize. The Alabama banking laws, and the local branch of the State Bank of Alabama thereby took some trenchant comment from the Planters' *Gazette* (dating from 1830); its predecessor, from 1821, the Montgomery *Republican;* and the later Alabama *Journal*. Each would have on occasion a marvelous story such as the centennial of the Methodist Church, on September 25, 1839; the meteor that exploded and fell near Cross Keys during the night of June 29, 1843; or how G. W. Noble got his leg, foot and best trousers burned when the Whigs were celebrating the inauguration of President William Henry Harrison on March 4, 1841. He was standing on the touch hole when Montgomery's cannon was fired.

The decade from 1840 to 1850 constituted the glory years of ante-bellum Alabama, even though there would be a continuing degree of prosperity and concomitantly, a genteel tradition of felicitous living through the outbreak of the War Between the States.

The era of King Cotton had begun haltingly as early as 1815, on marginal to good land in northern Alabama obtained through public sales even before territorial status was granted on March 3, 1817. Public lands were sold by section (six hundred forty acres) or fraction thereof, on easy terms. Solid, defensible deeds were obtainable, since all acreage had been surveyed; no longer was your holding described by "metes and bounds": ". . . from the big hickory to the next two white oaks, following the (meandering) creek to a fence (of sorts)." The bad news was that the nearest land office in pre-territorial Alabama was at Nashville, Tennessee—after a difficult, often dangerous journey over the primordial New Market Road that snaked its way north through the valley of the Tennessee River.

With an estimated thirty thousand slaves out of a total population of some one hundred twenty thousand, Alabama produced only one hundred sixty million pounds of cotton in 1820. This had almost doubled, at more than three hundred million pounds, ten years later; the number of slaves had quadrupled, at almost one hundred twenty-five thousand. By 1840, the cotton crop reached five hundred million pounds.

The billion-pound level of production that was thought to be an illusory goal was reached in 1850, but there were clearly recognizable problems, even as demand for cotton and the output of textiles both here and in Europe continued ever upward: overworked land and diminishing new acreage; a sharply-escalating slave population approaching fifty percent of all Alabama residents, and the expense of maintaining such a huge work force, even though its members were not paid wages; the mounting costs of storing and shipping cotton bales; and far more ominous, the spreading, seemingly irreconciliable national arguments over states' rights, slavery and abolition.

Even in the 1840s, Alabama newspapers had regular articles on the diminishing fertility of the soil, urging the use of blue marl, a prized natural limestone fertilizer found in some areas of the Black Belt including Russell County; more frequent crop rotation; and simply allowing exhausted fields to lie fallow, or to be planted in restorative grains or hay.

Slave labor was ideal in terms of its non-existent wages, of course (although some planters considered the cost of purchasing blacks as an expensive pre-payment of wages, and depended upon the natural increase of their slave population as much as possible); but indirect costs kept climbing steadily on the plantations. This trend was exacerbated when many growers, influenced by rising cotton prices, reduced the acreage devoted to corn, grain and vegetables as well as that set aside to feed milk cows and animals raised for slaughter. This could quickly result in having to provide far more expensive food, purchased from outside sources.

Railroads and steamboats were much more convenient and efficient than mule teams and barges, but planters soon found that the newer modes of transportation were also considerably more expensive. The need to warehouse larger crops of cotton, even temporarily, was also an increasing cost, along with the expense of ginning. No appreciable market for the huge output of cottonseed had been developed; the day of cottonseed cake for animal food and Chiffon (margarine) was not yet at hand. Ginning was essentially a means of separating lint from seed, at added cost.

Meanwhile, the secular trend in the price of cotton was persistently upward for much of the generation of time between 1820 and 1850. A steady succession of increases had brought the price per pound from ten to twenty cents between 1820 and 1840. There was a sharp, cyclical adjustment from about 1845 to 1848, when prices fell as low as eight cents per pound; but the market recovered strongly to fourteen cents in 1850 and averaged a somewhat weak, yet still profitable twelve cents per pound from 1840 to 1850.[15] And the planters had no highly competitive synthetics to contend with, or gimmicky government price supports which finally destroyed the natural relationship between price, supply and demand (and the cotton markets) a century later.

On balance, the cotton industry reflected mild optimism as the 1850s began. In Alabama, there was talk of the one thousand seven hundred fifty cotton mills reportedly to be operating in England by 1851; and of a seven hundred percent jump in imports of cotton to Great Britain in a generation. The Abercrombies and other leading planters, however, saw the growing shadow of, and the prospect of disaster in, the deepening gulf between slave and free states.

Suddenly, the illness of the older and aging Abercrombie brothers, Charles and Anderson; the unexpected demise of their nephew Milo Bolling, only fifty-four; and pivotal decisions by James, youngest of Charles Abercrombie, Sr.'s eleven children, and his nephew John Comer; would change the Alabama branch of the family forever, even before the earthshaking upheavals brought about by the formation of the Confederacy.

Anderson would have been seventy-five at the outbreak of the War Between the States, and Charles, almost seventy-one. Fortunately, neither of them, or Milo Bolling Abercrombie lived to see the birth of the Confederate States of America in the city they all knew so well, or the final catastrophe of surrender at Appomattox Courthouse in Virginia four years later. Delegates from South Carolina, Alabama, Georgia, Texas, Louisiana, Mississippi and Florida met in the Alabama capitol, reconstructed from the disastrous fire of 1849, on February 8, 1861, for the fateful decision to secede.

James was critically ill himself when the Confederacy was formally launched in the city that had been a second home for most of his adult life, and he would not live out the summer. In the preceding decade, however, he made some determinations that would be crucial factors in the decision of his nephews John Comer and

Charles Abercrombie, of his great-nephew James B. (the father of James S. Abercrombie), and of other members of the family, to move to Texas.

In 1849, James Abercrombie was the best-known public figure in central and eastern Alabama, with a long record of distinguished legislative service dating back almost thirty years, and a further reputation as one of Alabama's most astute planters and businessmen. He was in the midst of negotiations with his brother Anderson, members of the influential Bickerstaff family, and a syndicate of other Alabama and Georgia suzerains, for the intricate financing and early construction of what would become the Central of Georgia railroad, running through the middle of the Abercrombie plantations and the Bickerstaff brickyard.

James felt that at age fifty-seven, with ten grown children and a stable marriage in its thirty-third year, he was at a crossroads. He could either go into retirement (which the energetic youngest Abercrombie of his generation probably did not consider long); examine a new venture in brickmaking proposed by his close friends, the Bickerstaffs; or remain in politics.

He chose the third option, seeking an unexpired term in the United States Senate against John Cochran, who lived on the upper reaches of the Choctawhatchee near Eufaula, in Barbour County on the eastern border with Florida and Georgia. After a preliminary analysis, James (now widely known as Captain Abercrombie), pointed his campaign heavily toward Limestone and Madison counties in northern Alabama, on the Tennessee border. Much of the state's population was concentrated in this sector, and in nearby Birmingham were the strong beginnings of two vital new industries: coal and steelmaking. Both were attracting a steady influx of new residents, and new voters.

Consequently, Captain Abercrombie began to make extended visits to both Madison and Limestone counties. He found that he had a world-beater as a campaign manager in his future son-in-law, Lawrence Ripley Davis, scion of a leading family and one of the most able members of the state legislature. "Rip" knew everyone in the area, with its many attractions ranging from the highest per capita income in Alabama to the fishing around Capshaw Mountain. Representative Davis said later of his father-in-law, ". . . [He is] one of the most remarkable men the state has produced . . . a tower of strength to whatever cause he espouses, wielding an immense influence by his personal popularity and wondrous energy.''

Both James and his nephew John Comer were much taken with Huntsville and Madison County, and with adjoining Limestone County, all settled to a large extent by wealthy Virginia and Tennessee planters and professional men who came south looking for land in the fertile river valleys.

They found that Huntsville had a newspaper as early as 1812, a public library eight years later, and a half-dozen academies and as many churches before 1830. A cousin of the Abercrombies, Clement Comer Clay (later a governor and United States senator of Alabama) had been a delegate to the Constitutional Convention for the Alabama Territory in 1819, just as Charles Abercrombie, Sr. had served the new state of Georgia at the old capital of Louisville in 1789. Clay's descendants showed James and John Comer mementoes of a banquet preceding the Alabama convention, which was attended by President James Monroe and two of his cabinet officers.

They also had a store of anecdotes about Andrew Jackson at the Green Bottom Tavern, or bivouacking at Hunt's Spring with his regiments (including a young scout named Davy Crockett), enroute to the 1814 battle of Horseshoe Bend. Old Hickory, they recalled, had shown Senator Clay the sabre scar on his scalp once in Washington, D. C. after a few bourbons. It had been inflicted on him by an English captain of dragoons in the War of 1812. The future general and president was briefly a captive of the British while a young cadet, and had refused an order to clean the officer's boots.

James, the politician, businessman and investor, was even more impressed with the public buildings and palatial homes in the area, especially by the Parthenon-like Madison County courthouse, built of brick and marble at the then enormous cost of $36,000, and by the Bibb and Bradley mansions.

Governor Thomas Bibb (a long-time friend of the Abercrombies who succeeded his brother William when the latter died after a fall from his horse) had constructed a legendary home, ''Bella Mina,'' and then spent $32,000 on a showplace for his daughter, the widow of James Bradley, that was nine years abuilding. The most startling sight in the Huntsville area at the time, however, might have been a list of the assessed value of property owned by the nineteen thousand nine hundred sixty-five inhabitants of Madison County. Timepieces alone, mainly gold and silver watches, ran to $9264.25.

There was a similar level of prosperity in Limestone County, where James Abercrombie was often to visit the future home of his daughter Mary and Ripley Davis, a big, rambling structure near a flowing spring, with long porches, huge oaks and honeysuckle everywhere. James also saw Professor John Fraser's famed Classical Institute, where the graduate of the University of Inverness and Harvard College taught a rigorous curriculum to small classes; and the Federal architecture of the nearby mansions, with their Adam-style mantels, spiral stairways, fanlights and brickwork of the highest quality. Sometimes there were a half-dozen types of brick moulding in a single cornice, as if the brickmason sought to prove the high degree of his craftsmanship by almost impossible standards.

It was obvious that this northernmost part of Alabama had a unique and compelling range of attractions, along with the same gentility of manner and tradition found throughout the state in the ante-bellum era.

Yet when James Abercrombie and his nephew John Comer began to look into the hard economics of a possible move to the Huntsville, Alabama area, the uncle could not advise it. The cream had been skimmed off in land acquisitions going back to the very first surveys by Thomas Freeman, in 1809; and much of the land had been put to hard use for four decades. Now even the more fertile acreage was becoming depleted, and everything was at prices well beyond Colonel John Comer Abercrombie's budget. Another negative factor was the surprising degree of caution that the canny James had detected in conversations with some leading citizens of the area. There was evidently a growing body of opinion that the 1850s would never match the degree of prosperity, even of opulence, seen earlier in many parts of Madison and Limestone counties.

And then there were all those people who had left, and were still leaving, to join that cousin of David Gray's who had found fertile, cheap land in Texas. Few if any of them had come back, except to brag on their new holdings during a visit to what some of them now called "Old" Huntsville, and to urge their friends and neighbors to join them in the sister town in Walker County, Texas.

Back at Cross Keys, John Comer carefully weighed all of this, from James' logical analysis and advice to the positive reports he had been given himself of the opportunities in Texas, where excellent cotton land was still going at about $2 an acre, a fraction of the current price around Huntsville, Alabama.

Colonel Abercrombie had been given the name of James W. Winters, an early settler at Waverly in the deep southeast part of Walker County, Texas who had been joined by other emigrants from Huntsville, Alabama. He contacted Winters, and found that they had mutual friends including members of the Hamlin Lewis and John Lindsay Scott families in Montgomery who were considering a move to Texas.[16] After a brief correspondence, John Comer decided that he would ride to Texas on horseback for an inspection of the Winters land (about fifteen miles south of Huntsville), at first hand.

He made the trip; liked what he saw (including several visits to the little county seat of Huntsville, Texas, already reminiscent of the Huntsville of Madison County, Alabama); and was enroute to Waverly within the year with his family, slaves, farm animals, tools, equipment and everything else that could be packed into huge wagons. His wife Jane Minerva went to New Orleans by steamboat via Mobile, and then overland to Texas, accompanied by the four children. John Comer made the long, difficult trip with the wagons, slaves and animals; and then went to New Orleans from Waverly, to see the family safely to their new home. Soon, they would be followed by his brother Charles, and later by three nephews: Leonard Anderson, Milo Bolling, Jr., and James B. Abercrombie, the father of James S. Abercrombie. The nephews, respectively seventeen, fifteen and still unborn in 1850, would remain at Cross Keys or in Montgomery until the death of their father, Milo Bolling, Sr., on a nearby estate at Mount Meigs, Alabama on August 22, 1860.

The pattern had been established for the next move of the American clan Abercrombie, this a fourth and (to date) final migration, inexorably again to the west. But we must tie together the later history of Cross Keys, of Brickyard, of Captain James—and of the accomplishments of the talented and capable Abercrombies of the later generations in Alabama, before moving on to Texas.

Of Milo Bolling Abercrombie's six sons from his first marriage, only John Comer, II; Robert Haden (an early namesake of the brother who was closest to James Smither Abercrombie in another generation); and George chose to remain in Alabama. We saw earlier that Daniel Webster and Bolling, the sons of the second marriage to Sarah Greenleaf, and their sisters Winona and Talulah, went to the East with their mother after the death of their father and lived out their lives there.

John Comer, II, although barely twenty-four when his father died, was the only son to remain active in the management of the Cross Keys properties. An officer in the 45th Infantry Regiment of Alabama, CSA, he stayed at the plantation during most of the chaotic years of the War Between the States because of the extreme importance of raising corn and cotton for the Confederate forces.

On March 3, 1864 he married Miss R. A. Martin, daughter of a pioneer Russell County family whose grandfather, Thomas M. Martin, had served as an original county commissioner with General Anderson Abercrombie.

It fell to John Comer, II's bitter lot to preside over the gradual dismemberment of the Cross Keys plantations, during the despair-filled years of Reconstruction which began with Alabama being placed under martial law in 1867 and 1868. The state legislature refused to ratify the Fourteenth Amendment, which protected freed slaves through the concept of due process of law. Federal troops then garrisoned the Yellowhammer State until 1876, and the situation went from bad to worse.

John Comer and his peers had the impossible task of attempting to operate large plantations, in disrepair for years, without the resources to hire laborers, replace equipment or even to buy seed. Cross Keys was gradually sold off, the once vast holding having been greatly reduced earlier by portions allocated to the second Mrs. Milo Bolling Abercrombie and to Colonel John Comer and his brother Charles. The proceeds of these later sales provided temporary capital for start-up operations based primarily on tenant farming, but it was a losing battle. By the time of John Comer, II's death in Tuskegee on January 24, 1891, Cross Keys in effect no longer existed.

Robert Haden had just married Fannie R. Gary and begun the practice of law in Tuskegee when the Confederate states seceded. An officer in an Alabama cavalry unit, he fought through many campaigns and returned home unscathed to resume his practice. He was one of the most prominent members of the Alabama bar in Tuskegee and Montgomery for twenty-five years, and had just formed a new firm in Gadsen, Alabama when he died there June 9, 1891.

George, one of the very few Abercrombies who did not marry, was a physician who practiced at Snowdoun, now an exurb of Montgomery. He died suddenly on February 17, 1875 in his thirty-fifth year. Always close to the next-born sibling Sarah Comer Abercrombie Crawford as a child, he was buried by his beloved sister at Cross Keys.

The Brickyard properties also disappeared in the sad aftermath of war and Reconstruction. There is no record of Charles Abercrombie having children, and of the six sons of General Anderson, only John Grimes and his younger brother James Jackson, the brilliant judge and attorney, showed any real interest in the family plantations along the Chattahoochee after 1865. James Jackson provided legal counsel and advice for the older brother for a time at Brickyard, but this too was a losing battle. John Grimes soon joined his other brothers Charles Thomas, Robert and Wiley in various business ventures; and the sixth son, Everard, formed a law firm in Montgomery.

Similarly, two of James Abercrombie's three surviving sons (George Hargrave had died in childhood) chose to join their father in a brickmaking business in Pensacola, Florida. These sons, James, Jr. and Thomas Anderson, married Pensacola girls, and introduced their sister Clara to her Pensacola husband. The second eldest son, John Lucas, remained for a time at Brickyard, but soon went into business at Columbus, Georgia.

At least he and three other sisters (Sarah Edwina, Jane and Evalina Elizabeth) who had married into leading families of eastern Alabama and Columbus, continued to live in the area of what had been one of the great ante-bellum plantations. And Parthenia, the wife of General James H. Clanton, was a relatively short distance away in Montgomery.

But the great property of the Abercrombies at Brickyard was gone forever, perhaps to be remembered in time more for its centuries-old Indian mounds than for the tremendous fields of cotton and corn, and Billo the overseer's skilled blacks loading the first of thousands of bales of the new crop of good middling onto wagons in a September dawn. Then General Anderson and Mr. Charles would ride a little ahead of the big wagons on their blooded mares, anxious to see their cotton safely on the Mobile-bound barges on the Tallapoosa.

Captain James Abercrombie saw well before the fateful secession conference in the capitol at Montgomery that King Cotton's glory days in the South were coming to an end. He had won the race for the United States Senate in 1851 handily, but two years later, when campaigning for a full six-year term, he abandoned his long relationship with the Whig Party, which went back to the very beginnings of his political career, when he first sought election as a very young representative to the just-organized Alabama House of Representatives.

The Whigs, winners of the presidency in 1840 with William Henry Harrison (who lived only a month after his inauguration), and in 1844 with Zachary Taylor, were a curious political amalgam of eastern bankers and industrialists, western land developers and southern planters. The southerners questioned their role in the alliance from the moment the eastern Whigs began to rub elbows with the abolitionists, who were suddenly everywhere you looked (even in the Alabama legislature, where the extremely controversial James G. Birney had won a seat).

James Abercrombie awoke one day to discover even close friends in the Senate making speeches on the floor about the United States and Brazil being the only two countries in the western world still permitting slavery within their continental borders. In 1851 he switched to the Democratic Party, and supported the victorious Franklin Pierce, who overwhelmed the Whig, Winfield Scott, two hundred fifty-four electoral votes to forty-two, for the presidency.

In Washington, D.C., Senator James Abercrombie had won the respect of his colleagues including General Sam Houston, who served from February 21, 1846 to March 4, 1859 in the Senate. He and General Sam often raised their voices together in defense of states' rights, although the Alabaman and the Texan would disagree on secession, and on the bitter, chilling speech with which Houston warned of slow but inevitable disaster for the South in any armed confrontation with the North.

When he completed his full six-year term in the United States Senate in 1859, James Abercrombie was sixty-seven years old. He was in reasonably good health, but saw no real future for his sons, or for himself or other members of the family, at the Brickyard plantations. History was simply issuing some orders that could not be countermanded, and he was a realist.

Thus, he turned to his friends of many years, the Bickerstaffs, whose kilns were churning out bricks at an ever-increasing rate, for advice on organizing his own brickmaking company at Pensacola. He had successfully launched this, with James, Jr. and Thomas Anderson, when he died on July 2, 1861 in Pensacola, full of honors and memories of an unforgettable era in the Yellowhammer State he had adopted as his own.

The name of Abercrombie, as well as that of the numerous descendants of many Abercrombie daughters and granddaughters who had intermarried with other distinguished families, lived on in Alabama, Georgia and Florida. There were leading businessmen and attorneys and public officials, and one of the youngest presidents ever of the University of Alabama, founded at Tuscaloosa in the first beginnings of statehood. This was Dr. John William Abercrombie, a great-great-grandson of General Anderson and the distinguished educator who developed many of the fundamental concepts of primary and secondary education in Alabama. He became president of the state university in 1902, when just thirty-six years of age.

But the scene had shifted, perhaps inevitably for a family with the lemming-like, deep-seated urge to move on inexorably to the west. The new stage setting was to be in Texas for the next century and more, and perhaps down all the coming corridors of time and of life.

Colonel John Comer Abercrombie had left Cross Keys for a last time, headed due west for Waverly and New Huntsville, in far distant Walker County where the new cotton lands of Texas beckoned.

Notes

[1] There were two towns named Cross Keys in Alabama at differing times, almost two hundred fifty miles apart; neither exists as an established community today. The post office at Cross Keys in DeKalb County was opened March 12, 1832 and discontinued January 31,1907, presumably because of a lack of business. This Cross Keys was about six miles northwest of Athens, Alabama, near Elkmont. The Cross Keys to which the Leonard Abercrombie family moved in 1834 was equidistant between Montgomery and Tuskegee in Macon County. The post office at this Cross Keys was opened February 10, 1890 and was discontinued on August 15, 1906.

[2] Brickyard, Alabama was often described as being five miles south of Columbus, Georgia, the far larger and better known town just across the state line that is now the second largest city in Georgia. Some Alabama planters on the far eastern border maintained residences and offices in Columbus. James Jackson Abercrombie, the noted attorney and jurist, was judge of the Superior Court of the Muscogee District of Georgia, and practiced law for many years in Columbus, but had many of his clients in nearby Alabama, where he removed after the War Between the States.

[3] Alabama's Indian culture is thought to date back as far as ten thousand years, from recent carbon-14 dating of artifacts, some of them discovered in the burial mounds, which are found along the principal river valleys. At least four tribes inhabited the area when Hernando de Soto first explored it in 1540–1541 during the famed expedition which resulted in the discovery of the Mississippi River. These were the Muskogees or Upper

Creeks, in what became central and eastern Alabama; the Choctaws of the south and southwest; the Chicksaws, northwest; and the Cherokees, northeast. DeSoto's men, equipped with harquebus and sword, killed thousands of terrified Indians and their chieftain Tuscaloosa in a terrible and unnecessary massacre on October 18, 1540. Tuscaloosa's name proudly survives in the state's fifth largest city and site of the main campus of the University of Alabama.

[4] John Comer Abercrombie married Jane Minerva Sims of Charleston, South Carolina at Cross Keys in 1842, when he was thirty-three and she was twenty. Milo Bolling already had nine children at the time. John and Jane would have eight children in all, four of them (Lem, Sally, John and Carolina (Carrie) born in Alabama, and the other four (Eachine, Minnie, James and Charles) in Texas. Charles married Sarah Holeman July 15, 1833 in Montgomery County, Alabama, when he was twenty-three. Theirs was a long and apparently happy, but childless, marriage.

[5] Robert Abercrombie Jones was the son of Retinca Abercrombie, a daughter of Robert, Jr.'s second marriage, to Nancy Moore. Retinca married William Hardwick Jones on July 22, 1800. The Joneses, with many another prominent North Carolina family, were Royalist enough to receive high-ranking British officers sent on to Wilmington after Banastre Tarleton and his British Legion had overrun South Carolina and captured Charleston in 1780. Jane Elizabeth Jones is still remembered in Wilmington for an incident that was extremely embarrassing to the British. Miss Jones paid an unprecedented call on a "certain young British lord," an aide to General Tarleton, who was quartered with neighbors down the street. Claiming that this officer had made a "highly improper suggestion" to her while escorting her home from a ball, Jane Elizabeth proceeded to horsewhip him in the neighbor's drawing room. Her brother George Pritchard Jones then offered to kill the British lord on sight, and General Tarleton ordered him back to London on the next ship. The story spread like wildfire.

[6] Peter Maher claimed to be both a seminarian, who decided at the last moment not to be ordained, and a graduate of the University of Dublin (Trinity College). If so, he was an Anglican, not a Catholic, candidate for holy orders. Trinity College did not enroll Roman Catholics until 1873. In any case, Professor Maher and his fellow educators of the day gave marvelous value for the tuition dollar. The standard "three R's" curriculum went at $4 a term, but you could add algebra, advanced English grammar and world geography for another $2, or go the deluxe route (etymology, Latin, Greek and higher mathematics) for a total of $8.

[7] Twenty years later, with the continuing influx of Catholic planters, merchants and investors from New Orleans, Charleston and Mobile, Father James Pellicer (the pastor of St. Peter's) combined local contributions with major gifts he somehow raised in Mexico and Cuba to provide a greatly enlarged St. Peter's that was consecrated by the ordinaries of Mobile and New Orleans on Easter Sunday, 1854.

[8] The federal government at least set the toll rates on these ferries and bridges, and rickety though most of them were, anything was better than the alternative: going through land still held by the Creek Nation. The Indians had no set fee, but exacted anything from a small bag of cornmeal to what approached a ransom. Washington did provide, however, for a short, toll-less road of less than ten miles length from Fort Daniel in Gwinnett County to a hamlet called Standing Peachtree on the nearby Chattahoochee River. Of little significance at the time, the road would become extremely important to the future development of Georgia, and of the entire southeast. Standing Peachtree and a junction called Five Points a few miles south of the Chattahoochee became the boundaries of a town called Atlanta when it was decided to locate the southern terminus of a new railroad to Chattanooga there.

[9] Robert Fulton was an impoverished painter of miniatures from a Quaker community near Lancaster, Pennsylvania who attracted the attention of Philadelphia patrons. They

sent him to London in 1787, ostensibly to study with English masters of portraiture. Instead, he became interested in British canals, and was soon an expert on inland waterways. Back in the United States, he formed a partnership with Robert Livingston, a pioneer in the design of steamboats. Together, they built the first practical steamboats, one of which went into regular use in 1807 between Albany and New York City. Fulton also built the first submarine, in 1807.

[10] This fundamental law of economics, erroneously attributed to Sir Thomas Gresham, who founded the Royal Exchange in London, is based on the irrefutable fact that "cheap" money will drive "good" money out of circulation. Gold was systematically withdrawn from circulation in the United States from 1792 to 1834, while silver flowed into the Treasury and the nation was on the silver standard. The process was reversed in 1834, and we went on a gold standard.

[11] The Eastern connection had been made much more convenient by a remarkable new service inaugurated in Alabama on November 15, 1836. Termed the "Horse Express," this went to the east through Columbus, Georgia, and to the north through Huntsville, Alabama. It guaranteed, as a curious precursor of today's overnight air delivery services, guaranteed safe delivery of bills of sale, drafts, invoices, bills of lading, notes, correspondence and other vital papers in New York within six business days (five days to Philadelphia). The charges were $1 per letter, or $4 per ounce.

[12] It was a mark of distinction for an Indian to own slaves, and some of the chieftains willed as many as eight to members of their family. Arketeahhola, for example, left his eldest son Lonahholka two blacks worth about $1000; and less valuable slaves to another son, Telofhargo, and his daughters Chiholarkee and Chaneehoyah.

George Washington's former aide, Colonel Willem Marinus, was astonished when a black slave was assigned to him as a personal servant during a visit to Coweta, the capital of the Creek Nation, in 1790. He invited the assembled chieftains to send an envoy to Washington for a personal conference with President Washington, who was concerned over reports of continuing Indian raids against early settlements in what would become the Alabama Territory.

[13] From the time of their arrival along the Chattahoochee, Anderson and Charles Abercrombie had as their closest neighbors two other outstanding pioneer families of Russell County: the Frank Bickerstaffs and the Charles R. Dudleys. The Bickerstaffs discovered a sticky red clay, ideal for brickmaking, on their farms; opened a brickyard that gave the name to the vicinity and to its original town, and became an extremely important source of employment and of income during the trying years of Reconstruction; and are still expanding their business a century-and-a-half later. Bickerstaff Clay Products has two plants in the Brickyard area (which is now part of the two-state Phenix City, Alabama-Columbus, Georgia metroplex); and additional plants in Atlanta and in Birmingham, with a total of some seven hundred employees.

[14] James G. Birney was a fiery speaker and a master of persuasive tracts and letters to the editor which he supplied in plentiful quantity to newspapers all over the South. After somehow getting himself elected to the Alabama legislature, he raised enough hackles there to make him decide it best to return to his native Kentucky. Birney surfaced later in the East and became the candidate for president of the Abolitionist Party in 1840, but polled less than three thousand votes against the victorious Whig, William Henry Harrison, and the losing Democrat, Martin Van Buren.

[15] Prices quoted are averages from the great trading center at Liverpool, which dominated the world cotton market for most of the nineteenth century as the ever-increasing number of British mills hungered for production from the United States and the Caribbean.

[16] Hamlin Lewis, John Lindsay Scott and John Elliott Scott, with many family slaves they had decided to bring through New Orleans rather than overland, died in an 1851

cholera epidemic in the Louisiana capital while enroute from Alabama to Waverly. An earlier outbreak of the dread malady claimed the lives of many Irish immigrants on their way to Mexican land grants in Refugio and San Patricio de Hibernia, through the tiny port of Indianola.

Chapter 5

1850–1906

Huntsville, Esperanza and Richmond, Texas

Pleasant Gray learns of bountiful Mexican land grants . . . By horseback to Nacogdoches . . . Of Alcalde Adolphus Sterne and ex-Congressman, ex-Governor Sam Houston . . . The watershed land, and frustrating years of delay . . . An entry in the libro becerro, *and Huntsville, Texas is born . . . Early days and a gracious tradition . . . Colonel John Comer Abercrombie completes the long trek westward . . . General Sam returns . . . Colonel (and Senator) Leonard A. Abercrombie . . . The War Between the States . . . James Buford Abercrombie, II: superintendent of farms . . . Jamie Smither Abercrombie is born on July 7, 1891 . . . Boyhood in a well-ordered replica of an ante-bellum Southern town . . . Financial reverses: The Abercrombies move to Esperanza and Richmond in the spreading Panic of 1903 . . . A first job for barefooted Jamie . . . The decision to move to Houston*

Pleasant Gray read the story first in a New Orleans newspaper. Some cotton buyer had left the paper in the spacious lobby of the Green Bottom Inn during the fall ginning season of 1830. The buyers always frequented the Inn (General Andrew Jackson's hospitable headquarters for food, lodging, whiskey, horse racing and cockfights during his many visits to Huntsville, Alabama) as they bargained for the new-crop bales of cotton piling up in the nearby wagon yard.

Now it was almost Christmastide, and on a trip into town to seek modest presents for his wife Hannah and their little son and two daughters, Gray saw the same story, with further details, in the weekly newspaper from Mobile: the new republic of Mexico was offering very large grants of fertile land to settlers for little more than a filing fee.

Only weeks after gaining independence from Spain in 1821, the Mexican government had begun a study of the pressing need to colonize the vast empty stretches of territory between the Nueces and Sabine Rivers in what is now South, Southeast and East Texas. The reasoning behind the study was totally sound: empty territories bring in neither crops, livestock nor taxes; instead they invite confiscation by other nations.

A basic colonization law was not promulgated by the federal authorities in Mexico City until August 18, 1824,[1] but the bureaucrats involved should be praised for persevering toward their goal of placing selected settlers on millions of acres of vacant land, rather than being criticized for any delay involved. The marvel is that the new republic had any time at all from 1821 to 1824 to devote to colonization.

The three years between the signing of the Treaty of Cordoba (which granted Mexico independence from Spain on August 24, 1821) and the issuance of the colonization decree saw the ascendancy of the complex and uncompromisingly authoritarian General Agustin Iturbide, who declared himself Emperor Agustin I on May 19, 1822; Iturbide's overthrow by General Antonio Lopez de Santa Anna (of San Jacinto battlefield disgrace-to-be); the erstwhile Agustin I's abdication and exile in London and Rome; and his execution (after returning to Mexico unaware that he had been sentenced to death *in absentia*) on July 19, 1824.

Even after three years of such tumult, the new Santa Anna government published the colonization law less than a month after coming to full power with the death of Iturbide. Aside from federal control of areas within ten leagues of the coastline, or twenty leagues or less from the boundaries of other nations, the embryo Mexican states were allowed to legislate their own detailed regulations for colonization.

Understandably, the provisional state of Coahuila and Tejas, on Mexico's northern border, with its vast expanse of empty land and nearness to prospective settlers, was first to sign into law a decree of colonization. Under the decree, effective March 24, 1825, the state "invit(ed) and call(ed)"colonists to take up fertile lands for the "augumentation of population" and for the safe and profitable pursuit of agriculture, ranching, commerce and the arts.

When Pleasant Gray read again of what was reported to be good land for almost nothing that Christmastide of 1830, his earlier interest was immediately rekindled. Now he was determined to discover everything he could about the Mexican proposal. There were good reasons: life had its positive aspects in Huntsville, and throughout Madison County, Alabama in 1830, but it also posed many difficulties for an ambitious young farmer with no land of his own, little or no capital, and young children.

Although Huntsville had been laid out around John Hunt's flowing spring less than two decades earlier, most of the best land had been claimed at public auctions going back to 1809, or purchased at low rates with bountiful credit soon thereafter. By 1819, a combination of statehood, post-War of 1812 prosperity, $100 per acre income from cotton, and speculation fueled by wealthy Virginians flowing in from the north had sent Madison County land values skyrocketing to an average of $50–$55 per acre.

Pleasant's cousin David Gray, whose land he was farming, had acquired extensive holdings as early as Thomas Freeman's first land survey, in 1809, and at prices as low as $2 per acre; but there seemed to be little hope that Pleasant Gray would be able to buy his own land at 1830's highly-inflated prices. After discussing the matter with his bachelor brother Ephraim, with Hannah and with some of their neighboring friends, he decided to write the office for colonization at Leona Vicario in Coahuila,[2] requesting further details including the exact amount of land available to differing classifications of settlers.

Pleasant Gray had set into motion, slowly yet inexorably, on a winter day early in 1831, a chain of events destined to bring members of the Abercrombie family to Huntsville, Texas. There Jamie Smither Abercrombie would be born, on July 7, 1891; and in nearby Houston the American branch of the clan Abercromby, baronets of Scotland and of Nova Scotia, would complete a migration westward encompassing the thousands of miles between Pitmedden and Texas, and almost two centuries in time.

When the information he sought finally arrived from Mexico and had been translated with what must have been considerable difficulty, Pleasant Gray's interest increased geometrically. The offer of land was for one labor, or 177.1 acres, per family engaged solely in farming. If the colonist also agreed to a ranching operation, however, the grant escalated dramatically, by twenty-five hundred percent, to a *sitio* (or Spanish league) of 4428.4 acres.[3]

With this information in hand, Pleasant Gray now knew that a substantial amount of acreage might be available to him as a Mexican colonist; but the land was more than one thousand miles distant from Huntsville, Alabama, and he had no knowledge of its setting, fertility, suitability for specific crops or ranching operations, nearness to markets, average annual rainfall, etc. Also unanswered were such vital questions as living conditions for his growing family, relationships with the Mexican government, and the possible need for protection from hostile Indians or the other perils of harsh frontier life.

The answer was obvious: he would make his own on-site survey, even though this meant a difficult, possibly hazardous round trip of some twenty-five hundred miles, and weeks of absence from his family and his crops.

Pleasant Gray made the trip overland, on horseback. Traveling alone, there would be little point in the alternatives of: (1) a buggy or small wagon; or (2) a relatively expensive journey combining flatboats down the Alabama River and its tributaries to Mobile, thence by schooner to New Orleans or (if passage became available) to the new port of Galveston, and finally by horseback to his destination. There were no railroads south of Savannah in 1831, and few stagecoaches away from principal cities. Pleasant, an experienced horseman accustomed to riding all over Madison and adjoining north and central Alabama counties, probably saw the long trip west and south as a challenge.

As soon as the cotton crop was safely out of the ground, and past the danger of late frost, he made his final arrangements with wife, brother and cousin; said his goodbyes with what must have been a special hug for Hannah and the children; and set out on his strongest horse for distant Coahuila and Tejas.

He probably crossed the mighty Tennessee River just west of Huntsville at the busy cotton port of Decatur, detoured slightly around the base of Penitentiary Mountain to enter Mississippi, and began the long, slanting ride diagonally across the entirety of that neighboring state to reach Natchez. From there, he headed due west to the old town of Natchitoches, in northwestern Louisiana. Natchitoches, originally founded by the French in 1714 as Fort St. Jean Baptiste, was a traditional entry point for those seeking what would become East Texas, just as it had been for seventeenth- and eighteenth-century explorers, conquerors, smugglers and assorted adventurers.

Two days later, after resting himself and his horse at an inn near the cotton docks,[4] Pleasant crossed the Red River headed for Nacogdoches, another early settlement and hub for those not necessarily welcoming close inquiry into their past. Only twenty-five miles further west, he took a ferry across the Sabine River and entered Mexican territory. Now he was on the legendary Camino Real, or King's Highway, which ran raggedly (and roughly) from the far western reaches of the Rio Bravo to the Louisiana border at the Sabine.

Pleasant Gray had been told by one of the increasing number of Alabamans interested in Mexican land grants to be certain if in Nacogdoches to call on Adolphus Sterne. This was good advice, for Don Adolpho Sterne, the alcalde (chief administrative and judicial officer) of the old crossroads town, was an excellent man to know in that part of the world, especially if you wished to probe for the latest and most reliable information concerning Mexico and that country's policies toward prospective American colonists.

Sterne, a polylinguist (German, English, Spanish and French) and native of Westphalia in northwestern Germany, was only thirty years of age in 1831, but clearly destined for a significant role in Texas history. Married to Eva Rosine, a Catholic woman from Louisiana with close ties to governmental and ecclesiastical authorities through her family, Adolph Sterne had known Sam Houston when both men were residents of Nashville—Sterne a young, ambitious Jewish merchant with a flair for politics and statehouse intrigue; General Sam a United States congressman and governor of Tennessee.

By late December of 1832, Sam Houston himself was a resident of Nacogdoches. He was also a long-time guest in the Sterne home, captivated by the vivacious Eva and her Creole, French-speaking servants, and the rotund, gregarious Adolph. In the Sterne residence, he would be baptized a Roman Catholic, with Eva as his godmother, by Father Rene Chambondeau.[5]

In a tumultuous three years, General Sam (Co-lon-neh, or The Raven, to the Cherokees) had demonstrated again his resilient ability to rise phoenix-like from the ashes. First, he survived the mysterious break-up of his brief first marriage, a tidal wave of malicious gossip and resigning the governorship of Tennessee. He then returned to the tribal wigwams at the invitation of his admirer, Chief He-Puts-The-Drums-Away; lived through a devastating fever and the ministrations of Cherokee shamans; began a controversial liaison with Tiana, his Indian maid of the forests; renewed a close friendship with President Andrew Jackson; and was found not guilty of fraud at a sensational Washington, D.C. trial with some of the impact of an 1830 Watergate. At the conclusion of these adventures, Sam Houston showed up at a formal White House reception in full Cherokee regalia and accepted appointment as a secret high-level emissary for the United States government.

Pleasant Gray and Sam Houston, a pair of adopted Texans with sharply contrasting experiences, would be neighbors a dozen years down the calendar, in Huntsville, Texas. In the early 1830s, both men had greatly differing backgrounds, but were both drawn to Nacogdoches by that irresistible lure of the frontier: cheap, available land. General Houston ostensibly came to the old town to speculate in Red River acreage, while practicing law on the side. It is also possible that he was in Nacogdoches, a center of intrigue, for another purpose: to examine new aspects of prying Tejas loose from Mexico.

In any event, Sam Houston was as usual a popular and much sought-after addition to the frontier community of thirteen hundred souls (almost four hundred of them under sixteen years of age). Scant weeks after his arrival, Adolphus Sterne had him elected to a new post. General Sam would be the delegate from Nacogdoches to the constitutional convention opening at San Felipe de Austin on April 1, 1833. The convention would be seeking the status of a separate Mexican state for Tejas. Saltillo, the capital of Coahuila and Tejas, was a hard and perilous six-hundred mile ride, much of it through prairie, desert and the foothills of the Sierra Madre range, for the increasing number of colonists having business with state authorities.

We do not know what counsel Don Adolpho Sterne gave Pleasant Gray in Nacogdoches that late spring of 1831 when Gray came riding into town, aside from the standard (and sound) advice to put up at Brown's Tavern instead of at Miguel Cortenoz' Cantina del Monte, where noisy *bailes* and brisk trade in the downstairs saloon kept all but the most exhausted lodgers awake through most of the night. It is quite probable, however, that the knowledgeable Sterne told the visitor from Alabama to await further interpretation of a recently-publicized decree of April 6, 1830, and the resolution of a rash of claims and counterclaims by empresarios regarding boundaries and land titles.

The confusing 1830 decree, if strictly enforced, would terminate colonization by U.S. citizens, and abolish a significant prerogative granted state authorities less than a half-dozen years before. Now there were indications that it might be repealed as part of an effort to clarify the troublesome question of the jurisdiction of the central government within the Mexican states. Further, a welcome acceleration of official government land surveys, and rumors of pending compromises between some of the principal empresarios, strengthened hopes of resolving boundary and title disputes.

Pleasant Gray did delay actually filing for a grant of land, but he saw no reason not to push on farther west for a good look at some of the land that would hopefully soon be available. Don Adolpho could be helpful in this regard also, for among his acquaintances was the German empresario Joseph (Jose) Vehlein.[6] Vehlein, a Mexican citizen and wide-ranging entrepreneur, had acquired in partnership with David G. Burnet (the provisional president of the Republic of Texas in years to come), a gargantuan grant extending originally from Galveston Bay to the Sabine River, and encompassing much of East Texas. Part of this huge concession was quite near Nacogdoches, but these lands were in the main a thick forest of pine and scrub oak, unsuited for either farming or ranching without extensive clearing, and even then of marginal fertility.

Upon further inquiry, Gray found that far better acreage was held by Vehlein and Burnet about seventy-five miles south and west of Nacogdoches along the watershed dividing the San Jacinto and Trinity Rivers. A few days later, at a location almost midway between the two rivers, he was looking with growing appreciation at what seemed to be an ideal piece of land, among rolling hills and small valleys with interspersed level grazing areas. Pleasant must have sensed that he had found what he had been seeking.

The more he studied the site, the more he was reminded of north and central Alabama. The topography was quite similar, even to the size of the hills. The trees were of the same varieties: mainly pine, with groves of cedar and heavy clumps of post, red and water oak. He recognized many of the same birds he had known since childhood: flickers, mockingbirds, doves, woodpeckers, and huge hawks gliding noiselessly in search of prey.

The Alabaman was already aware, from questioning Sterne and the alcalde's fellow townsmen, that the Tejas climate was superior in terms of a much longer growing season, for frost was common in north Alabama through April, and it could be quite nippy in early

October. Average rainfall, he had found, was quite adequate, primarily because of prevailing winds that brought clouds, thunderstorms and moisture in regularly from the Gulf of Mexico, particularly during the summer when drought was an ever-present threat to farmers raising thirsty crops of corn and cotton.

Pleasant Gray was also seeking information on the availability of wild game and fish on his inspection trip. Frontiersmen had to depend heavily upon these sources of food—temporarily for actual sustenance until a first harvest was safely in the barn, and permanently as a source of variety in the family diet. Meals of corn meal and sweet potatoes, staples of the frontier menu, could quickly become monotonous.

From contemporary accounts, we know that wild game and fish were abundant in the East Texas-to-be of the 1830s. Pleasant must have caught sight of large herds of deer grazing on the prairies and in the undergrowth of the forests as he rode south and west from Nacogdoches. Buck, doe and fawn had practically no natural enemies, aside from a limited number of bobcats; the prolific herds suffered relatively minor losses from the Indians and a few professional hunters. Squirrels, a frontier delicacy, were everywhere in the trees, chattering noisily at the periodic invasions of wild turkeys nesting in the clumps of young pine. And there were occasional black bears, migrating from the nearby Big Thicket after a winter's hibernation to stun and capture perch, catfish and bass in the shallow waters of the creeks.

Fish were plentiful in the clear, unpolluted waters of both the creeks and the San Jacinto and Trinity Rivers, with huge catfish caught on trotlines strung across the deeper channels where these monsters lurked.

Even before his inspection of the watershed land was complete, Pleasant Gray had made up his mind. He would emigrate to the area with his family as soon as possible. Back in Nacogdoches, he called on Adolphus Sterne immediately; Pleasant told Sterne frankly of his high opinion of the watershed acreage and of his decision to become a colonist; then he asked for Don Adolpho's advice.

The alcalde's recommendation was for the Alabaman to return home and get his affairs in order in anticipation of a change in the controversial decree of 1830 and the resolution of title and boundary disputes. In the meantime, Sterne would tell Empresario Vehlein of Gray's decision, and do his best to stay in touch with the prospective settler, unreliable though the postal system of 1831 might be.

Pleasant Gray was both the talk of the town and an unofficial salesman for Coahuila and Tejas after his return to Huntsville, Alabama in the late summer of 1831. His enthusiasm for the distant Mexican frontier was undoubtedly a major factor in developing close ties between Huntsville on the Tennessee border, and the Huntsville-to-be in Texas. And he would be responsible in large degree for the rising tide of Alabamans who would settle in Texas.

Among them would be Colonel John Comer Abercrombie, Jamie Smither Abercrombie's great-uncle who would ride horseback from Cross Keys to Waverly, Texas in 1850, returning later that year with his family.

After two frustrating years of further delay, Pleasant Gray finally received the news he had awaited so long. The stagecoach from Decatur brought a letter from Adolphus Sterne telling of the repeal, late in 1833, of the decree of 1830. The empresarios were free again to bring in United States citizens as colonists, and they had in the meantime resolved virtually all of their disagreements, feuds and lawsuits regarding boundaries and titles to land.

Still, there was many a loose end to tie down in Alabama, plus the long overland trek to the west. This time it would not be a lone rider on horseback, but six people on slow march in and around a big, high-wheeled covered wagon. The awkward vehicle was heavily laden with tools, farm implements and rough frontier furniture, seeds, food and dozens of other things the family would need, including the peach tree seedlings and cuttings of her favorite flowers that Hannah jealously guarded. The brothers Gray alternated in driving the wagon, although Pleasant was more often a bit ahead on his horse, looking for the best trail to follow, or the easiest place to ford smaller rivers and creeks.

It was the fall of 1834 before the two brothers, Hannah and the three children arrived in Nacogdoches, trail-weary but excited at the prospect of a new life. They had even brought the family's best milch cow, lowing and complaining as she followed the wagon on a short tether for more than one thousand miles. Pleasant had remembered that the local breed of dairy cattle on the Mexican frontier were at best mediocre producers of bluejohn.

As soon as he could find a temporary home for his family, with the aid of Don Adolpho Sterne, Pleasant Gray held a long conference with his rotund German friend. He found from Sterne that Nacogdoches, and Tejas overall, had changed substantially since 1831. There had been a civil war in Mexico, with Lopez de Santa Anna as the victor, and a growing current of unrest among the neglected Mexican colonies on the border. The Texians, as settlers had begun to describe themselves, were in the main still loyal to Mexico; but the tide seemed to be turning.

Stephen F. Austin, a conservative, steadying influence from his prospering settlements between the Brazos and Colorado Rivers, had been in Mexico City for more than a year, and was now imprisoned there. During Austin's lengthening absence, Sam Houston was definitely in the ascendancy. Known to be a confidante of Andrew Jackson (and thought to be an agent provocateur for Old Hickory); adept at attracting wide attention, with his commanding presence, colorful garb and trappings of solid silver for his huge horses; skilled in the military arts; and a master of intrigue; General Sam was clearly a man to be reckoned with. Within the space of little more than a year, he had acquired almost a league of land on the Red River, won a sensational trial for his clients, represented his area in the constitutional convention at San Felipe de Austin and been named commander-in-chief of the militia for the Department of Nacogdoches.

Now, Adolphus Sterne reported, General Sam was in Washington, D.C., with stops in the Arkansas Territory, Cincinnati and St. Louis enroute. It was rumored that he would go to New York City soon, as counsel for the newly-organized Galveston Bay and Texas Land Company, to advise an Eastern syndicate on how to invest in as much as eight million acres of what was now Coahuila and Tejas land.

Pleasant Gray listened to all this with interest, but as an essentially apolitical man concerned with one overriding problem: how to obtain the grant of a league of attractive land. He too was intrigued with Sam Houston, and knew how fond Don Adolpho and Eva Rosine Sterne had become of him; but he probably saw General Sam more as Stephen F. Austin perceived him. Don Estevan de Austin, the name under which he had been officially booked into a Mexico City prison under mysterious circumstances, spoke of Sam Houston as "that adventurer, that Nacogdoches insurgent." Austin was far more interested in what he could do to protect his loyal colonists in the fertile Brazos River bottoms, and their promising crops of cotton, corn and grain, than in some coup d'etat launched from deep East Texas.

Pleasant had to hear a few more Nacogdoches stories from Don Adolpho, including a fascinating tale about Martin Parmer, the Ring-Tailed Panther,[7] before they got down to the real business at hand. Then Sterne showed him in detail how to apply to Empresario Joseph Vehlein, at Saltillo, for a land grant under the reaffirmed decree of 1825.

Pleasant Gray had ridden with Don Adolpho to the splendid location between the San Jacinto and the Trinity that so reminded him of his Alabama home. Sterne shared his enthusiasm for the site, all the more after they had discovered a significant additional attraction: two lively, bubbling springs on the edge of the nearby prairie. Now they were careful to include this area well within the metes and bounds of the land Gray was seeking, for the colonist-to-be saw a considerably broader opportunity developing.

Since returning to Nacogdoches, he had learned of three new settler families in the general vicinity of what he was already calling his watershed land. Further, there were two tribes of friendly Indians, the Bedias and the Coushattas, within a dozen miles, along the nearby creeks and the upper reaches of the Trinity to the north.[8] The Indians were said to be anxious to trade hides, medicinal herbs, venison and dried fish for the small tools and the staples such as flour, cornmeal and salt they were becoming accustomed to acquire by barter from a trading post. Why not, Pleasant Gray thought, establish such a facility at a location much more convenient for incoming settlers, and for the Indians, than Nacogdoches? Saving much of a round trip of from one hundred to one hundred fifty miles was in itself a powerful attraction for potential customers.

Gray's application for Mexican land, which now appeared to be more and more appealing, was finally completed and signed on November 24, 1834. It went to Jose Vehlein, recently awarded the title of special commissioner for the settlement of citizens, by courier. There was an accompanying note from the alcalde of Nacogdoches that was calculated to do no harm.

Pleasant Gray asked for the 4428.4 acres alloted to families agreeing to participate both in farming and in ranching. Following Adolphus Sterne's advice, he emphasized that he and his dependents were already residents of the municipality of Washington (the Mexican designation, paying homage to the hero of Mount Vernon, for what would become the huge extent of the original Montgomery

County). Gray also recited some of the provisions of the colonization decree of 1825 in laudatory terms, and was careful to mention that he would be "forever grateful" for the grant of land he was seeking.

Even with the intercession and the continuing friendship of Adolphus Sterne, it was almost eight months before Pleasant Gray's application was processed and approved. But late in July 1835, a copy of the original grant (dated July 10, 1835) was delivered to colonist P. Gray at Nacogdoches. He must have had marked difficulty in translating the traditionally elegant and sonorous Spanish text, but he could sense the overall tone of the document, which he adjudged to be positive. Don Adolpho soon confirmed his optimism.

"P." Gray was an unusual form of address for the Mexican bureaucrats, who tended strongly toward formality; they simply could not devise an acceptable translation of Gray's first name. Joseph (or Josef) Vehlein was obviously "Jose," but how could you call a man "Agradable" or "Simpatico" Gray? When the new settler asked about the original of his long-sought document, ex-Alcalde Sterne (he had agreed to pass the time-consuming office on to a friend, Rayford Berry) explained that the original was in the archives, and from there entered upon the *libro becerro,* or literally, the (official) "calfskin book."

More than four years had passed since the Alabaman and his weary mount, both caked with red mud from the thick dust and countless potholes of the Camino Real, had first arrived in the old frontier town of Adolphus Sterne and Don Samuel Houston; but now Pleasant Gray had his beautiful watershed acreage, all seven square miles of it.

The copy of the grant in the *libro becerro* had arrived just in time. Vehlein, Burnet and Lorenzo de Zavala (Burnet's vice-president in the first interim government of the Texian Republic) were already negotiating with the Galveston Bay and Texas Land Company for the sale of virtually all the acreage they still held under their combined contracts with the Mexican government. GB&TLC, in spite of its powerful friends in New York City, Washington, D.C. and Saltillo, would have an unhappy future clouded by misrepresentations, questionable titles to huge tracts and widespread claims of fraud.

Gray established his trading post just where he had envisioned it: six or seven miles southwest of the Trinity River, and a bit closer to the San Jacinto. Here the two springs he and Adolphus Sterne had admired bubbled and flowed close to a little prairie, and there was a fine grove of live oaks.

All around were the rolling hills and valleys, covered with lush, deep dark-green forests of pine, that had first attracted the new owner. Now, riding over the huge expanse of his property, Gray discovered small but valuable stands of hardwoods merging into the pine trees close to the rich alluvial soil along the creeks and rivers. Among other varieties, he identified sweet and black gum, hickory and walnut. And scattered as far as he could see across the undulating terrain, Pleasant noted again with satisfaction, were more of the level areas where his cattle could graze.

Aided by the first curious Indians who came hesitatingly forward, and by their nearest neighbors, George Lamb and John McAdams, Pleasant and Ephraim Gray began almost immediately to build two log cabins on the site. The first was the family home, badly needed against the biting wet northers of the Tejas winter. This would soon also shelter a second son for Pleasant and Hannah, named David for his cousin back in Alabama. The other cabin, much smaller, was the original trading post.

Late in 1835, the Grays named the tiny settlement Huntsville, after their Alabama home. The new Huntsville prospered from the beginning, just as their trading post. The original log cabin home quickly became an inn, to care for the increasing flow of settlers and travelers. The trading post was enlarged into a store, with far more items in stock for a growing clientele. Pleasant built his expanded family a new home across the street, and Ephraim put up his own cabin in a nearby cedar grove.

Huntsville's growth in those early days was a somewhat extraordinary phenomenon, in view of the relative isolation of Pleasant Gray's watershed grant, and for that matter, of the entire municipality of Washington. A visitor coming down one of the principal trails, from the northern reaches of the Sabine to Huntsville, in 1835 reported seeing only two cabins across more than two hundred miles of desolate wilderness.

The phenomenon could probably be explained in large measure by three principal factors: (1) keen interest in this part of Texas-to-be, especially in Alabama, Tennessee, Georgia, Mississippi and the Carolinas; (2) growing knowledge that a settler could quickly make not only a first subsistence crop, but a marketable cash crop as well; and (3) the conviction that Texas might soon be free from Mexico, and under a new government providing both generous grants of land and exceptional opportunities.

Pleasant Gray himself had a role in the widening attention accorded Texas—not only in Huntsville, Alabama, but in other parts of the Yellowhammer State including Talladega, Montgomery and Macon County. The latter area, long a stronghold of the Abercrombie family, would soon send its first settlers to Texas. Sam Houston's influence, of course, was salient, pervasive and increasingly felt in a widening arc. Co-loh-neh had been named commander-in-chief of the Texian army (such as it was) on November 3, 1835. Now The Raven's pilgrimages and mysterious missions, concentrated in the southeast United States but ranging as far afield as New York City, began to pay off in financial support, sharply-increased immigration and volunteer militiamen.[9] There were those who pointed out that the influx of adventurers, fugitives and just plain rogue rapscallions was also markedly higher.

The fertile, alluvial soil in the best parts of the municipality of Washington, and elsewhere in south and southeast Texas-to-be, combined with an average growing season of almost three hundred days and adequate rainfall, made it possible for a settler to plant early and harvest enough for his own needs plus the market, even in a first season as a colonist. This advantage was enhanced substantially in Pleasant Gray's area by the port of Cincinnati, named in honor of their former home by settler-entrepreneurs from Ohio. This potential city would have a significant history, attenuated though it was to be.

Settlers could haul their corn, cotton or sorghum (in many cases less than a dozen miles) to Cincinnati, northeast of Huntsville on the Trinity, and send it most of the year to ready markets in Houston and Galveston on flatboats, barges or tiny steamboats. Even before 1840, the prospering Trinity River port had five blocks of wharves plus accompanying civic attributes and potential. It rapidly became both the export and import center for a wide swath of East Texas. You sent out cotton, corn and milo; but unbelievably, you could get back not only commonplace needs such as Barbados sugar and Louisiana rock salt (with a Galveston commission tacked on), but Hebrides woolens and Parisian bonnets.

The prospect of free land and widening opportunities under a new and more sympathetic government was a potent lure for prospective settlers. This was understandably much reinforced after Sam Houston's stunning victory over Santa Anna at San Jacinto on April 21, 1836.[10] Nor did the Texian officials, or those who succeeded them when statehood came nine years later, disappoint anyone in their willingness to parcel out the public lands, and thereby opportunity. The disposition of the enormously large public acreage may be an example of bureaucratic profligacy unmatched in history, helpful though it undoubtedly was in the development of Texas at the time. Here is the record:

The General Land Office in Austin shows that the public domain of Texas consisted originally of one hundred seventy million acres of surveyed land. This was far larger than the total extent of many major European nations at the time, but the Republic of Texas began the run on the land bank almost immediately by disposing of forty-eight million acres. This vast expanse went to stimulate immigration, reward the veterans of the War for Independence, pay the Republic's debts and finance governmental operations. Recognition of all Spanish and Mexican land grants, as stipulated by the constitution of 1845, swallowed another twenty-six million acres. An additional eleven million were allocated to construction of the vast State Capitol, with its walls of rough-hewn granite (cost: three million acres), other major building projects, further grants to veterans, and the sale of scrip.

When the railroads were alloted thirty-two million acres, the exchequer was technically down to fifty-three million; but adjustments, vacancies and the addition of the tidelands[11] brought the total back to fifty-nine million acres. At this point, an irrevocable grant of fifty-two million acres to public education, surely one of the more prudent decisions in the long and sometimes unfathomable history of the Texas Legislature, left the balance in the seven-million acre range, but ensured substantial and increasing support for Texans seeking education at any level from kindergarten through doctoral and professional degrees.

As Huntsville continued its substantial growth through the 1830s and into the next decade, it was quickly apparent that the frontier community would not be content with materialistic progress alone. This was obvious in the early and persistent emphasis upon churches, schools, newspapers and the overall quality of community life.

There were meetings of church groups in various Huntsville homes before Texas joined the Union in 1846, and the Cumberland Presbyterians built a first house of worship soon thereafter. Reverend A. J. McGown, a veteran of San Jacinto, was the Presbyterian pastor.[13] Baptist, Methodist and Episcopalian churches were built next, in that order.

A handsome private school, the so-called Brick Academy, was built by public subscription in 1845; two years later, a public school opened next to the Academy. Another private institution, the Huntsville Male Institute, began classes in 1848. Few Texans realize that one of their oldest and most distinguished institutions of higher education, Austin College, was chartered in Huntsville in 1849 and remained there until it was moved to Sherman. The graduates of Andrew Female College, established in 1853, were noted for both their comeliness and their ladylike deportment. One of their instructors was Miss Rowena Crawford, the future wife of Judge James A. Baker (whose son and namesake would save the endowment of The William Marsh Rice Institute after a sensational series of legal proceedings and serve five decades as first chairman of the board of trustees of what is now Rice University).

A first issue of the Montgomery (County) *Patriot* appeared on May 11, 1845, but was replaced by General Francis L. Hatch's *Banner* eight months later, and by the Huntsville *Item,* which was to become one of the state's oldest and best-regarded weeklies, in 1850. Huntsville had also one of the earliest church newspapers, the Texas (Cumberland) *Presbyterian* edited by the Reverend Mr. McGown, from 1850 to 1860.

It is true that the leading citizens of Huntsville (many of them from the early days bankers, experienced merchants and members of the professions) sought and demanded material progress. They constructed residences of the best lumber from William Wyser's sawmill, instead of log cabins, even in 1841; and they were building fairly large brick homes by 1846. But a central concern was the establishment of a way of life based upon tradition and gentility that they had known elsewhere, many of them in Alabama. They understood instinctively that this required an investment in the precious intangibles of human existence, rather than solely in what was tangibly measureable.

The way of life they sought was already apparent to some degree as the men in the families, and colonies, of new settlers rode into Huntsville ahead of the huge, overloaded, ox-drawn wagons. These men, readily distinguishable from frontier drifters, often rode on blooded horses. The wagons they escorted were packed with implements and tools, but also with fine pieces of furniture. In the chests of mahoghany were embroidered linens of exquisite design, and heavy silver.

Trudging behind the major wagon trains, as convincing evidence of a total commitment to the decision to move on irrevocably far to the west, were dozens of slaves and sometimes entire herds of cattle.

On a frontier where the average level of formal education was less than that offered in the solid, yet limited, curriculum of the grammar school, a considerable percentage of the new Huntsvilleans were professionals—attorneys, physicians and teachers. But professionals or not, they had been driven inexorably west by the dwindling opportunities and exhausted farmlands of the southeastern United States, a full decade and more before the cataclysm of the War Between the States. They brought with them invaluable training and experience, and assets that sometimes included private libraries rivaling, both in quality and in quantity, the sum of the books available in all of Montgomery County when it was organized in 1837.

After the immigrants of the 1830s and 1840s had reached the promised land of Huntsville, entire convoys pitched camp and began to recover from a journey usually encompassing seven or eight weeks, but as much as three months. The first inquiry, however, was for a guide to Galveston; there the womenfolk and children were waiting, having come down the Alabama rivers by packet to Mobile to await a big schooner or early-model steamboat making for Galvez Town.[14] Jean Lafitte's old headquarters was a good three hundred miles closer than the thriving Mexican port of Matamoros, even though far fewer vessels called at Galveston.

For a town barely past its tenth anniversary, 1845 was a signal year for Huntsville.

President John Tyler, under pressure from the incoming chief executive James K. Polk and the dying Andrew Jackson, had signed an annexation resolution on March 1, 1845—just three days before Polk took office. This was approved by the Congress of the Republic of Texas on June 21, and by the United States Congress on a date later established by the Supreme Court of the United States as December 29, 1845.

Of equal if not greater import in Huntsville itself (for Texans had first voted for annexation as early as 1836), was Sam Houston's decision to make his home there. After two terms as president of the Republic,[15] General Sam had drawn the plans for Raven Hill, a home fourteen miles east of Huntsville at Point Blank. The location was too isolated for the General, who was getting in too much whittling time and too little talking politics; for the countless stream of visitors who were barely surviving the stagecoach ride down from Nacogdoches, or up from Houston, without another fourteen miles of bouncing discomfort; and for Mrs. Margaret Lea, an ardent Baptist who wanted to be in the midst of friends and church at Huntsville, not at Point Blank. The Houstons moved in 1845 to what is now Sam Houston Park, in a little valley just south of the public square.

Also in 1845, it was decided that Montgomery County (from which was finally carved out portions of six other Texas counties) was simply too big. Under terms of an act of the State Legislature, much of the northern reaches of Montgomery would be made into Walker County. There was immediate competition among several towns, including Huntsville, Cincinnati and Waverly, requesting the designation as county seat.

As a practical matter, the competition was virtually over before it was launched. Pleasant and Hannah Gray ''sold'' more than an acre of land for use as a public square and the site of the Walker County courthouse for one cent. The land was in the immediate vicinity of their original log cabin home. Pleasant and his brother Ephraim had earlier laid out the four principal streets bounding the square: Cedar (Eleventh Street today), Main (University Avenue), Spring (Twelfth) and Andrew Jackson (Sam Houston Avenue) with rudimentary surveying instruments. Now the streets were widened and graded.

When a committee raised $1750 in cash toward the construction of the first Walker County courthouse (which unfortunately had to be torn down a few years later because of a defective foundation), and voters all over the county began to recall Huntsville's early emphasis upon education, churches and other intangible values plus the town's importance as a center for area business and transportation, there was no question as to where the county seat would be located.

Once the courthouse battle was won, civic pride and good works continued to multiply. The Grays were in the forefront, donating land for several of the earlier churches, for Austin College and for the original Oakwood Cemetery. A committee was even formed to seek the removal of the temporary state capital from Austin to Huntsville, since the constitution of 1845 mandated an election to determine the permanent capital ten years after annexation. This campaign, however, was lost.

We have an indication of early land values in Huntsville, incidentally, from a deed wherein Pleasant and Hannah Gray purchased "a Negro wench by name Keziah (or Kesiah)" from General Hatch, publisher of the *Banner,* for one hundred eighty-one acres of land in an area known as Smede Park on the south boundary of the P. Gray League. Keziah, presumably acquired to help with Hannah's increasing duties as mistress of a six-person household without the manifold benefits of electricity, gadgets, supermarkets or flash-frozen dinners, was valued at $600. This works out to $3.31 per acre. This same piece of land, now part of Sam Houston Park, was sold by General Hatch to Sam Houston in 1844.

Huntsville, Alabama and indeed much of the Yellowhammer State had maintained strengthening ties with the sister town in Texas, and with communities such as Cincinnati and Waverly in the Huntsville area. The Alabama branch of the Abercrombie family, at Cross Keys in Macon County, had many friends who had emigrated to Huntsville and to Waverly.

In the late 1840s, just as much of Alabama was beginning to experience increasing economic woes and the first indications of the eventual collapse of a way of life based upon (once) inexpensive, fertile land and a slave economy, two Abercrombies from Cross Keys, John Comer and Charles Anderson, decided to leave Macon County for Texas.

John Comer Abercrombie (the middle name was for his mother, Sarah Comer, a member of another distinguished Revolutionary War family who had married the first Leonard Abercrombie in 1804 in the old Abercrombie home in Hancock County, Georgia) was born in 1808 in Hancock County. He came to Alabama in 1834 with his father and his uncle, General Anderson Abercrombie. A cotton planter and accomplished horseman, he had also followed the family tradition of military service, and became a colonel in the Alabama militia before marrying Jane Minerva Sims in 1842.

In 1847, Colonel Abercrombie had three children, and another on the way, after five years of marriage. There was the prospect of a considerably larger family, but his share of the Cross Keys estates was not bringing in the increasing income he foresaw that he would need. Further, John Comer's brother, Milo Bolling, had married in his early twenties. His wife, Sarah Lee Haden, had already borne Bolling thirteen children (five of them dead at birth or as infants), and was still of child-bearing age. There were many demands on Cross Keys, and it was not likely that they would lessen.

John Abercrombie had noticed with deepening interest that a number of his planter friends, following the early settler James W. Winters, were buying rich alluvial land at about $2 an acre near Waverly, in the deep southeast corner of Walker County some fifteen miles from Huntsville, Texas. This was reported to be cotton country, with a long, hot, humid spring, summer and early fall; good rainfall; and an easy market haul to nearby river landings on the Trinity, or on to the thriving port of Cincinnati above Huntsville.

Colonel Abercrombie decided to make the difficult journey to Texas by horseback, to see for himself how true the glowing reports from emigrating friends really were. He evidently liked what he saw, because he began planning a move to Texas as soon as he returned to Alabama. In 1850, he arrived at Waverly with wife Jane Minerva; Levi (Lem), eight; Sally, six; John, Jr., three; and the baby Carolina, two. She would be called Carrie.

The Abercrombies had come over the longer but more comfortable land route through New Orleans, fortunately before the 1851 cholera epidemic which would claim the lives of their emigrating friends Hamlin Lewis, John Elliott Scott, John Lindsay Scott and many accompanying family slaves. Less than twenty years earlier, Irish colonists headed for Refugio and San Patricio de Hibernia had been decimated by an earlier outbreak of cholera in the Louisiana capital.

A letter awaited the Abercrombies at Waverly. Bolling and Sarah had their fifteenth and last child, a boy named James Buford Abercrombie, II. It was joyful news indeed, after three little sons in succession had been stillborn.[16] James Buford, II was Jim Abercrombie's father, who would come to Huntsville as a young man to join the Texas branch of the clan Abercrombie.

There was further news. The younger brother Charles Anderson, lacking much of Colonel John's commanding presence and initiative, would soon be enroute to Waverly with his childless wife Malinda; but he asked for any additional information concerning their new home. A few months later, he did arrive with Malinda. They would spend almost the next forty years living quietly on Walker County farms, first on the outskirts of Waverly, and then near Harmon Creek in the eastern portion of the county. Charles Anderson Abercrombie, II, a nephew and namesake who was to be the eighth and last of John Comer's children, was a roughneck and driller in the Houston area as early as 1897. He would give James S. Abercrombie, his cousin, Mr. Jim's first job in the Oil Patch, in 1908.

Still to join the Texas Abercrombie contingent was a most significant addition who was still a teenager back in Cross Keys in 1850. This was Milo Bolling's first son and John Comer's nephew, Leonard Anderson Abercrombie. Born December 1, 1832, he was destined for a brilliant career as an attorney, senator, banker and Confederate officer.

The first time he could get into Huntsville after arriving in Waverly, Colonel Abercrombie carried out a sad duty. He called on Hannah Gray to express his condolences. For some still unexplained reason, Pleasant Gray had left his prospering town of almost five hundred souls and his family one day in 1848 bound for the California gold rush, on horseback. He died enroute somewhere near Santa Fe—some say of a fever, others of a powerful curse called down upon him by a shaman for having ridden off west on the best horse of a Coushatta chieftain.

Colonel Abercrombie would never have cause to regret his coming to Walker County, if we examine the 1860 census report for the Huntsville area. It indicates that in a short ten years he had amassed real estate worth $41,650. Unless the colonel was trying to impress the census taker (one C. H. Murray), he must have acquired a great deal of land. The best acreage was going for up to $10, although good land was available at $4 an acre and the average cost was around $2.50. With the influx of settlers and an enormous increase in the number of slaves in Montgomery and Walker counties from 1850 to 1860 (from slightly more than twenty-one hundred to almost four thousand), the production of cotton had risen spectacularly. Statewide, the jump was from 58,072 to 431,463 bales of five-hundred pound weight. Prosperity was not only in sight; it was everywhere you looked.

Then suddenly it was 1861, Abraham Lincoln had been elected president without a single official vote being tallied for him in Texas, and Sam Houston was removed as governor of the state for refusing to take an oath of allegiance to the Confederacy. Life in Huntsville, Texas—and for that matter, anywhere in the United States—would never be the same again.

Houston's abrupt removal from office was a telling blow for the hero of San Jacinto, who had just celebrated his sixty-eighth birthday. He had sat stubbornly on the portico of the Executive Mansion in Austin while the Secession Convention duly noted his absence, declared his office vacant and rejected him that early afternoon of March 16, 1861.

President of the Republic of Texas for five years, and United States senator from February 21, 1846 to March 4, 1859, he had won the governorship from Hardin R. Runnels (a former supporter) in a bitter campaign that raged across the state. Now, as he was turned out of the office, he told a reporter with gallows humor, "Well, they didn't get a greenhorn, anyhow."

The emotional, war-thirsty Secession Convention probably reminded ex-Governor Houston of his description of Governor Runnels' campaign manager during the 1859 campaign: "That fellow," he charged, "has all the characteristics of a hound dog. Except fidelity."

Sam Houston had predicted coming tragedy, in a brilliant and courageous speech at Galveston. In the maelstrom of criticism that followed, he was threatened with assassination. "Let me tell you," he warned, "what is coming. Your fathers and husbands, your sons and brothers, will be herded at the point of the bayonet." Southern independence, he said, might be gained by the "sacrifice of countless millions of treasure and hundreds of thousands of lives," but victory was a "bare possibility." "Much as I believe in states' rights," he concluded, "the North is determined to preserve the Union . . . when they begin to move (it will be with) . . . the steady momentum and perseverance of a mighty avalanche . . . What I fear is, they will overwhelm the South."

General Sam went home from Austin (a town, he noted, originally named Waterloo) to Huntsville. He and Margaret had sold the

Smede Park property to finance campaign debts; now they leased the "Steamboat House," an architectural curiosity near old Oakwood Cemetery. The general had but two more years of his extraordinary life to live, surrounded by his loving wife and his young children. Only Sam, Jr. was old enough to enlist, and enlist he did without protest from his father, who visited him with pride at Galveston. The old soldier was asked to review young Sam's unit, the Second Texas Infantry Regiment; this he did with some foreboding, for he had learned that the regiment would soon be ordered to the front, in Mississippi.

Sam Houston died at Steamboat House on July 26, 1863. His last words, just at sunset, are said to have been "Texas . . . Texas . . . Margaret." He was buried in a heavy rain on July 28 at old Oakwood, after a guard of honor including Colonel John Abercrombie had brought the coffin to the gravesite near a huge live oak.

The day was full of omens: the newspapers had the first full accounts of two grievous Confederate losses occurring almost at the same time, at Vicksburg and at Gettysburg. The capture of Vicksburg literally cut the Confederacy in two. General Robert E. Lee's shattering defeat in Pennsylvania was an even worse development for the South. Lee's invading forces had inflicted heavy losses upon the Union forces, but after regrouping in Virginia, their own casualties were reckoned at more than twenty thousand. Too many Southern infantrymen had died in Union counterattacks and devastating artillery fire at Cemetery Ridge. A spearhead of Lee's men had gained the top of the ridge on raw courage, but they were quickly killed or captured. The fate of the Confederacy was sealed, in spite of two more years of gallant effort and increasing sacrifice and loss.

In contrast to other states both North and South, Texas suffered comparatively little in the loss of property or lives during the war years of 1861–1865. Certainly there was not the anguish of a Georgia, with countless plantations and entire towns—even cities, devastated; or anything approaching the human losses in Alabama, where one hundred twenty-five thousand served in the Confederate ranks and thirty-five thousand (twenty-eight percent) died in addition to the maimed and the wounded.

The height of 1926 fashion, cloche hat and all, at Myrtle Bank.

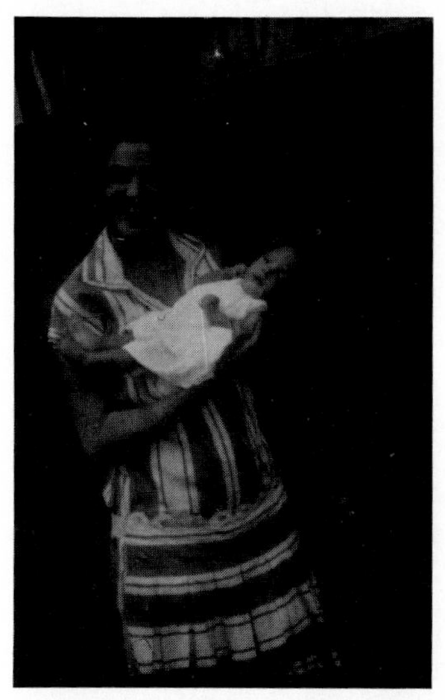

Josephine and Miss Lillie before leaving Kingston via motorboat.

Bringing the rigs and equipment for the Colombian expedition through the Panama Canal.

On the verandah overlooking the Myrtle Bank gardens.

The Flora burns out of control at Spindletop.

Goose Creek.

Mr. Jim at Hull, of blowouts and bad luck.

Humble.

West Columbia.

Conroe.

Wildcatting in Colombia

A native fishing village near Puerto Escondido, center for unloading operations.

Burro power for Mr. Jim at Montería.

Leaving on horseback for the Tubara lease.

Jim and Milo, spudding in at Tubara.

Christmas dinner out of cans at Lorencita, 1925.

The Owen #3 at Lorencita, near the Sinu River.

Cartagena, Colombia

Miss Lillie shops for baskets in the Cartagena market, 1925.

Ancient San Fernando Castle, at the harbor of Cartagena.

Milo, Bob and Bob, Jr. with a friend, on a Sunday outing in Cartagena.

The Little Grandmother (Josephine Mitchell Wood) and six great-grandchildren at 3402 Audubon for the traditional family Sunday dinner, in 1930. Left to right (back row): Bob Abercrombie, Jr.; Mrs. (W. B.) Wood; and Max Rotholz, Jr., Lavinia (Vinnie) Abercrombie Rotholz' son; (front row): the twins, Bolling, Jr. and John, Bolling Abercrombie's sons; Joe Dick, Joe Rice Abercrombie's son; and Josephine, Mr. Jim and Miss Lillie's only child, named for her great-grandmother and grandmother.

The Cameron-Davant Company's branch at Humble in 1918. Armed soldier on guard because the company was machining parts for the government under War Industries Board contracts.

Harry Cameron and Mr. Jim at 711 Milby in 1920. Note three-piece suit and natty hat.

Harry Cameron poses with the entire 1922 Cameron Iron Works product line.

The machine shop in 1925, with new warehouse addition. The pick-up and delivery fleet includes Mr. Jim's reliable Dodge touring car and a surplus World War I truck, both parked outside.

Daniel Jefferson Harrison and James Smither Abercrombie of Harrison and Abercrombie, the effective, powerful, synergistic quasi-partnership.

Cartoons courtesy of John R. Suman, Jr.

George Strake, who discovered the great Conroe field, points with dismay to the H(arrison) & A(bercrombie) #1, which cratered after adjoining wells owned by Standard of Kansas blew out of control. The Alexander #1 was spouting 10,000 barrels of oil a day, threatening the entire Conroe field, before Humble Oil's John R. Suman, aided by his own engineering staff, Jim Abercrombie and Harrison and Abercrombie crews, came to the rescue. Suman brought in John Eastman, whose new technique of directional drilling saved the day.

Those are crocodile tears being shed by Jim Abercrombie and Dan Harrison. The Humble Oil team of Suman, Eastman and Scott is triumphant over killing the wild Alexander #1, but Jim and Dan have more than a flooded well. They have $300,000 in cash for their lease, and about $3 million in crude oil trapped in a giant crater and channeled into a nearby pipeline.

The J. S. Abercrombie home at 2221 River Oaks Boulevard, where Mr. Jim, Miss Lillie and Josephine moved in 1937. The picture was taken just after Houston's rare and spectacular snowfall of January 19,1940.

Miss Lillie's home at 421 Broad Street, the showplace of its time in Lake Charles.

Holiday decor at 2221 River Oaks for the traditional and memorable annual Christmas party, which spilled over in time to huge tents in the back yard.

The Saga of Mustang Motte

So, now is come Jim's Cuero hunt; Will Blackwell's birds are ready. And hitting them is quite a stunt, so let your aim be steady. Put on your finest hunting hat, just for Blalock to shoot at, He'll keep on shooting 'til it's flat. So come, let's all hunt quail.

Get up, now oil that blunderbuss, and load it with those nine shot. Don't dally or Milo'll surely cuss. Drink that coffee while it's hot. Jim wants us out before sunrise, he won't take no alibis from you or any other guys. Though it's dark, we'll still hunt quail.

Herman, show Chad old Polly's point, don't let Ernest wipe our eye. Bill Smith may creak in every joint, but for one shot he might try. Well now, let Pete get that dead bird, Suman shot o'er Will's prize herd while old Cumming was a poor third. It's late, so let's kill those quail.

Bob's big-talking in Mustange Motte; Naurice just bought one more ranch. Those two yak-e-ti-yak a lot, ain't none here who them can stanch. There's champagne, scotch and bourbon too, barbecue beef and darn good stew; Watch Sayles' Leach, he sure can chew. Drop that drink, and let's hunt quail.

Reiffert takes us where aint no quail, and yet we hard shots don't fret; just turn out King, he'll never fail, we'll bet Jim and Ernest yet. Lorehn put on his Sunday look, guess he wants his picture took. You bet he hopes it's in The Book. Let's go home; Will's out of quail.

E. D. Cumming

The "charter" of Mustang Motte, locus of the annual quail shoot that began on the Blackwell Ranch at Cuero in 1938, by the poet laureate of the shoot, Ed Cumming, senior vice-president of Shell Oil and one of the most popular men in the Oil Patch.

Jim gives Elwood Fouts the game plan before the climactic Texas Railroad Commission hearing of February 20, 1939 on Old Ocean: ''You and Joe Moore be fair, but plenty tough. How can they cut back the allowable on a field where we've lost $2,648,903 in five years?''

The Abercrombie Engineering Laboratory at what was then Rice Institute, planned and built with a $500,000 gift from Mr. Jim, Miss Lillie and Josephine.

Edmond L. Lorehn (right) is congratulated by Rear Admiral William H. P. Blandy, chief of the Bureau of Ordnance, United States Navy, after accepting Navy ''E'' Award for Cameron Iron Works in Washington, D.C. on July 25, 1941.

Test firing at sea of twenty-millimeter Oerlikon gun equipped with Cameron Iron hydraulic mounts.

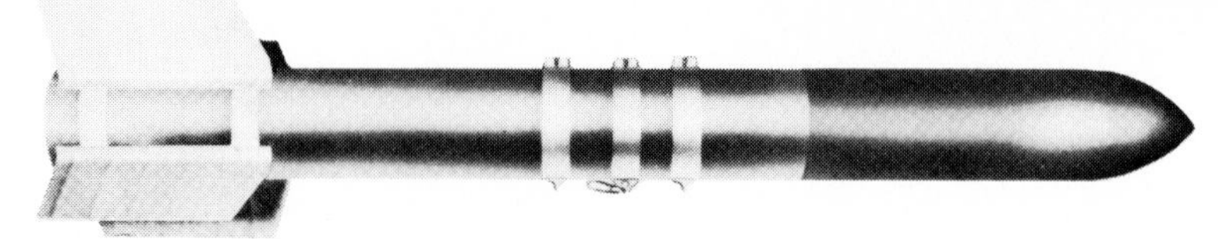

Cameron Iron produced thousands of these ''Tiny Tim'' rockets for Navy fighter planes.

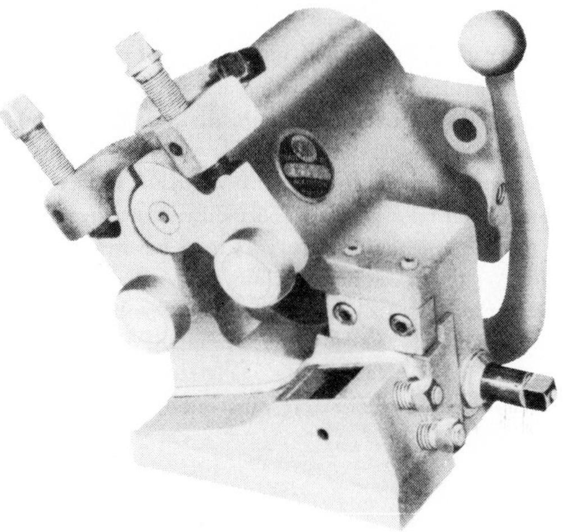

A roller turner, high-priority part for turret lathes needed throughout the nation, produced by CIW under sub-contracts.

A CIW ''K-gun,'' the deadly anti-submarine weapon, with arbor and depth charge loaded and ready for firing.

Actual battlegrounds in Texas were spectacularly few and far between. Galveston was lost to Union forces for three months in the fall of 1862, but was retaken by General John B. Magruder on New Year's Day, 1863. Nine months later, five thousand men on Union gunboats moved determinedly on Sabine Pass, only to be repulsed somehow by a tiny force of the Texas Navy commanded by the Irish hero and Houston saloonkeeper, Dick Dowling. General Nathaniel P. Banks brought Union troops as far as Natchitoches in early April of 1864, but was defeated by Confederate cavalry under General Richard Taylor before reaching Texas soil. Finally, Colonel John C. Ford captured eight hundred surprised Northern soldiers at Resaca de las Palmas, near Brownsville, on May 13, 1865, only to learn that Robert E. Lee had surrendered at Appomattox Courthouse five weeks earlier. The Union troops, who had infiltrated from Mexico to stage sporadic raids on the border, were trying to find their way home after being told in Matamoros that the war was over.

Nevertheless, the war was felt most keenly in Huntsville, Texas, which was essentially a copy of an ante-bellum town in the Deep South in 1861. People throughout Walker and Montgomery counties had deep and remaining ties with Alabama in particular, but also with the other southern states which had sent settlers and colonists to Texas. Montgomery, the capital of the Confederacy, was less than twenty miles from the Abercrombie plantations at Cross Keys, Alabama. Chickamauga, where thirty-four thousand men were killed and wounded in a climactic battle to control Chattanooga, was just over the Tennessee border from Huntsville, Alabama.

The Huntsville (Alabama) Volunteers who had come to help in the Texian War for Independence in 1835 and 1836 were still well remembered, and young men of their sister city in Texas felt a keen obligation to enlist in similar units. Most of the fourth and fifth regiments of the Texas Infantry, CSA were recruited in Walker County for service with General John B. Hood's famed Texas Brigade, which fought with great distinction in the Army of Northern Virginia. The Texans found, however, that it was not just as General Louis T. Wigfall had told an enthusiastic meeting in Huntsville. "Why you fellas," he is reported to have said, "could whip those Yankees with cornstalks."

Huntsville recruits with Alabama connections found that the flickers of Texas were the same as Alabama yellowhammers. They plucked a tail feather from these birds to wear in their campaign hats, just as their cousins in the Yellowhammer State.

Benjamin Franklin Terry's legendary Texas Rangers, organized in Houston at the beginning of the war, also drew many Walker County men to the colors. This unit was the famed 8th Texas Cavalry, CSA which kept Terry's name even though the fiery leader was killed in an early series of battles in Tennessee and Kentucky in the fall of 1861.

Colonel John Abercrombie, kept from active duty by his age and the critical need to increase cotton production, saw his nineteen-year-old Lem off late in 1861 to a war from which he would never return. Margaret Houston wrote Sam, Jr. of Lem's death while serving with Hood's Brigade. She added the names of nine other of her son's "friends and classmates," all from prominent families, who had been killed. She mentioned that "old Mrs. Thomas" had lost five sons. This was probably Mrs. Leroy Thomas, who came to the "Trinity landing area" from Selma, Alabama in 1854 with her husband and fourteen children.[17]

Leonard Anderson Abercrombie, twenty-eight years of age when the war broke out, had completed his law studies ("reading Blackstone") with Chief Justice W. P. Chilton of the Alabama Supreme Court. He married the justice's daughter Lavinia on New Year's Day, 1860 at Talladega, Alabama, and the new couple set out for Huntsville after a brief honeymoon. Leonard immediately launched a long and successful career as an attorney, after learning to his surprise that Austin College had already opened the first law school in Texas. The career was quickly interrupted when the young lawyer accepted an appointment in General Magruder's brigade, where he rose rapidly to the rank of lieutenant colonel of infantry.

On his third wedding anniversary, Colonel Abercrombie was in command of the brigade infantry unit as General Magruder recaptured Galveston and brought his Yankee prisoners back to the new state penitentiary in Huntsville. Typically, Leonard Abercrombie was always quick to point out that his infantrymen took no active role in the battle, which was waged solely by the brigade artillery regiment. Most men would have claimed escalating credit for the victory, finally staking out the title of liberator of Galveston and environs.

Finally, the war was over. The people of Huntsville, grieving over both their own losses and the casualty lists and accounts of fearful destruction in the heartland of the Confederacy, began slowly to rebuild their lives. Recovery was not easy, and it was complicated terribly by a calamitous yellow fever epidemic that struck in 1867.

Huntsville had escaped yellow fever when the dread disease, transmitted by the droves of *Aedes aegypti* mosquitoes in nearby marshes, literally wiped out the prospering port of Cincinnati in 1853. Now, fourteen years later, it was brought back by a passenger on the stagecoach from Navasota who fell ill at the Sims Hotel. Already evidencing the classic symptoms of high fever and yellowing of the eyes from destruction of liver cells, he died five days later. From early August until late October, when the first sharp norther killed off the mosquito crop and brought the epidemic under control, an estimated one hundred fifty persons died in Huntsville and the surrounding area.

Entire families simply fled not only Huntsville, but neighboring counties as well. Others burned foul-smelling smudges and heated their incoming mail in an oven. One treatment for the disease, widely recommended, involved staying in bed under heavy blankets, mustard foot baths and chest poultices, castor oil and absolute rest. An alternate procedure was based upon bathing the back with kerosene and the administration of choloroform and carbolic acid.

Among those who succumbed to yellow fever, controllable today only through the eradication of virus-bearing mosquitoes or the administration of vaccines made from live virus, was Margaret Houston. A resident of Independence since 1865, she had come in from the family summer home at Cedar Point on Galveston Bay to serve as a volunteer nurse.[18] Three physicians and a number of nurses also died, but basic medical care and round-the-clock nursing to reduce fever saved hundreds of patients. Once recovered, they had gained one boon: lifelong immunity from yellowjack, as the disease was called. The victims, most of them resting forever in Oakwood, ranged from members of the best-known families to convicts, federal prisoners and freed slaves who had refused to leave their former masters after Lincoln's Emancipation Proclamation.

The beginnings of real recovery, then, were delayed until almost 1870. At this point, the innate strengths of Huntsville came again to the fore: a stable, responsible community willing to establish and maintain essential values; a core of competent, energetic professional and business leaders; proficient farmers and artisans; an excellent location; and a long tradition of getting along together.

The tradition of a peaceful and cohesive community became more and more significant in the Reconstruction era, when some towns and cities, and even entire states, in the Deep South were under martial law. It must have been extremely difficult, for example, for a onetime staff officer in the Army of Northern Virginia to look up from the plow he was awkwardly guiding for the first time in his life, and see his former mulatto field hand departing for his new post as a member of the State Legislature. Or to have armed black guards at the polling places on election day. This and more came to pass in Huntsville, but the town's sturdy social and economic fabric was able to repair itself.

With a far more difficult situation in Alabama, additional members of the Abercrombie clan began to emigrate to Huntsville, where Colonel John Abercrombie continued to be a leading citizen, and his nephew Leonard's star was constantly on the rise. Throughout Alabama, there was widespread remaining destruction, and even chaos, along with martial law; federal troops would remain in the state until 1876. In Huntsville, there was good order, a recovering market for cotton, and both part- and full-time jobs at the state penitentiary, which was already developing into a national model for agricultural as well as manufacturing production at a correctional institution.[19]

One of the first new emigres was James Buford Abercrombie, II, Leonard Abercrombie's much younger brother and Colonel John's nephew. The last of fifteen children, his mother had died when he was barely three, in 1853. His father, Milo Bolling Abercrombie, who had continued to manage the Cross Keys properties after the departure of his brothers for Texas, married another Sarah: Sarah G. Greenleaf of Boston. They were to have four children, all born at Cross Keys between 1855 and 1858.

The following year, Milo Bolling died, scant months before the outbreak of the War Between the States. James Buford, only ten, was raised by his older brothers and sisters of the whole blood, and by the numerous slaves on the Abercrombie plantation; his stepmother and her children (Daniel Webster, Bolling, Winona and Talulah, with one ''l'') went back to Massachusetts and lived out their lives there and elsewhere in New England. Daniel Webster Abercrombie, later a Phi Beta Kappa graduate of Harvard College, was headmaster of the prestigious Worcester Academy from 1882 until 1918.

In Huntsville, J. B. (as he was called far more frequently than James or Jim) worked with his uncle until Colonel John died in 1877. He had in the meantime taken a job with the Texas Prison System, where he was eventually promoted to the very responsible position of superintendent of farms.

J. B. Abercrombie had been calling on Lina Wood, the daughter of a prominent Huntsville family, for some time. He was welcomed on Sunday afternoons at the Wood home, and escorted Miss Lina along the board sidewalks (which could have broken boards to stumble into in the dark without a strong man's supporting arm) after evening socials. They went on picnics to Harmon Creek with their friends and to occasional plays staged by touring companies of actors. After many months, J. B. and Lina were seen attending the local St. Stephens Episcopal Church together, this being regarded as a penultimate step in Huntsville's tradition of courting. Their friend, the Reverend Jeremiah Ward, was the Episcopalian priest, but he was transferred to Grace Episcopal Church in Galveston because the small congregation he served in Huntsville found it difficult to maintain him and his family. The Reverend Mr. Ward, however, kept his former flock well in mind, and made frequent visits to Walker County as marriage records will attest. On November 27, 1879, he came back to Huntsville to marry James Buford Abercrombie, II and Miss Lina Wood.

For Leonard Anderson Abercrombie, 1879 was also a signal year. He was elected to the State Senate while practicing law with Judge James A. Baker, another of the coterie of eminent lawyers increasingly gathered at Huntsville. He and other community leaders had been much disturbed by a post-war decision of the Presbyterian Church to move Austin College to Sherman, and they decided to do something about it.

The decision to move Austin College, chartered a full generation before what its more chauvinistic graduates term "The University," was irrevocable. Colonel Abercrombie had learned from Colonel George W. Grant, however, of a proposal from the George Peabody Education Foundation to the Texas Legislature. The Peabody trustees would make a major contribution toward a teacher's college of the first class, if the legislators were willing to establish such an institution by statute and operate it.

With key assistance from Colonels Grant and Charles Stewart, and from Judge J. R. Burnett, Senator Abercrombie saw the enabling act through the Legislature, Governor Oran M. Roberts (a staunch supporter of higher education) signed it, and the Sam Houston Normal Institute, now Sam Houston State University, was a reality.[20]

In the same year of 1879, one of Huntsville's most distinguished contributions to the upcoming century of new Texas leadership, a student at Sam Houston as the 1800s came to an end, was born. He was James A. Elkins, the son of A. J. Elkins, the sheriff of Walker County who lived west of New Waverly in precinct five.[21]

Walker County continued its economic recovery in the last quarter of the nineteenth century, after a serious blow when the International & Great Northern (IGN) railroad by-passed the county seat by locating the main line seven miles southwest of Huntsville at Phelps, in 1872.

This was remedied somewhat when a "tap" line was constructed down from Huntsville, with connections by stagecoach. When IGN was unable to obtain right-of-way to extend its line south through Waverly, however, a relocation ten miles to the west sounded the death knell for John Abercrombie's little town, a stronghold of the more prosperous planters from Alabama since its founding in 1835. The freeing of the slaves who had planted, cultivated and harvested the huge cotton crops had already dealt a severe blow to Waverly. When the IGN established its new station ten miles to the west, people began to move there almost at once. The station became New Waverly and the original settlement became a ghost town. Colonel John lived only a few more years, but they were increasingly difficult ones for him and for the other big planters in the area, who watched a way of life come to an end.

J. B. and Lina Abercrombie were to have thirteen children, three of whom died at birth or during infancy. Will was the first-born, arriving during Christmas week of 1880. Then came Ella and Bolling. Jamie Smither, the fourth child, was born on July 7, 1891. The middle name was either for Major Robert Goodloe Smither, pioneer member of a large and prominent family, or his brother, Judge James L. Smither. The Smithers were Episcopalians, founding members of St. Stephen's Church, friends of both the Abercrombie and Wood families, and related to half of Huntsville.

We know a great deal about how Jamie Smither Abercrombie and his contemporaries must have perceived Huntsville, where he spent the first nine years of his life from 1891 to 1900 and first attended school. This is primarily because of a gifted writer, born less than two years after Jamie, who took time from a splendid career in the Marine Corps to paint his beloved hometown in glowing, intensely human word-pictures that capture the moment and then live on. Here is how Huntsville, Texas was at the turn of the century, in excerpt and paraphrase, from Colonel John W. Thomason, Jr.'s essay entitled "Huntsville," in the April 1934 issue of the *Southwest Review*[22]:

> The town, grown like all southwest towns around a central square, spread its wide shady streets over the wooded hills. The houses were low and white, with wide verandas where one sat to taste the Gulf breeze in the cool of the evenings . . . Here were peach orchards, grown from seedlings brought out of beloved (Alabama) gardens . . . and the mockingbirds sang in the pear trees all the moonlit nights . . . Here the young gentlemen rode blooded horses, and there was good horseflesh on the roads . . . The family Sunday drive was in a surrey or carriage . . . Huntsville remained sleepy and contemplative, with its schools at each end of a mile-long street, and many churches in between . . . The old and pleasant ways remained; young gentlemen "waited" on young ladies, or paid them court with bouquet and serenade.
>
> Saloons were passed with averted face, and small boys strictly enjoined to stay away from the wagon yard, especially on Saturdays . . . Dining rooms of old silver and gleaming wood, with as many as twenty seated, and the pickaninnies waving chinaberry branches against flies and mosquitoes . . . The fragrant smokehouse and the barns, with a great woodpile to heat the entire house . . . the smell of leather and sweat and polish in the harness room and the wise, patient horses in the stalls . . . My gray pony Nellie; and Daisy, the blooded saddle mare; the tall bays that drew the carriage; the big mules, stolid and obstinate.
>
> (And I remember) driving the cows to pasture amid the low-flying, redheaded woodpeckers; the blue darters; the bluejays and flickers in tall trees; the sharp-shinned hawks, killers all . . . Hunting as soon as you could hold a gun, and the wild, V-formed geese in the fly-bys of late fall and early winter, honking relentlessly . . . Murmurous tall pines . . . my

> pony's hooves silent on fragrant, fallen needles . . . thickets of wild plum, tall corn, rows of cotton marching off like the files of an infantry battalion.
>
> The Negroes—there were always Negroes: Aunt Sue Semmes, who alone cooked my game; Uncle Ed, born in slavery in Alabama; Elbert, the small, spry old carpenter (who suffered from young, flighty wives); Lafayette (LAY-FAT) Williams, who resolved to name a child for each president (whereby Garfield Cleveland McKinley Williams as Lafayette grew older but still short of his goal); Aunt Jane Ward, levying on her white folks for the Juneteenth; and still an annual dinner for all the former slaves . . . A compliment to my mother: 'Miss Sue, I do declah, you treats us as good as if you was a niggah yo'sef.'

We know, too, of those early days in Huntsville that Jamie Abercrombie was a hardworking, serious youngster, respectful of his father but considerably closer to his mother and maternal grandmother (Mrs. Josephine (Josie) Wood, wife of William B. Wood), with a precocious, ingrained sense of the need for the family to stay close together. He was fond of hunting and of wandering for miles over Pleasant Gray's prairies and rolling, pine-clad hills in search of quail and whitewing. Yet he was one to seek out odd jobs such as cutting firewood, or helping with farm chores, or earning other small sums sweeping out the stores and offices on the public square. Perhaps there was a premonition that he would have to accept a leadership role within the family at an early age. If so, Nature was clearly cooperating. Tall for his years and well-muscled, Jamie appeared at eight to be ten, and at ten to be a teenager. His quiet, confident demeanor also belied his years, and seemed to move Jamie toward premature responsibilities.

The Huntsville public school system which Jamie attended was clearly the best in Walker County and demonstrably superior to most such systems in Texas at the time, thanks to Huntsville's long tradition of excellence in education. There were, unbelievably, seventy-five public schools in the county in 1900; the overall scholastic population was four thousand eighty-five, or twenty-six percent of the total population, distributed over fourteen school districts plus Huntsville itself; about half the students were black.

Most so-called "intermediate" schools in Walker County had only six grades, but a few had added a seventh. These included Crabb's Prairie, Black Jack, Pleasant Ridge, Hawthorne, Bath (formerly 'Possum Walk), and three negro (colored, in the idiom of 1900) schools, at Galilee, Rosa and Jasper. Public education from the eighth through the eleventh grades was available only in Huntsville.

Classes usually began in late September, after most of the cotton crop was picked, and concluded in March before spring planting. The schools in Huntsville, however, had advanced the school term to seven months before 1900. In contrast to institutions over the county, some of which taught all classes in one room, there was a small library, running water and individual desks in most Huntsville schools, but no such modern, newfangled notions as indoor plumbing, air conditioning, cafeterias or athletic programs. The boys amused themselves at recess by fighting, shooting marbles, playing mumbledy-peg or watching the girls; the girls amused themselves by gossiping, playing hide-and-seek or watching the boys.

Sometime about 1900, the J. B. Abercrombie family came upon hard times. There had been devastating freezes in both the winters of 1898 and of 1899, followed ironically by a boll weevil infestation of the cotton fields that cut the 1899 crop by fifty percent. It had taken the weevil, which attacks the boll or pod of the cotton plant, seven years to work its way up from Mexico.

Walker County had a population of 15,813 in 1900, but less than 2,500 lived in Huntsville itself; this was still a heavily rural county, and when half the cotton crop was lost, things were immediately bad. The new oil mill was in trouble because there was a shortage of cottonseed to crush; the price of timber, a traditional source of additional income for farmers, was off sharply; the rock quarry was shutting down until construction picked up.

Soon, there were layoffs in the penitentiary farm system, and even the position of superintendent became insecure.

J. B. Abercrombie had come to depend upon his uncle John for advice and assistance in the early days when he first came to Huntsville as a young man. When Colonel John died, he sought out his older brother Leonard (eighteen years his senior) who had become probably Huntsville's leading citizen before moving to Houston for new successes as an attorney and businessman. Now Leonard was gone, dead in a Philadelphia hospital at the relatively young age of fifty-nine, and buried in Oakwood Cemetery.

Pretty much on his own, with a wife and nine children to support, J. B. felt that he had to make a move. Perhaps, he reasoned, he could find security back on a farm. He had heard of the possibility of raising and processing tobacco just north of Willis, at a little town called Esperanza which also had a sawmill, tobacco barns and a large gin. The unusual name came about when the founder, William F. Spiller, had first decided to call his settlement Ada, only to discover from the postmaster general that there already was an Ada, Texas. Under postal regulations, there would have to be a change.

Spiller's partner, Colonel Julius Oppenheimer, wanted to make it Spillerville, but they agreed on Esperanza (the Spanish word for hope) because their innovative plans were based upon the hope of launching a new industry: growing and processing Cuban tobacco, and manufacturing fine cigars from it.

The scheme showed some promise after sturdy tobacco plants were raised from seed brought from Havana. A cigar factory was built, and production actually started; but problems in processing the Cuban leaf and very high freight rates caused the entire operation to be abandoned.

J. B. Abercrombie was among many farmers at Esperanza, and in the nearby Willis area, who had depended upon a combination of the innovative crop of Cuban tobacco (the prized Vuelta Abajo variety), and yields of more prosaic cotton, corn and grain for income. Suddenly, there was no market for tobacco leaf, and early symptoms of what would deepen into the Panic of 1903 had seriously depressed all agricultural prices. The 1902 cotton crop, for example, brought in less than eight cents a pound, or an average of $38 per bale. Cottonseed fell to fourteen cents a pound, and prices for corn and grains were correspondingly low. Even the sources of small, but important day-to-day cash income were drastically affected: eggs sold for a penny each, butter for twenty cents a pound; fryers brought only thirty to thirty-five cents each, or less than the cost of raising them from chicks.

After the school term at Esperanza was over in the spring of 1903, it was decided that the family would move to Richmond. A position was available at the new Sugar Land unit of the Texas Prison System, where J. B.'s earlier experience at Huntsville would be valuable in helping to operate the new twenty-five-hundred acre Harlem Farm.

Jamie's father found a big, roomy old two-story house by the side of the Richmond-Sugar Land highway for his family, surrounded by huge live oaks. There were flower beds for Miss Lina, and a spacious vegetable garden flanked by robust, heavy-bearing fig trees. The move from Esperanza was completed as soon as possible, because the planting season at Harlem Farm was already underway.

The Abercrombies had once again chosen a town with strong overtones of ante-bellum tradition, where those with roots going back to Alabama and other states of the Old South, as well as to the first beginnings of Huntsville, Texas, would feel instinctively at home. Richmond had been founded by Colonel J. W. Handy (reputedly the handsomest man at the battle of San Jacinto), in 1837. Situated on a high bluff overlooking the Brazos River (el Rio de los Brazos de Dios), which winds its way back a twisty three hundred twenty-eight riverbank miles to Waco, the town was still the headquarters for many of Stephen F. Austin's ''old 300'' colonists, who had arrived at the mouth of the Brazos on the good ship *Lively*, Texas' so-called *Mayflower*.

As the Abercrombies arrived, Richmond's population was estimated at almost one thousand five hundred. There was a waterworks, three railroads, an oversupply of cotton gins (fine ''bottoms'' land would ''make'' two-and-a-half bales of cotton to the acre, or one hundred bushels of corn), grist mills, a dozen or more churches, electricity, and almost two hundred telephones. Some of the prominent names were T. B. Wessendorff (lumber and undertaking), Sheriff Robert Darst (a relative of Daniel Boone), August Meyers (dry goods and groceries) and Dr. William Pettus, physician and grandfather of Governor William Pettus Hobby.

Over-enthusiastic land agents were still describing Richmond in 1903 as the ''second richest city in Texas,'' with ''opulent'' plantations of cotton, corn and sugar cane and adjoining ranches where purebred cattle munched on succulent grass and grain stubble. Fifteen years would soon have passed since the showdown of August 16, 1889, when the Jaybirds (dedicated to a ''government of whites by and for whites'') shot it out with the Woodpeckers, a coalition of blacks and ''carpetbagger'' (Yankee) planters. And it was a full generation since Sheriff and State Senator Walter Burton, an intelligent but contentious black who started life as a field hand, had teamed up with ''Bossman'' Henry C. Ferguson to control politics in Fort Bend County.

As soon as the Abercrombie family had settled in, Jamie was enrolled in the Richmond grammar school for the 1903–1904 term and began seeking a job. A literal example of John Greenleaf Whittier's ''barefoot boy with cheeks of tan'' (shoes were reserved for church in the summertimes of the early 1900s), he must have impressed the very few prospective employers he could locate.

By afternoon, he was the new "soda jerk" at Cranston's Drug Store. Cokes were a nickle, but you could have a squirt of cherry, vanilla or even chocolate added for the same price. Phosphates were a dime, milk shakes and malts fifteen cents, and the top of the line, a vast banana split, was twenty cents. The homemade ice cream in the shakes, malts and splits was the real stuff, however, almost as rich as whipping cream; and two friends could share a banana split at a dime each.

The barefoot soda jerk would never forget that first job and recalled it over the years to close friends. He had always loved ice cream, and ate it in sometimes remarkable quantity throughout his life.

Three years later, in 1906, Jamie had left school. He was working at whatever jobs a youngster soon to be fifteen could find to supplement the income needed by a growing family. J. B. Abercrombie was not in the best of health, and there seemed to be little real opportunity in Richmond. Why not, he asked himself, move to Houston, already a prosperous small city, and one where several of his Huntsville cousins were doing well? Houston was in the midst of unprecedented growth that would jump the population from 44,633 to 78,800 (an increase of seventy-seven percent) between 1900 and 1910.

Among the city's leading citizens were Abercrombie relatives who were the son and son-in-law of J. B.'s brother, Senator (Colonel) Leonard A. Abercrombie. The son was Leonard Anderson Abercrombie, Jr., a prominent attorney and developer; the son-in-law was Robert Scott Lovett, principal in the law firm of Baker & Lovett. Robert Scott's grandfather was Chief Justice W. P. Chilton of the Alabama Supreme Court. A graduate of Yale and the Harvard Law School, Lovett won the Navy Cross as a World War I pilot; he became assistant secretary of war (1941) and undersecretary of state (1947) before being named secretary of defense in 1952. Leonard A. Abercrombie, Jr.'s son, Lovett, a grandson of Senator Abercrombie, was to graduate from Rice Institute and become a prominent stockbroker and investment counsel in Houston.

The Abercrombie home between Richmond and Sugar Land was near the Phenix Dairy farm, a major source of Houston's milk. J. B. became friendly with some of the employees and was soon interested in opening a small dairy of his own on the outskirts of

Houston. The plan would be to develop customers for home delivery, and to sell excess milk or cream to Phenix or other Houston dairies. Will, the first-born, was twenty-five now, and on his own; but Bolling, nineteen; Jamie, almost fifteen; and Bob, eleven; could be very helpful in the new venture. John, nine; Charles (Milo), six; and Joe Rice, the four-year-old baby, were still too young; Annie, twelve; and Lavinia, ten; were students and babysitters who helped their mother constantly with the never-ending tasks of running a large household with many children.

With very limited capital, J. B. Abercrombie had to look carefully to his needs. First, he had to locate an inexpensive property on the outskirts of Houston that he could lease for his dairy; next would come the acquisition of some good milk cows. In Scotland, he would have chosen the big, brown-and-white Ayrshires that some of his cousins had taken by ship as far as Barbados two centuries before; in the Houston area, he looked for the increasingly popular short-horned Jersey cows. The latter, being imported by the Lasater family at Falfurrias, had almost fifty percent more butterfat in their milk than did the popular Holsteins.

In the summer of 1906, J. B. leased a property on old Almeda Road, where the Sisters of Charity of the Incarnate Word had recently opened St. Anthony's Home for the aged.[23] The owner was George Hermann, a recluse who would soon become Houston's first philanthropist of note. There was a reasonable amount of pasture land on the lease, although it would be necessary to feed a dairy herd some silage throughout the year, and certainly during the winter. Adjoining the location he had chosen was a magnificent stand of thick, tall pines, with interspersed oaks, hawthorn and other native shrubs and trees. This tract of two hundred seventy-eight acres was also owned by George Hermann, who would fortunately give it to the city of Houston as the now priceless Hermann Park in 1914, just months before his death.

Soon J. B. had a herd of cows, although smaller than he might have wished, and was looking for equipment for his dairying operation, a sturdy delivery wagon and some good horses. Used equipment and a wagon were acquired and, finally, the prospective new entrepreneur went in search of horses. Jim and Bob (the smallest of the Abercrombie brothers and by far the best rider among them) went along on the horse-buying expedition. Bob insisted on a three-year-old gray that his father thought might be a bit too spirited for the dull and patient job of pulling the delivery wagon over a milk route, but the son prevailed.

Now the Abercrombie dairy was about to be launched, as soon as some customers could be found. If someone had told the family salesmen (Bolling, Jim and Bob) that there were already eighty-three dairies operating in Houston in 1905, they might have been completely dismayed. As it was, they began to round up customers throughout the south and southeast parts of the city at a steady clip, while their father moved on with operational details.

The final step was to rent a new home for the Abercrombie family in Houston. As in Richmond, it would have to be fairly large: when you included Mrs. Josie Wood, the ''Little Grandmother'' who was a frequent and welcome visitor, the total at home was eleven.

Late in the summer, another roomy, rambling two-story home was found, on the south side of Chocolate Road in the Fourth Ward. It was reasonably close to the dairy, but in an area still so sparsely settled that the telephone (when finally installed) was outside the regular switchboard, with the number A- (for Automatic-) 91. Now the move from Richmond was completed as soon as possible, in order for Bob, John, Milo, Annie and Vinnie to start the fall school term on time. Annie, just turned thirteen, and ''with a good head on her shoulders,'' wanted to go job-hunting; but she was persuaded to stay in school.

Jim Abercrombie (the Scots variant ''Jamie'' had been supplanted, and no one ever called the big teenager ''Jimmy'') had his fifteenth birthday on July 7, 1906. A few weeks later, the future Whale of Old Ocean was officially a Houstonian, and on his way to the Oil Patch. There would be a two-year delay, however, involving the family dairy and milk route.

Notes

[1] There were earlier, but unsuccessful, attempts to begin colonization of what is now Texas, under both Spanish and Mexican rule. Father John Barry, a Carmelite priest (or ''White Friar,'' a member of the medieval order distinguished by their white robes and strict vows of poverty), applied from Baton Rouge as early as 1804 for a large grant on which to settle immigrants from his native Ireland. Diego Barry and Felipe O'Reilly, two other Irishmen who had taken Mexican forenames as well as citizenship, teamed up with one Tadeo Ortiz in 1823 on an ambitious scheme to bring as many as twelve thousand Irish and Spanish settlers to an enormous concession of six thousand leagues in the new Mexican republic.

Both proposals were rejected, the application of Father Barry and his Louisiana partners, quite summarily. The Spanish still remembered their difficulties with Philip Nolan, an adventuresome Irish ''mustanger,'' cartographer and conniver at high levels of intrigue. Ostensibly in what was then New Spain to capture wild (mustang) horses and to prepare accurate, long-needed maps of what was pretty well *terra incognita*, Nolan had another mission. After secret meetings with James Wilkinson, the ranking general of the U.S. Army at the time, he also took careful notes on the lack of adequate garrisoning by the Spanish. The general, an enigma who seems to have been at various times in the pay of the United States, the Spanish and the British, had in mind capturing large portions of New Spain with the aid of Philip Nolan.

Nolan actually invaded the Texas coast in the early fall of 1800 with two dozen other soldiers of fortune; a co-conspirator, Peter Ellis Bean; and a group of Negro slaves who had been promised their freedom plus land for their help. The Spanish governor, Juan Bautista de Elguezaba, had become suspicious of Nolan, and ordered his arrest on sight. After a brief skirmish in present-day McLennan County, the invaders were defeated and marched away for eventual imprisonment in Mexico City. When Nolan attempted to escape near the mouth of the Brazos River, he was shot to death; his ears were reportedly cut off, and sent to Governor Elguezaba. Bean did escape, to resurface as a figure in early Texian history. As Pedro Elias Bean, he became a colonel in the army of the Mexican revolutionary hero Jose Maria Morelos and died a rich, highly respected leader in Mexico City.

[2] In their understandable enthusiasm over gaining independence from Spain, Mexican revolutionaries renamed Saltillo, an important settlement since 1575 and the capital of Coahuila to this day, for Leona Vicario, a renowned heroine of the struggle for freedom. After less than four years, the name of Saltillo was officially restored on April 2, 1831—to the further consternation of mapmakers and keepers of records.

[3] Ranching was naturally a favored occupation under the regulations, which seem to have been deliberately framed to minimize the amount of vacant land, and to maximize the number of colonist families. Married settlers who declared only for ranching, without a commitment to farming, were allowed a sitio less a labor, or 4251.3 (4428.4 minus 177.1) acres. Those opting for ranching plus farming received a full league, or 4428.4 acres. As a practical matter, you applied for both grants if you were married, since at least minimal farming would be necessary for subsistence.

Bachelors were given only one-fourth of a league less a labor, or 1062.8 acres. The difference of 3365.6 (4428.4 minus 1062.8) acres must have caused even the most hardened bachelors to reconsider the single life as they prepared to file for the Mexican land.

There was a twenty-five percent bonus for foreigners married to Mexican nationals. Empresarios, or land agents (many of whom were former citizens of other nations long resident in, and now citizens of, Mexico), were awarded five leagues plus five labors, or 23,027.5 acres of "premium" land for each one hundred families they brought as settlers to the new state of Coahuila and Tejas.

The basic unit of land measurement under the colonization plan was the vara, defined by the General Land Office of the State of Texas as 33.333 inches, or "three geometrical feet." The following table shows the conversion of "varas square" to league (sitio), section and the usual fractions of a section:

5000 varas square	= one league (sitio)	=	4428.4	acres
1900.8	= one section	=	640	acres
1344	= one-half section	=	320	acres
950.4	= one-quarter section	=	160	acres

A labor was 1000 varas (not varas square), or one twenty-fifth of a league (sitio). It was equivalent to 177.1 acres.

[4] Natchitoches, the first permanent settlement in Louisiana, was already a booming market and transportation center for cotton, and an important inland port, in 1831. One year later, the Red River (which had made all this possible), inexplicably shifted its course

almost five miles to the east; Natchitoches' bright prospects as a focal point for commerce in the southeast region went glimmering.

[5] The isolated, somewhat xenophobic Mexican government was wary of all foreigners, and downright suspicious of U.S. Protestants, even though Moses Austin and his son Stephen Fuller (quite fluent in Spanish and loyal to Mexico City) were the exception to the rule. Religious liberty would become a significant issue in the Texian war for independence. Adolphus Sterne, a man of discernment, had married a Catholic of prominent family; he undoubtedly explained to his guest Sam Houston the advantages of at least nominal membership in the Church of Rome, especially if you were seeking large parcels of Mexican land.

An obviously superior procedure, not available to Messrs. Sterne and Houston, began with being born an intelligent, resourceful and ambitious Irish Roman Catholic, as James Power and James Hewetson, his physician partner. Each took the Christian name Santiago, Mexican citizenship and a wife of consequential family after settling in Saltillo, the capital of Coahuila and Tejas. Power married Dolores Portilla, an ancestor of the Welder family, members of which still own original Portilla land grants in Nueces and San Patricio counties near Corpus Christi; he learned of the birth of his first child, a son, on April 17, 1833, just as his ship was weighing anchor at Port Aransas for Ireland, where he would recruit three hundred Catholic colonists. Dr. Hewetson married a rich widow, Josefa Guajardo Rosillo, in the splendid Cathedral of St. James in Saltillo on April 20, 1833, less than a week later. The Power-Hewetson colony centered on Refugio (birthplace of my friend of so many years, James Power Heard). Refugio was part of a vast original grant extending from the mouth of the Nueces River to Lavaca Bay, and from Galveston Bay to the juncture of the Trinity and Sabine Rivers. This was augmented later to include all littoral lands between the Nueces and Lavaca Rivers.

Sam Houston, incidentally, died a Baptist. This was due in large part to a relentless campaign by his pious wife Margaret. After several near escapes, the General was received into the Baptist Church of Independence, Texas on November 19, 1854. He was baptized by immersion in the waters of nearby Rocky Creek, which were running definitely cold in a blustery norther. The officiating minister was the Reverend Rufus C. Burleson, later president of Baylor College (and the great-great-grandfather of Eleanor Tinsley, Houston city councilwoman).

The ceremony aroused a great deal of interest in the religious press of the day, and the claim that over three thousand Baptist ministers had been praying for General Sam's conversion; the very scope of this project must have commanded Sam Houston's attention as well. Formal admittance into the church did have a considerable, and positive, emotional and religious impact upon the aging hero of San Jacinto. Nevertheless, the General could not resist injecting a little wry humor into the situation. When a close friend asked him how it felt to realize all his sins had been washed away in the cold waters of Rocky Creek, he reportedly replied, "Well, if it got ALL my sins, then I say the Lord help the fish below, and downstream."

[6] Vehlein, a German rather than an Irishman, followed the pattern established by James Power and James Hewetson in terms of Mexican residence, citizenship and marriage, but his business and political activities were considerably wider in ambit than those of many other empresarios. With some training in the developing sciences of geology and metallurgy, he mined iron ore near ancient silver deposits at Monclova and had other concessions in the name of Jose Vehlein y Compania. More important for Texas, Vehlein had a significant role in the reassignment of a major grant to John McMullen and James McGloin. These Irish empresarios, residents of Matamoros, had originally sought East Texas lands that went instead to Vehlein and David G. Burnet. Now they would become the founders of San Patricio de Hibernia, near Corpus Christi. This came about when Empresario Benjamin Drake Lovell told Vehlein of his intent to abandon a concession he held with John Purnell, after Purnell drowned in Aransas Bay. Vehlein apparently con-

vinced Jose Antonio Saucedo, commissioner for the forfeited Lovell-Purnell grant, and Saucedo's superiors that the McMullen-McGloin plan to colonize lands adjoining the South Texas coast with Irish Roman Catholic settlers was preferable to other proposals.

[7] Colonel Martin Parmer, a central figure in the abortive Fredonian Rebellion of 1826–1827 at Nacogdoches that foretold the future Texas Revolution, led Hayden Edwards' colonists in an armed confrontation with Mexican troops. Parmer was a certain cynosure in Nacogdoches, or wherever he happened to be. Born in Virginia in 1775, he had a career which curiously tracked that of Sam Houston, although at a lower level of involvement and achievement. Parmer lived among the Sioux and Chippewa for almost a decade in the Missouri Territory and served both as an Indian agent and as a member of the territorial legislature, where he gained a reputation as a contentious, but skilled and logical debater who could be handy with his fists in a showdown.

A legendary frontiersman and hunter who once paid $50 in gold for a storied bear dog, Parmer was fond of his marvelous sobriquet, "The Ringtailed Panther." It was apparently given him by Chippewas who both feared and admired him. The Nacogdoches newspaper, however, had carried a gossipy item that seemed to portray a quite different Colonel Parmer. The gist of the story was that Parmer, "as is knowed," had been living "in bond" with the Widow Smith, pending arrival of the circuit preacher and the marriage ceremony. Captain Smith, long assumed dead after failing to return from a hazardous mission in Mexico, suddenly returned very much alive. Whereupon The Ringtailed Panther, the newspaper account succinctly concluded, "tuk out" for parts unknown.

[8] Ironically, the Coushattas (now the Alabamas and Coushattas) were driven from their Alabama homeland early in the nineteenth century, allegedly as enemies of the United States. There is little evidence, however, that they sided with the British in the War of 1812, as did many of their cousins in the Upper Creek Confederacy. A so-called "woodland" or peaceful tribe of Muskhogean stock, they drifted west after the Creek Nation ceded almost half of Alabama and much of Georgia to the United States. The Coushattas ended up along the Neches River in East Texas, and then in the forests near the Trinity and San Jacinto Rivers. Sam Houston recommended in 1854 that the Coushattas be given 640 acres of arable land, and their more numerous kinsmen, the Alabamas, twice as much. The Alabamas received 1280 acres, but the grant to the Coushattas was never made, and the two tribes lived together in dire and mushrooming poverty until 1928, when they were down to about two hundred malnourished, disease-ridden (yet still proud), aboriginal Americans. At this point, the federal government finally provided three thousand acres of additional land plus small cabins and deep water wells; from this assistance plus an appropriation of only $40,000 by the 1963 Texas Legislature, the Alabamas and Coushattas have built a new life for a steadily increasing population on their small holding near Livingston on Highway 190. More than one hundred thousand visitors a year now purchase unique examples of arts and crafts, take various tours, eat in the Inn of the Twelve Clans and see *Beyond the Sundown*, Kermit Hunter's drama of tribal life one hundred and fifty years ago, in a sixteen-thousand seat amphitheatre in the deep woods of East Texas. Paul Yeager brought the story of the Alabamas and Coushattas to a national Public Broadcasting System audience with his *Journey to the Sun*, produced at the University of Houston's pioneer station, KUHT-TV.

[9] Volunteers came first from the sister city of Huntsville, Alabama, where Pleasant Gray retained and strengthened his contacts with correspondence, newspaper stories and advertisements, and public notices concerning his new home in Texas. The Huntsville Volunteers, one hundred and eighty-one strong, landed at Copano Bay and were in training at nearby Refugio when militiamen were allowed to vote for delegates to the 1836 Constitutional Convention whether they were Texians or not. They supported the winners, General Sam Houston and Empresario James Power, who represented Refugio. Tragically, many of the Huntsville Volunteers perished in the Goliad Massacre, where three hundred and ninety Texian prisoners under Colonel James W. Fannin were marched out on Palm

Sunday (March 20), 1836 to be executed in cold blood under orders of General Lopez Antonio de Santa Anna. Only twenty-eight escaped after Mexican troops began firing indiscriminately into Fannin's men, who had been told that they would be released and sent home after losing the battle of Coleto Creek. There were volunteers from other areas of Alabama, and from Louisiana, Mississippi, Georgia, Tennessee and Kentucky—even from Ohio and New York. After editorials supportive of the Texian cause appeared in New Orleans newspapers, Adolphus Sterne told a meeting in Nacogdoches that he would purchase the finest rifles available for the first fifty men to join a proposed volunteer unit in the Louisiana capital. Six weeks later, Sam Houston noted that members of the crack New Orleans Grays, a newly-arrived unit, had the best weapons in his ill-equipped Army of the Republic of Texas.

[10] Sam Houston himself had a preponderant role in setting the tone of marked generosity in grants of Texas land. He insisted, and properly, that the temporarily bankrupt Republic of Texas, unable to do anything else for the veterans of San Jacinto, give those champions of a new nation bountiful portions of the public domain. Little did he foresee that vulturine speculators would often acquire potentially priceless land warrants from impoverished soldiers for a spring planting of seed corn, a few jugs of whisky or a pitifully small amount of cash.

General Sam made special provision for Erastus (Deaf) Smith, the genius scout and strategist who made such formidable contributions to victory at San Jacinto. Scout Smith (a litmus test for newcomers to Texas today would be whether they call him "Deef" (correct) or "Deaf") was awarded a lot and house of his choice in San Antonio de Bexar, the honor of having one of the state's most prosperous agribusiness counties named for him and (curiously) an oil portrait to be commissioned by, and paid for by, the hard-up Republic of Texas.

After providing peerless information gleaned from captured Mexican soldiers and his own extremely perceptive observations, Smith insisted that a bridge over Vince's Bayou, near the battlefield-to-be, should be destroyed. He then saw that it was cut down and burned it himself. This strengthened the resolve of the outnumbered Texians substantially, since Deaf Smith next spread the word that the bridge had been the last avenue of escape. The destruction of this span was far more significant, however, because it led directly to the capture of General Santa Anna, who was attempting desperately to escape from the disaster of San Jacinto in time to intercept the forces of his subordinate, General Juan Filisola, already within a march of two hours with twenty-five thousand fresh troops. Fleeing on horseback toward Filisola's headquarters, Santa Anna had his mount go lame only minutes before Allen Vince of Vince's Bayou and bridge rode by on a splendid black stallion named Old Whip. He pointed a pistol threateningly at the astonished Vince and appropriated Old Whip.

The pursuing Allen Vince soon came upon Old Whip mired in the silt-laden bayou, with Santa Anna nowhere in sight. Vince removed the handsomest saddle he had ever seen, a fabulous example of the leatherworker's art chased in silver and gold and reckoned to be worth about $300, before coaxing Old Whip back to solid ground. He remarked for posterity that it was "a purty good fee for a purty short ride." Antonio Lopez de Santa Anna escaped on foot and donned the uniform of a private; but he was captured in a few hours when a scouting party collared the vanquished dictator. Other Mexican captives then recognized him, and began indiscreetly to shout his name. Within the hour, he was standing before the wounded Sam Houston, to whom he formally surrendered. Santa Anna then made another escape, this time from Texians crowding around, shouting "Remember the Alamo," and offering to dispatch him on the spot with their deadly short knives. In the end, Sam Houston sent the Mexican general and head of state to President Andrew Jackson under heavy guard. Old Hickory packed him off to Mexico.

[11] Texans will be forever in the debt of Price Daniel, whose children are direct descendants of Sam Houston. As attorney-general, Daniel saved the tidelands when the Depart-

ment of Justice claimed that most of these offshore holdings rightfully belonged to the federal government. He directed a brilliant and tenacious legal battle to uphold the unique agreement of 1845 under which Texas tidelands were to extend three leagues, or ten-and-a-half miles from shore. General Daniel finally won for his state and her people in the Supreme Court of the United States, a victory that vaulted him into the United States Senate (1953–1957) and into three consecutive terms as governor (1958–1964).

[12] There are obvious parallels here between Huntsville, Texas and Huntsville, Alabama that reflect the early, vigorous and prolonged influence of the earlier settlement, and of Madison and Limestone counties in Alabama, upon those who came west to found another Huntsville.

[13] The Cumberland Presbyterians (taking their name from the Cumberland Plateau of the Appalachians which extends into Alabama and the valley of the Tennessee River) are a sect of considerable interest, both historically and theologically. They were prominent in early Huntsville because many of the early settlers in the area (including Colonel John C. Abercrombie) were of Scots descent, with a dual tradition of staunch Presbyterianism and rock-ribbed independence. The sect actually arose in 1810, when dissidents on the Kentucky-Tennessee border left the Presbyterian Church, USA. The immediate cause was a shortage of ordained ministers; the Cumberland Presbytery of the PC/USA had ordained men between 1799 and 1802 considered by the ruling Synod of Kentucky to lack full and proper theological training. The dispute gathered steam until 1806, when the Synod dissolved the Cumberland Presbytery and the rejected ministers formed a separate group reorganized four years later as the Cumberland Presbyterians. The new sect emphasized evangelism and decentralization of church government, while rejecting the current interpretation of predestination. After almost a century, the PC/USA changed the Confession of Faith in 1903 to include an explication of predestination acceptable to Cumberland Presbyterians. Most of the then two hundred and twenty-five thousand members of the dissident sect rejoined the PC/USA in 1906, but there are about one hundred thousand Cumberland Presbyterians today, scattered through the South with a concentration in Memphis. Even with the added strength of their own newspaper, Huntsville's Cumberland Presbyterians disbanded after the emergence of the ''Old School'' Presbyterians, and their historic church was taken over by the Church of Christ's members.

[14] Although Galveston was not formally established until 1838, it was well known for its natural advantages as a port from the days of Don Bernardo de Galvez, governor of Louisiana and (later) viceroy of Mexico. He occupied all of Galveston Island for a time in 1777, and named the central portion of the present city Galvez, or Galvez' Town. Jean Laffite and his buccaneers headquartered there as late as 1821. They renamed the settlement, with its excellent harbor, Campeche, but burned it before leaving the area in some haste. The legendary pirate and smuggler, issued a full pardon by President James Madison for heroic assistance in the War of 1812, had been accused of new attacks on U.S. shipping that made him again a *persona non grata*.

[15] President of the Republic of Texas from December 22, 1836 (when he succeeded Joseph Vehlein's former partner, David G. Burnet) until December 10, 1838, Sam Houston was ineligible to succeed himself under the constitution. This was a matter of concern to many Texans, and especially in Huntsville. General Sam had brought the leaky ship of state through some unexpected squalls, and even through a near-hurricane or two; now he would be succeeded by Mirabeau B. Lamar, a man of proven valor and ability leading a cavalry charge, but a novice in politics and government, especially in finance.

Lamar, promoted from private to colonel on the battlefield by General Sam, had been vindictively criticizing his former superior for everything from drinking too much of the ''ardent'' (spirits) to dealing too leniently with the Cherokees. All of this came to Houston's ears soon enough, but he did not respond; he simply had himself elected to the Congress of the Republic, meeting in the squalor of muddy Austin. Here he could whittle, hold court, engage in thickening intrigue with representatives of the French and British governments, watch Mirabeau B(uonaparte) from close up, and bide his time. It came soon enough; the calamitous Lamar presidency ended on December 13, 1841, with the Republic of Texas in debt by an undetermined amount between $6 and $12 million dollars, and the economy in shambles.

Sam Houston was elected president again by a thumping majority, to serve until December 9, 1844. By that time, when he retired temporarily before new careers as U.S. senator and governor, the economy was much improved. President Houston slashed expenditures, burned all the worthless "printing press" money he could find, severely limited the issuance of a sound, new currency and benefitted greatly from two years of bountiful harvests that sharply augmented income throughout the Republic. Meanwhile, he had patiently negotiated a treaty with Santa Anna, back in power in Mexico and threatening constantly to invade Texas; and pacified the Indians. Most significantly of all, General Sam had a key role in complex maneuvering to bring about the annexation of Texas by the United States. This came about through a resolution of March 1, 1845, which President John Tyler signed three days before leaving office. He acted on the strong insistence of Sam Houston's close friend, incoming President James K. Polk, and the critically ill Andrew Jackson, General Sam's political mentor and protector.

[16] The children lost at birth were Charles Anderson Abercrombie I, born May 9, 1846; Charles Anderson Abercrombie II, born September 9, 1847; and James Buford Abercrombie I, born July 27, 1850. It was not unusual for parents, when infant mortality rates were far higher, to name a later child for one who had died. Franklin Delano Roosevelt, Jr. was preceded by another Franklin Delano Roosevelt, Jr. who did not survive.

[17] Margaret Houston and the General almost lost Sam, Jr. at the fearful battle of Shiloh (Pittsburg Landing), with its casualty list in excess of twenty thousand men, but he was saved by a series of providential happenings. Ashbel Smith, the Yale-educated blueblood and physician who had served Texas in posts ranging from surgeon-general to envoy to England and France, had come by Raven Hill while on furlough. A captain in the Confederate forces, he was headed back for duty with young Sam's outfit (Company C of the Second Texas Infantry Regiment) at Corinth, Mississippi. Margaret Houston asked Captain Smith to take a small Bible to her eighteen-year-old son. Two weeks later, both Sam, Jr. and Ashbel Smith were wounded at Shiloh as the Second Texas attacked and overran a Union unit. Young Sam was left for dead, but attracted the attention of a Yankee medical officer and a chaplain when he moaned and began to return to consciousness. As they carefully rolled him over to inspect his wound, a Bible, shot through completely, fell from inside his loosened tunic. Inside the front cover was an inscription from Margaret Houston. "Are you General Houston's son?," the chaplain asked. "Yes," Sam replied. The chaplain then recalled that he had known Senator Houston when he was one of very few Southern legislators with the courage to protest the pro-slavery Kansas-Nebraska bill of 1854 (for which action Houston was censured by the Texas Legislature).

Young Sam was given special medical attention, and ultimately recovered, to be invalided home. The Second Texas Regiment carried him for weeks on the Killed in Action roster.

[18] Just as almost everyone in Walker County, Margaret Houston was in straitened circumstances after the War Between the States. General Sam had left her and the children an estate reckoned to be worth almost $100,000, but most of this was in land and slow-paying notes. She decided to move to Independence, where living would be less expensive. One day she had a visit from Joshua Houston, the General's personal servant for decades and now a free man. Josh brought her several thousand dollars in gold, his life savings, explaining that General Sam had made it possible for him to have the money anyhow, and that he had learned that she might need it.

Mrs. Houston of course refused this extremely generous offer. Josh Houston then used the money to establish a blacksmith shop and store in the Huntsville area, and to educate his son Samuel W. Houston. Professor Houston, a pioneer Negro educator, founded the highly successful Sam Houston School for Industrial Training at Galilee, a black community some five miles west of Huntsville.

Ironically, Margaret Houston would have been quite safe from yellow fever at Cedar Point, the family home on Galveston Bay where she always spent the summer months; Cedar Point was almost one hundred and twenty-five miles from the raging epidemic in Huntsville, with its deadly *Aedes aegypti* mosquitoes. But General Sam's widow went where help was needed; and paid with her life for courage and devotion to the needs of others.

[19] A committee of the Congress of the Republic of Texas chose Huntsville as the site for a central prison in 1842. The First Legislature of the State of Texas formally established the state penitentiary at Huntsville on May 11, 1846, and provided for the purchase of not more than one hundred acres of land as a site. Pleasant Gray and others then sold the prison committee ninety-nine acres for $495, or a special price of five dollars an acre. The first facility opened in 1848; it was vastly overbuilt, with a total of two hundred and forty cells. Only four hundred and twelve prisoners were admitted in the first ten years, most of them on terms of two to five years for cattle rustling, thievery of other variety and aggravated assault. "The Walls," as the facility became known, was almost empty part of the time (in stark contrast to today, when Texas counties have been told on occasion to stop sending prisoners because of extreme overcrowding). The inmate who attracted the most attention in the early days was the Indian chief Santana. Brought to the penitentiary in 1868 under sentence of death for raiding settlements in West Texas, his sentence was commuted to life imprisonment three years later, and he was released in 1873. When returned to the prison later in 1873, he committed suicide—some say after hearing the first flight of winter's wild geese honking as they flew, free, high above him.

There was a prison farm as early as 1850, and the remarkable development of large-scale agriculture with inmate labor, part of a deliberate policy of keeping costs as low as possible, began with the purchase of the twenty-five-hundred acre Harlem Farm in Fort Bend County by the Texas Prison System. Total holdings are now in excess of one hundred thousand acres. Manufacturing started in 1854, when $40,000 was invested in textile equipment which later produced cloth for thousands of Confederate uniforms. The System even tried mining iron ore and making metal products at Rusk, until the operation lost money and was shut down.

Until 1875, when the practice was stopped because of abuses, escapes and increasing public objections, state prisoners were hired out for the day to do not only common labor but carpentry, blacksmithing and other skilled work under the shotgun of a nearby guard. This is said to have delayed the development of a body of trained artisans in the Huntsville area.

[20] Sam Houston graduates have been known to point out to graduates of "The University" that the Huntsville institution was underway two years before the charter for "The University" was issued in 1881.

[21] Few men have had more impact upon Houston than did James A. Elkins, one of a remarkable group of attorneys who left their native Huntsville for brilliant careers in the mushrooming metropolis seventy-five miles south of their birthplace. Judge Elkins' influence was dominant in Houston for almost a half-century, in law, banking and politics. Born September 25, 1879, he was the son of A. J. Elkins, a native of Georgia who came to Walker County as a cotton farmer and was elected sheriff while still in his twenties. He married Sallie Mays, the daughter of a neighbor near 'Possum Walk and East Sandy, when she was seventeen; there were two children: Fanny, born July 7, 1870, and James.

Sheriff Elkins was killed in 1880, and young James worked part-time to help support the family from an early age. He was the newsboy for Huntsville, delivering and selling the *Houston Post* before and after school. While only fourteen, he had saved enough to set up a little store in a rented building in 1893. J. A. opened for business in the early fall, when money was pouring in from the cotton crop, and did well until the store burned several months later. Without insurance, young Elkins had to abandon the field of merchandising.

James A. was a good enough catcher and hitter to play semi-professional baseball as a teenager, on a team that included Charles I. Francis, a noted attorney himself later in Houston. After competing in the Piney Woods League, he was given a tryout by the Houston Buffs. Fortunately, he turned down an offer of $300 a season in 1898 in favor of completing his studies at Sam Houston State Teachers College, where he was a pre-law major. Elkins, who had worked his way through Sam Houston, then financed his law school training at the University of Texas by landing the job of business manager of the *Cactus*, the UT yearbook. After completing law school in 1905, the young barrister opened a successful practice in Huntsville, where he also served as city attorney, county attorney and county judge. In 1917, he heard the call of the city, and formed a partnership in Houston with William A. Vinson. A decade later, the firm of Vinson & Elkins (now one of the largest and best known in the nation) leased an entire floor in that startling new skyscraper, the Neils Esperson Building, with its marvelous cupola and other detailings.

Meanwhile, Judge Elkins had teamed up with a long-time friend of his Huntsville days, J.W. Keeland, to organize the Guaranty Trust Company in 1924. The original capitalization was for $110,000 and the bank operated out of eighty square feet of space adjoining the Vinson & Elkins law firm in the Rusk Building. After receiving a charter as a national bank in 1934 (as the City National Bank), the Judge built a new twenty-four story home for his financial institution in 1947. Nine years later, he merged it with the First National Bank and began planning a far taller and larger skyscraper to house what is now a multi-billion dollar institution. There are those who say that the architects were put to work immediately after the first meeting of the executive staff of the newly-merged First City National Bank. Judge Elkins had noticed that there were not enough chairs for all the vice-presidents, some of whom had to remain standing. In any event, the splendid new bank was ready in 1960.

Judge Elkins became a dominant figure in the political life of Houston and of Texas through his potent legal and banking connections, plus a well-earned reputation for sage, effective advice. He was a central figure in Suite 8-F at the Lamar Hotel, the nexus of political power in the state and city where he met so often with his peers including James S. Abercrombie (his neighbor at the Warwick Hotel for many years), George and Herman Brown, William A. Smith, Wesley West and Gus S. Wortham.

In 1950, the Judge passed the scriptural life span of seventy, and became chairman of the board of the First City National, with his son James A., Jr. succeeding him as president (just as Jim would take his father's place later as a regent of the University of Houston, chairman of the board of the "Elkins bank," and a preeminent leader in the Houston community). Another son, William Sims, was a partner in Vinson & Elkins for many years, and now lives in retirement at Elkins Lake, the beautiful development near Huntsville which was once a private retreat for Judge Elkins and his friends.

The Judge lived on to ninety-two, in a wheelchair at the end, but sharp of mind and indomitable. He was badly shaken by the death of his wife, the former Isabel Mitchell of Galveston (on September 28, 1969), and the end of a marriage that spanned sixty-four years; but he survived Mrs. Elkins almost three years before his own death, on May 7, 1972.

The end came only one day after another Kentucky Derby at Churchill Downs, where Judge Elkins and his closest compadres from Suite 8-F had enjoyed so many memorable weekends. A horse with the improbable name of Bee Bee Bee, little remembered but fortunate enough to come along the year before the incomparable triple crown winner Secretariat, won the ninety-seventh running of the Derby in unremarkable time.

[22] John W. Thomason, Jr., first-born of the nine children of his physician father Dr. John W. Thomason and Sue Hayes Goree Thomason, came into this world at Huntsville on

February 28, 1893 when James Smither Abercrombie was twenty months old. The paternal grandfather, Joshua A. Thomason, was also a doctor of medicine, and a Huntsville pioneer who had come west from Alabama in 1841. The maternal grandfather, Captain Thomas J. Goree, was another pioneer of Walker County; he served with distinction on the staff of General James Longstreet, a Confederate immortal, from First Bull Run to the final surrender at Appomattox Courthouse.

After attendance at Southwestern University in Georgetown, Sam Houston Normal, the University of Texas and the Art Students' League in New York City, John Thomason, Jr. was a high school teacher and principal before writing briefly for the Houston *Chronicle*. With the outbreak of World War I, he began a brilliant twenty-seven-year career with the United States Marine Corps. This included action in France in 1917 and 1918, attendance at both the Army and Navy War Colleges, postings abroad, top assignments as World War II became a reality, and winning the coveted Navy Cross and the Silver Star of the U.S. Army among other decorations. Colonel Thomason died on active duty at San Diego on April 12, 1944; a Navy destroyer, the USS *John W. Thomason, Jr.*, was named for him as was a park at the Marine Corps base at Quantico, Virginia. Gifted as an illustrator as well as a writer, Colonel Thomason's memory is perpetuated both in the Graphic Arts Building and in the Thomason Special Collections at Sam Houston State University. The collections, housed separately on the fourth floor of the library, include his illustrated books and short stories, manuscripts, pen and ink sketches and watercolors.

John W. Thomason, Jr. was married to Leda Barbara Bass of Huntsville. They had one child, John W., III, born in 1920. Colonel Thomason is buried in Oakwood Cemetery.

A decade after the Thomason essay on Huntsville appeared in the April, 1934 issue of the *Southwest Review*, no less a critic than J. Frank Dobie saluted the author and said of his work, ". . :because of what you have written, (people) are richer inside themselves and live more abundantly on the soil they belong to . . ."

[23] The Sisters of Charity of the Incarnate Word had operated St. Joseph's Infirmary since 1887, to a large extent in the earliest days from a contract with Harris County to care for indigent patients at the munificent rate of fifty cents per day. This institution, which survived crisis and catastrophe including an 1894 fire in which two heroic nuns perished in an attempt to rescue patients, was the beginning of today's St. Joseph Hospital. St. Anthony's Home, now expanded into the St. Anthony Center, was administered for many years by Mother Augustine (Sister Mary Margaret McKeever), superior general of the Sisters of the Incarnate Word.

J. B. Abercrombie came to know Mother Augustine and the other members of the order at St. Anthony's. They operated a tiny dairy, and grazed their cows near the Abercrombie herd. Three-quarters of a century later, J. B.'s son John Abercrombie, the sole survivor of his generation of the family, lived for several years at St. Anthony's Center.

Many prominent Houstonians, among them Jim Abercrombie and his friend of more than fifty years, Judge J. A. Elkins, were quiet or anonymous contributors to St. Joseph Hospital and to St. Anthony's Home. Judge Elkins and Mother Augustine had unusual life spans that were remarkably similar. He was born September 25, 1879 and died May 7, 1972; she was born November 1, 1879 and died October 17, 1972. Both ended their long and impactful lives in a wheelchair, but alert of mind and indomitable.

Chapter 6

1906–1920

The First Years in Houston and the Oil Patch

Lumber, cotton, magnolias—and Oil (Spindletop!) . . . A young milkman, Old Gracie and a fast street car . . . "Doc" Neuhaus watches a quarter-pony win . . . Jim goes roustabouting at Cypress . . . The Abercrombies lose both parents, but stay together as a family . . . Bet-A-Million Gates and "Sweet Sixteen," saved by an all-around well man . . . Jim and Big Chan find a new hand at Goose Creek . . . The first Abercrombie rig, at Burkburnett . . . The brothers Abercrombie, independent drilling contractors . . . Harry Cameron, who works magic with iron, Edmond L. Lorehn, and Cameron Iron Works . . . Paterfamilias *at 3402 Audubon . . . "Grits" gets a feel for a rig and bit . . . Early and late at 711 Milby*

Houston in 1900 was in its sixty-fifth year since the Allen brothers staked out their lots in the midst of some prime mosquito-breeding bayous. It was ready to qualify for Social Security, yet still a big, bustling, overgrown town rather than a city, an aging St. Bernard puppy with the promise of surpassing but unrealized growth in its huge paws and loose-skinned frame.

Lumber still ruled the roost in 1900, in more ways than one; the streets had even been laid out eighty feet curb to curb, that being the distance necessary for a skilled mule skinner to make a U-turn with a fully-loaded wagon of pine logs at the first pass. Cotton and rice were not far behind, however, as the leading products of the area; and breweries were catching up with a formidable annual output of almost two hundred thousand barrels of beer, in spite of dramatic visits by Carrie Nation herself.[1]

King Nottoc, a tall, handsome young Tennesseean with fine, piercing eyes and a commanding presence, ruled the annual cotton festival; this was Jesse Holman Jones, who would soon open his own lumber yard after learning the business under his uncle, and announce his first big contract: constructing the Texas Building at the St. Louis Exposition everyone was talking about.

The 1900 rice crop was reckoned to be worth $6 million; this and the established, profitable traffic arising from lumber and cotton (plus speculators coming down to buy rice land) would soon make Houston the largest railroad nexus in the South and accelerate even more the building of the Ship Channel. Two sections of this bedrock foundation for future and lasting economic expansion of startling dimension had already been completed, at the then enormous cost of $4 million.

Yet there was a distinct remaining flavor of magnolia and honeysuckle—of a more felicitous, and far less stressful, time in Houston at the turn of the century. No longer did the socially elite dress in velvet tights and doublet to joust at a knightly ''tournament'' before dancing Virginia reels at the Hutchins House; but at the cotillions of the Houston Light Guard, there was still some discussion of what might have happened at Second Manassas, the favorite dance was the quadrille, and eagle-eyed matrons peered intensely under the new incandescent lights[2] for any trace of rouge on young debutantes lightly dusted with rice powder.

As written elsewhere, another prime reason for the persistence of the ''old'' Houston of earlier generations was the tradition of the leisurely life of the Old South that countless colonels (some of them self-appointed in non-existent regiments) brought here after the War Between the States.

On Quality Hill, the River Oaks of the Victorian era, wealthy bankers and merchants recreated an ante-bellum world of spacious gardens and big, colonnaded homes painted dazzling white every other spring. Quality Hill, just northeast of the downtown area and south of Buffalo Bayou, was only ten or fifteen minutes by carriage from the business offices of a beginning King's Row along Main, Commerce and Franklin. The master of the house would be driven down in splendor for a few hours of work, top-hatted and chomping on a fresh cheroot, after a splendid, unhurried breakfast reading what had caught everyone's attention in the morning Houston *Post*, a new column (''Postscripts'') by a witty young reporter named Sidney Porter. Breakfast was uncomplicated by early long-distance calls from the Eastern money mills, or that latest abomination of the 1980s, a direct computer hook-up with a terminal at home.

Then Spindletop literally exploded upon the scene, at midmorning on January 10, 1901.[3] Not quite five miles south of Beaumont, Captain Anthony F. Lucas and a persistent, one-armed, self-educated geologist named Patillo Higgins had brought in a roaring gusher of oil that would change Houston, and all of the world—but particularly Houston—for all the years to come. And although he was only a nine-year-old schoolboy in Huntsville, Texas at the time, Spindletop would affect Jim Abercrombie as much as any individual who lived through the three-quarters of a century he was fortunately to have remaining to him.

By 1906, Houston was forever transmuted, even transmogrified, with the elements of extraordinary change the latter term indicates, by that tremendous strike of January 10 and the forests of derricks it engendered just eighty miles to the east.

Only Beaumont could offer the frenetic spectacles in which curbside "boomers" arriving by the dozen on the morning Southern Pacific, traded in big-denomination cash for good leases anywhere within Spindletop's golden bounds. They would drop a $10 or $20 bill and leave it trampled in the mud as they rushed to record their latest transaction at the Jefferson County courthouse, which looked more and more like the pit of the Chicago Board of Trade after winter wheat had plummeted on confirmation of drouth-breaking rains in the Dakotas.

Here, too, you saw the silk-smooth operations of James Roche, heir to an English earldom, as he put together a prime block of leases for John W. (Bet-A-Million) Gates, enroute from Kansas City on his own special train. And it was Beaumont's Spindletop that took the early Texas oil play away from Corsicana; the gigantic new Jefferson County oilfield was chiefly responsible for running up the state's production from 836,000 barrels of crude in 1900 to an astounding 17,852,308 in 1902. This enormous increase, incidentally, gave world leadership in petroleum output to the United States, which surpassed Czarist Russia at 88,766,916 barrels to 80,540,045—long, long before the Middle East, and Venezuela, and Mexico, and the North Sea.[4]

Houston, nevertheless, reaped the truly prime and most enduring benefits of Spindletop. There is not a doubt that the Lucas-Higgins gusher and nearby fields such as Sour Lake changed Beaumont from town to city, while literally creating Port Arthur, with its unbelievable complex of refineries. Similarly, Beaumont was potentially the energy capital of the nation, or even of the world, when Governor Jim Hogg (whose Scots ancestors had traded with the Abercrombies at Hogg & Campbell's branch in Orange County, North Carolina), John Gates, Walter Sharp, Buckskin Joe Cullinan, W. T. Campbell[5] and others organized what would become the

Texas Company (Texaco) in the very shadows of Spindletop. But the headquarters of this and other great oil companies would inevitably move on to Houston, where the vast infrastructure of what would become such a dominant industry began to emerge as early as 1900. Within a decade, products and services virtually unheard of at the turn of the century were providing thousands of jobs in Harris County and beginning to create great new fortunes in addition to those based solely upon the discovery of an oilfield.

Harris County had its own gusher on November 28, 1904, when Walter Sharp's legendary Moonshine #1 roared into production at Humble, less than twenty miles north of downtown Houston, after years of difficult, costly and discouraging drilling that had more enthusiasm than oil, however; technical problems emerged and multiplied. Production then dropped drastically, but special trains brought hundreds from Houston to the tiny community of Humble, some of them the very same "boomers" who had thronged Beaumont after Spindletop.

The entrancingly-named Moonshine #1 (commemorating a local hill long known for the production of "corn squeezings") created continuing excitement in Houston, in spite of problems with the discovery well. This was reflected by the organization of new corporations for petroleum exploration and production, among them the Landslide Oil Company. With the experienced Sharp and W. T. Campbell among its directors, Landslide Oil paid as much as $5000 cash per acre for prime Humble leases. Their faith in the area was vindicated when the Beatty #2 came in on January 9, 1905 with an initial flow of twelve thousand barrels per day, helping in time to establish the Humble field as one of the most prolific in Texas history. There would be continuing problems with those bugaboos of the early days of the industry: high pressure, blowouts and lost wells—but Humble has now produced more than three hundred million barrels of oil and moved into the state's petroleum Hall of Fame.

The little Harris County town, which had an official population of thirty in 1905, also gave its name to another giant enterprise of tremendous importance to the Houston area, Texas and the nation: the Humble Oil Company. Its incorporation would soon confirm again Houston's central position in the developing Oil Patch, reinforced by the superb qualities of integrity, experience and leadership within "The Humble's" founding directors.

So it was that James Buford Abercrombie and his sons launched their little dairy in the fall of 1906 in a yeasty, challenging atmosphere that would see their new home of Houston grow by seventy-seven percent, from 44,633 to 78,800, between 1900 and 1910. They knew little or nothing of the oil industry, and yet had come to its very pivot and hub of the future, at a particularly opportune time when petroleum would soon provide unparalleled opportunities, not only in Harris and surrounding counties, but throughout much of the Gulf Coast. They were on the scene, and early in the game.

Jim Abercrombie took an increasingly central role in the operation of the family dairy from the beginning. Maturing ever more rapidly as his big frame filled out, he appeared to be eighteen when the new business first got underway, although barely fifteen. A year later, he could pass for a grown man, and well that he might: his father's illness persisted, limiting his physical activities; while Bob, at twelve; and John, ten; tried to help in every way they could, both were mere boys under a strict family requirement of unfailing attendance at school, along with their sisters Annie and Vinnie. (The baby, Joe Rice, would start his own education at age seven, in 1909, although already learning to read and write at home.)

This meant that Jim and the nineteen-year-old Bolling were left with growing responsibilities and plenty of hard work. Will, who would become one of the best-liked businessmen in Galveston, busied himself at the dairy on many weekends, coming in on the marvelous new Interurban that made the fifty miles from Broadway and the Strand to the Rice Hotel in less than an hour; but Will, in his mid-twenties, was contemplating marriage and had his own obligations, much as he respected and loved his parents and younger siblings.

Dairying meant unusually long hours, in a business that can approach round-the-clock duties when you include herding cows to and from pastures; feeding and preparing them for milking; sterilizing the metal containers; separating cream for sale to special customers, and for butter-making; loading the containers; actually delivering the milk; and as many more related chores. At least the Abercrombies did not have to wash and sterilize individual milk bottles back in 1906. The deliveryman carried a row of heavy ten-gallon cans, sterilized with live steam, with a spigot at the bottom; each customer supplied his own milk bottles, which were left on the doorstep to be filled from the spigoted cans.

Jim was usually the deliveryman, leaving the dairy an hour or so before dawn. He was helped greatly by Old Gracie, a particularly intelligent young gray mare who quickly memorized the early morning stops. This allowed the driver a series of catnaps, plus a reasonable little snooze into town and back. (A round trip of more than ten miles from Old Almeda Road.)

Young Jim always awoke as they came up La Branch to Preston Avenue, turned left and stopped at Stude's Bakery and Coffee Saloon, which stayed open all night and was a good customer for coffee cream and milk. Often he would see George Hermann, a perennially early riser, coming in for warm doughnuts that must have reminded the philanthropist-inventor of the good Swiss-German *kuchen* of his father, an immigrant baker who had come to Houston in 1838 with less than $10 in his pocket. The young milkman came to know Mr. Hermann, who would inquire about the Abercrombie dairy and the family Jerseys grazing on his leased pastures.[6]

One fateful morning, when the oil industry almost lost a preeminent leader of the future, Herman Stude's customers had to take their coffee black. Jim Abercrombie and Old Gracie were proceeding due north on La Branch in the penumbra of predawn, just six blocks south of Preston at McKinney, and Jim was having his customary forty winks, trusting to the reliable gray mare for safe arrival at 810 Preston. The next thing he knew, he was lying in the middle of McKinney Avenue with a smashed ten-gallon milk can in his lap, thoroughly bathed in Grade A milk but otherwise unscathed. The delivery wagon was on its side, one damaged wheel spinning askew. Old Gracie, terrified but little harmed, was struggling to get up while firemen who had come running over from the nearby station on Caroline were trying to calm her.

One of Houston's new-fangled electric street cars, considerably faster than the earlier models and without their harshly clanging bells or familiar noise of overhead trolley, had reached the intersection of La Branch and McKinney Avenue just as Old Gracie and her catnapping driver were about to leave it northbound. The mare's keen ears were attuned to a different-sounding street car, and the 1906 version of a Metropolitan Transit Authority bus hit the rear end of the Abercrombie milk wagon, spinning it completely around, as Gracie went through what she thought was an empty intersection.

Both horse and driver were *hors de combat* for a few days, while Bolling and another horse took over after emergency repairs to the wagon by a wheelwright; but Jim and Old Gracie were back on the job soon, little the worse for wear. He did tell them at Stude's that he and the mare had learned a thing or two about the new street cars; and Gracie, smart horse that she was, now stopped for a look-see before crossing McKinney Avenue, or any other thoroughfare with those steel rails that could bring sudden disaster.

At the big, rambling house on Chocolate Road, there was a change that would influence all the Abercrombie family, Jim perhaps most of all. This was the arrival of Jim's maternal grandmother, Mrs. William B. Wood, who was asked to make her home with her daughter Lina, son-in-law James Buford and their eight children still at Chocolate Road, soon after the death of her husband at Huntsville in 1907.

Josephine (Josie) Wood's impact upon people was directly inverse to her size; this remarkable woman was barely four feet, ten inches in height, but she was literally looked up to throughout her long life for wise counsel and guidance, and a warm, enveloping spirit of love and togetherness that seemed to be wherever The Little Grandmother was. As indicated briefly before, she was doubly related to the Abercrombies, through ties going back to Alabama, and even to eighteenth-century North Carolina and Georgia.

Apart from being grandmother to Jim and his siblings, her husband William B. Wood's great-great-grandfather was none other than Charles Abercrombie, planter and Patriot of Orange County, North Carolina and of Hancock County, Georgia. Through this very direct connection, J. B. Abercrombie's great-great-aunt Nancy Abercrombie Barnes (Charles' daughter) was his wife Evalina Wood Abercrombie's great-grandmother. Husband and wife were distant cousins.

Evalina Wood Abercrombie's own grandmother had been a central personality in her generation, and as Mrs. Green Wood, a leader in central Alabama's farming and social circles. Her long and detailed will, disposing of assets ranging from prime cotton land through slaves to silver to cash through the executorship of her son, Green Wood, Jr., was carefully drawn so as to emphasize the preservation of her own family as an integral unit, with special attention to the oncoming generations.

Josie Wood herself became the amalgam for two generations of Houston Abercrombies, subtly yet powerfully reinforcing a natural tendency, inculcated from Orange County, Sparta, Brickyard, Cross Keys—and even from centuries before, to remain together as an extended family. We trace clearly to her Jim Abercrombie's own abiding inclination to keep the Houston clan together as long as possible, on Chocolate Road, at Graham Avenue West and particularly at 3402 Audubon, under the banner of The Little Grandmother and—as we shall see, of another strong and positive personality soon to emerge: Miss Annie Abercrombie.

The Little Grandmother must have felt a closeness, and a happiness, in spite of a difficult economic situation exacerbated by J. B. Abercrombie's recurrent poor health when she arrived on Chocolate Road late in 1907. The work at the dairy was hard and seemingly never-ending; but it was done, and without complaint, in good spirit and humor.

The school-age children were preparing to enter the new Charlotte Allen Elementary (named for Mrs. Augustus C. Allen, wife and sister-in-law of Houston's two founders) at Chenevert and Elgin. It would open in September 1907, an exhilarating half-hour ride distant on two of the dairy's horses, if you took short cuts through pine groves and open fields. Bob, John and Milo could negotiate the trip five minutes sooner than Annie and Lavinia, but the girls claimed that this was because they had to be more careful; Baby Joe Rice, barely seven, rode with them. The children were outgoing, likeable youngsters and favorites of Jane Caradine, the "lady principal" who was one of the first women to administer a public school in the city.

We know from one of the closest friends of the Abercrombie children something of how it was at the Charlotte Allen School in that last decade before the outbreak of World War I. This is Vernon Frank (Doc) Neuhaus. He was in particular a pal of Bob, and an exact contemporary of Joe Rice; but he knew all of the Abercrombie youngsters and would be in the oilfields later with five of the brothers.

Doc Neuhaus was born in Schulenburg of fine, old-line German stock, to one of a group of families that dominated farming, banking and cotton-buying in the elegant little city halfway between Houston and San Antonio. A cousin, Lillie Cranz, had married Hugh Roy Cullen, then a young cotton buyer, who was destined to become a legendary leader in the Oil Patch. Many of the Neuhaus clan came to Houston, where they quickly gained and maintained prominence in the professions as well as in banking and stockbroking, and in the cultural and social life of the city.

Among the welcome immigrants from Schulenburg was young Vernon Frank, immediately dubbed "Doc" because his father was a physician. Doc tells us now, across three-quarters of a century, how it was at the Allen School with the Abercrombie clan: "Most of all, they were fun to be around. They worked hard and played hard; they always stuck together; and it was just fun to be with them."

One Saturday, Doc went over to visit Jim and Bob, and they asked him to come with them to a little three-eighths-of-a-mile race track laid out in the middle of what is now the Hermann Park Zoo. It turned out that Bob, smallest by far of the Abercrombie brothers and a natural-born jockey, knew exactly what he was doing when Old Gracie was originally purchased for the family dairy in spite of some misgivings by his father. Far from being either old, or just an ordinary draft horse, Gracie was part "quarter-pony," an early version of today's fleet and extremely valuable quarter-horses. Bob had apparently detected this in a test ride, before he persuaded his father to buy the horse.

While Doc Neuhaus watched wide-eyed, Jim and Bob went up to a man named Sidney Long, who ran the informal little racetrack in Hermann Park, and apparently arranged for Gracie to be entered in a series of what were six hundred sixty-yard dashes. Bob had washed and curried the horse carefully after feeding her a generous portion of corn and oats at the dairy but had ridden her over bareback from Chocolate Road while Neuhaus and Jim walked alongside. Now, Doc could not believe that his friend would ride her without any sort of saddle, especially since he thought that there had been an exchange of hard betting cash between the Abercrombie brothers and Sidney Long. Gracie's trappings at the moment included only a light bridle.

The mystery was soon solved. Bob pulled a many-times-patched, ancient inner tube out of a little ditty bag he had been carrying, while Jim fitted it snugly around Gracie's middle. Bob, who then weighed "about a hundred pounds, dripping wet," stuck his legs through the inner tube and moved on over to the starting line.

Doc Neuhaus could not remember if Bob and Old Gracie ever lost a race at the Hermann Park futurity, consistently outrunning

Sidney Long's "quarter-ponies" and all comers, some of them valued at $500–$600.

And from those days, Jim and Bob in particular would retain an abiding interest in horseracing, which brought them so much pleasure and recreation. They were disappointed, as were all true *aficionados* of the Sport of Kings, at Epsom Downs, Houston's racetrack on the Humble Road which drew almost thirty thousand to its opening on Thanksgiving Day of 1933 but failed to attract world-class horseflesh. They and some of their closest friends, however, began pilgrimages to Saratoga, Hialeah, New Orleans and in particular to Churchill Downs for the Kentucky Derby. As a later chapter will recount, they acquired in time some splendid racehorses, and Mr. Jim purchased a showplace horse farm in Kentucky.

Doc would be in and out of the Oil Patch with the Abercrombies for much of a generation before leaving for a new and resplendent career in the Rio Grande Valley, where he has become a titan in banking, land and other investments (in the Neuhaus tradition). But he still remembers, nearing eighty-five, Old Gracie, and Bob Abercrombie racing her to victory on an inner-tube saddle, amidst the gnarled oaks of what would become George Hermann's park, now such a priceless asset of the city he benefitted so greatly.

By his seventeenth birthday, on July 9, 1908, Jim Abercrombie had learned a great many things, including more than he really wanted to know about dairying. Gradually, almost imperceptibly, he had assumed the role of leadership in the family, without in any way denigrating, or surpassing, the authority of his parents; above all, he would never harm the image of his father, who had less than four years to live.

Jim had a plan, probably after consultation with The Little Grandmother, and a sound plan it was. He and Bolling, with the help of their father, although he continued in questionable health, had the dairy operation reduced in the main to a routine. Meanwhile, oil fever was hitting new highs in Houston every day. The discovery of what appeared to be a major new Harris County field at Goose Creek, on June 2, 1908, had created many new jobs; some of these would pay per month as much as the total net income from the dairy. It seemed logical for Jim and for Bolling (now twenty-one) to look for work in the Oil Patch.

They would earn between them enough to hire the manpower to keep the dairy underway, and the family firmly established at what had become a congenial new headquarters in Houston, the oil capital-to-be.

The Little Grandmother remembered that an older cousin with the traditional family name of Charles Anderson Abercrombie had left Huntsville years before to make his way in Houston, and was somehow "in oil." He had become vice president of the short-lived Goose Creek Production Company, but he and his brother Claude were essentially drilling contractors and had been in the oilfields as early as 1898.

Jim found that Charles lived at 807 Heights Boulevard, in the separate little town of Houston Heights that Oscar Martin Carter and Daniel Denton Cooley, respectively president and cashier of the First National Bank of Ashland, Nebraska, had established on 1,800 acres just northwest of the Houston city limits in 1892. "The Heights" was actually just fifty-two feet higher than downtown Houston, but there was a tradition dating back to earlier epidemics of yellow fever that life was healthier in the area of the new community traversed by the old West Montgomery Road. It was indeed healthier during outbreaks of "yellowjack"; you were several miles away from Houston's bayous and swamps and their disease-bearing *Aedes aegypti* mosquitoes.

One of the basic attractions of The Heights was a master plan based upon an exact north-south orientation of wide, sweeping streets dominated by the broad, landscaped esplanade of Heights Boulevard. On the Boulevard, and on east-west streets such as Yale and Oxford would soon appear imposing mansions, some of them challenging the standards of Quality Hill and the newer "bois d'arc" district[7] further downtown. At one showplace home, at 1802 Heights Boulevard, Arthur and Ralph Cooley would grow up with their world-famed, surgeon-to-be brother Denton. The boys stayed inside at night in their earlier years because prowling wolves from the nearby prairies were still seen occasionally in the neighborhood.

Jim Abercrombie arranged to visit his cousin Charles after a preliminary telephone conversation and started at first to splurge on a forty-cent trip to the Heights in one of Houston's several new taxicabs; he found, however, that trips outside the city limits could cost an entire dollar and settled for a nickel ride on the Houston Heights Street Railway with famed motorman Sam Danna. "Mr. Sam" stopped right in front of 807 on the Boulevard, and Jim went in to meet Charles, his wife and their children, a daughter named Jolly and a son, Eckart.

Charles Anderson Abercrombie must have instinctively liked the big, quiet, capable-looking youngster; everyone did. When Jim left an hour or so later, to wander past the nearby "Katy" (Missouri, Kansas & Texas) railroad station at Yale and Seventh, he had his first job in the Oil Patch. Cousin Charles had hired him as a roustabout, whatever that was, to work with a drilling crew on a wildcat they were spudding in near Cypress, some fifteen miles northwest of downtown Houston.

There was no place to stay in Cypress, a hamlet dating from an 1832 settlement along nearby Cypress Creek. In 1908, it was little more than a country store and a blacksmith shop, and transportation immediately became a major problem for Jim. Luckily, cousin Charles had a brand-new Model T Ford, the first that the young roustabout had ever seen; he and his drilling crew packed into the car at sun-up for the trip out West Montgomery Road and what is now Highway 290. Still, it was a good eight miles from Chocolate Road to Heights Boulevard before dawn, and the same distance back after work, even though the street cars ran early and late. Jim would have to find lodgings near his cousin's home. The older Abercrombie had offered to let his new employee stay with his own family; Jim, shy and fiercely independent, was grateful; but he thought that this was an imposition and refused.

He found that he could have room and board at the Heights Hotel on Ashland and Nineteenth for $3.50 a week. This was too much for his budget, based upon taking as much as possible of his pay home to Chocolate Road. Instead, he negotiated a lesser rate for a tiny room and fewer meals, since he headed for Houston at noon Saturday for the weekend.

Jim Abercrombie found out quickly about the term "roustabout," which had originally meant a deckhand; it involved doing all the unskilled operations around a drilling rig while you climbed the occupational ladder to roughneck, and hopefully on to toolpusher, driller and field superintendent. During the next decade, he learned all these jobs, and how to perform them superbly well, at fields throughout southeast Texas.

Bolling, the older brother, found work also in the new industry that would soon dominate Houston, but as a clerk in the expanding

Texas Company. Only he and Will, of the Abercrombie brothers, would stay out of the Oil Patch itself.

Jim Abercrombie was at Spindletop, where it all began; at Goose Creek, with its early disappointments; at Sour Lake, which produced almost nine million barrels in a single year after a disastrous blowout; and at Hull and Dayton and Barber's Hill. Within months after taking his first job at Cypress, he was a roughneck, and a good one; by 1910, although still a teenager, he was a driller; in his early twenties Crown Petroleum hired him as field superintendent.

Clearly, here was a most unusual man. What made Jim Abercrombie such a success at this early stage in his career, and throughout decades of sharply-escalating accomplishment in various fields of endeavor? Naurice Cummings,[8] perhaps his closest friend outside the family, recalls in revealing detail the physical characteristics and personal attributes that must have been key factors in Mr. Jim's ascendancy. Naurice (possibly the only man in the world with that forename, so consistently mistaken for Maurice) was born in 1900 in Beeville, Texas, which would become the fiefdom of Judge James Daugherty. As a teenager, he came to Houston looking for work in the oilfields and heard that Crown Petroleum was hiring at Goose Creek. Over he went to the little east Harris County boom town, which lost its marvelous name[9] when it and Pelly were both swallowed up by a larger Baytown after Humble Oil & Refining had located the world's biggest refinery there.

Naurice found the Crown Petroleum lease, but not a soul was around; finally, he came upon a giant negro, well above six-and-a-half feet tall, stacking pipe and pipe fittings all by himself. This, he learned later, was Big Chan. "I hear you people are hiring," Naurice said. He could hardly believe the size of the black man's biceps. "Yeah, they're puttin' on hands." "You know where the employment office is?" "Here he comes now," Big Chan replied, nodding toward the deeply-rutted road.

It was Naurice Cummings' first sight of Jim Abercrombie. His initial impression, reinforced by the reaction of many other people, was that Abercrombie was clearly over six feet tall. Actually, Naurice found later, he was five feet, eleven inches; however, there was something about the way in which Jim carried himself. He came quietly onto the scene in a manner that made you realize immediately his presence and impact. And his clean, starched khakis had a fresh crease; the shave was so close you would think he had just come out of the Rice Hotel barbershop.

Naurice was further impressed. Without profanity, but mincing no words, Jim Abercrombie began to inquire in the strongest terms as to why the rig was running short of pipe. Big Chan replied patiently, without either anger or undue deference; it was plain that employer and employee respected and understood one another. "Boss, I'm doin' all I can; but I'm working alone; my helper quit." "Well," Mr. Jim responded, looking straight at Naurice for the first time, "why not get this boy here to help; we're stringing pipe, and we need plenty of it."

That was how Naurice Cummings started his own career in the oil industry, now running well into a sixth decade: Jim Abercrombie didn't even know his name; there was no discussion of pay or hours or even if there was enough room in the bunkhouse for the new hand. All that was worked out later, to Naurice's satisfaction, and he was soon all over the lease, helping Big Chan, working with the blacksmith, learning to roustabout and later, to roughneck.

Jim Abercrombie, Naurice Cummings recalls with great clarity, was "just an outstanding example of what we called a 'first-class well man.' He could do anything: drill his quota of footage and more on any shift, literally smell out oil, loosen a stuck drill stem, keep a good crew together—even fight fires; and there were plenty of them in those days, at Goose Creek and everywhere else, with those oil- and grease-soaked wooden derrick floors ready to burn like a tinder box."

Mr. Jim was especially popular on the rigs "because he would never ask anyone to do anything he wouldn't do himself. And he was always teaching someone how to do things—sort of ran his own school for roughnecks and future drillers, right on the job."

Naurice claims that Jim Abercrombie "was the original Red Adair; the best man on an oilfield fire you ever saw, and long before anyone ever heard of asbestos suits and foam and fancy chemicals and explosives. He would just put on some horsehide gloves, grab the biggest, thickest piece of corrugated iron he could handle, and shield himself with it while he tried to get in close and douse the heart of the flames with water. The crew stayed back, keeping another hose on him and that corrugated iron while we sprayed the derrick floor and anything else that started to smoke."

Wells were quite shallow in those days, of course, and firefighting was not nearly so complicated. Nevertheless, Jim Abercrombie fought both with courage and with ingenuity. One day, a slow but stubborn fire started on one of the Crown Petroleum wells, endangering crew, derrick, rig and adjacent production. Supplies of fresh water were a little low anyhow, and soon there was no pressure left for firefighting. The crew pulled the derrick floor apart, stacked it well out of the way, and did everything else they could to minimize risk and damage, finally skidding the wooden derrick out of the immediate area.

Jim studied the situation awhile, and quickly had a little pipeline laid over to nearby Goose Lake. As soon as the new water supply was available, the fire was put out in short order. Actually, the Goose Lake impromptu pipeline was so effective that it was soon realized that Jim Abercrombie had a new firefighting tool: salt water. Goose Lake was partly fed from Galveston Bay, and water from the lake, heavily saturated with sodium chloride, was more effective than fresh water against the rig fire.

After the firefighting was all over, Jim Abercrombie would reappear in a fresh set of the starched khakis that he always kept at hand. "He was the hardest-working, and the cleanest-looking, man in the oilfields," Naurice remembers. "It became a habit, and then a tradition, with him, that neat appearance; and it definitely made an impression on people. While most of the men on a rig in those days changed clothes on Saturday, and shaved when they went into town, he was a leader, and he looked the part."

Jim and Naurice Cummings became fast friends despite the fact that Abercrombie was almost ten years older. One great tie between them, and it would remain so the rest of Jim's life, was their love of hunting. They shot quail in the fall, and ducks and geese in the winter; plus, Naurice remembers, woodcock and snipe—anything but the mud hens that some of the Cajun roughnecks would bag, hang for days outside the bunkhouse, as the corpses drip-dried, and then eat with great relish after showing cook how to prepare them a special way.

Then new opportunity struck for both Jim Abercrombie and Naurice Cummings. They would leave for differing parts of the Oil Patch, but meet again in a few years to resume a friendship that was to span more than a half-century. But before leaving Goose Creek, Jim would complete a unique project of great significance to two areas of his future career.

Bet-A-Million Gates' "Sweet Sixteen," a hoped-for-extension to the important Goose Creek field, had blown in as a gusher, out of control. Gates remembered three wells that Abercrombie had drilled for him at Port Neches; now he was hearing more and more what Naurice and so many others knew: Jim Abercrombie was as good an all-around well man as you could find.

Jim was called in, studied the well a day and most of a night, and capped it on the first try. Gates did not forget the "Sweet Sixteen," and his all-around well man began to think increasingly about the problems, and the advantages, of high pressure. You needed pressure to bring in a well and keep it flowing; but that pressure had to be under constant control.

Meanwhile, there were many changes within the Abercrombie family; most difficult to bear, the loss of both parents. James Buford and Evalina were buried side by side in Huntsville's old Oakwood Cemetery, with many another Abercrombie.

Jim had been a major source of income for the Chocolate Road home since leaving there in 1908; many times he gave his entire paycheck to his mother, making enough for his own meager needs by working extra "towers," or shifts, on the rigs. At least the titular head of the household since his father's death on March 6, 1912, he was clearly *paterfamilias* after his mother's passing, on January 10, 1918.

The loss of his mother, Jim revealed to close friends and associates in later years, was a source of deep and lasting grief, almost of psychological shock. The grief seemed to be assuaged by the role of keeping the Abercrombies together, which he gladly assumed, and by hard work. Jim took much comfort from the continuing presence of The Little Grandmother, and from how quickly Annie and Vinnie had become surrogate mothers to the younger children, while helping so much to maintain a central family home.

The dairy was closed after J. B. Abercrombie's death, and the family moved to a much more convenient location on Graham Avenue West, a continuation of Ennis from Roseland Avenue. Now the Abercrombies were within the city limits (with a new telephone in regular service, Hadley 2214). Milo and Joe Rice remained in school, and Vinnie was at home to help her mother and grandmother; but all the other children had jobs.

Annie, soon to become one of Houston's first women executives, was a clerk (and later, treasurer) of the Gerten-Meyers Supply Company (oilwell and mill supplies, successors to Houston Belting & Supply); but she always found time to assume more and more responsibilities in running the family home, as her mother's illness became more serious. John was a blueprinter for the Texas Company, and Bob a clerk at the Southern Pacific (SP) Lines. There he found direct descendents of slaves who had come over from Alabama with Colonel John Comer Abercrombie, on the long trek with the big wagons from Cross Keys, in 1850. As most of the family blacks, they had taken the Abercrombie name after emancipation; now Ozey and Reuben Abercrombie, freight car loaders, were on the same SP payroll with Colonel John's great-great-nephew.

Will remained in Galveston with his family, and Bolling had joined the Army in the billowing enthusiasm that followed the declaration of war against Germany on April 6, 1917, when there were hundreds of enlistments in Houston every week. Jim, just promoted to superintendent of production by R. L. Young, president of Crown Petroleum, talked to Will and to Bob about the war; everybody wanted to take a crack at the Hun, and those memorable posters (Uncle Sam Wants YOU!) were everywhere you looked. Then Bob talked to a recruiting sergeant, who was ready to sign him up before he asked where he worked. The Army had already been told to leave railroad employees alone, and a superintendent of production for an oil company was in a key position far more important to the nation than having him in training with an infantry squad at Camp Logan[10] or Fort Sam Houston.

As Jim Abercrombie moved up the oilfield ladder, he was watching for an opportunity to invest his savings in a good second-hand rotary rig. He had heard that the oil play in Burkburnett, right on the Red River border with Oklahoma a few miles north of Wichita Falls, had every indication of turning into a boom. An overnight train trip through Dallas confirmed this; Burkburnett reminded him of the boom days at Humble and Goose Creek, with lease traders jamming the town's little hotel and derricks beginning to sprout like a new forest on the horizon.

Back in Houston, Jim redoubled his efforts to find a suitable rig, and came upon one that he financed primarily from his savings. He had arranged earlier for a line of credit from John Crotty, president of the Republic Supply Company. Jim explained that he had no collateral, and no credit record, but would pay for needed equipment and supplies as soon as possible, with interest. Crotty approved this arrangement personally, was paid every dime sooner than he expected, and had all of Abercrombie's supply business as long as he remained president of Republic. Mr. Jim very rarely asked for a favor, and he did not forget anyone who helped him.

Next, he went to President Young of Crown Petroleum about an unusual proposition. He would stay on as superintendent of production for the time being, especially in view of the nation's emergency need for oil in World War I, but would appreciate the chance to send his own rig to Burkburnett, in charge of an experienced driller and crew.

R. L. Young could not recall many arrangements of this type, if any; he was certain of one thing, though: there was not a better man around than Jim Abercrombie. His latest accomplishment had been to save a Crown Petroleum well at Hull that was showing seven hundred fifty pounds of pressure at three thousand feet—an almost certain indication in those days of a costly and life-threatening blowout.

Young agreed to the arrangement; he wanted to keep Jim on the Crown payroll as long as he could, on any reasonable basis; and he knew that Abercrombie would not fail to do his job and do it right, even though he was branching out on his own on a part-time basis. Jim's rig was spudding in at Burkburnett within the week.

Two years later, in 1920, Mr. Jim was ready for the big move. His one rig had been constantly busy at Burkburnett; now he had enough capital and credit to buy three more, and the contacts, know-how and reputation to keep them running also. At a meeting of the brothers Abercrombie, Jim told them that he was leaving Crown Petroleum to organize his own independent drilling company, to work primarily in South Texas and the nearby Gulf Coast fields. There would be a job for everyone. Bob, Milo, John and Joe Rice (who was barely two years out of school but had already been roughnecking) elected to go along with their brother, for whom they all had great respect and affection. Will and Bolling were also close to Jim, but Will had already decided to remain in business in Galveston, and Bolling, back from the Army, also had other plans. He wanted to establish a company that would sell carbonic gas and other supplies to soda fountains, bottlers and creameries. This was to be the Houston Carbonate Company, which Jim helped to finance. Both he and Annie would also assist Bolling later in managing this venture, but it was never to be really successful.

With four rigs running, Mr. Jim found that he needed his own machine shop for almost constant repairs to equipment, adapting non-standardized pipe threads and flange connections, or even designing completely new tools. This was an increasing problem until he remembered a man who could work magic with iron: he was Harry S. Cameron, a native of Indianapolis who had studied architectural and mechanical engineering at a little college operated by the Christian Brothers in Memphis. After a thorough apprenticeship in a machine shop in Little Rock, Cameron invented and patented the first hydraulic cotton bailer.

While still in his twenties, Harry Cameron heard the clarion call of the oilfields; he went first to Spindletop, then to Goose Creek and to Humble, earning a sound and deserved reputation as a machinist of high skill and inventive ability. He could not only repair and refit all types of oilfield gear and equipment, but the work was superbly done and ready when promised; and any time a driller needed a specially-machined tool or gadget, Harry Cameron was your man. He could work from a set of blueprints, or from a sketch drawn on the back of a greasy envelope during the graveyard shift.

Jim Abercrombie knew Cameron at Goose Creek and brought Harry plenty of business until Crown Petroleum sent him to West Columbia to nurse a troublesome well back to health. On his return, he found the machinist at the Humble Iron Works, where he had become a partner.

Soon, Harry Cameron saw much more of a future in Houston than in Humble. He and John Davant bought out the Humble Iron Works, changed the name to the Cameron-Davant Company, and opened a little branch at Goose Creek and two locations in Houston. The first was a downtown office at 519 Washington Avenue, next to the Macatee Hotel; the second a machine shop in a rusting metal building at 711 Milby in the East End equipped with a drill press, a shaper and a couple of lathes.

Cameron-Davant also attempted to enter the new oilfield supply business at its Washington Avenue office, stocking various types of fittings, a small inventory of pipe, and belting, packing and gauges. For good measure, they also carried a line of automobile and truck tires.

Jim Abercrombie soon discovered that he was spending more and more time, and money, with Harry Cameron as his drilling contracts expanded. Often he would be at 711 two or three times a week, impeccably dressed in a gray-flannel, vested suit with a fine-looking hat, in sharp contrast to the machinist's work clothes. He took these opportunities to watch Cameron more and more closely, and he liked what he saw. In the early summer of 1920, he came to the machinist with a proposition. The two of them would buy out Davant, close down the Washington Avenue office, and concentrate on what was the little company's real strength, Cameron's high skills in working metal. Jim would continue as a best customer and see if he could bring in additional business from his legion of friends in the Oil Patch.

The papers were signed on Jim Abercrombie's twenty-ninth birthday, July 9, 1920, when he and Harry Cameron bought the 711 Milby operation lock, stock and barrel for $17,324.31, counting some odd tools and a set of fine hacksaws. Harry wanted to name the new enterprise the Abercrombie Iron Works, or at least the Abercrombie-Cameron Company. Jim's reply was typical: "Aw, I already have an outfit named for me; you take this one."

So, the Cameron Iron Works, Incorporated was officially launched, on August 20, 1920, with $25,000 in capital. Harry Cameron put up $6500; and Jim Abercrombie, $14,500; with Annie, Vinnie (now Mrs.·J. S. Calloway), Bob, Edmond L. Lorehn and Philip E. Davis, providing the remaining $4000 between them. A total of two hundred fifty shares was issued, with a par value of $100. Jim received one hundred forty-five; Harry, sixty-five; Annie, twenty; and the other investors, five shares each. Mr. Jim was named president, at zero salary; Harry was vice president and general manager, at $300 a month; Ed Lorehn, business manager and secretary, received $175 a month; and Philip Davis, bookkeeper, $225 a month. Annie was elected treasurer, but received no salary.

Ed Lorehn was the twenty-six-year-old son of Olle J. Lorehn, a talented architect who had come to Houston in 1900 from the beer capital of St. Louis to design a local brewery. Here he became one of the city's busiest and best-known practitioners, and a prominent Catholic layman. The elder Lorehn would be commissioned to make the first additions to what is now Sacred Heart Cathedral, across from the huge Scanlan oak at Fannin and Pierce, where the carpetbagger and widower Thomas H. Scanlan lived with his seven spinster daughters. He would also remodel an old structure moved from the original St. Thomas College to Father John T. Nicholson's Sacred Heart School, where the curriculum included Latin, Greek, etymology and a little beginning Gaelic for budding linguists who were up to it and Father Nicholson's exacting standards.

Ed Lorehn was the second manifestation of Jim Abercrombie's uncanny ability to identify those of marked ability and potential in technology, management or political leadership. The first had been Harry Cameron, who could work magic with iron.

Young Lorehn studied engineering for three years with one of the first classes admitted to Rice Institute, under such immortals as Lewis Babcock (Pappy) Ryon, James Stephen Waters, Joseph Horace Pound and Arthur Hartsook, after preparing at St. Thomas and at Dean Academy in Franklin, Massachusetts. With the outbreak of World War I, he joined the famed First Officers Training Class,[12] which would furnish so many of Texas' future leaders. After serving as a lieutenant at Fort Sill, Oklahoma, Ed Lorehn was out of Army khaki and his wide-brimmed artilleryman's hat by the last days of 1918.

He thought about returning to Rice to complete his degree in engineering, but saw the advantage of getting a start in the oil industry before hundreds of other former servicemen were also out looking for jobs. Then someone told him, just as they had told Naurice Cummings, that Crown Petroleum was hiring over at Humble. He decided to go on over and apply.

Ed Lorehn did not have to stack pipe with Big Chan, but he was sent to talk with Jim Abercrombie, who still did most of the hiring for Crown both at Humble and at Goose Creek. Jim liked the quiet Lorehn and his training in engineering, plus his experience as an Army officer, brief though that had been. In less than a year, after Abercrombie saw that Ed was both technically competent and skillful in handling people as well as paperwork, he promoted him to foreman.

Jim had told Harry Cameron that they would need a man such as Lorehn, whose obvious talent dovetailed so well with what he and the master machinist could provide at Cameron Iron Works. Abercrombie had temporarily lost contact with Ed after striking out on his own, but he thought that he could find him on one of the Crown Petroleum leases. Later that same day, Ed Lorehn was concentrating on the best ruts to follow as he drove along on a terrible road between Humble and the Montgomery County line. When he looked up for a moment, he saw a car pulled over by an old bridge just ahead. There was a familiar figure by the car waving his hand. As he pulled over to stop, he saw that it was Jim Abercrombie.

Lorehn, surprised, greeted his former boss: "Hi, what's up?"

Jim came right to the point: "Ed, I've bought into a machine shop with Harry Cameron, who used to do our iron work over at Humble. You know how good he is—repairs, pipe adapters, fishing tools, refitting, special orders; he can do it all." Lorehn nodded; he remembered Cameron, and very favorably.

Abercrombie continued: "But we need someone like you to manage details, help on engineering problems, handle personnel and paperwork. The kind of stuff you do so well. That would leave Harry free to keep the shop moving and concentrate on special orders, while I help to bring in new business besides throwing all the J. S. Abercrombie work in there. I believe we could make a real good team; what do you think?"

Jim looked straight at Lorehn. He had liked the man instinctively from the moment he first met him and had a strong hunch about Ed's potential for the future being plenty high; he wanted to get him away from Crown Petroleum. Ed hesitated a moment. He knew that anything Jim Abercrombie was starting up in the Oil Patch had an overriding chance to succeed, and perhaps make it big; but he had just been promoted by R. L. Young, from toolpusher to field superintendent for the Humble area. Still, he really liked Jim, could take a chance, at twenty-five with few if any responsibilities, and there was a powerful, even a compelling, urge to join the Abercrombie-Cameron team in what seemed to be a promising venture.

"OK, Boss," Ed Lorehn answered, and he and Abercrombie shook hands on the deal. Thus began a career of thirty-four years at Cameron Iron Works that brought great satisfaction and deserved honors to him, and major contributions to the success of the company. Lorehn told Jim, and others, in later years that a major factor in his decision to join the new enterprise was how Abercrombie had tracked him down so quickly in the boondocks of far northern Harris County. "He must have really wanted me to come along with them," he recalled; "sort of flattering to a man."

Meanwhile, Jim Abercrombie, ever conscious of his accepted role as *paterfamilias*, had purchased an ideal home for his clan at 3402 Audubon in the developing Montrose area, after a brief move to nearby 606 Fargo. The new residence, on the corner of Harold, would be home for many years for Jim and his brothers and sisters, beginning in 1920. Some of them would continue to live there even after they were married, in a warm and comfortable setting presided over by Miss Annie, as she was now called, and The Little Grandmother, still a central figure in the family in spite of her advancing age.

It was a fine and friendly neighborhood, with J. H. Farbar next door, and Melvin E. Kurth, Congressman Joe Eagle and Roy Huffington down the street. The decline of Montrose was still a generation away.

Annie was now working for the family drilling company, along with everyone except Will and Bolling. In the oilfields, the baby brother Joe Rice had demonstrated unusual talents as he moved on rapidly in what would become an outstanding career as a driller and superintendent of operations. Bob, although also adept in the field, tended increasingly to handle administrative details. John and Milo were valuable and experienced men who would also become field superintendents, but neither seemed to have the ability to "smell oil," make extra drilling footage shift after shift, or free a stuck drill stem quickly. Joe Rice had somehow learned all this from Jim. "Grits" (Joe Rice's nickname on the rigs) was a natural, and his brothers were proud of him.

Jim Abercrombie had offices for his independent drilling company at 206-208 Rodgers Building. He had hoped to be in the more popular Binz Building with his cousin and former employer Charles Abercrombie, but there were no vacancies. The Binz Building had been designed by Ed Lorehn's father, with many innovations: "skyscraper" construction, with load-bearing walls; a six-story structure with a twenty-story foundation for any later additions;[13] "express" elevators; and a twenty-eight-day wait between concrete pourings, ordered by owner Jacob Binz to assure maximum strength.

When the Binz Building was opened late in 1895, with its own artesian well and fire protection system, it had cost a phenomenal $60,000. People came from all over Texas to see it and to claim they could see Galveston Bay from the sixth floor.

Jim told his cousin Charles that he was sorry not to be able to move into "the Binz," but Houston being Houston, better buildings would be coming along. Little did he know how many and how relatively soon, or that Jesse Jones would invite him to lease half an entire floor in the towering, resplendent new Gulf Building (first named for "Mr. Jesse" himself) in a few years. But that is getting ahead of our story.

Jim Abercrombie had predicted that he, Harry Cameron and Ed Lorehn would make a fine team at Cameron Iron Works. He could not have been more correct, and this became evident even in the earliest stages of the reorganized machine shop at 711 Milby. Jim had never required much sleep; this was a considerable blessing, with the Abercrombie rigs increased again to five and on locations often a hundred miles or more apart that he visited regularly. Determined to make Cameron Iron as successful as his drilling operations, he formed a habit of coming by 711 Milby very early, or quite late, for meetings at which his experience in the field, knack of getting to the heart of equipment problems, and ever-widening contacts were invaluable.

Often Jim would bring in something from the Abercrombie rigs, or from a favorite customer, for a quick repair job or refitting. He had bought a big, roomy, dependable Dodge touring car that would carry a small piece of equipment in the back seat without any difficulty, after looking over such long-forgotten makes as the Case Six, National Sextet and McFallon 90 offered by Houston's many automobile dealers.

The timing of these meetings at 711 Milby must have been at least a minor problem to Ed, and at times almost a dilemma for Harry; yet they both saw that the sessions with Jim were of great value—almost indispensable. Lorehn would remain a bachelor until 1928, and did not have Harry's personal responsibilities, although there were conflicts, and it was a long drive from the East End across town in 1920, well after dark or early in the morning, to or from his home.

Harry and Isabel Cameron, however, had five stairstep children, the oldest barely nine; fortunately, they lived only minutes from 711 Milby, at 4524 Rusk near Hurst Street, but Harry must still have had many a warmed-over supper and some hurried breakfasts as he and Ed and Jim saw Cameron Iron off to a solid beginning.

The company had gross sales of $27,741.94 through December 31, 1920, after only six months of operations, four as a chartered corporation. More significantly, there was a net profit of $4609.13. The Cameron Iron Works was underway.

It had been an eventful decade-and-a-half for the Abercrombies, since the family came to Houston to operate their dairy on land leased from George Hermann, Bob raced Old Gracie on a six hundred sixty-yard track, and Jim decided to lead the way into the Oil Patch. There had been the retained sadness of losing both parents, but as Jim promised his mother and grandmother, he had kept the family together; now they were together in a new home at 3402 Audubon that reflected heart-warming closeness.

From roustabouting on Charles Abercrombie's rig at Cypress as a teenager, Jim Abercrombie now headed a thriving independent drilling company with five rigs, all busy on contracts throughout South Texas and the nearby Gulf Coast counties. Not yet thirty, he had an enviable, and deserved, reputation as an expert driller, gifted troubleshooter, and "good all-around well man." Bob, Milo, John and Joe Rice, the baby brother with the natural flair for guiding a bit to oil-streaked cores, worked successfully and happily with him, even though he was insisting that Milo continue his studies in petroleum engineering at Texas A&M College during the academic year, returning to the rigs only during vacation.

Dynamo Jim (his new sobriquet in the Oil Patch) also had Cameron Iron Works underway, with much promise, as 1920 came to an end.

Yet the approaching two years of the so-called post-war depression would test even Houston's burgeoning prosperity, while the Abercrombies confronted both economic recession and a near-tragedy that would in time point the way to tremendous new challenge and success in the decades to come.

Notes

[1] Carrie Nation, who often depended more upon hatchets and rocks than upon prayer in her unique attacks on saloons, kept coming back to Houston as the consumption not only of beer, but of the hard stuff, continued to climb. She was particularly aggravated by a prosperous operation in the old "Bloody Fifth" (Ward), where the owner had the effrontery to rename his drinking establishment the Carrie Nation Saloon. She marched in one evening with a full house on hand, smashed every mirror in sight with rocks out of a stout handbag after disposing of a fancy glass door with her name etched on it, and was going after the barkeeper with a hatchet when subdued. Owner Terence O'Brien claimed that repairs would run to $750, but the publicity was "worth every penny, and more."

[2] Houston was more "electrified" than most Southern cities at the turn of the century, and the incandescent lights had been on longer here. Houston Lighting & Power opened a major generating station in 1897 (without battling rabid environmentalists and licensing bodies), and there was a new and substantial surge in the already widespread use of both commercial and residential electricity; but a few "electric arc" street lamps were in place as early as 1880, the first at Main and Preston.

[3] Anyone interested in the history of the petroleum industry, and especially in its development in Houston, Beaumont and southeast Texas, must read the classic *Spindletop* (now in reprint), by James A. Clark and Michel T. Halbouty. Jimmy Clark, who grew up in Beaumont and was the industry's most knowledgable and readable chronicler, teamed with the world-class geologist Halbouty (who was warning of the energy problems of the

1980s a generation ago: "*sum vox clamantis in deserto*") on this superb book, one of many by the late oil editor of the Houston *Post*.

[4] The entire world production of petroleum in 1902 was 185,150,000 barrels, which would have run the United States just 8.75 days at our all-time consumption level of 21,150,000 barrels a day in February 1979. Four years later, we are using a third less overall, thanks to OPEC, the inexorable laws of supply and demand, and emphasis on conservation.

[5] W. T. Campbell was a cultured and highly intelligent Englishman who came to Texas as a newspaper publisher and ended up as one of the organizers of the Texas Company (Texaco). His daughter, Sarah Campbell Blaffer, a lady of distinction, taste, accomplishment and independent mind, married Robert Lee Blaffer, another giant of the petroleum industry who helped bring Humble Oil & Refining Company to the heights through a rare combination of foresight, initiative and fiscal caution.

[6] City employees having their brown-bag lunch in front of City Hall are in Hermann Square, a lesser-known gift by the donor of Hermann Park. Hermann Square was once the site of the tiny home and bakery of the elder Hermann. Contemporary accounts indicate that the little park was also a sanctuary for early-century winos, who were allowed to sleep off their hangovers there undisturbed.

[7] The "bois d'arc district," south of Quality Hill and a little east of Main Street, was paved with blocks of extremely hard and durable wood from the native bois d'arc (osage orange) tree. During Houston's frequent and heavy rains, the blocks sometimes floated away while inadequate storm sewers tried to cope with sudden, torrential downpours known as "frog-stranglers." Whereupon General-to-be Maurice Hirsch and other youngsters in the neighborhood would help to recover the blocks, which were then dried and replaced, pending the next monsoon-like frog-strangler.

[8] Naurice Cummings, as we are to see in later chapters, became and remained a friend, and a close one, of many Houston giants in addition to James S. Abercrombie. At his office in the First City National Bank Building, where it is difficult to believe that the man you are interviewing is eighty, and not sixty, is a prized photograph of Judge J. A. Elkins. It is the only copy that Judge Elkins, in his nineties when the picture was made, allowed outside his immediate family. George and Herman Brown were his intimate friends as Cummings came to know them and Houston's other titans of business, oil and the professions.

When Hugh Roy Cullen decided late in 1956 to form a Board of Governors to expand community support for his University of Houston, he had his choice of Houston's power structure. He called Naurice Cummings at the top of his list, and Naurice, always frank and honest, said that he was flattered, but didn't know much about universities. "Let me think about it, Mr. Cullen," he concluded. "Well, come on down," was the reply. Mr. Cullen was a direct action man, and his office, the headquarters for Quintana Petroleum, was on the next floor. Naurice went directly down, and told Mr. Cullen essentially what he had said on the telephone. He would think about it, and call him in a few days.

Two hours later, Cummings saw Mr. Cullen upstairs in the Ramada Club, having luncheon with a small group. As he left, Mr. Cullen waved to him, and he went over to say hello. Mr. Cullen immediately introduced Naurice to his guests as "the first member of a new bunch we're getting together to expand the Board of Regents out at the University." After a firm handshake from Hugh Roy Cullen, and congratulations from the guests, Cummings reflected a moment on how determined Mr. Cullen could be. He was an active and valuable member of the Board of Governors until August 31, 1963, when the group was dissolved as the University of Houston entered the state system of higher education.

[9] Sherwood Stewart, possibly still the world's finest doubles player when he chooses to compete, confounds tennis committees and sportswriters everywhere by listing his home as Goose Creek, Texas. He is a native, and proud of it.

[10] Camp Logan, opened in today's Memorial Park area in the late summer of 1917 as a mobilization and training center for selective service registrants, was also utilized by National Guard and by Regular Army units. The Thirty-Third Division would leave from there for duty in France in May, 1918.

Tragedy came to Camp Logan, and to Houston, before the installation was fully open. A battalion of black soldiers from the Twenty-Fourth Infantry Division, a Regular Army outfit, was sent to guard construction sites at the camp, and there began to be disturbing incidents with National Guard units, as well as civilians in various parts of the city. Tensions grew, and on August 23, 1917, the very day that the Houston Chamber of Commerce had set aside for a picnic honoring members of the negro battalion, riots involving the black unit, other soldiers, civilians and the city police force broke out. Martial law was declared before order could be restored, and seventeen persons including four policemen were killed. The Army charged many negro soldiers with mutiny and rioting, and after a tempestuous trial at Fort Sam Houston in San Antonio, seventeen of them were hanged.

[11] Before the American Petroleum Institute brought about the standardization of pipe threads and flange connections, there was a constant need for adapters, or for refitting, on the drilling rigs. Many a driller or toolpusher spent half his time at the nearest machine shop, usually at some critical stage in the attempt to complete a well successfully.

[12] The First Officers Training Camp was organized soon after the declaration of war against Germany, to convert a group of outstanding volunteers from area universities into "90-day wonders" after three months of intensive training at Leon Springs, near San Antonio. They were sworn in as second lieutenants upon graduation, in a special ceremony held in front of the Alamo, and transferred to various commands, often to help shape up the flood of raw recruits being channeled into new divisions. FOTCers with a background in engineering and mathematics usually ended up in the Corps of Engineers, at Fort Belvoir, Virginia; or at Fort Sill, Oklahoma, headquarters for the field artillery.

Rice Institute seniors called to duty with the FOTC in April 1917 were presented their diplomas by President Edgar Odell Lovett at a special convocation at Leon Springs.

Among First Officers Training Camp graduates who later held high political office in Texas were Governor Beauford Jester; Adjutant-General Ike S. Ashburn; Robert Lee Bobbitt, speaker of the House of Representatives, attorney-general and justice of the Court of Civil Appeals; Railroad Commissioner Ernest O. Thompson (a close friend of Jim Abercrombie in the years to come); and Congressman Maury Maverick.

Houstonians in the FOTC, which would become a super "Old Boys" network, included James A. Baker, Jr., Rex G. Baker, Lewis R. Bryan, Jr., W. T. Campbell, Jr., Francis G. Coates, Sam H. Davis, John K. Dorrance, Raymond P. Elledge, Sr., David Frame, Gillette Hill, Mike Hogg, George B. Journeay, Ardon B. Judd, Frank A. Liddell, Edmond L. Lorehn (as noted earlier), Perry Moore, John E. Price, George E. B. Peddy, John T. Scott, Jr., Robert A. Shepherd, Micajah S. Stude, Howard S. Warner, Ewing Werlein and Colonel William B. Bates, who remembered an FOTCer from Mercedes, Texas and Texas A&M College who had risen to the rank of lieutenant-general almost forty years after Leon Springs, and brought Andrew Davis Bruce back to Texas to be president of the University of Houston.

[13] The Binz Building has just been reopened, with the addition of a dozen stories on Olle Lorehn's sturdy original foundation and a complete exterior and interior refurbishing of the eighty-eight-year-old structure, once again in demand because of its central location just east of the incredible forest of new skyscrapers that dwarf it as well as the Gulf Building. And leases per square foot that reflect at least in part 1895, rather than 1983, building costs.

Chapter 7

1920–1929

Problems and Progress, Here and Abroad

Spectacular growth for Houston . . . From a "boll weevil" and near-tragedy at Hull comes U.S. Patent #1,569,247 . . . Mr. Jim meets his future bride, Miss Lillie, at Lake Charles . . . A phantasmagoric trip to London . . . The English syndicate hires a world-class driller for one hundred thousand quid . . . Marriage and a honeymoon on another continent . . . Wildcatting and Christmas dinner in a Colombian rain forest . . . A non-British subject is born in Kingston, Jamaica . . . The death of Harry Cameron . . . Drilling in alligator country, and the first offshore well . . . New dramatis personae *in the wings as a tumultuous near-decade comes to an end*

Houston, the aging St. Bernard puppy, entered an era of spectacular growth in 1920, fed by record lumber sales, three-million-bale cotton shipments, eight oilfields producing a total of almost one hundred thousand barrels a day, eighteen railroads, the state's largest concentration of cattle in a single county and more than ten thousand ships calling annually at the bustling Port of Houston.

From 1920 to 1924 alone, the city's population soared almost fifty percent, from 138,276, to 202,590; there was a need for ten thousand more homes, plus a substantial increase in apartments, that relatively new development in housing; the Ship Channel was lined with the first wave of industrial plants that would in time rival Germany's *Ruhrgebiet*; $1 million was being spent on the over-ornate Majestic Theater, complete with giant pipe organ and unbelievable decor.

Cameron Iron Works shared in this burgeoning prosperity through most of 1922. Sales reached an annual level of $65,000, and net profit increased enough to raise salaries substantially; the original work force of five was doubled.

Then the inevitable post-war recession came to the Oil Patch, in the fall of 1922, and the same phenomenon the industry was to see in disturbing cycles (most recently from 1982 through 1983) appeared: a substantial drop in operating rigs. The next two years became increasingly difficult; salaries were reduced to original 1920 levels, and then reduced again over protests by Jim Abercrombie; he received no compensation himself at Cameron, but knew that Harry Cameron in particular, with five growing children, was already on a tight budget. At least there were no layoffs, and the hourly wage scale was maintained, although some days the work force had to occupy themselves by making pieces of standard equipment for inventory, or by overhauling shop equipment. Cameron Iron Works sales barely hit $40,000 in 1923, and then fell further to $33,000 in 1924 before the welcome turnaround.

In the meantime, near-tragedy struck Jim Abercrombie's drilling company; as a direct result, however, one of the most serious problems confronting the nascent petroleum industry would be largely resolved, and Cameron Iron could take a giant step toward future leadership among the manufacturers of specialized oilfield equipment. The problem was pockets of gas under high pressure, hidden for eons in underground formations until suddenly pierced by a drilling bit.

Jim knew as much as anyone in the industry about high pressure. He had saved the "Sweet Sixteen" for Bet-A-Million Gates, and many another well that had been about to crater for R. L. Young and Crown Petroleum. The old-timers on the rigs said that pressure was just like women: "You can't live with 'em, but you can't live without 'em, either." Pressure brings oil and gas to the surface and keeps them flowing. Under control, it is an indispensable ally; but let it get out of control, and you run the constant risk of a blowout; fire; injury or even death for the drilling crew; and the loss of derrick, rig and equipment, or an entire oilfield.

The problem was being compounded in the early 1920s by deeper and deeper wells, with concomitantly greater danger of suddenly hitting much higher pressure underground, and a resulting emergency at the wellhead. Neither sophisticated exploration techniques, nor reliable control devices, were yet available.

In the late fall of 1921, Mr. Jim had been given a substantial contract by the Monarch Oil & Refining Company to work over a troublesome well in the Hull field about forty miles northeast of Houston in the far reaches of Liberty County. Abercrombie attached particular significance to the contract for several reasons: everyone was talking about Hull and its potential, as they had been since Buckskin Joe Cullinan brought in the discovery well, the #3 Dolbear Fee, on July 26, 1918 after months of rumors about an expected big strike in the area, and a ''tight well'' situation that involved armed guards prowling the nine-hundred-acre lease day and night; further, Jim was human; he enjoyed his widening and deserved reputation as a top troubleshooter, and especially wanted a shot at the Monarch well, which had attracted more and more attention.

Three years after the original discovery, production at Hull was running an amazing eight million barrels annually from a tricky, shallow salt dome with a history of blowouts and workovers.[1] The Monarch well was in a strategic part of this suddenly prolific field, which was producing more than one hundred fifty thousand barrels of good-quality crude a week.

The importance of bringing the Monarch test under control was obvious. It related directly to the ongoing development of what was obviously a real bonanza of gas and oil, if only Hull's bounteous but volatile underground formations could be tamed. Jim had a hunch too that the workover might lead to new drilling techniques, or new types of equipment with a much wider use in the industry.

During the first week or so of the Monarch contract, Mr. Jim stayed on the job almost constantly; he found a room in the little hotel in Liberty for the few hours of sleep he could spare. Suddenly, there was a blowout just as the day crew was ready to take over. There were no injuries, but some loss of equipment and a real mess downhole.

Concerned, yet undaunted, Jim was as usual the calm optimist. The toolpusher and driller were really upset; one of the roughnecks claimed that the well was jinxed, as was Hull overall; a buddy had told him to stay away from the field. The boss was only heard to say what he often said: ''We'll work it out.''

Abercrombie drove back to Houston to check on some other matters and to think about the Monarch workover. He now did more and more of his thinking while driving by himself in the big Dodge—away from the telephone, chomping away on one of the good cigars that he increasingly relished. When he returned to Hull in a few days, he brought with him Sam Cantrell and John Bass, two top drillers who were running other Abercrombie rigs and had encountered pressure problems.

They walked around in the mud and mosquitoes of east Liberty County while the last of the debris from the blowout was cleared away, Cantrell remarking often on the size and ferocity of the Hull mosquitoes that were everywhere. "Gallinippers," he pronounced, swatting at a huge specimen on his neck; "salt marsh gallinippers; if this here field is up to the size and bite of these monsters, old Buckskin Joe has brought him in another Spindletop, for sure."

Later that afternoon, Sam and John had seen enough of Hull to understand its present significance and future potential; they had previously quizzed their boss and the crew on duty about the blowout, in detail. Now they discussed it and similar mishaps they could recall with Jim, and talked with some area drillers and field superintendents they knew, noting how many major companies were active at Hull. But neither Sam or John, or anyone else, seem to have any concrete advice to offer.

If there was consensus, it was to the effect that the Liberty County strike was just a tricky field where you took all prudent precautions against pockets of high pressure, yet still had to trust to luck and the feel and smell of the drilling bit when you went below the twenty-two hundred-foot level where trouble lurked. One widely-held opinion was that if anyone could handle that Monarch workover, it was Jim Abercrombie.

Soon, everything was ready for another try. Things went smoothly for several shifts, and then—a second blowout, on evening tower just after Jim had returned to Houston. Luckily, there were again no injuries; the loss of equipment and other damage was even heavier, however.

The boss took the news calmly enough, as was his fashion; Jim Abercrombie was a patient man, if you accepted a variety of patience mingled with tenacity and being accustomed to success; but Hull and the Monarch job were about to become an obsession.

Characteristically, Jim decided to stay away from the Hull situation for a while in order to get a new perspective, after doing two things: he sent Bob and Milo over to help clear the wreckage and to get to know the territory a little; then he telephoned his contact at Monarch Oil & Refining, to assure him that the Abercrombies would get the job done, although they had admittedly run into a few underground detours. He told Joe Rice, who had stopped by the Rodgers Building office for a quick visit, that even the best bird dogs went to point on a porcupine occasionally, especially when chasing fat quail in heavy brush. And finally, he just drove around for much of a day, attempting to clear his mind and to discover a new approach to the Monarch workover.

One idea that Jim had earlier, then discarded, was the use of an elementary blowout preventer called a "boll weevil." This was essentially a piece of heavy-gauge pipe surrounded by a thick lead casing, with an attached stopcock at the top of the device. If the driller suspected trouble downhole, he dropped the gadget over the casing, closed the stopcock and hoped that if this did not shut off the rising pressure, it would at least give everyone time to get off the derrick floor and away from the rig. The "boll weevil" was simply impractical; there was a later version of a blowout preventer, however, that he thought might work with some modifications, even though it had been on the market for some years with indifferent success.

Jim ordered the later-model preventer, with his own modifications; he thought it worth at least a try. When it was ready, in the first week of 1922, he had come to another decision: he, Bob, Milo, John and Joe Rice would take over the Hull workover themselves. Jim Abercrombie sensed a real challenge; he wanted to meet it head-on with his best shot. There would have to be absences on other company rigs and jobs, but he wanted to be on the Monarch well as much as possible himself and to have his brothers with him, particularly when the workover was at crucial stages.

The five brothers worked carefully for weeks on the Monarch well, expending experience, initiative, ability and just plain sweat as they probed slowly again toward the contract depth. By mid-March they were at about twenty-one hundred feet, almost sixteen hundred feet into the huge salt dome of the Hull field, with its diameter of more than a mile.

Then it happened. Jim had asked everyone to be on hand as he himself drilled cautiously ahead. Suddenly, the derrick floor began to shake; he ordered his brothers away from the rig while they yelled at him to get away himself. The next thing Jim saw was that his modified blowout preventer was absolutely useless; the well was not only going to blow, but blow big. He joined his brothers in a sturdy nearby toolshed just in time; any or all of them could have been maimed or killed.

A contemporary account, not lacking in hyperbole, gives us one version of what started happening seconds after everyone reached the comparative safety of the toolshed:

With a roar like a hundred express trains racing across the countryside, the well blew out, spewing oil in all directions. There was a dull explosion and a tongue of flame leaped into the air, followed by billowing torrents of black smoke.

The derrick simply evaporated. Casings wilted like lettuce out of water as heavy machinery writhed and twisted into grotesque shapes in the blazing inferno.[2]

The near-tragedy could not have happened at a more inopportune time for Mr. Jim's independent drilling company. Hull simply compounded a worsening situation. The 1922-1924 recession, soon to be evident at Cameron Iron Works, was already spreading throughout the Oil Patch and was to affect even Houston's booming economy. It was apparent that there would be some stacked derricks and lean budgets, just when Jim had lost his best rig and was facing major equipment replacements from what was now a total of three blowouts at the Monarch workover, each of them increasingly dangerous and costly.

Jim Abercrombie's reservoir of inner strength and self-confidence made his reaction to this stress-laden situation predictable. He was grateful of course that he and his brothers were unharmed, but even as they watched ongoing disaster from inside the toolshed, his mind raced ahead to the real problem: high pressure. Who can gainsay that just as Rabelais, he saw opportunity lurking behind misfortune and grabbed it by the forelock before it went past and was forever gone?[3]

Jim's practical nature had already accepted the reality of heavy financial loss; this could, and would, be dealt with. Beyond temporary reverses, however, he now saw uncontrolled pressure as an industry-wide problem, and one of transcending impact as wells were drilled deeper and deeper. Most of all, perhaps, his underlying tenacity hated to admit defeat, and the score on that March day in 1922 was high pressure, three; Abercrombie, zero.

As soon as it was safe to do so, he lit up a fresh cigar and went over with his brothers to confirm what they already knew: the Monarch workover was a total loss—cratered and gone. Luckily, there was no fire, or danger to nearby wells. Bad as it was, he told Bob, Milo, John and Joe Rice, things will work out. He asked the youngest brother to telephone home and tell The Little Grandmother that everyone was fine, and they would be home in a couple of hours.

Then he drove back alone, on the miserable road down to Daisetta, over to Liberty and due west, looking again and again into his mind's eye for a glimpse of some new design that would make a blowout preventer practical and reliable. At 3402 Audubon, where Grandmother Wood and Miss Annie had a good steak dinner in preparation (with plenty of grits and gravy for Joe Rice), he relaxed with a couple of stiff drinks of the best bourbon Houston's leading bootlegger could provide, enjoyed dinner with the family, and played bridge until midnight. There was no mention of Hull.

Not able to sleep, Jim tossed and turned, thinking of some variation in existing blowout preventers that would make them really work. Without the rigorous training in engineering and hydraulics that might have hampered his far-ranging imagination and innate creative ability, he came upon a new, common-sense approach that might just do it. Why not try a ram-type preventer with the faces of the rams (simple hydrostatic pistons) closing in on the drilling stem to form a seal against rising pressure? He sketched the elements of such a design quickly and roughly on the back of an envelope before finally falling to sleep.

The next morning he was up unusually early and waiting for Harry Cameron when the master machinist walked over from his home to 711 Milby. Harry asked about the blowout; Jim, who had telephoned him the night before with the barest details, told him that it had been pretty bad but had at least given him an idea.

As they walked into the shop, Abercrombie reached for the envelope on which he had sketched his rough design, only to find that he had left the envelope at home. More and more excited as they talked about the design, he took a soldering rod and drew the outlines of his idea in the sawdust and dirt of the machine shop floor. "It probably won't work at all," he told Cameron. "I'm certainly no engineer." "Well," Harry replied, "engineers can prove that a bumblebee can't fly, because of the laws of aerodynamics; but nobody has told the bees yet."

Harry Cameron had a casting made over at Howard Hughes' nearby shop, and as soon as it was ready, he machined a working model of Mr. Jim's new concept. Later, he and Abercrombie sat in the ramshackle office looking it over from all angles; they knew they had something good, but had no idea just how good. A formal patent application was filed on April 14, 1922 and quickly acknowledged, even though the basic patent would not be issued until January 12, 1926 as number 1,569,247.

The Patent Office, which reviews some pretty outlandish applications, must have been impressed by the logical design of what would be called the ''Type MO'' blowout preventer at Cameron Iron Works.

The straightforward description, already reflecting Jim and Harry's developing policies regarding product integrity, was also a big plus. It read in part: ''Another object(ive) is to provide a blowout preventer which will be composed of a minimum number of parts of simple and rugged construction.'' Jim Abercrombie could still see the soft metal alloy (babbit) of the modified preventer he had installed at the Hull workover flying apart under the first indication of real pressure.

It would be January of 1924 before Mr. Jim and Cameron were confident enough about their new blowout preventer to allow it to be generally available, or widely advertised; tests and major improvements had extended over almost two years. During the interim, it was discovered that the original ''Type MO'' preventer was fundamentally sound but allowed some fluid to escape between the ram faces and drill stem as pressure increased. This pushed the ram upward, further aggravating leakage and decreasing the tightness of the seal.

Harry Cameron resolved this by adding specially-fabricated packing between the ram faces and the stem, and in a further refinement, completely around the rams. The packing contained an ingenious V-shaped notch cut into an area near the corner of a ram face. Rising pressure would force the notch to open, effecting a far better seal. Extensive testing showed that leakage was almost totally controlled by the revised design, which was granted patent number 1,498,610—as an improvement on the original ''MO'' concept that Mr. Jim had sketched out on the floor at 711 Milby, on June 22, 1922.

The relative speed with which patent 1,498,610 was approved indicates how the revisions strengthened the basic design and must have impressed government engineers and patent examiners. Now Cameron Iron was no longer merely a very good machine shop; it was a manufacturing concern, producing a dependable, widely-needed device that would become standard equipment throughout the oil industry. And Jim Abercrombie had indeed seized opportunity by the forelock, before it could get away.

The Cameron blowout preventer led the way back for the still infant company, particularly after the testing program had added steel and cast iron components, and Cameron Iron Works could guarantee two thousand pounds of water pressure in final tests. When Cameron preventers became available for six- and then ten-inch diameter casing, soon advanced to twelve inches, the improved Type MO had captured the market.

South Texas quickly became the proving ground, with new high-pressure fields and the problems that Jim Abercrombie had foreseen at Refugio, and in Live Oak, Nueces and Matagorda counties; soon, 711 Milby had even the first inquiries from abroad: Vera Cruz and Tampico, and a lake called Maracaibo, in western Venezuela. Everyone wanted to know about the new blowout preventer; sales were back to $67,000 in 1925, and then broke out sharply to new six-figure levels.

Within the next few years, the Cameron product line expanded to more than thirty "pieces of iron," including a patented casing cutter and ingenious joints, clamps and shoes. Mr. Jim demonstrated his high-level creative ability again by devising a system for closing the rams on the blowout preventer almost instantly through the use of steam or water pressure. Manual closings had always involved delays that could be increasingly dangerous to personnel and equipment.

As vitally interested as he was, and would remain, in Cameron Iron, Jim Abercrombie realized after months of intense preoccupation with the company that he must reorder his working days (and nights) so as to spend far more time as a drilling contractor. In the five years between 1924 and 1929, a crucial period in his personal development and in the growth of his financial resources, Mr. Jim would be in such far-flung ports of call as Lake Charles and Tullos, Louisiana; London, England; Cartagena, Colombia; and Kingston, Jamaica. Lake Charles would always remain the most important of these locations to him, because there he would find his wife of the next half-century, and an enduring marriage of two persons "as close as husband and wife could be,'' in the words of his best friend.

In the spring of 1924, Mr. Jim agreed to drill a series of wells for Socony-Vacuum, one of John D. Rockefeller's original ventures in the then minuscule petroleum industry. The wells were to be just outside Lake Charles, scene of an expanding new field. The day he checked into the aging but comfortable Majestic Hotel, he ran into his friend Naurice Cummings in the lobby. Naurice had just been hired as Socony-Vacuum's area representative, and both men were delighted at the renewal of a friendship that would last for the remainder of Jim's life.

The Majestic, a landmark in Lake Charles and Calcasieu Parish, was owned by Colonel Charles Calvert, one of the best-known men in the area, but was managed by his daughter Emma Calvert Mickey; everyone called her Mrs. (Mizz, in the pleasing Lake Charles *patois*) Mickey. Emma's confidante and best friend was Lillie Frank, the daughter of a leading family long in the city whose imposing residence was a local showplace. Mrs. Mickey was determined to have a major role in a project that Miss Lillie, a very attractive and personable young lady, could obviously see to on her own: finding a suitable husband. And the manageress had a prime candidate in her sights—none other than the quietly imposing, handsome and immaculately dressed Jim Abercrombie.

There was this difficulty: as courteous as Abercrombie was, he seemed to live only for his work, with free time limited to poker sessions and bird hunting, or predawn duck shoots, with that pal of his, Mr. Cummings. Introductions were soon arranged, however, in the homelike atmosphere of the Majestic, and the match-making Mrs. Mickey was encouraged by how the drilling contractor kept looking at Lillie.

Jim must have been attracted to Lillie Frank from the moment he met her: obviously intelligent, and pleasant to be around, the vivacious young woman was dressed in the fetching style of the mid-1920s, with bobbed hair framing her pretty face.

Mrs. Mickey began to ask each day when Jim planned to return from the field, and Abercrombie noticed that if he came in at any reasonable hour, Miss Lillie was usually there for a visit with the manageress. Mrs. Mickey would have his meal served piping hot, even if the kitchen was about to shut down, and it usually included favorite foods she had heard him order. The chef was instructed to save the prime cuts of beef for the guest from Houston and to find his bowl of gumbo Creole in the rich depths of the simmering pot, among the succulent, thick bits of shrimp, oysters, crayfish and okra.

Soon, Mr. Jim was calling regularly at the big, ornate Frank home at 421 Broad Street, where he was always cordially received by the family; Naurice noted that something significant was happening to his pal Abercrombie: he was leaving the rigs before dark, and coming in to talk quietly to Lillie, fresh in crisp white organdy in the porch swing before they had dinner together; Jim's absence from the poker table, where he had been such a regular, was remarked upon. Manageress Mickey, coming out to the porch to tell them that dinner was ready, just beamed as the three of them paused a moment before going in, to watch the stunning, blood-red sunset above the Calcasieu River. Her campaign was obviously making progress.

In the fall of 1924, Jim Abercrombie was paid a most unusual compliment. A syndicate of English businessmen and investors with heavy political impact in the capital city of Bogotá had obtained a very large concession in the northern plateau of Colombia, primarily in Cordova, Bolivar and Antioquia provinces. This was due south of Cartagena,[4] and less than a hundred and fifty miles from Lake Maracaibo, the Venezuelan bonanza-to-be. There were indications of sizable deposits of oil and gas, but the syndicate had a severe problem: they knew almost nothing about the petroleum industry, and even less about where to locate a world-class driller to put down test wells.

J. C. Walker, a managing partner of the English group, was acquainted with several of the J. P. Morgan executives in New York and sought the advice of this pre-eminent firm. One of the House of Morgan's principal clients was United States Steel, which in turn owned the Oil Well Supply Company, a leading "supply house" for the expanding petroleum industry. Oil Well Supply was well entrenched in Texas and Louisiana, and Mr. Jim had bought many a ton of pipe from them; their top men knew him well and recommended Jim Abercrombie above anyone in the entire Oil Patch, in the strongest terms of endorsement. Thus the letter that arrived a few weeks later, setting forth the outlines of the proposition and inviting Jim to come to London for detailed conferences at the expense of the syndicate.

He was of course flattered; any citizen of the Oil Patch would be. He had often wondered what it would be like, drilling in a foreign country—especially one virtually unexplored with little or no existing production; a major strike would surely enhance his crescent reputation and earning capacity. And he sensed that the men who had contacted him were willing and able to pay a large, even a very large, fee; it was obviously a project of great magnitude and enormous potential profit to the syndicate.

Yet there were countervailing problems and complications, both personal and financial. He and Lillie Frank had pretty well come to an understanding, although there had not as yet been a proposal; he planned to marry the charming Lake Charles girl, if she would have him, sometime in the next several months. There was also the J. S. Abercrombie Company, recently organized with his brothers and sisters as substantial shareholders.

The rigs were all busy, and drilling operations and cash flow had almost recovered from the distressing losses at Hull. The other thrust of the company, finding and developing oil wells of its own, also seemed promising; but beginning production at West Columbia and Stratton Ridge, plus some ongoing expansion he had in mind, would require a great deal of attention in the next several years. He wanted, for example, to have a look at some production near Tullos, Louisiana. The oil was sour crude, but leases were relatively inexpensive and further development of a field with your own rigs could provide at least coverage of your costs with the possibility of substantial profits.

Jim was determined to make a go of the new Abercrombie enterprise, not only for himself but particularly for the remainder of the family at 3402 Audubon. Of all the differing roles that he would accept, and had already assumed, that of *paterfamilias* was of prime importance. He continued to welcome the responsibilities that he had taken upon himself while still a teenager. Moreover, the emerging young executive and industrialist had attempted to communicate to Bob and to The Little Grandmother (his closest links within the clan) that he expected to be called upon in times of concern, not merely when the hurricane flag was already whipping wildly about onshore.

Seemingly gruff, yet innately shy, he was razor-sensitive to the needs and problems of others as well, once the family had been seen to. This characteristic of wanting instinctively to help his fellowman would continue to broaden and deepen within Jim Abercrombie's psyche, shaping his future life to a major degree.

Mr. Jim's first reaction to the offer from London was to thank J. C. Walker and the other members of his group, as well as the top brass at Oil Well Supply who had so strongly recommended him, but simply decline. Then he left the hotel to walk alone along the meandering Calcasieu River, watching for the flights of canvasback ducks and Canadian geese that honked their way south in the deepening twilight of late November, propelled jet-like by a strong, biting norther that spat with rain and mist, threatening sleet.

Finally, he turned back, after thinking many times of similar walks on Pleasant Gray's prairie, long ago in Huntsville; his subconscious, aided perhaps by the isolation and bracing air along the Calcasieu, had turned up another approach to the British offer. The more he thought of it, the more attractive the possibility of a fresh source of major capital for future expansion appeared, if the negative aspects of the proposition could be overcome. He decided to discuss the entire situation with Lillie Frank, who had become so important to him and central to his thoughts and plans. She, predictably, told him in effect to seize opportunity once again by the forelock. Go to London and discuss the Colombian project with the English syndicate; then, whatever the decision, she would be waiting.

Jim departed Houston's old Grand Central Station[5] on the forty-hour trip to New York on a rainy afternoon in December. He had already decided what he would propose to J. C. Walker and his colleagues in London, and would review his recommendations plus some related materials he had in a briefcase while enroute East; but he had promised himself that once on the high seas, he would put business behind him for once in order to rest and refuel his psychic batteries. It was too good an opportunity to miss.

Two days later, with some aid from Thomas Cook's world-renowned travel agency, Jim Abercrombie was at a New York City pier, fascinated by the spectacle of a midnight departure on the Cunard liner *Mauretania*. For the next six days, the lad from Huntsville, whose ocean-going had been limited to red snapper fishing in the Gulf of Mexico, was in a new world on the seventy thousand-ton luxury liner. The *Mauretania,* although launched in 1906, had been beautifully refurbished, with imposing staterooms and vast public areas; its powerful turbines, recently converted from coal to oil, propelled the great ship along at a cruising speed of twenty-five knots. He toured the engine room the first day out, noting the smooth thrust of the turbines and the almost surgical cleanliness everywhere.

For an hour or so each day he walked the long, elliptical deck of the *Mauretania,* impervious to the raging wintry belligerence of the North Atlantic that kept almost everyone else below. On one of these circular marches, he encountered a Jesuit ordered back to Rome for reassignment. They spent much of the voyage in long discussions ranging over everything from how to train bird dogs to Thomistic theology. Unfortunately, Mr. Jim knew nothing of his Jesuit kinsman (alias Robertus Scotus), another James Abercrombie who had landed on that stormy Fifeshire coast in the late sixteenth century, bearing secret messages from Pope Paul IV to the beleaguered Catholic barons of northeast Scotland. That would have provided rich new fuel for conversations that lasted over many hours as it was.

The *Mauretania* docked at Southampton in a marvelous Dickensian snowstorm, leaving the pre-Christmas Hampshire countryside in a light blanket of glittering white. Jim was met by a respectful emissary of the British syndicate who had marked difficulty understanding the Texan's fine Walker County accent, but was himself quickly identified by the pragmatic English device of a small sign hanging around his neck. It read: "Seeking Mr. Abercrombie of Texas," as if anyone could mistake the handsome, sun-tanned driller in the brand-new XXXX Stetson, even though he was attired in his best blue pinstripe suit and foulard tie. The Englishman understood how quickly his quarry had gone through customs when it was explained that Mr. Jim had only the small yet elegant black leather suitcase and matching briefcase Miss Annie had selected for him. Both were politely yet firmly wrested from him by the sign-bearer, who signaled for the liveried chauffeur waiting nearby in a black Bentley limousine. It was already regarded as a bit ostentatious, or certainly a cut below the better levels of *savoir vivre,* for well-regarded private bankers in The City to be seen in a Rolls-Royce.

Two hours later, after a marvelous drive through Surrey's North Downs and the ancient crossing of the River Wey at Guildford, Mr.

Jim was quite comfortably established in a splendid suite at the Savoy, looking out at the snow-clad Embankment. It was difficult to get to sleep, but he finally dozed off after a final review of his proposal, to be put before the syndicate the next morning at nine, and was up at dawn for a hearty breakfast in the dining room soon after it opened. He had never before seen a head waiter in a morning coat. The food was fine, but the coffee mighty weak for a man used to the thick chicory blend they served in Lake Charles.

Back in the suite, there was plenty of time to scan both the *Times* and the *Daily Telegraph:* someone named Josef Stalin was winning a power struggle for control of Russia after the death of Lenin, and a German court had sentenced the leader of what was termed the "Beer Hall Putsch" in Munich, the former Corporal Adolph Hitler, to five years in prison.[6] The concierge called with a brief message: "Mr. Abercrombie's driver was waiting." He gathered up a fistful of the excellent Cuban panatelas he had discovered at the newsstand in the lobby, along with his briefcase, and went on down.

Jim was in the appointed place, the conference room of a private bank between Threadneedle and Cornhill Streets in the heart of The City, just as the first of his hosts, J. C. Walker, arrived; after a handshake, he offered Mr. Walker a panatela, and they lit up. He made a mental note to find out quietly where Walker, in his own hundred-guinea pinstripe from Henry Poole of Savile Row, had his tailoring done.

The meeting began after further arrivals and introductions, and a hospitable welcome to the visitor from Walker, who quickly summarized Jim's very considerable qualifications and experience and the current status of the Colombian concession plus the syndicate's objective of putting down a series of hopefully successful exploratory wells. The Texan learned for the first time of the relative inaccessibility of drilling sites in Colombia, and of remaining ill will there against the United States. Many in the South American nation still blamed Washington for the loss of Panama, once a Colombian satrapy, in 1903. They claimed that President Teddy Roosevelt instigated a victorious Panamian revolt in order to overcome Colombian resistance to the establishment of the United States-dominated Canal Zone, which was absolutely true—as was the fact that the often bellicose Rough Rider won the Nobel Prize as principal peacemaker in the Russo-Japanese War at almost the same time he was stirring up trouble in Panama.

After Walker's presentation, Abercrombie was asked to respond. He answered with a brief, very concrete proposal that still omitted one highly significant factor: the amount of his fee. He emphasized that in drilling test wells in the plateau of the Andean range, he would prefer that the choice of sites, and the details of operations, be under his control. There were some preliminary questions, most of them revealing the syndicate's lack of knowledge about oil wells, and then J. C. Walker made a pertinent enquiry that had somehow never surfaced in earlier correspondence: how long would they have the pleasure of Mr. Abercrombie's company, both to see to his proper entertainment as their guest in London, and to discuss the project in proper depth?

Jim pulled out his watch; it was barely mid-morning. "Well," he responded, "depending upon the exact time of full tide, which I understand is about nine your time tonight, we have around ten hours, less what it takes for me to check out and get back to Southampton. I'm on the last ship that can get me back for some meetings in Houston that I just can't miss."

He had decided before making travel arrangements that if the syndicate really wanted his services, they could prove it on two counts: a quick decision leaving details of the operation in Colombia pretty much up to him, and paying a very substantial fee. Then, in order to reinforce his position, he had asked the Thomas Cook agency to find him a ship returning to America twenty-four hours after his arrival. This had created much puzzlement at the agency, but they had dealt with these unpredictable Americans before. There was passage available on a Boston-bound Italian liner drastically below the standards of the *Mauretania*. The matter of comparability of accommodations coming and going was tactfully yet explicitly gone into in a longish cable confirming the return booking.

After Jim had revealed his schedule to the assembled members of the syndicate, there was a long moment of silence; then ingrained British good manners and breeding took over. A hell of a note that the fellow would only be here for a night and a day, but then no one had really asked. "Well," Walker remarked as chief spokesman, pausing ever so briefly, "we had certainly looked forward to a much longer visit; but no matter, if your plans have been made, and they certainly seem to be definite. I do suggest that we substitute a working luncheon right here in the conference room." A male secretary was already scurrying toward the nearest telephone, after the merest nod from Walker; he would cancel some rather elaborate arrangements at a posh club nearby and engage the services of a caterer on an emergency basis.

Just before nine that evening, Mr. Jim was in a tiny stateroom on the Italian liner, ordering a nightcap from a Sicilian steward who apparently spoke fluent English; he wanted to reflect alone on the almost kaleidoscopic happenings of the crowded last twenty-four hours, rather than in the ship's bar. "Whisky," he said, "and plain water on the side." He had learned how distinctly this meant Scotch, rather than bourbon; but the good Highlands malt blend he had been served in London did have an appealing taste. The fierce 120-proof Irish *usquebaugh,* however, was something again; he had sampled it by mistake as a liqueur, after the hastily-arranged but ample luncheon with the syndicate.

On balance, he thought that the meeting in The City had gone well enough; at its conclusion, he had been told that he would hear from J. C. Walker by cable, probably in the first days of 1925, "or a fortnight hence." There had been another little moment of silence when he was asked about his fee and disclosed that this would be $20,000 à month, for something over two years, or $500,000 in round numbers. One banker had whispered to his neighbor in a respectful tone, "that's a hundred thousand quid!" It was, at the then-existing exchange rate of five-to-one. There had been no protest or attempt at negotiation; however, he was actually more concerned over ongoing management of the project, and such vital questions as who was to decide specific drilling sites, depths and procedures. This had not been too clear, although he had attempted to resolve the matter several times during the long day of discussions with the Englishmen.

Win, lose or draw, Jim concluded, it had been a tremendous adventure, and one he was still enjoying; moreover, whether he realized it or not, the London expedition (brief though it had been) was already broadening and deepening his experience and ability to deal with people of consequence on matters of potentially great significance. Suddenly very tired, he did not leave a morning call and slept almost until noon, awakening to a gray, rolling sea three hundred miles west of Land's End and a mediocre luncheon of veal piccata with unidentifiable vegetables.

The cable arrived at 3402 Audubon on Christmas Eve, delivered by a youngster who had bicycled it across town from Western Union's main office on Franklin Avenue through a blustery wet norther. He gave the astonished boy a $5 bill, and then decided not to open the radiogram until he could share it with Lillie and the remainder of the family. She and her sister Carrie were due within the hour at the Southern Pacific station, for a holiday visit with all the Abercrombies at which she and Jim would announce their engagement. Miss Annie was prowling through 3402 with the housekeeper they had recently hired, looking for any spot of dust against the long-awaited visit of the Frank sisters. The handsome old oak floor in the guest bedroom had been waxed and rewaxed for Lillie and Carrie, and new curtains had just been hung. The Little Grandmother, a spry, alert seventy-two years of age, was in the kitchen mixing up her own Alabama version of dressing for tomorrow's huge turkey.

The news from England was good. Contracts were being prepared by a distinguished firm of London solicitors, but James S. Abercrombie, Esq. was authorized to proceed soonest with setting his plan in motion, under the terms and conditions discussed. Mr. Walker was the official liaison; a drawing account had been established at the Morgan bank in New York City.

There were congratulations, and a kiss and a hug from Lillie; Jim himself was quite pleased but as usual did not show it too much outwardly. Then the emphasis shifted quickly to the holiday festivities and his visitors.

Mr. Jim enjoyed the time with his bride-to-be and her personable sister very much, and particularly the ease with which Lillie fitted naturally into the family group at the big house on Audubon. From the moment the Franks boarded the eastbound Southern Pacific for the return to Lake Charles, however, he plunged into the enormous task of getting together the imposing collection of drilling equipment and supplies that would have to be taken to Colombia via the Panama Canal. At night he pored over the sparse data available on the syndicate's huge concession, studying geological maps of the northwest coast where the Sinu River emptied into the Gulf of Uraba. The Sinu, he noted, was less than fifty miles from Panama's Darien Province; but it was in an area of impenetrable rain forests that still prevented the construction of a land route between Cartagena, on the north Caribbean shore, and Panama City. Rugged country, and no doubt about it.

He was as busy as he had ever been in his life for the next five months, but the Colombian expedition was ready to roll, on schedule, in the very first days of May 1925. As May approached, Jim and Lillie faced the dismal prospect of his absence for at least another month or so, after a time during which his visits to Lake Charles had been necessarily limited. The basic plan was for him to go to South America with Bob and Milo, get things underway; and then come back to be married, with a brief honeymoon before seeing to the newly-expanding operations of the J. S. Abercrombie Company and Cameron Iron Works in the domestic Oil Patch. Thereafter, he would alternate between Colombia and Houston, where he and Lillie planned to make their first home in comfortable rooms at 3402 Audubon until the anticipated completion of the South American contract in 1927.

Joe Rice and John were to take on added responsibilities in ongoing drilling operations, as would Harry Cameron and Ed Lorehn at Cameron Iron; but Jim Abercrombie would continue to be looked to for overall direction and for key decisions; this was already a clearly-established pattern. Even though he seemed to know instinctively how to select capable ensigns and to give them both guidance and the degree of freedom necessary for proper development as executives, he was—and would continue to be—captain of the ship.

Plans can be altered, and as Jim thought of melancholy weeks a continent apart from his beloved Lillie, he saw the solution: a wedding now, followed immediately by a honeymoon in Colombia, with brief stops enroute at Lake Charles, New Orleans, Havana and Kingston, Jamaica.

So it was that Mr. and Mrs. James Smither Abercrombie were married on May 8, 1925, and the young bride was writing her brothers Edwin and Maurice and sister Carrie from Havana just a week later: ''Hope the rest of the trip will be this wonderful; it was so calm coming here from New Orleans we didn't even know we were on a boat. We leave in the morning. Havana is beautiful, and I think we covered it all today. Love to all. Lillie.'' On May 21, the new couple was at San Cristobal in Panama after a day in Kingston, where Lillie was taken with the beautiful contrast between the sugar-white beaches and the towering Blue Mountains behind them.

The Colombian project was headquartered in Cartagena, even though Mr. Jim found it necessary to be in Bogotá, the capital some four hundred miles to the south, on a number of occasions because of relationships with government bureaus and officials and the United States embassy. Luckily, Colombia had one of the world's first commercial airlines, dating from 1919; the two-hour trans-Andean flight could be hair-raising, especially as you approached Bogotá's airport, so often shrouded in mist and fog at eighty-six hundred feet in the lofty eastern *cordillera*; but the only alternative was a three-day trip by automobile, crossing the treacherous Magdalena river plus mountain passes at altitudes in excess of thirteen thousand feet.

Jim flew every time his presence was required in Bogotá and enjoyed every minute of the flight over some of the world's most beautiful scenery. Years later, he was enthralled by the movie *Night Flight,* which depicted so accurately the first years of intercontinental air travel between the Americas.

The old city of Cartagena, with its impregnable walls and fortresses of thirty-foot-thick stone, was a captivating place. A gallimaufry of differing races, cultures and traditions, it had Javanese and seventeenth-century English amid blacks, mestizos and haughty Spanish. The Javanese, from nearby Surinam, bought dried fish from the English-speaking descendants of Puritans who had settled the San Andres Islands three hundred years ago, and married their daughters with elaborate Muslim ceremony in a mosque across the street from the 1603 monastery renamed for the Spanish missionary priest and Jesuit saint, Peter Claver[7]; elsewhere in the city and area, mestizos overwhelmingly dependent upon agriculture were still ruled by the proud, indolent progeny of Asturian *hidalgos* increasingly confronted by the stirrings of modern industry.

Lillie thoroughly enjoyed the city, with its ancient forts of San Felipe, "Tenaza" and San Fernando Castle; and lovely old churches, monasteries and homes of Spanish (even Moorish) architecture. The Hotel Cartagena was nothing to write home about, yet it was clean and comfortable with excellent service; Jim told her it was like the new Roosevelt in New Orleans when compared to the Hotel Patio in Montería, his field headquarters on the Sinu River a hundred and twenty miles due south of Cartagena; or the camps at nearby Lorica and Lorencita. He did not tell her about the heat and mosquitoes and sand fleas at the native town of El Salto, where he and Bob and Milo had worked through a dismal night overseeing unloading operations at the boat landing.

By late June, the difficult lightering of heavy drilling equipment by barge at Puerto Escondido, and its delivery by truck and tractor to the Owen lease near Lorencita (sometimes after building or shoring up their own roads and bridges through the rain forest) was done. As soon as Bob and Milo's drilling crew had spudded in under his expert supervision, Jim booked a stateroom on the next steamer out of Cartagena for New Orleans. He was overdue on his first promised return to Houston, but there was a far more significant reason to get back: Lillie was now certain that she was expecting, after a second visit to the English obstetrician recommended to her by the house physician at their Cartagena hotel.

Jim left Lillie in Lake Charles, where there was a festive family dinner at 421 Broad Street celebrating the joyous news. He hurried on over to Houston on the Southern Pacific the next day. Things were going well enough, but he noted a considerable pile of paper on his desk, both in the Rodgers Building office downtown and at 711 Milby. He disposed of most of this in separate conferences with Joe Rice and John, and then with Harry Cameron and Ed Lorehn; but he made it abundantly clear, in his calm and nonoffensive yet direct and unmistakable manner of communicating, that he never read anything more than a page long and far preferred letters (or brief memoranda) of two or three succinct paragraphs. It was a position he would maintain, and reinforce, as his career moved upward and on.

In a week or so the cables from Cartagena began to stack up, and Jim knew that he would have to return to the rain forests, where a new lease at Tubara (even more inaccessible) was next for exploration. He had been thinking constantly of Lillie. She would obviously be more comfortable, and she and the child safer, at 421 Broad Street or in Houston, much as she liked their part-time life in Cartagena where Jim was so much nearer. He started up the Dodge sedan, and drove immediately to Lake Charles; there he confirmed what he already knew. The couple was so close, as they always were to be, that there was no question of the young wife staying behind. They both wanted to be together, and especially at such a meaningful time.

There was a compromise, however, and a wise one. Cartagena's one hospital was adequate, but few members of the staff had been trained to United States, or English, standards. Lillie remembered that her young London-trained obstetrician had told her of the hospital at the new University College in Kingston, recently opened at

Mona in the northeast suburbs toward Morant Bay. And they both recalled the pleasant, elegant and beautifully-landscaped Myrtle Bank Hotel in downtown Kingston, where they had dined during the brief stopover in Jamaica.

Within a week, Jim had a referral to a highly-recommended obstetrician at the University College Hospital and a reservation at the Myrtle Bank. It was two days from the drilling sites at Tubara or Lorencita back to Kingston, or twenty-four hours with luck; but it was not the journey of a week or ten days back to Lake Charles or Houston. Lillie would stay at the Myrtle Bank, and he would be in Kingston as much as he could—more and more as the time for her delivery was at hand.

What a contrast between Christmas Day of 1925 and the warm, big family gathering at 3402 Audubon just a year ago! There were all sorts of problems at Lorencita that fall, as he had told Lillie in his short but frequent letters between visits to Kingston. Her response, as the holidays neared, was for Jim to stay at the camp until things were better; she would of course miss him, but by this time they had a circle of friends, mainly English planters and businessmen, at the Myrtle Bank and at the outlying Mona Hotel. One of the wives had invited them to their family gathering, but would understand if she came alone.

Jim reluctantly agreed to stay at Lorencita and had a Christmas dinner that came strictly out of cans, other than a tasty young suckling pig roasted on a makeshift outdoor spit; the meal was served on rough planking under tall coconut palms. There was some pretty good eggnog, although he had never tried it before made with goat's milk instead of cream.

The Lorencita well was moving along much better by the second week in January, although he was privately beginning to question the role and effectiveness of a geologist the syndicate had sent over from the University of Manchester "to consult with him on the project." He had decided to leave in the next few days for Kingston, where he was to remain through the birth of their child, when the little camp truck came roaring up suddenly with a cable sent to Montería through the American consulate in Cartagena. The message was from Lillie. She was fine, but the obstetrician thought it best for him to come to Kingston as soon as possible. He noted that the envelope was marked "urgent," and he was on his way back to Cartagena in a matter of minutes, trying to remember the schedule for departures to Kingston, or the name of the fellow who had just started up a little air charter service to the Guineas and Jamaica.

The baby arrived at eleven in the morning on Friday, January 15, 1926. Jim was there for the event, but only by a matter of hours. It was a beautiful little girl; they named her Josephine Evalina, for The Little Grandmother (the baby's great-grandmother) and her maternal grandmother. The birth certificate, issued later in Texas, spelled the second name a bit differently: Everlina. The obvious love and closeness between Jim and Lillie Abercrombie, already noted so often by members of their families as well as friends, would now be intensified and expanded by the advent of their little daughter.

The English can be an efficient lot in administrative matters, if they put their mind to it; indeed, some areas of the world might be immeasurably better off if British administration had been retained indefinitely. Jim and Lillie thought differently back in 1926, however. A few weeks after Josephine's arrival, there were some discreet inquiries at the Myrtle Bank about the new little citizen, presumed to be a Britisher, but not registered. The reason was that the Abercrombies were determined to have Josephine's birth recorded first and only in the States, where her citizenship clearly resided.

The nursemaid was instructed to tell any and all unexpected callers that the Abercrombies were not at home; Lillie timed her daily outings with the baby, in the beautiful gardens at Myrtle Bank, for unusual hours when consular officials were unlikely to be about. Soon, Jim had a better solution: Josephine was three months old, and fit to travel on the high seas; he booked passage to New Orleans on a small but comfortable United States ship and went looking for a friendly Colombian who had once taken him and Lillie on a motorboat ride around the harbor. He had been told that the man was acquainted with all of the pilots who guided ships in and out of Cartagena, and often brought them back to shore.

Jim told the motorboat operator it was imperative that he make a departure for New Orleans, but was almost certain he would miss the scheduled sailing time by fifteen or twenty minutes. Would it be possible, he asked, to be taken out with his wife and baby and be transferred aboard when the pilot was picked up? As he posed the question, Jim brought a peso bill of very large denomination out of his wallet and thoughtfully smoothed one crinkled corner. The motorboat operator thought the matter a little puzzling; bills of that size might easily delay a sailing on their own; but he was a man to assist those who sought his services and could pay for them.

Two nights later, Jim took Josephine up the little ladder hooked firmly to the rail of his departing ship, now just beyond the breakwater and deep channel, handed her to the smiling pilot for a moment, and went back to help Lillie to the deck.

At United States immigration offices in New Orleans, Jim suggested to Lillie that she answer any questions truthfully of course, but as briefly as possible.

"Where were you born?" "Huntsville." "Texas?" "Yes." "And you, ma'am?" "Lake Charles." "The baby?" "Kingston." A pause, but no further questions. Perhaps the official had thought Lillie said, "Kingsville"; or meant one of the 19 Kingstons in the United States. At any rate, Josephine Abercrombie's birth certificate was issued in Houston, Texas and not in Kingston, Jamaica.

The project in Colombia lasted until early in 1927. Natural gas was discovered in several locations, along with marginal quantities of oil. Colombia still produces barely enough petroleum products for her own use—about five to six percent of the giant output of her neighbor Venezuela; the trans-Andean pipeline, however, will substantially increase the production of natural gas from hitherto inaccessible fields in both Colombia and Ecuador.

Mr. Jim treasured the experience in Colombia for many reasons, chief among them being in South America with Lillie and the birth of their beloved daughter; although he seldom if ever voiced criticism of the English syndicate, others have said that he might have had far more success if allowed full freedom in where he drilled and to what depths.

A few weeks after returning to Houston, Jim and Lillie took an apartment at the splendid new Warwick Hotel, only a stone's throw from where he and Bob had raced Gracie against Sidney Long's quarter-ponies. One of his neighbors for the next decade would be another Huntsvillean, Judge Elkins. The rest of the family remained at 3402 Audubon, except for Vinnie (now married to Max Rotholz, a handsome ex-World War I flying ace) and Bolling and his wife. They had moved nearby to 1512 Westheimer.

Jim Abercrombie had not been back in Houston a full day, however, before he discovered a major crisis at Cameron Iron. He had headed straight for 711 Milby, where he barely recognized Harry Cameron when he came in well past his usual time of arrival. Jim knew that Harry had suffered from the recurrence of a tubercular condition that had bothered him for a time again in 1925, but had returned to full duty; he had seen him several times later in 1925, and during another trip to Houston from Colombia, less than three months before. Now the illness was suddenly far more pronounced, with marked loss of weight and of energy.

There had been a serious relapse in the last several weeks, but Cameron had insisted that his partner and good friend of many years in the Oil Patch not be told, since he knew how extraordinarily busy Jim must be winding up things in Colombia; in any case, he would be home soon. Now Harry Cameron was a very sick man, and Mr. Jim demanded that he rest completely away from the shop.

Yet Abercrombie, with his innate sensitivity camouflaged by seeming gruffness, knew that Harry could not, and should not, be kept completely away from 711. His life blood was there, and in the fields where his well-made iron was functioning, whether he was to recover or not. Jim kept the magician of iron advised of what was going on, brought him problems that would excite his curiosity rather than tax his waning strength, and overlooked his visits (brief though they soon had to be) to his beloved machine shop.

Harry rallied for a few months, in the sometime inexplicable pattern of his disease, and was allowed to return part-time to his duties at Cameron Iron; but as 1928 began, he was confined to his home.

When Harry Cameron died on May 20, 1928, the Oil Patch was in mourning for one of its own. The *Oil Weekly* spoke in its issue of June 8 of " . . . the passing of one more of the practical shop men whose genius and energy have contributed materially to the progress of drilling and operating methods."

Ed Lorehn, who had matured even more rapidly under the stress of Harry Cameron's extended illness, was made vice president and general manager, in addition to his post as secretary-treasurer at Cameron Iron. Only thirty-four, he was indeed proving the potential that Jim Abercrombie, keen judge of top-level talent, had seen in him. As Lorehn took his new post, Cameron was just completing its most successful year to date, with record sales of $156,000 and a profit of $21,000 for the fiscal year ending June 30, 1927. A patent was expected momentarily on Mr. Jim's new blowout preventer, the improved model with rams closed by either water or steam power, and capable of being locked into place almost instantly.

Jim also found that "JSA," the family drilling and production company, was in good health, even though production was pretty well limited in 1927 to the sour crude wells at Tullos and some declining oil and distillate output at West Columbia. Now, with the five Abercrombie brothers of the Oil Patch reunited, they and other JSA top hands would move quickly into significant new drilling ventures, especially in Louisiana. Jim and his brothers now had with them such stalwarts as John Bass, M. G. Early and J. M. (Red) Teague,[8] some of them on the rigs since before Spindletop. And Jim had added substantially to his overall firepower by placing the formidable law firm of Amerman, Fouts and Moore on retainer. Judge Fouts and his younger colleague Joe Moore were already specialists in petroleum litigation, and Fouts especially had far-flung contacts in the industry that were invaluable.

The contracts to drill in Louisiana came about through a visit to the new JSA offices at 616-618 West Building by R. C. (Toby) Stewart, superintendent of operations for the Texas Company in the Pelican State. He knew Jim Abercrombie's track record and wanted to discuss with him some promising acreage under long-term lease from the Louisiana Land & Exploration Company (LLX).[9] The difficulty was that the acreage, a huge tract, was in the midst of what the Cajuns called "real alligator country"—inaccessible swampland in Terrebonne, Vermilion, Lafourche and adjoining parishes. As always, Jim listened carefully, without interruption, to Stewart's description of the leases and the problems they presented. Then he was silent for several minutes—so long that the Texaco official began to wonder. At this point, Abercrombie asked two particularly cogent questions, one about geophysical exploration in the area, the other about water transportation to and from it. Stewart responded, and they made a deal.

JSA crews were spudding in on schedule in the spring of 1928 and would keep up to five rigs busy for years on the prolific Texaco-LLX leases, helping the Texas Company to add enormously to its reserves and LLX to become a major independent with skyrocketing prices for its thinly-held stock. It was during this time that Jim Abercrombie drilled what was probably the first offshore well, a good producer in Timbalier Bay set on concrete pilings. "They'll be drilling a lot farther out," he told Joe Rice one day, as they looked out into the Gulf toward Raccoon Point and Isle Derniere. "Nothing to be afraid of on the water, if you use common sense, good men and good equipment—and mind the hurricane warnings.''

Jim was right about drilling a lot farther out, but neither he nor Joe Rice could envision a half-century ago catastrophic losses such as that of the ocean-going rigs *Alexander I. Kieland* and *Ocean Ranger.* The *Kieland* would sink in a raging storm one hundred eighty miles out in the North Sea in 1980, with a loss of one hundred twenty-three men, many of them neighbors in the old port of Stavanger, Norway. Two years later, the *Ocean Ranger* went down thirty miles off Newfoundland in a fierce gale lashing the Atlantic; eighty-four men died.

Jim Abercrombie was fundamentally a Satchel Paige[10] man; he looked ahead, not behind. Yet he must have realized, as the sometimes tumultuous 1920s drew to a close, just how eventful the nine years had been since he left Crown Petroleum to become a full-time entrepreneur.

Like a kaleidoscope, the months and years spun through his memory: Burkburnett and Hull, and sketching the design for the blowout preventer in the dirt and sawdust at 711 Milby; Naurice and Lake Charles, and coming to love Lillie; the still-phantasmagoric trip to London; his marriage to Lillie and the unforgettable honeymoon in Colombia and enroute there; Christmas dinner in the rain forest at Lorencita and the hurried, worrisome trip back to Kingston, followed by the joyful birth of their daughter; the return to Houston, and after that, the still-gathering sorrow over the loss of his good friend and partner, Harry Cameron. Finally, there was the promise of robust new growth for both the JSA Company and Cameron Iron, in a life now highlighted both by crescent achievement and by the happiness Lillie and little Josephine brought to it.

How could he know that the next dozen years to 1941 would dwarf the near-decade he had just lived through, in their ups and downs of contrasting problem and solution, challenge and achievement? He would face the harsh realities of the Great Depression as well as the excitement of an emergency meeting with FDR at the White House; the discovery of a giant oilfield and bureaucratic misunderstandings that threatened its proper development; converting Cameron Iron to war production almost overnight; and many another test of his maturing judgment and abilities.

The curtains were about to open on a new act, with stellar new performers who would figure heavily in the ongoing story of Mr.

Jim. Much of what was to be accomplished in the next crucial period of his career, from 1929 to 1941, would depend heavily upon his rare capacity for discovering people with extraordinary talents that meshed with his own. Among them would be Dan J. Harrison, a former district attorney with a fine grasp of the oil business that would bring him mushrooming success in it; Ralph H. McCullough, the fiscal expert and all-round administrator the Abercrombie forces had needed; and Herbert Allen, a big, black-haired engineer whose inventive genius in tandem with Mr. Jim's myriad talents would propel Cameron Iron to spiraling new heights.

Notes

[1] Hull, although it would remain a major field and the site of significant new discoveries by R. S. Sterling, John W. Mecom and other legendary oilmen, was never again to reach 1921's phenomenal production of 8.2 million barrels.

[2] The quotation is from a valuable early history of Cameron Iron Works published in 1946 to commemorate the company's twenty-fifth anniversary.

[3] In *Gargantua I,* Rabelais tells us: ''Opportunity hath all her hair on her forehead; when she is past, you may not recall her. She hath no tuft whereby you can lay hold on her, for she is bald on the hinder part of her head, and never returneth again.''

[4] The author was involved in a much later episode involving the Houston oil industry and Cartagena. I had a call one Saturday in 1959 from a Monsignor Mallouk, representing the papal Congregation for the Propagation of the Faith in Rome. He had a letter of introduction to me. It was difficult to predict what this was all about, but I arranged to see the monsignor that evening. Monsignor Mallouk was a small, intense man; he presented his card, which listed that distinguishment, M.A., Oxon. (Oxford) plus a doctorate in sacred theology from Louvain. Next came a letter of introduction in a sealed envelope addressed to me; but before I could open it, he held up his hand and began shuffling through a briefcase. Out came a letter which he handed over with understandable pride, pointing to the signature. ''Roncalli,'' he announced. It was indeed from Angelo Giuseppe Cardinal Roncalli, before that man of impact became Pope John XXIII. Now that the monsignor was accredited, he waited for me to open the letter. It was from the secretary to Francis Cardinal Spellman, asking me to assist Monsignor Mallouk in a mission he was undertaking in Houston. The mystery was growing until I recalled that Cardinal Spellman had been instrumental in having a cousin of mine named to President Eisenhower's cabinet, when Ike was seeking a Roman Catholic appointee. Somehow, my name had ended up in the archdiocesan files in New York, under ''Houston.''

Finally, the monsignor revealed what he hoped I could do for him: arrange an introduction to George Strake, a papal knight who had hit it really big at Conroe. Oilman Strake, a marvelous man and most generous contributor to Catholic causes, was a major prospect in the eyes of Monsignor Mallouk's superiors for support of a unique project. They did not, however, want to go through ecclesiastical channels where there might be other plans for George Strake's generosity. The project involved the establishment of a new center, located halfway around the world in Cartagena; under the guidance of Catholic scholars such as Monsignor Mallouk who were natives of the Middle East, it would have the long-term objective of bringing the leaders of the Arab world closer to the Church of Rome.

I located Strake the next day on the first tee at the River Oaks Country Club and managed to get a word with him before his foursome went off. Without going into any details,

I told him that a monsignor had come from Rome to see him on what I assumed was papal business. "Run him by the house about 2:30 this afternoon," George said. "I'll be glad to see him." As agreed, I took Monsignor Mallouk by 3214 Inwood on schedule, and introduced him to the prospect. My assignment was complete, but I often wondered about the good monsignor and Project Cartagena without necessarily wanting to reopen the question with George Strake.

[5] The old Grand Central Station was near Tin Can Alley, just north of Preston Avenue. The squalid, crime-infested Alley was run by a huge woman who went by the name of Aunt Cocaine. She sold the stuff cheap, long before it emerged as the devastating problem it has become today.

[6] Hitler remained in prison less than a year before being released. He used the time to write *Mein Kampf*, the Bible of his brown shirts and source book for the madness that would spread over Europe less than fifteen years later.

[7] Peter Claver was a Spanish Jesuit who went to Cartagena as a twenty-nine-year-old missionary, in 1610. Appalled at the condition of slaves in the Colombian city, then the biggest slave market in South America, he spent the next forty years ministering to the African blacks, bringing them food and medicine and attempting to ameliorate their miserable existence in the pens where they were held like cattle. He and the growing number of his helpers met arriving ships from Africa and went down into the holds where slaves died enroute by the dozens, bringing what help and comfort they could. Canonized almost three hundred years after his death in 1654, St. Peter Claver is credited with converting as many as four hundred thousand slaves to Catholicism.

[8] J. M. (Red) Teague, a legend in the Oil Patch, was a muleskinner at twelve and a roughneck at sixteen. A mainstay of the Abercrombie drilling teams for years, in between repeated attempts to establish himself as a farmer, he became a key member of the Cameron Iron Works sales and troubleshooting force in later years. He will reappear in following chapters.

[9] The Louisiana Land & Exploration Company was organized by far-sighted investors, including Ambassador Kenneth Franzheim's grandfather Colonel Edward F. Simms and Robert A. Welch. Welch once offered to loan his employees money to buy the shares, but they had advanced from fifty to seventy-five cents and many felt that LLX stock had "had its run." During one three-year period in the 1950s, the stock ran up from $36 to $600 after shares split a total of twelve-to-one and climbed again to $50.

[10] Satchel Paige, the unbelievable black pitcher who was still going strong at fifty, struck Rogers Hornsby out five times in one exhibition game and out-dueled the Dean brothers, Jay Hanna (Dizzy) and Paul. Satchel's motto was "never look back; they might be gainin' on you."

Chapter 8

1929–1941

Key Reinforcements for Turbulent Years

Harrison & Abercrombie of dovetailing talents . . . Jesse Jones finds some tenants . . . Invaluable new recruits: Ralph McCullough and Herb Allen . . . Tough sledding in the Great Depression . . . George Strake, Conroe, John Suman and the saga of the Alexander #1 . . . *Dan and the Whale of Old Ocean find a billion-dollar oilfield . . . Brilliant new techniques of recycling and reservoir protection . . . A significant victory with J. R. Parten and Sam Rayburn over FDR and Harold Ickes . . . A stomping saves the Railroad Commission . . . Joe Moore and Mr. Jim win a battle of proration over the Big Fish of the Black Giant . . . Cameron Iron turns the corner and moves quickly to K-guns . . . Herman and George Brown and Suite 8-F . . . A last quail hunt before Pearl Harbor with an old friend from Goose Creek and Lake Charles . . . Five years of complex problems approach*

Daniel Jefferson Harrison and Jim Abercrombie were never close to one another; they had quite disparate backgrounds, personalities, goals and approaches to life; they were not legally partners, although Harrison & Abercrombie would become a trail-blazing company during a crucial, controversial decade-and-a-half in the inchoate petroleum industry. Yet these two physically imposing, highly intelligent men—dissimilar though they happened to be in many respects—were blessed with dovetailing talents that each recognized (and prized) in the other.

This was a relationship founded on mutual respect and admiration for the other's differing abilities, rather than upon closeness; on the realization that despite marching to unsynchronized beats of dissonant drums, they could achieve together a synergism wherein two plus two equaled five—or more. In tandem, they recognized and seized opportunities that might well have escaped them as individuals, worked their way through extremely trying situations and became hallmarks of success in the Oil Patch.

Dan Harrison was born in Williamson County, near Georgetown, in 1880; he was the son of Williamson County pioneers, W. D. and Elizabeth Victoria Anderson Harrison. The family moved to nearby Lampasas while Dan was a youngster; there they met W. T. Campbell, an Englishman who came to Texas to become a newspaper publisher and ended up as an incorporator of the Texas Company, and his children W. T., Jr. and Sarah. Dan and "T" and Sarah, who was to marry R. Lee Blaffer, would live out long lives as Houstonians.

Young Harrison was a good student; he was graduated from the University of Texas with the B.A. degree in 1902, and the LL.B. in 1904. In law school, Dan was a year ahead of Judge J. A. Elkins, better known at the time as the business manager of the UT yearbook, the *Cactus*; and a contemporary of many later luminaries of the state bar. While studying law, Harrison was varsity center on the 1902 and 1903 Longhorn football teams; this was in an era long predating the NCAA, when you could play as long as you were enrolled, whether a graduate or undergraduate student, and might find yourself lining up alongside a few "ringers" whose last enrollment was in grammar school.

It was only nine years before that the first UT football team was organized, and a manufacturing executive named Walter Camp had recently completed five years as volunteer coach of the Yale eleven with a win-loss record of 67-2 (.971). He had begun thirty-five years of selecting All-American teams which were to appear in *Collier's* from 1897 to 1924. The Southwest Conference, with Oklahoma as a charter member, would not be established for another decade-and-a-half, in 1917.

The moment he was licensed as an attorney, Dan Harrison headed for Liberty, the prosperous county seat between Houston and Beaumont. Not far from Spindletop, Liberty already had an oil play and was to be near other significant discoveries and fields including Anahuac, Hull and Barber's Hill. It was a likely location for a young lawyer, and Harrison soon built up a good practice. He served as city attorney from 1910 to 1914, and as district attorney (75th Judicial District) from 1914 to 1918; but he also kept his eye increasingly on oil leases and developments in the area and resigned as district attorney in 1918 to become an independent oil producer. He had married Ethel Louise Hedeman, daughter of a Yazoo County, Mississippi couple who had settled in Llano after moving there from Beaumont, in 1917. Mrs. Harrison was a 1913 graduate of the University of Texas.

Jim Abercrombie had heard of Dan Harrison as early as 1920, when the attorney-oilman was buying leases around Dayton, Daisetta and Hull, and Jim was drilling in Liberty County. They met soon after Harrison moved to Houston in 1926 and opened an office at 521 Mason Building. Jim claimed that a mule brought them together, just as his milk-wagon-pulling Gracie, the quarter-pony, might have hastened his own decision to abandon dairying for roustabouting when the street car ran into her at McKinney and La Branch.

Harvey Mecom, John W.'s father, had a livery stable just off Commerce Street on Buffalo Bayou where he did a thriving business in mules. He sold or rented the stubborn, hard-working hybrids to drilling contractors, and through this got into the oil business himself.[1] One of his livery stable customers was Dan Harrison, who was operating some leases in north Liberty County, where even mules found it difficult to navigate during the rainy season. Dan and Mecom started talking oil, tried a joint venture or two, and soon went together to form the Harrison Oil Company.

Soon after this, one of Harvey Mecom's best mules was hit by a street car. He had been represented by Elwood Fouts and Joe Moore on some tricky title work (where they had a growing reputation), and decided to let their relatively new firm sue the transit company when he was unable to obtain a satisfactory settlement. His new partner, the oilman-attorney Dan Harrison, was either not up on mule law or showed little interest in the matter. In any event, Joe Moore took the case and won it. During the proceedings, Jim Abercrombie, who had made Elwood Fouts vice president of the JSA Company and saw a good bit of both Fouts and Moore, was introduced to Harrison and Mecom.

Dan Harrison was apparently impressed from the beginning by Abercrombie, and the feeling was mutual. Harrison knew of Abercrombie's reputation as a driller and was aware that he was well acquainted with the Hull field, and generally with Liberty County. There was soon an agreement under which the JSA Company drilled two exploratory wells for Harrison Oil in the North Dayton (Old Liberty) field on a joint interest basis. Both hit, early in 1929, and there was soon a firm relationship between Harrison and Abercrombie, even though both men would maintain separate companies as distinctly individual entities.

A great Houstonian who knew and liked both Jim and the more recently arrived Dan Harrison was looking at this time for what he described as "a few more high-class tenants" for his new building, which would be ready for occupancy in the summer of 1929. This was Jesse Jones, who had recently decided to call his new Main Street skyscraper (tentatively named for him) the Gulf Building.[2] Gulf Oil, in one of its perennial episodes of attempting to decide whether to headquarter here or in Pittsburgh with all the other principal Mellon companies, had leased half the structure, and the remaining space was filling up in Houston's prosperous economic climate.

The entire twenty-first floor was open, however, and Mr. Jones convinced Jim and Dan to take it jointly. The JSA Company would occupy the southern half; Harrison Oil, together with the allied Harrison Investment Company, the northern; there was a combined reception area and telephone system, with Dan Harrison having Fairfax 5317 through 5320 plus a special long-distance line; the Abercrombie operation got along with two local numbers. Jesse Jones pointed out how convenient it would be for both companies to do all their banking downstairs at his National Bank of Commerce.

Meanwhile, pleased though he was with the evolving new quasi-partnership with Dan Harrison, and new record sales ($228,000) and profits ($30,000) for fiscal 1929 at Cameron Iron, Jim Abercrombie's eagle-acute recruiting eye was about to discover two men who would assume key positions at JSA and Cameron, respectively. He was not aware that they would become indispensable—first in getting through the totally-unexpected Great Depression, and then over decades of tremendous subsequent progress for the Abercrombie enterprises they would serve with such signal devotion and effect.

The first new recruit was Ralph McCullough; the second, Herbert Allen.

Ralph H. McCullough, a native of St. Louis, moved to Houston with his parents and two sisters in 1911, when only four years old. His father became one of the first tax accountants in the city, and the JSA Company was among his clients. Young Ralph, following in the elder McCullough's footsteps, studied accounting and finance at the University of Texas; while in Austin, he had part-time and summer jobs with the State Highway Department and with the Railroad Commission, gaining valuable experience with both agencies. In 1928, he joined an accounting firm in the state capital.

Ralph's father had sent one of his staff, A. E. Fincher, to work full-time on the Abercrombie account; in the fall of 1929, Fincher needed someone to help him. Young McCullough was advised of this, came over from Austin for an interview and was hired. He began almost immediately to handle some particularly important matters, including the long-established Texaco-LLX drilling contracts in Louisiana and joint ventures with Harrison Oil. Skilled in finance, he also asked some pertinent questions about cash flow and lines of credit that attracted the attention of both Jim and Bob Abercrombie.

By 1931, the Great Depression had finally reached Houston. There were no bank failures, primarily because Jesse H. Jones[3] simply merged the weak with the strong in a historic weekend session behind locked doors; but there were business failures everywhere, high unemployment and general economic malaise. Mayor Walter Monteith had the distressing experience of opening a city relief headquarters in the Hampshaw Building.

Both the JSA Company and Cameron Iron were affected by the delayed, yet severe, economic downturn, of course; the oil industry was especially vulnerable because the vast East Texas fields were running wide open, with crude falling as low as a nickel a barrel. At the Gulf Building, Bob Abercrombie knew that as office manager and budget watchdog, he would have to recommend to Jim that they cut administrative costs to the bone. Jim agreed, but they had both already seen enough of Ralph McCullough to know that he would remain on the payroll.

Ralph himself came to Bob, told him that he was a twenty-three-year-old bachelor living at home, was aware that times were tough and would be willing to work for nothing until things were better. Bob appreciated this but told McCullough that he would continue to draw $100 a month. Ralph never forgot this, coming as it did when a roast beef entree with potatoes thrown in would run nineteen cents at the Forum cafeteria down Main Street, and Ethyl gasoline was going for seventeen cents a gallon.

Less than two years later, A. E. Fincher and his wife were killed in an automobile accident near San Antonio. Within the week, Bob Abercrombie told Ralph that "The Boss" wanted to see him. Jim had already decided that McCullough should be offered Fincher's position.

Ralph and The Boss talked for a few moments, recalling Fincher's death with sorrow. He had been a good and valuable man, and a long-time friend and colleague of Ralph's father. Then Jim told McCullough that he had made an excellent impression and could have Fincher's position if he wanted it. "You're young, son," he told him, "but you can handle the job. If we didn't think you could, we wouldn't offer it."

Abercrombie went on for a few minutes: "You know pretty well how Fincher operated, but you may not know something about me. When I hire a man for a job this important to us, I expect him to make his own way until he hits a problem or a situation he wants to bring to Bob, or to me."

"Couple of other things," he continued, in what was becoming a longish speech for Mr. Jim, "you have some special training and experience. Not just tax accounting, either; I noticed that you worked at the Railroad Commission, and know something about cash flow and bank loans. I expect I'll want to bounce some ideas off you." Jim was silent, and Ralph thought that the interview was over; then he saw through the cigar smoke that The Boss was still thinking and was about to add something. "Then there's detail," he said. "I'm no good at it, but I'm often in need of someone who can carry out the details of a plan and do it right. You seem to be good at that."

McCullough told Jim that he wanted the job, was glad to have it and appreciated the faith he and Bob had shown in him. They shook hands, cementing a relationship already in place that was to last another forty-four years.

Herbert Allen had licked polio as a child, and now the big, affable youngster with the burly shoulders and anthracite-black hair was not about to allow lack of funds to prevent him from getting a good engineering education. Excellent grades at little Nacogdoches High School had sent him on to the gifted professors at Rice Institute, where William Marsh Rice's original concept of no tuition would still be in effect for many years when he matriculated in 1924. A partial scholarship as a freshman football player and a campus job rolling tennis courts would take care of his board and room.

After a year in which he lettered both in freshman football and as a shotputter on the track team that would soon include the world champion sprinter Claude Bracey, Herb decided that he would drop athletics. It was impossible for a man to be on the practice field and in an afternoon engineering laboratory simultaneously, much as he liked football and track and the Institute's first full-time football coach (none other than the immortal-to-be John Heisman). All during the next academic year, he got up at dawn to roll the campus tennis courts before his 8 a.m. class; and as soon as his laboratory sessions were over, he headed downtown to operate the switchboard at the old Methodist Hospital until midnight. In those far more tranquil days, a man could do a lot of homework at a switchboard, especially as the evening lengthened toward midnight.

Herb remained out of Rice in his junior year (1926–1927). He was barely nineteen and younger than most of his classmates; he decided that some time in a good machine shop would provide both some down-to-earth experience and a little nest egg with which to complete his engineering degree. When he returned to the Institute after fifteen months at the Lufkin Foundry, he had learned not only how to do almost anything on a lathe, shaper or drill press but some invaluable things about forging, casting and shaping metal. Although he would not realize this until later, he had also learned a great deal about how to get along with blue-collar workers.

In his senior year (1928–1929), young Allen's professors recommended him for a project that was to affect the remainder of his long and tremendously successful career. Will Hogg, son of the legendary Governor Jim Hogg, wanted to test the feasibility of an oscillating (rather than a rotating) drilling bit; the bit would be driven by the hydraulic flow of mud. An experiment was set up at Rice, on the banks of a little bayou that then meandered through the southwest portion of the campus, with Herb in charge.

The project continued after Allen's graduation in May 1929 but was suddenly terminated early in 1931. David Picton, attorney for the Hogg interests, kept Herb on the payroll a month to clean up remaining details, and gave him permission to continue to work on his own on a variation of the oscillating bit that had occurred to him: he called it a "relief valve," designed to lower and control pressure. Allen was soon urged to show his relief valve to Joseph A. Tennant, a brilliant consulting engineer.

Tennant was not greatly impressed, but indicated that he might want to keep in contact with Herb. "What about?" the young engineer inquired. "Well, I'm just not at liberty to say, right now," was Tennant's reply. Allen's curiosity was thoroughly aroused by this time; he went to a good friend, Lyle Cashion, who was in charge of petroleum equipment for Gulf Oil in the area.

Cashion had the answer: Joe Tennant, Jim Abercrombie, Dan Harrison and Lenoir Josey were in the process of acquiring the rights to a new type of slush pump being developed by Charles Stevens of San Antonio. If perfected, it would be a major improvement over the steam pumps then generally in use on drilling rigs; steam pumps wore down valves, liners and pistons alarmingly because drilling mud was constantly swirling around these operating parts. As a consequence, most drillers kept one or even two reserve pumps on standby. The new Stevens design had a cylindrical sleeve to keep mud and moving parts separated.

A few days later, Cashion and Allen were looking at an early model of the Stevens pump on a Gulf Oil rig in the North Liberty field. Herb studied it carefully and soon had some ideas for improving performance of the device. Back in Houston, Allen called on Joe Tennant and told him with a straight face that he had seen a piece of equipment that might interest the consulting engineer; he then gave Tennant his ideas concerning the Stevens pump. A week later, Herb Allen was hired as the first employee of the newly-organized Abercrombie Pump Company. It was just in time; off the Hogg payroll for more than three months, he was down to his last $5 bill.

Allen borrowed some space at Rice Institute and went to work with Tennant and Charles Stevens. Their assignment was to get the bugs out of the new slush pump, so that it could be manufactured at Cameron Iron Works; engineering and sales would be handled by Abercrombie Pump.

Herb soon had a visitor at Rice. It was Jim Abercrombie. He had never met the man, but recalls vividly his first impressions: "I knew him by reputation as already being one of the great men in the oilfields. I was a little awed by him, but found at once that although he had little to say, he and I could communicate. In a sort of mental shorthand, I suppose. We didn't say a lot to one another; we just thought in sync."

In a month or so, Allen moved out to 711 Milby; he had a tiny office opening directly on the street, where Jim Abercrombie became a regular visitor, usually between six in the evening and midnight—often until two in the morning if he and Herb were discussing something of particular interest or looking at a newly-machined part. Mr. Jim, as the young engineer called him, "was a born engineer who just never got around to taking his engineering degree.'' He noticed early on that Abercrombie had to know everything about a problem, and as soon and succinctly as possible. ''He got to the heart of the matter, in a hurry,'' Allen remembers. ''The man had no interest in written reports; just 'what is this all about, in a few words'.''

Mr. Jim was establishing more firmly his unbelievable working hours and patterns that would persist for many years: six to eight hours at Cameron Iron Works after a full day occupied with problems at the JSA Company, and now with Harrison & Abercrombie business as well.

Ironically, the Stevens slush pump was never developed commercially; it had some inherent problems that were never satisfactorily resolved. Yet from it came the first two of what were to be more than three hundred patents from the fertile mind and innovative genius of Herbert Allen: (1) a reliable pressure gauge for use in the field; and (2) a ''shear relief valve'' based on modification of the concept he had first brought to Joe Tennant. Both gauge and valve became standard equipment, widely used in the petroleum industry.

Jim Abercrombie would soon have additional proof of the significance of his two new recruits, as Ralph McCullough as well as Herb Allen made growing contributions at the JSA Company and at Cameron. McCullough had broadened his role and greatly expanded both his present value and future potential. This came about after Jim reminded him of their earlier conversation in which he had told Ralph he would look to him as a sounding board for ideas, in addition to his day-to-day duties and carrying out the details of special projects. But, Abercrombie mildly reproved him, McCullough always seemed to be surrounded by papers and whirring calculators.

Ralph got the idea; he made himself more available to The Boss even if it meant running the calculators after normal office hours. And he learned how to delegate less important functions. Soon McCullough was on track for more and more important assignments, even though advancement would be delayed for him and rising young executives everywhere by the spreading economic malaise of the early 1930s.

At 2105–2116 Gulf Building

Ralph H. McCullough, The Boss' right-hand man for forty-four years.

Miss Vinnie (Lavinia Abercrombie (Mrs. Max) Rotholz).

Joe Rice Abercrombie, who had Mr. Jim's feel for a drilling bit.

The invaluable Freda Bowen, now in her thirty-seventh year with the Abercrombie organization she has served with ability and dedication.

Charter members of the governing body of the Texas Children's (Hospital) Foundation, in 1947. Their unrealized dream (and that of the Houston Pediatric Society) of a specialized hospital for children in the Texas Medical Center was brought to Mr. Jim, first by his physician, H. J. (Jack) Ehlers, M.D., and then by Leopold Meyer. The result was the Texas Children's Hospital, which treated almost fifty-seven thousand children, many of them with complex pediatric disorders, in 1982. Standing (left to right): A. Lane Mitchell, M.D.; John K. Glen, M.D.; George W. Salmon, M.D.; H. J. Ehlers, M.D.; George A. Butler, secretary; Raymond Cohen, M.D. Seated: Miss Nina J. Cullinan; David Greer, M.D., president; Mrs. H. Malcolm Lovett; and Leopold Meyer, treasurer.

The present interlocking facilities of the Texas Children's Hospital, St. Luke's Episcopal Hospital and the Texas Heart Institute.

Mr. Jim and Lep Meyer with a friend at the opening tour of the Texas Children's Hospital. Jesse Holman Jones liked the picture so much he autographed it.

Bob Hope, gifted supporter of good causes, Texaco salesman and would-be golfer, admires Jim Abercrombie's portrait in the lobby of the Texas Children's Hospital.

Ralph McCullough, standing at right, surveys another sell-out crowd at the 1946 Pin Oak Horse Show.

Mr. Jim and Walter Pidgeon indulge in a little horse (burro) play to publicize the Pin Oak Horse Show, at Seven Falls, Colorado.

Four Pin Oak champions: M and M, Mr. Jim and Josephine.

Jim and brother Milo welcome a Viennese beauty to an opening night party at Pin Oak Stables.

Hunting Quail on Mustang Motte

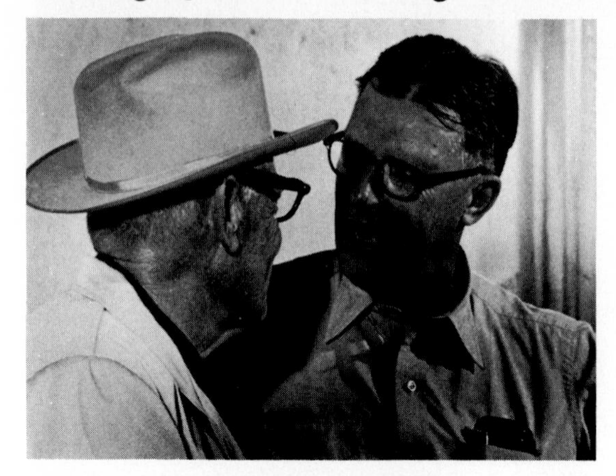

"You remember when we shot that snipe, over at Goose Creek?"

Jim and Bob Abercrombie, shooting in front of a rapidly-approaching blue norther with Colonel Ernest O. Thompson.

The color-blind W. A. (Bill) Smith in his hunting gear, but who enjoys Mustang Motte more, or is more popular there?

L. F. (Mac) McCollum in the midst of a friendly, hungry group. Note the luxurious table setting including sterling bread trays and Baccarat crystal; but that is Dom Perignon champagne Naurice Cummings is inspecting at the far end, and the broiled quail and porterhouse steak cannot be beat.

The hunters of 1949.

Sitting: Sayles Leach, Ernest Thompson, Jack Blalock, Jim Abercrombie, Naurice Cummings (Big Business), Herman Brown, John Suman, W. A. (Bill) Blackwell, Ed Cumming.

Standing: Bob Henderson, Reiffert Blackwell, Lem Buderstadt, Fred Muegge, Jack Suman, Milo Abercrombie.

Herman Brown zeroes in on one.

J. Sayles Leach, refugee from a Texas Company board meeting any time he can get to the Blackwell Ranch with his hunting pals.

Naurice's murdered hat; never wear a new one to Mustang Motte.

Ed Cumming (left), the poet laureate of Mustang Motte, and W. A. (Bill) Blackwell, host for a series of great gatherings that extended over a quarter-century until his death in 1962.

Mr. Jim and his good friend R. W. (Cotton Bob) Henderson look over a fine picture of Cotton Bob Henderson.

Bob Abercrombie and Mr. Jim with two promising new dogs from the Cuero Academy for Well-Trained Pointers.

Mr. Jim finds Hugh Roy Cullen, another giant of the Oil Patch, in a contemplative mood. Thinking of Tom O'Connor versus Old Ocean?

With a successful Suite 8-F candidate, Governor-to-be Beauford Jester, landslide victor over Homer P. Rainey in the 1946 Democratic Party runoff.

GEORGE R. BROWN
and
WM. A. "BILL" SMITH
are honoring
LEOPOLD L. MEYER
with a cocktail party
upon the occasion of his
90th birthday
Monday, June 21st, 1982
5 pm — 7 pm
The Brown Apartment
8-F Lamar Hotel

No gifts please
Please phone 223-5721 if declining

Greeting another key participant in the historic proration hearings on Old Ocean, Colonel Ernest Thompson. That is a former King Nottoc between Mr. Jim and the colonel, with the Old Gray Fox (Mayor Oscar Holcombe) at far right.

LBJ towers over Lep Meyer and Mr. Jim at a Mid-Continent Oil and Gas Association reception, shortly after beginning the vigorous campaign that resulted in his election as United States senator by a margin of 87 votes, on November 2, 1948. At left, Hampton C. Robinson, Jr., M.D., and Corbin J. Robertson, partially obscured; at right, Naurice Cummings.

A relaxed moment with a Suite 8-F compadre *and even closer friend of then-President Lyndon Baines Johnson, the modest tycoon-philanthropist and marvelous Houstonian, George Brown.*

Jim Abercrombie, uncanny judge of political ability and potential, with John B. Connally, another winner he backed early on and in the stretch, when $75,000 committed at the Stephen F. Austin by Ralph H. McCullough in the nick of time probably bought the radio time that meant the difference in dark horse candidate Connally's winning campaign for the governorship.

The President and Mrs. Roosevelt
request the pleasure of the company of
Mr Abercrombie
at a buffet luncheon at the White House
on Monday, January the twentieth
nineteen hundred and forty-one
immediately after the Inaugural Ceremonies
at the Capitol

The honor of your prese
is requested at the ceremonies
attending the Inauguration of the
President of the United Stat
January twentieth,
Nineteen hundred forty-five.

Harry Flood Byrd, Chairman,
Kenneth McKellar, Arthur Vandenberg, Sam Rayburn,
Robert L. Doughton, Joseph W. Martin, Jr.,
Committee on Arrangements.
Edwin A. Halsey, Secretary.

Please present the enclosed
card of admission.

THE WHITE HOUSE

Mr. and Mrs. J. S. Abercrombie
Gulf Building
Houston, Texas

Mrs. Roosevelt
At Home
on Friday afternoon
January 19, 1945
at three o'clock

The White House
Admit at East Gate
NOT TRANSFERABLE
January 20, 1941

DISPLAY ON WINDSHIELD OF CAR

The Inaugural Committee
requests the honor of your presence
to attend and participate in the Inauguration of
John Fitzgerald Kennedy
as President of the United States of America
and
Lyndon Baines Johnson
as Vice President of the United States of America
on Friday the twentieth of January
one thousand nine hundred and sixty-one
in the City of Washington

Edward H. Foley
Chairman

WESTERN UNION

D A WA011 GOVT NL PD
THE WHITE HOUSE WASHINGTON DC 25
J S ABERCROMBIE (CARE ASST HOTEL MGR ON DUTY)
LA FONTAINE ROOM WARWICK HOTEL HOU
THE LUNCHEON IN YOUR HONOR IS HIGHLY REGISTED AS AN EXPRESSION OF GRATITUDE FOR YOUR CONTRIBUTIONS TO HEALTH, AGRICULTURE AND INDUSTRY AND FOR YOUR MANY ENDEAVORS ON BEHALF OF YOU CITY, STATE AND NATION. YOUR ACCOMPLISHMENTS WILL ENDURE LONG BEYOND THIS HOUR. I AM HAPPY TO JOIN IN THIS TRIBUTE AND SEND MY BEST WISHES UPON YOUR DESIGNATION AS KEY HOUSTONIAN OF THE YEAR. I HAVE LONG KNOWN THAT YOU ARE ONE OF TEXAS MOST RESPECTED AND DESERVING PATRIOTS -- AND WE WHO LOVE OUR STATE ARE THANKFUL THAT YOU CAME OUR WAY
LYNDON B JOHNSON

The post-war Katy Road plant of Cameron Iron Works, ready for enormous expansion into what will become a world-wide manufacturing, service and distributing organization with more than $1 billion in annual sales.

Herbert Allen and "The Boss" when Allen was named a fellow of the American Society of Mechanical Engineers for his many and distinguished contributions to his profession, on September 9, 1964.

Herb Allen's twenty thousand-ton multiple ram forging press, the world's largest when it was built at Cameron Iron Works in 1960 in less than six months, to anticipate new problems and demands of the jet-atomic age. The frame is fifty feet high, and the press weighed in at 3,158,250 pounds.

Mr. Jim receives a recognition he especially prized, from a friend and colleague he holds in high regard. John R. Suman, president of the Texas Mid-Continent Oil and Gas Association, presents him the TM-CO&GA Distinguished Service Award for 1952.

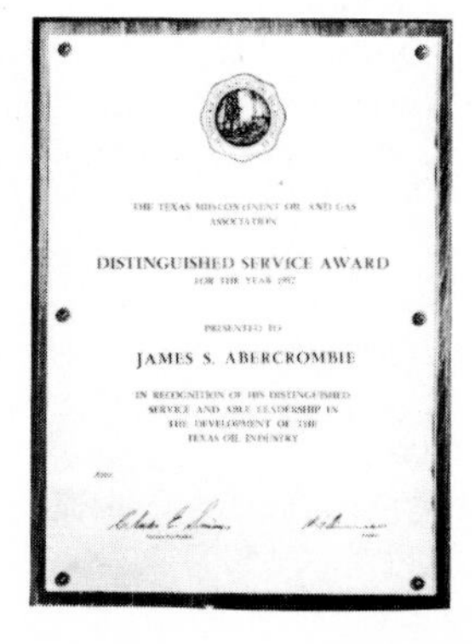

Jim Abercrombie's historic 1922 blowout preventer, on exhibition for many years at the Smithsonian Institution, is now on permanent exhibition at Cameron Iron Works. Four feet long and two feet high, it could withstand three thousand pounds of cold-water pressure per square inch.

A land-based Cameron Iron Works Christmas tree that looks like a handsome piece of modern sculpture but is a rugged, very effective "piece of iron."

"Christmas trees," to control producing wells, are engineered to withstand pressures many times higher than the original blowout preventer of 1922. This underwater model has a fascinating but thoroughly practical design which led one customer to claim that CIW had Rube Goldberg on its engineering staff.

Mr. Jim points the way ahead as he and Miss Lillie enjoy a visit with grandsons Jim and George, first of the eighth generation of Abercrombies in these United States.

As the Depression tightened its harsh grip on the economy, Jim Abercrombie's attention was focused on potentially disastrous turnarounds at Cameron Iron and at the JSA Company. After another record-breaking year at Cameron in fiscal 1930 (sales, $479,000; profits, $114,000), sales fell fifty-one percent to $234,000 and then a catastrophic further sixty-three percent to $87,000 in 1931 and 1932, respectively. Profits plummeted from $114,000 to $6000 in 1931, and then to a loss of $29,000 in fiscal 1932. The drilling business was so slow that Milo, John and Joe Rice helped Cameron Iron personnel dig slush pits for a new pump warehouse on Clinton Drive.

Still, no one lost his sense of humor. When Jim, enroute to a meeting with Dan Harrison, stopped by, his brothers were ready for a little horseplay. They put down their shovels and made toward the nattily-dressed executive. "Let's see how old Jim will look in the pit," someone shouted. As they advanced, the intended victim suddenly took off his coat and laid his Stetson carefully on it. Then he rolled up his sleeves and got ready for battle. The game was over; no one really wanted to test Brother Jim, whose ability in enforcing discipline on the early rigs was still remembered. He had been to Fist City, as necessary, at Goose Creek and Spindletop and Humble and elsewhere—although his wider reputation was as a peacemaker.

Abercrombie soon found that Dan Harrison could be a major factor in improving the situation for the JSA Company and its stacked rigs. Dan was quite adept at finding potentially profitable drilling deals, or in helping to close deals that Jim had discovered. Both men were known as fair, but extremely tough, traders; in the Oil Patch, things were very slow, but a few big lease brokers, then some independents and majors began to call on Harrison & Abercrombie (H&A). They brought propositions that combined reasonable risk with the possibility of substantial profit; you did get hard trading, but a definite yes or no; plus a clean, legally tight contract drawn by Harrison, and Abercrombie's experience in drilling, expert knowledge of equipment and nose for oil.

Late in 1932, H&A acquired a promising lease near Luling and brought in five good producers in the new Darst Creek field. With part of the proceeds, they made two investments, one of lasting importance to the future of both Jim and Dan and their companies.

First, they went into the gigantic East Texas field before the situation there became chaotic, yet they had to store more than one hundred fifty thousand barrels of crude before gradually disposing of it on a roller coaster market. The second investment involved a lease on fifteen acres in the potentially spectacular Conroe field, "smack dab in the middle," as Abercrombie described it, of more than ten thousand acres held by Humble Oil & Refining and George Strake. Strake had brought in the discovery well six miles southeast of Conroe on December 13, 1931.[4]

The Harrison and Abercrombie Alexander #1 came in at Conroe as a good producer, after being completed at 5160 feet in George Strake's discovery shale. Two weeks later, the Standard of Kansas #1, on the lease immediately adjoining the H&A well, blew out and caught fire, apparently from a combination of high pressure and improperly-set casing; it then cratered, and an offset well also belonging to Standard of Kansas went through the same cycle.

Jim Abercrombie was determined to save his own well. He simply lived day and night with the Alexander #1 after he and Red Early, the driller, ordered a deep moat built around it to lessen the danger of fire. But on January 26, 1933, the Alexander also cratered while the Standard of Kansas wells continued an intermittent bombardment of rocks and jagged bits of casing. Jim knew it was coming: he and Red had figured out that if they could examine the Christmas tree still in place atop their well, they would know a good bit more about the chances of saving the Alexander. They built a sort of tunnel out of tin and crawled up through it for a look, but the news was all bad. The Christmas tree was leaking steadily, portending an imminent blowout and cratering.

When the well blew the next day, it began one of the legendary sagas of the Oil Patch and, happily, a chain of events that brought Harrison & Abercrombie several million dollars of badly-needed income.

Within hours, the Alexander #1 was sitting in a deepening, already enormous hole festooned with the remnants of Jim's best rig and assorted equipment. Gas bubbled around some ruined casing and sub-surface rocks. Abercrombie, for once really discouraged and bordering on physical exhaustion, went into Conroe to telephone Dan Harrison. When he came back, an amazing thing had happened: a tremendous volume of oil was flowing from the remnants of the seven-inch casing in the cratered well; it would soon spill over into the moat surrounding it.

Jim estimated the flow at perhaps two hundred barrels an hour; actually, it was double that and more: ten thousand barrels a day. Now he and Dan were in a completely new ball game, involving George Strake, Humble Oil & Refining, the Texas Railroad Commission and every operator in the already gigantic Conroe field, which would dwarf everything on the Gulf Coast if it could be saved.

Officials of Humble Oil had acquired almost half of George Strake's eighty-five hundred acres under lease at Conroe, through their preeminent geologist Wallace Pratt, plus another three thousand acres on their own. They and Strake saw the ten thousand barrels a day flowing from the Alexander #1 as life blood draining from their bodies. If continued long enough, it could cause other operators to insist on running wide open, thus depleting in a few years underground pressures and reserves estimated to last generations.

The Railroad Commission, in a crucial fight for proper proration and spacing, had to watch one well (due to no fault of Harrison & Abercrombie) use up the allocation for a hundred wells and increase the possibility of demands for exceptions. Independents such as C. M. (Pete) Frost (who had managed to wander into Strake's discovery location just when a revealing drill stem test was going on and began leasing heavily the same day) also had much at stake.

Fortunately, Humble Oil saw the vital importance of the Alexander #1 crater and assigned one of their very best upcoming executives to remedying the situation as equitably and quickly as possible. This was John R. Suman, a highly capable young geologist-administrator from the University of California who would soon be promoted to a vice-presidency.

Suman was a staunch advocate of conservation, and an innovator, who left his positive mark on "the Humble" as well as on Standard of New Jersey. He remembered directional or "whipstocked" wells that he had seen at Huntington Beach in California, and the expert in this procedure, John Eastman. W. W. Moore, Humble Oil's chief engineer, agreed to support Suman's plan to bring Eastman to Conroe to kill the Alexander #1 with an extremely accurate directional well through which enormous quantities of water could be pumped. Moore and Suman then got the controversial plan approved by Humble's board of directors, in spite of such problems as a serious fire hazard and having to spud in only four hundred feet from the cratered Alexander.

Suddenly, three weeks after it started, the billowing flow from the Harrison & Abercrombie well dropped to almost nothing, then stopped completely; but four months later, on June 19, 1933, it inexplicably resumed and was soon back to its old and tremendous volume. John Suman had in the meantime negotiated a fair and even generous contract with Jim and Dan. They would be paid $300,000 for their fifteen-acre lease; allowed to sell all the oil in their crater, moat and creek bed (which was not subject to proration allocations); and provided extraordinary protection against fire resulting from a directional well. This last provision was quite consequential: The Alexander crater had grown to an amazing diameter in excess of one hundred fifty feet, and a depth of one hundred eighty feet. To diminish the risk of a fire, Humble engineers were to provide six huge boilers to keep a layer of steam atop the oil in the crater, shields of steel and asbestos sprayed constantly with water, and wooden housings for all metal drive chains on the rig (to prevent sparks).

Suman headed for California, prepared to pay John Eastman virtually anything he asked for a directional well. Eastman said that he would handle the job for $3000 plus expenses. He wanted to prove his technique, which had been widely criticized, and this was the perfect opportunity; the money could come later. Suman told him that he was not charging enough, because he thought that he should. Eastman repeated that the price was $3000 plus expenses; they shook on the deal, Texas-style, and began to discuss details of equipment and timing.

John Eastman put his bit within twenty-two feet of his target, an exact location at the bottom of the cratered Alexander #1. John Suman had followed the whipstocking experiment very closely, without interfering in any manner with operational personnel. When preliminary tests indicated the high probability of success, he took off for Avery Island, Louisiana to shoot ducks with the famed geologist Everette DeGolyer, keeping in touch by telephone. Suman returned with his limit of ducks to watch the death of the Alexander #1; the murder weapon was ninety-six thousand barrels of water, and the time of execution, just before five on the afternoon of January 9, 1934.

The cratered well had poured out an estimated 1.5 million barrels of oil, virtually all of which Harrison & Abercrombie crews had trapped in their moat and adjoining dry creek bed, the creek bed having been carefully dammed and sprayed with gunite to minimize absorption. The crude was then pumped into a nearby pipeline. Jim and Dan had escaped the possibility of financial disaster, primarily through John Suman and Humble Oil; they had found instead a sorely-needed source of major income to complete their emergence from the perilous years of the Great Depression.[5]

Now they would move on to tremendous accomplishments at a treacherous, trouble-full field in southwest Brazoria County—Old Ocean.

Jim Clark, king of the oil writers, called his good friend Jim Abercrombie "The Whale of Old Ocean." The sobriquet was singularly appropriate: the discovery and proper development of the historic field on the boundary between Brazoria and Matagorda counties involved years of effort by many men, yet turned directly upon the innovative skills; long, arduously-gained experience; technical know-how; and granite-like perseverance of Abercrombie.

Not yet forty-five, and fortunate enough to have almost four decades of life before him, Mr. Jim may have been at the peak of his unique career when he finally deciphered the labyrinthine riddle of Old Ocean. This is the inevitable conclusion when you consider in retrospect all that Abercrombie had a key role in accomplishing at the gigantic new field: unprecedented advances in the control and constructive use of pressure through experimental equipment and procedures; recognition of the invaluable concept of reservoir protection by recycling and unitization; maximum conservation through efficient separation of various component products; and further confirmation of still-controversial procedures in exploration and drilling. It was as if the dank, forbidding marshes near Sweeny, once thought to be unconquerable by the drilling bit, had become a vast proving ground for further advances by the petroleum industry, many of them either pioneered or perfected by the Whale of Old Ocean.

Yet the new field also demonstrated anew the viability of that unusual quasi-partnership, Harrison & Abercrombie; for it was Dan Harrison, who could smell a good oil deal from counties away, who really brought Old Ocean to Jim Abercrombie's attention.

It had all begun years before, with William H. (Hod) Hodnett, who was chief of one of the first geophysics "shooting" crews back in the mid-1920s. Hodnett himself was not a geophysicist, but he became one of the legendary oil scouts along the Gulf Coast through friendships with great earth scientists such as Everette DeGolyer (with whom he formed the Atlatl[6] Royalty Company in 1929), and literally hundreds of contacts in and out of the industry.

Hodnett, who admittedly operated on hunches overlaid with Dr. DeGolyer's incomparable knowledge and experience, had a major role in discovering the Van Vleck and Spanish Camp fields. Time and time again, however, he came back to the marsh near Sweeny that was to become Old Ocean. Hod was fascinated by surface indications of oil: oozing gas underneath rotting vegetation, brackish water hinting at hidden salt domes, marsh grass identical to that along the Brazosport beaches further to the west. "Everything but a pterodactyl from the Lower Jurassic, flying right at you against the sunset," he once told Everette DeGolyer.

Then he came upon an old-time, crippled-up Texaco driller, Clyde Jones, drinking coffee one morning in Bay City; Jones took him to the site of two abandoned wells he had helped complete in the marsh, at depths just under three thousand feet. "Yeah, they produced," he told Hodnett; "but they sanded over after a while. Nothin' could bring 'em back." After that, Hod knew there was oil at Old Ocean; the problem was how to get it out of there.

Hod was not the only one fascinated with those dank, gaseous marshes near Sweeny; a lease broker named Bill Minchen soon turned up with one of the relatively new torsion balance surveys[7]; it showed an enormously extended underground structure that actually reached into the next county, under the marshes. Minchen also had about ten thousand acres available for lease in the area; the difficulty was that he wanted almost $60,000 cash for the package. Hodnett took the proposition to Dr. DeGolyer; the earth scientist liked the look of things, but demanded seismographic confirmation of the apparent structure. This was available from J. C. Karcher, another leading geophysicist who controlled the Coronado Exploration Company, for an additional $60,000.

Minchen had also shown his wares to Dan Harrison, who knew that Hodnett was quite knowledgeable about anything in the Brazoria-Matagorda area. Harrison consulted Hod, who was honest to tell Dan he and Dr. DeGolyer were interested, and clever enough to work out an arrangement agreeable to everyone that would not cost

Atlatl Royalty a dime: Harrison & Abercrombie agreed to put up what turned out to be $56,000 for half of Minchen's leases, if Hodnett guaranteed to find $60,000 for the seismographic survey; H&A would then own half the leases, and Atlatl the other half.

Not having $60,000 handy, the resourceful Hodnett next traded Dr. Karcher half the Atlatl leases (one-quarter of the deal) for the required seismographic work. Now Atlatl had a free ride.

Seismography revealed an even larger subsurface structure, of the incredible dimensions of nine by four miles. Jim Abercrombie was soon on a very carefully selected location with Red Early, John Bass and Sam Cantrell, ready to spud in the #1 Bernard River Land Company. He was about to embark upon a project of many years that would test his courage, ingenuity, experience and patience to the ultimate limits before bringing enormous and well-merited success.

The more Jim and Dan pored over reports on the St. Bernard test and conferred with Drs. DeGolyer and Karcher (possibly the two most formidable partners you could have in probing for a new major oilfield), the more they resolved to lease up more acreage quietly and to keep the well plenty tight. Jim, with the intuition coming from what was now more than a quarter-century on the rigs, seemed to feel that they were really on to something.

There were many delays as the drilling crew continued to register record pressures downhole. Mr. Jim spent more and more time with Herb Allen, as the depth approached and then exceeded one mile. They huddled together in the tiny office at 711 Milby, modifying equipment or sketching possible new gadgetry as The Boss munched on peanuts and swallowed innumerable Cokes. Finally, with the heaviest blowout preventer ever made in place, plus special-order lines and expansion joints, the discovery well was completed at 8651 feet on November 8, 1934; the potential was measured at two hundred forty barrels a day, from a Frio formation.

What interested Abercrombie particularly was the gas-oil ratio (almost thirty-five hundred-to-one) and the enormous (approaching four thousand pounds per square inch) pressure in the St. Bernard #1. Harrison seemed discouraged at the high gas-oil ratio, but Jim had a hunch it meant that tremendously greater production was available at lower depths, once pressure (extraordinarily high for 1934) could be controlled. He told Dan, "This may be a new kind of oilfield, if we can figure out how to handle it." He added, prophetically, "I know you're a 'black oil' man, and how you just don't like all that gas; but the day may be coming when gas is worth more than crude. We won't be flaring it much longer."

Now what was becoming a field laboratory for Cameron Iron Works (and for that matter, for an entire industry) really went into operation. Jim was determined to go deeper and deeper, drilling ever more carefully with still heavier equipment, as pressures continued to increase dramatically. It was midsummer of 1935 before the discovery well was confirmed and extended with an offset producer. Then, over a year later on September 11, 1936, they hit the bonanza: the first of what would prove to be four separate producing sands in the main reservoir of a huge, saddle-shaped salt dome. The St. Bernard #3 was flowing from a thick formation in the Armstrong, at 9824 to 9954 feet. Now there was a rising tide, then a flood, of publicity about Old Ocean, a field overshadowed hitherto by big strikes at Anahuac and at Dickinson; but Harrison and Abercrombie had increased their lease holdings to above twelve thousand acres. They could stand a little publicity, although both men instinctively shunned it.

By this time, Jim Abercrombie knew that he was dealing with an entirely different type of oilfield. While the industry raised its collective eyebrows and Dan Harrison worried about the sometimes staggering costs at Old Ocean, he pioneered with new concepts and procedures that have now become commonplace.

Mr. Jim was soon determined to turn the H&A wells at Old Ocean into an efficient, long-term, self-renewing petroleum factory. In doing so, he would have to move into *terra incognita;* but it would be with the comforting and invaluable support of Bob and his other brothers; of Dan, sensitive though he was to rising cost; of the sturdy triumvirate of Ralph McCullough, Ed Lorehn and Herb Allen; and of two new members of his cadre, Stanley Gill and Olle Lawrence Lorehn, Ed's brother.

The JSA rigs, with Milo, John and Joe Rice as field superintendents, were busy again after a brief period during which things looked as bleak as in 1921 and 1922; then Abercrombie crews led by J. M. (Red) Teague had come to Mr. Jim and told him they would wait on payday, since most of them owed him personal loans he had forgotten anyhow. "Just give us a little eatin' money for now," Red said.

Harrison could be, as the lawyer Joe Moore once described him, "a vigorous customer," yet he had faith in Jim and accepted his decisions even if sometimes with reluctance. "I told you so" was not in the Harrison vocabulary, and there were no recriminations. Mr. Jim appreciated this because "you are going to take some hickeys[8] in the oil game," as he pointed out on occasion to colleagues bringing him bad news.

McCullough worked well with Bob Abercrombie and did anything and everything as his duties at both JSA and Cameron Iron Works (CIW) melded into the unofficial post of executive assistant to The Boss. One special duty was to keep cash flow and lines of credit in sound health; he was good at this, even though Jim and Dan had to storm the banking citadels from time to time. Lorehn, the steady, all-around engineer turned administrator, teamed well with the brilliant Allen, who was finding as a newlywed that the post-midnight conferences with Mr. Jim at 711 Milby made for a difficult schedule.

The new men were Stanley Gill, a gifted consulting engineer who had graduated from MIT with honors, and Olle Lorehn, another product of Rice Institute. Gill would work for years on complex projects at Old Ocean and elsewhere, primarily in process and design. Lorehn was to become more and more valuable in a series of administrative jobs that would finally bring him to a vice-presidency at CIW.

The Old Ocean "factory" consisted of a dozen large separators, a complete repressuring plant for recycling and a series of injection wells. The overall installation was primarily designed by Stanley Gill, with constant input from Jim Abercrombie, Joe Tennant and Herb Allen. The separators divided the rich liquid and gaseous hydrocarbons into distillate, condensate, butane, propane, methane and other components. These were then sent to appropriate storage tanks, while residual gas went to ten powerful compressors in a nearby facility. There the gas was repressured and sent back into the reservoir through the injection wells.

Today, almost fifty years after this innovative system was first put in place, and four decades since unitization of the entire field was accomplished, Old Ocean ticks along like a well-maintained 1934 Rolls Royce. Bottom-hole pressures are essentially what they were when Jim Abercrombie first insisted on protecting them to ensure the fullest possible recovery from one of the most significant reservoirs of hydrocarbons ever discovered.

The production of oil from the field crossed the magic one-hundred-million-barrel mark in 1964, with highest output (6,111,030 barrels) in 1945, and continues at a steady rate in excess of 1.5 million barrels annually. The real story, however, is in the output of gas and gas condensate. Gas production per year is in excess of a hundred trillion cubic feet, and condensate averages above one million barrels. There are no really accurate figures on overall reserves at Old Ocean, but the great Harrison & Abercrombie find is in every sense a multibillion-dollar discovery.

Old Ocean was obviously of crucial importance in Jim Abercrombie's career and was to have a tremendous impact throughout the petroleum industry.

Some of the spinoff from the unique development program at the Brazoria county strike was to be markedly meaningful to Mr. Jim, both personally and professionally. This was particularly true in terms of his waxing interest in government and in politics. Jim had been concerned from his first days as an entrepreneur about getting men of high integrity and competence in public office and was supporting conservative Democrats for election from the early 1920s. His concern grew as the petroleum industry felt the increasing handicap and cost of a mounting maze of laws, regulations and constantly changing interpretations.

Abercrombie had a graduate course in lobbying during parts of 1933 and 1934, complete with a thirteen-week period during which he and Major Jubal R. Parten worked with Vice President John Nance Garner and Speaker Sam Rayburn to defeat the infamous "Ickes Bill." With some East Texas wells running wide open at ten thousand barrels a day, at an "official" price of a dime a barrel which could be negotiated as low as a nickel, most of the big petroleum associations and major companies were clamoring for federal control. This would be achieved by making Secretary of the Interior Harold L. Ickes, the "old curmudgeon," oil czar. FDR was all for the plan, coming as it did on the heels of similar legislation to establish the National Recovery Administration.

The opposition ranks siding with Rayburn and Garner were thin numerically, but they had Mr. Sam and Cactus Jack, plus courage, ingenuity and perseverance of a high order.

Jim Abercrombie was in the forefront of the battle for several reasons. His belief in states' rights and local control went back to his Alabama kinsman and namesake, Senator James Abercrombie, and had intensified over the generations; he knew too that it was better for Texas to work out its own regulatory provisions; and he was essentially a conservative, not a New Deal, Democrat. The quarterback for the anti-Ickes forces was Major Parten, moving toward the beginning heights of a long and distinguished career during which he would become a national figure as chief executive of Woodley Petroleum Company and a leading independent oilman, chairman of the Board of Regents of the University of Texas, confidante of men of impact and a political intellectual of rare foresight.

The major had on his side, in addition to Rayburn and Garner, Attorney-General (and later Governor) James V. Allred,[9] Railroad Commissioner Ernest O. Thompson, and a small yet potent collection of what were termed the ''independent independents,'' men who ''sure didn't want old Harold Ickes hangin' around our necks.'' The major, still active, alert and ramrod-straight in his eighties, liked Mr. Jim from the moment they first met. He characterizes him today as ''one of the finest men I ever knew.'' It did not take long for Parten to introduce Mr. Jim to Rayburn, Garner, Allred and Thompson, thereby establishing lifelong friendships and launching Abercrombie's first substantial contributions to, and fund-raising for, carefully-chosen political candidates.

The Ickes bill was finally defeated, FDR and most of the petroleum industry notwithstanding; the powerful and resourceful ''Mr. Sam'' Rayburn simply watched for the legislation to come out of the Senate and had it re-referred from a friendly committee to Interstate and Foreign Commerce. There, he promised Parten, Abercrombie, Dan Harrison, Hugh Roy Cullen, Jim West, Mike Hogg, Myron and Jack Blalock (the Speaker's close friends from East Texas) and some other diehards Mr. Jim had helped round up, ''it will die a merciful death.'' And the bill did die; three months later, ''Mr. Sam'' and Vice-President Garner asked Abercrombie to come by Garner's office. They ''struck a blow for liberty,'' with some of Cactus Jack's best bourbon, in honor of the meaningful legislative victory.

Jim Abercrombie had made, and Major Parten had reinforced, enduring friendships at the highest level of national and state government. Now, exhausted from the weeks in Washington interspersed with hurried train trips home to tend to their normal pursuits, they had to go to Austin on another lobbying assignment of special significance. Another ''bad bill'' had been introduced with strong support from the petroleum associations and most of the major companies. It would provide for the appointment, rather than election, of the three members of the state Railroad Commission who had such broad authority over the oil business in Texas. It could allow the governor potentially disastrous power over the petroleum industry.

Parten and Mr. Jim bore the brunt of this battle, also; and they apparently lost it late one night in the House of Representatives after a bitter fifteen-hour struggle. It was clear that the opposition had the votes in the Senate, too; the two-thirds margin to get the measure up, and to send it on to final passage was there. Then, Major Parten recalls vividly, there was a real piece of luck: a legislator from the winning side, angry from the long and acrimonious debate in the House, "jumped Howard Burns and started to stomp him, right in the lobby of the Stephen F. Austin Hotel." Parten and Abercrombie had just returned to the Stephen F. Austin, downcast and worn out, and had been talking to Burns, a representative from Huntsville who had been one of their floor leaders. Before the fight could be stopped, Burns was seriously injured. The word spread quickly, and support for the bill melted away in the Senate. It was never passed.

Mr. Jim had his real baptism of fire, political and regulatory, before the Railroad Commission in hearings extending through parts of 1938 and 1939, a crucial time in the development of the Old Ocean field when all that he had fought for there could easily have been lost. Railroad Commissioner Jerry Sadler, spurred on by his friend and supporter F. W. "Big Fish" Fisher (the operator of many shallow, prolific wells in East Texas), made an all-out attempt to reduce substantially a special two-hundred-barrel allowable at Old Ocean. This was unfair, it was alleged, if wells in the "Black Giant" (East Texas) field were held at twenty barrels per day.

Abercrombie, ably represented by Elwood Fouts and especially by Joe Moore, who had become an expert on Railroad Commission hearings, explained the matter. He and Dan Harrison, in almost five years at Old Ocean, had spent $5,711,903 while taking in $3,063,000, for a net loss of $2,648,903. In contrast, he continued, he had netted $162,000 in the Black Giant and $772,000 in Conroe during the same period of time. The big difference, Mr. Jim continued, in his forthright and convincing manner, was the depth of the wells at Old Ocean (then well past ten thousand feet) and the stringent field rules worked out in conjunction with the Commission's staff engineers by Stanley Gill and Joe Tennant. The rules made it possible, he pointed out, to save 99.5 percent of the gas in the field and to preserve the reservoir for full recovery over many years; but it was impossible to operate under anything less than a two-hundred-barrel allowable.

There was a silence, and then the alert Joe Moore asked his client Mr. Jim: "So, you lost $2,648,903; was that the amount?" "Yes, sir; $2,648,903." Lon A. Smith, chairman of the commission, indicated that the deal was hardly a bonanza, so far. Sadler, a tungsten-hard opportunist always playing the country bumpkin, looked at "Big Fish" Fisher and asked if he had any comment. "No comment," was the reply. "Well, it looks as if you're going to lose your case," was the realistic Sadler's retort.

Abercrombie, with Joe Moore's invaluable help, had defended his procedures at Old Ocean, and the concept of relating allowables to the realities of engineering and economics, even though there would be further hearings, lawsuits and injunctions. He had also told the industry that hydrocarbon reservoirs must be carefully preserved for the future.

There were meaningful extra dividends from Mr. Jim's activities in the legislative and political arena. First of all, he formed a staunch friendship with Sam Rayburn, who appointed Major Parten and Jim his unofficial, unpaid but carefully-heeded counselors on anything having to do with petroleum. This was a lasting, close relationship that would thrive throughout the remaining quarter-century of the remarkable "Mr. Sam's" life. Rayburn finally piled up twenty-five terms as a congressman; his tenure as speaker of the House of Representatives was twice that of the storied Henry Clay, and finally eclipsed that of Joe (Cannonball) Cannon; majority leader and the confidante of eight presidents, his influence was vast.

The petroleum industry would finally realize the value of Jim Abercrombie's ties to Mr. Sam, long after the rotund little dynamo was laid to rest in Willow Wild Cemetery at Bonham on November 18, 1961—with Harry S. Truman, Dwight D. Eisenhower, John F. Kennedy and LBJ among the mourners. Their closeness may have saved attacks on the depletion allowance more than once; and to demonstrate how strongly Mr. Sam believed in Abercrombie, as well as in Jubal R. Parten, in his papers were found two handwritten notes from none other than FDR urging him to let the Ickes bill out of committee.

Mr. Jim also came to know Herman and George Brown far better through his crescent interest in politics in the mid-1930s and thereafter. Soon he was a regular member of the unique salon in Suite 8-F of the Lamar Hotel which the Browns launched in 1940; Herman Brown and Jim were very similar in personality and approach to life, and became fast friends. George, the younger brother, saw this immediately. Here is what he told me about Mr. Herman and Mr. Jim at the Houston Club, while I sat with him at the 1982 annual meeting:

> Neither man spoke much; they thought things out from insight and experience before you heard from them; then, everyone listened. They liked small groups of close friends; Herman and Jim were probably as happy on that quail shoot at Cuero as they ever would be. Much integrity and wisdom in both men, and quiet brilliance, too. They knew how to enjoy things—often the same things: hunting; horseracing; a good, important political campaign; big, complicated business deals. Good men, and much alike. Long remembered, I hope.

We will read in following chapters of the famous ''hatchings'' at Suite 8-F, where many a political candidate of consequence and success first scratched his way out of the shell. The group Judge/Mayor Roy Hofheinz once called ''the fat cats'' (to his regret) came quietly to dominate the selection and financing of candidates for the principal offices in the Houston area, and over the state and nation. And there will be words, but principally pictures, of the Cuero quail hunts; plus accounts of horseracing projects and excursions, especially of what came to be an annual pilgrimage to the Kentucky Derby.

Cameron Iron Works had turned the corner in 1935, when sales went back to $321,000 and there was a profit again ($4000) following the loss of $29,000 in Depression-plagued 1932, and two break-even years. Herb Allen became chief engineer in 1935, after working out a new advance in packing for hydraulic rams that saved the Humble Oil account. Mr. Jim now insisted that Herb be given a new contract to include personal royalties on his future inventions. ''It's only fair,'' Abercrombie said. ''He earned it.''

With the introduction of the SDA ("short double-acting") blowout preventer and a pressure-operated gate valve, sales at Cameron skyrocketed to $1.118 million for the fiscal year ending June 30, 1937; profits reached $153,000. The machine shop at 711 Milby was expanded substantially, and working space doubled by purchase of adjoining property and the building of a steel structure; the total number of employees reached almost two hundred. The Oil Patch was being "Cameronized."

No dividends had been declared at CIW since modest payments of $10 per share in 1929; profits were simply reinvested in plant and equipment. Now a new federal tax on undivided profits made it necessary to recapitalize. After dividends of $500 (1937) and $240 (1938) per share were paid, $575,000 was transferred from surplus to capital, bringing the latter account from the original $25,000 to $600,000; the shares issued in 1920 were then split, two hundred forty-to-one.

When Germany's Panzer units invaded Poland on that fateful Labor Day weekend in 1939, Jim Abercrombie became convinced that the new *blitzkrieg* would spread, drawing the United States inevitably into a worldwide conflict. The farsighted Mr. Jim had Ed Lorehn and Allen draw up a list of parts or products needed by the United States Armed Forces which CIW would be most able to manufacture. The Boss and Lorehn then headed for Washington, D.C. and a series of meetings with ordnance and procurement officers; but they had no success: neither the Army nor the Navy (the Air Force was still a part of the Army) knew anything about CIW. They had their own established sources of supply.

Mr. Jim decided that the route to take was subcontracting for prime suppliers with a history of dealings with the Armed Forces, at least until Cameron could get its foot in the door. By early 1941, CIW had an agreement with the Gisholt Machinery Company of Madison, Wisconsin to make roller turner attachments for turret lathes, already a high-priority item.

Once Gisholt and the United States Navy's Bureau of Ordnance saw how well Cameron performed on this first subcontract, Commander A. D. Blackledge asked for a meeting with CIW representatives. He was the Navy's top expert on ordnance, and he was looking for someone to manufacture a really hot item not even in production: "K" guns, or depth charge projectors for antisubmarine warfare, plus "arbors," the attachment fired out of the projector. Crete, the "battleship of the Mediterranean," and convoys attempting desperately to supply it, were under joint attack by Adolph Hitler's Stuka bombers and his wolfpack submarines. This and the developing battle of the North Atlantic were perfect examples of the need to get ready for antisubmarine operations with all possible haste.

Herb Allen and Ed Lorehn met with Commander Blackledge and his staff on March 18, 1941 at naval ordnance headquarters in Washington, D.C. Some preliminary drawings of both the projector and arbor were ready, without cost estimates. Herb and Ed headed back to Houston that night, worked furiously for two weeks, day and night, and were in Washington again on April 5, with actual models of the projector and arbor.

After minor changes because of some possible patent involvements on the arbors, Lorehn and Allen were back at Cameron on April 8 with the promise of a letter of intent (which arrived April 10) for twelve-hundred-twenty-eight K-guns and ninety thousand arbors. The actual contract was signed April 14, 1941 in a further demonstration of how bureaucracy can move when it has to.

Admiral Chester W. Nimitz,[10] an expert on submarine warfare since World War I, described June 13, 1941 as a ''very unlucky day for German commanders.'' He was referring to some tests taking place on a blazing hot day in Houston in an isolated pine grove north of Old Katy Road. Two days before, there had been pieces of K-guns all over 711 Milby, but in a tradition of staying exactly on, and even ahead of, schedule, Cameron was completely ready for the test firing before Navy brass.

Everything went off without a hitch, and six weeks later the stocky, red-faced, efficient Frank Knox (secretary of the Navy) was awarding Ed Lorehn the Navy ''E'' for exceptional achievement. Lorehn accepted the award ''on behalf of all our employees,'' and CIW joined a group of elite United States companies in the first of what would be a succession of ''E'' awards for Cameron Iron Works: General Motors, Bausch & Lomb, E. I. Du Pont de Nemours, Ford and others.

Cameron finally produced all 14,826 of the K-guns procured by the United States Navy between 1941 and 1945. From time to time, Mr. Jim would receive a report of great interest to him, as one restricted communication from Admiral W. H. P. Blandy, chief of the Bureau of Ordnance. It recounted how CIW K-guns 865, 893, 895 and 897, on the USS *Spencer,* had fired depth charges that forced a German submarine to the surface. The *Spencer* then finished off the submarine with deck guns.

Busy though he was, in those absorbing years between 1937 and Pearl Harbor, Mr. Jim always found time for his own immediate family and for the remainder of the clan. He and Miss Lillie had purchased a beautiful home at 2221 River Oaks Boulevard which became the scene of a traditional Christmas party that simply grew and grew in size. Josephine was a bright, attractive young teenager attending the Kinkaid School, a long-established preparatory of excellent standing near their home. She was interested in riding, and very good at it; Jim had bought her a little polo pony named Lomita.

The Little Grandmother was gone, happy and alert to the end, which had come in 1932 in her eightieth year. She had the marvelous gift of being able to know and to love her great-grandchildren, who surrounded her every Sunday at the traditional family dinner at 3402 Audubon. The brothers had separate residences now, and only Miss Annie and Miss Vinnie and her husband Max Rotholz were at the old home; but the brothers visited there often. When Ann Joiner, a secretary at the JSA Company, told Bob how displeased she was with where she was living, he told her to call Miss Annie and just move on out to 3402. "Plenty of room there," he said. Ann lived there happily for years, absorbed into the clan Abercrombie.

Lillie was always concerned with how hard Jim drove himself, durable and seemingly indefatigable though he was. The late 1930s had been particularly stressful: months upon years of effort at Old Ocean, overlaid with vital legislative concerns and now, major new expansion at Cameron Iron. She realized that he was content only at full throttle, but insisted that he leave time for his favorite sport, hunting. Mr. Jim did this whenever possible. He loved to hunt, in close comradeship with his best friends, and was aware how the open fields, with long hikes in bracing weather, helped to refresh him both physically and mentally.

Jim was probably as good a shot with a 28-gauge as anyone who ever fired a shotgun; and this was true also for anything from a .22

to a deer rifle. Milo was not far behind his brother; the two of them sometimes gave a little demonstration lighting kitchen matches stuck in a fence post at fifty yards.

Mr. Jim often honed his shooting eye before the traditional quail hunt at the Blackwell Ranch near Cuero with an expedition to a ten-thousand-acre lease at Campbellton in Atascosa County. This brought him on a morning soon after Thanksgiving of 1941 to the downtown office of Naurice Cummings,[11] who had just returned to Houston to take charge of area operations for the National Supply Company.

Naurice was on the telephone for a few moments before he came out of his office, rather preoccupied, to greet Abercrombie; it was apparent some things had come up that might interfere with a quail hunt.

"You ready?," said Jim. "Milo's downstairs with the station wagon, all packed." He looked at his watch and added, "I want to get in a few shots before sundown." Naurice hesitated a moment and began to explain how busy he was. Abercrombie took the cigar out of his mouth, and pointed with it for added emphasis. "Now, Cummings," he began, "you know my opinion of a man who can't arrange his business to accommodate a little hunting . . . . "

Naurice could hardly remember the last time his good friend had called him Cummings, but he had the message. "I'll get my hat," he said; and they were on their way to Atascosa County.

It was a marvelous hunt, and a weekend of relaxation that Mr. Jim really needed. When he and Naurice returned, Pearl Harbor was only days away. Jim Abercrombie was about to be plunged into five years of the most complex problems he had ever faced. These would include the dissolution of the Harrison & Abercrombie quasi-partnership, the sale of Old Ocean and the inception of a quite different pattern of life for him.

Notes

[1] Harvey Mecom was not only responsible for bringing his son into the oilfields but for the phenomenally successful John W.'s later entrance into the hotel industry. John's parents took him regularly to the elegant new Warwick for Sunday dinner, and he liked the place so much that he bought it a generation later, expanded the small apartment hotel tremendously and filled it with splendid antiques and rare tapestries selected by his wife Elizabeth.

[2] The thirty-four story Gulf Building, on the site of the home of Augustus Allen (one of Houston's founding Allen brothers) and his charming wife Charlotte, was at the time the tallest building west of Chicago. It had its own fifteen thousand-candlepower aeronautical beacon, radio station (KXYZ) and special red-and-green lighting system for the Christmas season. After World War II, the structure had a gigantic rotating Gulf Oil sign that

became an early target for environmentalists. Following publication of a marvelous satire about a fifteen hundred-seat aircraft (one of a worldwide fleet sent to Houston nightly to cruise among dozens of such signs) crashing to earth in the year 2000 A.D., Gulf gave up and dismantled the sign. Mild inflation having set in, it reportedly cost more to take it down than it had to fabricate the sign and install it.

[3] William A. Kirkland, grandson of the founder of the First National Bank he later headed, revealed the details of how Jesse Jones prevented Depression bank failures here in his engrossing book, *Shepherd's Bank*.

[4] George W. Strake was a native of St. Louis and graduate of the Jesuit St. Louis University who went to Tampico after World War I service in the Army Air Corps. An employee of Gulf Oil, he resigned, set up his own drilling company during the early Mexican oil boom, and left Tampico with a $250,000 grubstake. He came to Houston in 1924 and married Susan Kehoe, daughter of a prominent Catholic family. Her uncle was a well-known cotton broker and land developer (and chairman of the author's draft board until I joined a reserve unit at Harvard College).

The Kehoes were pleased to have Strake, bright young graduate of a fine Catholic university and already a crackerjack oilman, in Houston, up-and-coming petroleum center that the city already was. They assumed he would stay right in Houston, but Strake took his bride to Cuba. Havana was in the midst of unprecedented prosperity fueled by the sugar industry, and Strake believed there was oil and gas to be discovered in Cuba, where gasoline was retailing for as much as fifty cents a gallon. When the sugar market collapsed and he had hit a series of dry holes, he came back to Houston in 1927 with little capital remaining; but on December 13, 1931, after surmounting formidable obstacles, he brought in the George W. Strake #1 in an area six miles southeast of Conroe where geologists had assured him there was no oil. He sold half the eighty-six hundred acres he had under lease to Humble Oil after Wallace Pratt congratulated him on his "fine discovery" and hinted he might have asked for more than the $4 million he received.

Four times a papal knight, Strake was personally awarded the Grand Cross of the Order of St. Sylvester, most coveted of the Catholic orders of knighthood, by Pius XII. He developed Conroe into one of the great oilfields and became one of the most popular leaders of the Oil Patch. Mr. and Mrs. Strake gave unstintedly of their wealth, which George said was "just loaned to us by the Good Lord, anyhow": a twenty-seven-hundred-acre camp for the Boy Scouts, microfilming the entire Vatican Library for St. Louis University and innumerable other magnificent contributions, especially to St. Joseph Hospital in Houston. After Strake died of a sudden heart attack in Columbus, Texas while enroute to the installation of a new archbishop at San Antonio, the family foundation gave another $5 million to St. Joseph. Susan Kehoe Strake is gone now also, but they both left a marvelous heritage for son George, Jr. and daughters Susan Dilworth and Georgianna Parsley.

[5] Jim Abercrombie was never to forget the Alexander #1, or John Suman, whom he praised up and down the Oil Patch in his quiet but meaningful manner, for the whipstocking victory at Conroe. George Strake, another big Suman booster (and well he should have been) fulfilled a promise to give Suman "a nice dinner" at the River Oaks Country Club. It was a memorable affair, and George Strake enjoyed it immensely after getting over the shock of the popular Suman's invitation list, which ran to three hundred fifty guests.

[6] The erudite Dr. DeGolyer, who carefully selected the name "Atlatl," must have been amused by those unacquainted with either Uto-Aztec or Nahuatl, who probably thought Atlatl was a unique abbreviation for Atlantic Refining. Pronounced with the stress on the initial "t", *atlatl* was the *spear-thrower* of Aztec and Nahuatl mythology.

[7] The great English scientist Lord Henry Cavendish discovered the principle of measuring gravitational acceleration, the basis for torsion balance surveys, in 1798—a full century and more before the surveys came into general use in the oilfields.

[8] "Hickey," a pimple in today's adolescent jargon, originally meant to "take a hickey" for failing to make your bid in the marvelous domino game of "shoot the moon." Roughnecks played the game endlessly in the bunkhouses between shifts ("towers"). A variation of "42," "shoot the moon" could be played with all the nuances of tournament bridge, which it roughly resembles. In time, "taking a hickey" came to mean taking a big loss in the oilfields, usually drilling a dry hole.

[9] J. R. Parten, then a resident of Shreveport, met James V. Allred when the future attorney-general, governor and federal judge was smart enough to buy radio time on Shreveport's powerful fifty-thousand-watt KWKH, which covered East Texas like a blanket. Instead of placing his political commercials at a much higher overall cost on a combination of small local stations in the area, Allred was thus guaranteed far better coverage at lower total outlay. When atmospheric conditions were right, KWKH's potent signal could be picked up over half of Texas, including most of the thickly-populated areas.

[10] Fleet Admiral Chester W. Nimitz, a Fredericksburg, Texas lad who became a legend in the World War II Navy, was assigned to submarines soon after graduating from Annapolis in 1905. He was never to forget the strategic impact of the underwater vessels, which sank almost three-fourths of the Japanese shipping fleet while he commanded our naval forces in the Pacific during World War II. The Japanese high command helped enormously when the Germans convinced them of the necessity of transmitting a schedule of anticipated "noon day positions" as their convoys departed the embarkation center at Moji for the long voyage to the South Pacific. We had most of these messages decoded at a top secret intelligence installation (formerly a girls' finishing school) in Washington, D.C. before they were processed in Tokyo; they ended up in the hands of our submarine commanders, who torpedoed the Jap supply ships with ease once they knew their expected positions.

[11] Naurice Cummings had come back to Houston, ironically as a top official of the supply company that had refused Jim Abercrombie $5000 worth of credit at a crucial stage in his career. When Naurice told Jim that he had decided to take a very attractive position with National Supply which included sales bonuses, Abercrombie was non-committal. After thinking about the matter, Mr. Jim reacted characteristically. First, he managed to find out the amount of his good friend's annual salary. Next, he called up Cummings' new boss in Pittsburgh, congratulated him on hiring Naurice, and told him that although the JSA Company had a policy of never doing business with National Supply, Cummings could expect a call from the JSA purchasing agent. The agent was then instructed to requisition a long list of supplies that added up to the amount of Naurice Cummings' annual salary.

Chapter 9

1941–1946

World War II's Weapons, Oil and Avgas

From "pieces of iron" to K-guns and "Tiny Tim" rockets at Cameron Iron . . . The new plant on Katy Road . . . Herb Allen and Mr. Jim save the Navy $1,741,230.10 . . . Old Ocean avgas after an emergency meeting with FDR at the White House . . . The price to Uncle Sam remains $1.34 per barrel . . . Natural gas is worth sixty cents, not two cents . . . Dan Harrison wants to sell out . . . An Abercrombie response to a point of honor . . . Naurice Cummings hears Dan leave $6 million on the table . . . Fifty thousand acres at Campbellton are divided twenty-seven to twenty-three . . . A $54 million decision at Cinco Ranch and a one-word telegram . . . The Pin Oak Horse Show also makes page one in the Houston Press.

Many employees of Cameron Iron, the JSA Company and Harrison & Abercrombie heard the first unbelievable news bulletins about Pearl Harbor while working overtime, even though what FDR would denounce so eloquently and accurately as a "day of infamy" was on a Sunday.

CIW had been producing dramatically increased amounts of the vital K-guns and would soon be adding other high-priority defense armament and equipment[1] as output for the petroleum industry was severely curtailed, then prohibited, by the War Production Board. One of the most difficult assignments for Ed Lorehn, his brother Olle and Herb Allen almost immediately after Pearl Harbor was explaining the sudden shutdown on "pieces of iron" manufactured by Cameron for years, without disclosing still-confidential plans to replace blowout preventers, core barrels and casing cutters[2] with K-guns.

The JSA Company and H&A also had some crews on overtime. There was an escalating demand not only for crude, but for all hydrocarbons, the basis of everything from aviation gasoline (avgas) to synthetic rubber. Wells would be running "flat out" for years, as selected oilfields were expanded throughout the Oil Patch.

The Navy, understandably impressed by CIW's performance on the K-gun contract, sent Bureau of Ordnance officials to Houston to determine if Cameron could turn out another critical item: three-inch barrels for .50-caliber guns. Mr. Jim, together with Ed Lorehn and Herb Allen, had encouraged the visit; they were convinced that the big three-inch gun barrels, traditionally manufactured in a lengthy sequence of machining operations, could be produced far more rapidly by innovative procedures.

The ordnance experts were almost in shock when they arrived in Houston on December 8, 1941; they had left Union Station in Washington, D.C. Saturday afternoon and found out about Pearl Harbor at a stopover in Atlanta. There they managed to buy a battery-operated radio, and sat huddled around it for the remainder of the journey, gradually piecing together details of the catastrophe at Honolulu in which three U.S. battleships were destroyed, one (the USS *Arizona*) with the loss of eleven hundred men. Wherever the southbound train stopped, the Navy men rushed to telephones for another attempt to get through the jammed switchboard at the Pentagon for further reports about the treacherous Japanese attack on main elements of our Pacific fleet.

CIW proposed to turn out one hundred of the intricately-machined .50-caliber gun barrels per month. Jim Abercrombie knew that if Cameron received this contract, it would be necessary to expand manufacturing capacity, and soon. Herb Allen asked him if 711 was to be further enlarged, or if The Boss preferred a new plant. Abercrombie opened another Coke and took a long, contemplative swallow. "I'll think it over," he replied.

The ordnance experts completed their meetings with the CIW staff the next day; they told Mr. Jim they were very positively impressed with the enthusiasm and obvious ability of his key men and work force, but were frankly concerned with Cameron's ability to deliver on as difficult an assignment as rifled gun barrels. The Navy representatives then proposed a unique contract under which CIW would guarantee fifty gun barrels per month, and the Bureau of Ordnance would also take anything above that.

The letter of agreement arrived from Washington January 15, 1942. Mr. Jim brought it by Herb's office and handed it to him. Allen looked it over quickly. "OK?," Abercrombie inquired. "Looks fine." Mr. Jim took a pen from his pocket and signed the agreement, while Allen thought again that he had heard nothing further about a new plant versus more expansion at 711 Milby.

Abercrombie then said, "About the new plant; where do you think we should build it?"

Herb thought for a moment before answering. Preliminary staff discussions had centered upon the Ship Channel area and the increasingly industrialized East End, if the decision was for a new plant; but he was well aware that The Boss was asking now for a personal opinion, different though it might be from the consensus. "I think we might do better out west of town," he answered. "Lots of space out there, and more pleasant surroundings—both for the plant and for all of our people. I saw some acreage north of the railroad when we were test-firing the K-gun, around Katy Road and Silber."

"Why don't you look into it?," The Boss replied.

A fine tract of one hundred acres was soon found on Katy Road, at an attractive price of $500 per acre. Production began at the new "gun plant" seven months later; it was built under wartime certificates of necessity, with an accelerated rate of depreciation.

The gun barrels were soon being turned out at one hundred, then at one hundred fifty barrels per month; and without going to the extra shifts the Bureau of Ordnance had predicted would be necessary for this level of output. This came about after Herb Allen reduced rifling time from twelve to two hours, with a differing technique he demonstrated to Mr. Jim in one of their countless post-midnight sessions. Herb simply substituted a broaching operation, or a series of cuttings, for traditional and far slower procedures. Next, Allen shortened the time for machining the breech end of the gun barrel from fourteen hours to forty-five minutes.

These two improvements could have provided Cameron almost spectacular profits under the original Navy contract, which paid at the rate of $1200 per finished gun barrel. Jim Abercrombie of course passed the savings on to the government by having the agreement negotiated down from $1200 to $526.41 per barrel. Total savings to the Navy when the last of 2585 gun barrels was delivered in 1945: $1,741,230.10.

Late in 1942, Bureau of Ordnance officials asked Cameron to consider manufacturing other defense items, among them yokes for four-inch guns on convoy vessels, and .20-millimeter hydraulic gun mounts. A new and controversial procedure was recommended for producing the yokes, but the Navy was so concerned over the possibility of a high rate of scrappage that only tentative approval was forthcoming. When less than one percent of the CIW yokes had to be scrapped, the Bureau of Ordnance was convinced again of Cameron efficiency. Herb Allen had already set up a miniature laboratory for experimentation in polymer chemistry (reminiscent of his student days at Rice Institute under George Holmes Richter and Frank Hurley), in order to discover the exact type of synthetic rubber required for the hydraulic gun mounts.

At this point, the Navy brass capitulated; they signed a unique agreement on November 5, 1942 whereby Cameron Iron would develop new types of ordnance or improvements in existing weapons or equipment under the direction of Allen, who had been promoted from chief engineer to the new position of vice-president for manufacturing and engineering as of February 1, 1942. Supreme Court Justice St. John Garwood, afterward a high-ranking officer in Naval Intelligence, was a prophet with honor. He had predicted four months before Pearl Harbor that the U.S. Navy had found an outstanding partner in the Cameron Iron Works. Justice Garwood was the speaker on August 21, 1941 as CIW employees received individual ''E'' pins and the company was awarded the first of seven ''E for Excellence'' awards.

Among other World War II weapons manufactured at Cameron were the deadly ''Tiny Tim'' rockets, designed to be fired from Navy fighters during the invasion of enemy-held beaches. Fleet Admiral William F. (Bull) Halsey wrote Mr. Jim after the fierce battles for Guadalcanal and for Okinawa: ''(Your Tiny Tim) rockets are doing a terrific job . . . We cannot have too many of them . . . or too soon.'' Abercrombie had Olle Lorehn give him four thumb tacks, and posted the letter himself on the main bulletin board in the gun plant, during one of the nightly tours that allowed him to know every CIW employee in those days, by first name, and just what he did. Herb Allen used to tease him: ''Boss, if we're ever short a man on the graveyard shift, I may have to ask you to fill in.''

Ralph McCullough discovered, especially after Pearl Harbor, that the weekends were pretty much like the work week. Secretary of Cameron Iron since 1933, he found this essentially nominal position expanding into that of secretary-treasurer and special assistant for matters involving taxes, cost accounting or contracts at the gun plant—plus his duties with the JSA Company and Harrison & Abercrombie. He was more and more the liaison between Mr. Jim, Ed Lorehn, Herb Allen, Olle Lorehn (who had become a vice-president of Cameron, charged with procurement and other administrative duties) and Bob Abercrombie. Ralph's position could also be described as quarterback of a small management team working closely and constantly with The Boss on a wide range of problems affecting the Abercrombie interests.

So it was that McCullough was in the Gulf Building office of the JSA Company the afternoon of the first Saturday in March of 1942. He and Mr. Jim had been going over some cash flow projections before Abercrombie went on to the old Houston Country Club off Wayside Drive, to play golf with J. Sayles Leach, president of the Texas Company and a next-door neighbor on River Oaks Boulevard; Naurice Cummings; and Fishback Wheless[3] of Gulf Oil.

The telephone rang in the silence, as Ralph wondered, in the innocence of 1942 prime rates, whether JSA would have to pay three-and-five-eighths or three- and three-quarters percent for some short-term money. The call was for ''Mr. Jim Abercrombie, the oilman.'' ''He's not here, but I can reach him if it's important,'' McCullough said. ''This is the White House,'' the operator responded. ''President Roosevelt is calling; he wants very much to talk to Mr. Abercrombie.'' Ralph took the call-back number and set about finding The Boss as soon as possible.

The locker room at the Houston Country Club is traditionally run by alert, long-time employees such as the current Henry Henderson; among their varied qualifications is knowing virtually every one of the Club's golf players and how to locate them quickly in an emergency if they are on the course, or in the locker room or the men's grill. The Henry Henderson of the 1940s was Leo Harvey, who found Mr. Jim in a matter of minutes, just turning the ninth hole on the beautiful old layout along Country Club Bayou.

When McCullough told him of the call from FDR, The Boss said he would come in to the Gulf Building immediately. There was no Gulf Freeway (until 1947), but Mr. Jim made it through the East End on Polk, and then downtown on Telephone Road and Leeland as quickly as possible. He parked on Rusk, just across the street from his office, and walked self-consciously to the Gulf Building elevators, his golf cleats loud in the comparative silence of a Saturday afternoon.

The Boss was talking to President Roosevelt in a matter of minutes. FDR wanted to see him at 10:30 the following Tuesday morning, in the White House. Mr. Jim of course agreed to be there; he asked permission to bring Ralph McCullough, which was immediately granted. No indication of an agenda, but it seemed obvious that the meeting had to do with petroleum: President Roosevelt had mentioned that the secretary of the Army, Robert Patterson; his executive assistant James Forrestal, recently named under-secretary of the Navy; and Secretary of the Interior Harold Ickes, of Ickes Bill fame; were to be present. The guest list had the smell of crude oil, rather than some further expansion of Navy armament contracts; Abercrombie suspected that his close friend Sam Rayburn might be involved.

Ralph and The Boss went up on the train. They were able to reserve a drawing room, which allowed them to relax a bit, spread out some of McCullough's papers and conjecture again about why the president of the United States and three of his busiest cabinet ministers wanted to see them.

Mr. Jim was not much for guessing games; he told Ralph that the agenda looked to him to be heavily slanted toward Old Ocean. McCullough agreed; he had brought along some very recent data on the Brazoria County field, boiled down to a single page. Abercrombie studied this for a time, and then watched the East Texas countryside roll by in the deepening dusk; the train was just leaving Walker County, headed for the deep Piney Woods. Could it be forty years, he thought, since he was a boy in Huntsville, with its memories and traditions of the old days before the War Between the States? And almost a generation since his parents were laid to rest in Oakwood Cemetery? The busy years were flying by, ever more rapidly.

Jim broke out some Bell's twelve-year-old Scotch and a deck of cards. They played gin rummy until the first call for dinner, and then headed for the dining car early. Railroad steaks were still very good in early 1942, but they were already scarce on crowded trains; after downing a succulent ribeye each, they had the good fortune to run into two Dallas bankers who were excellent bridge players, in the club car. The bankers paid off with a check, explaining that they were short of cash.

The train was right on time at Union Station on Tuesday morning; Ralph and The Boss were in their suite at the Mayflower a little after eight. McCullough called White House protocol, confirmed their arrival and was told that a limousine would be at the front entrance at exactly ten o'clock.

They rolled silently down Connecticut Avenue and K Street to Lafayette Square, then across Pennsylvania Avenue to the White House, Jim wishing all the time that they could have walked over instead on such a beautiful spring morning. The journey was barely five minutes by Cadillac, and he and Ralph could have made it on foot in a half hour, with a stopover in Lafayette Square. He had walked there often during his lobbying days in Washington with Major Parten.

Now, Jim remembered reading somewhere recently; the Square was visited daily by the great financier Bernard Baruch.[4] Baruch, FDR's ''elder statesman'' and expert on economic mobilization for war, often thought out his plans while sitting on a bench near Lafayette's statue, slowly feeding the pigeons from a little bag of parched corn as they whirred constantly about him.

They were ushered into the Oval Office at precisely 10:30. After quickly introducing Patterson, Forrestal and Ickes in his precise Grotonese, President Roosevelt turned again to Jim Abercrombie. ''I want to thank you and Mr. McCullough very much for coming here, especially on such short notice,'' FDR said. ''Our pleasure,'' Jim replied. ''It's a great honor to be asked here, Mr. President.'' ''(Secretary of the Navy) Frank Knox has told me how Cameron Iron is performing on those Navy contracts,'' FDR continued. ''We may have to move the Bureau of Ordnance to Houston.'' Abercrombie smiled and nodded, without replying; but he made a mental note to tell Ed and Herb and the men on the night shift what President Roosevelt had said about the K-gun contract.

FDR then came immediately to the point: ''Mr. Abercrombie, you and the Old Ocean oilfield and the hydrocarbons there have been highly recommended. We need a 100-octane avgas plant at Old Ocean just as soon as it can be built and put onstream.'' Mr. Jim looked quickly at Ralph for a moment; The Boss' hunch about the agenda had been correct. ''Our organization will do anything we can, Mr. President,'' Abercrombie replied.

Within the hour, Mr. Jim and McCullough were in Secretary Patterson's office with Forrestal and Ickes. For once, Abercrombie spoke first: "I didn't want to say this at the White House;" he said, "but you gentlemen must know that our companies have no experience in operating refineries. With the necessary priorities, our people and some specialists, I believe we can build you an avgas refinery. Operating it is something else."

Both Patterson and Forrestal started to reply. The secretary of war spoke first: "We'll get you anything you need to build this plant, and get it now; when it's ready to go onstream, you pick the organization or individuals you want to operate it, and we'll get them, too." Forrestal (who would later succeed Frank Knox as secretary of the navy, become the nation's first secretary of defense and die a suicide after a brilliant career, a victim of depression and overwork) then added: "Mr. Abercrombie, you may not have any experience in operating a refinery, but Jesse Jones and Sam Rayburn and the man from Uvalde (Vice President John Nance Garner) tell us there's very little about petroleum products you don't know or can find out or have done. We can't have Bill Knudsen[5] turning out planes and not have plenty of avgas to fuel them."

Everyone looked at Abercrombie. If you listed Mr. Jim's attributes, modesty would always rank very high among them; the conversation was getting downright embarrassing. He lit a new panatela while they waited, and then delivered what was almost a major speech for him: "Gentlemen, we'll of course do everything we can. Why don't you tell us exactly what you want done, the principal agencies involved in addition to Army, Navy and Interior, plus some idea of timetables and budgets." "And," he added, "the deal will have to be approved by the man who owns the other half of our joint interest in Old Ocean, Dan Harrison."

Harrison had no objection; he was just as enthusiastic as Mr. Jim about an opportunity to provide a signal service for the nation in a time of dire emergency. The avgas facility was actually a project of Jesse Jones' Reconstruction Finance Corporation (RFC), although under the jurisdiction of an RFC subsidiary, the Defense Plant Corporation (DPC). To complicate things further, the end product would be sold to another RFC subsidiary, the Defense Supplies Corporation (DSC). DSC was just what the name indicated, a huge government purchasing agency for critical items needed for national defense.

Ralph McCullough sighed to himself as he heard the game plan unfold and envisioned the future flood of forms from Washington agencies. As he furiously took notes, he realized again why The Boss refused to get involved in details.

Jim Abercrombie's responsibility was to assure that the Old Ocean refinery, to be located at nearby Sweeny, was properly planned and built, amid a growing avalanche of engineering reports and recommendations, blueprints, flow charts and construction schedules. He would then have oversight regarding the proper operation of the facility, as H&A hydrocarbons became the 100-octane avgas so desperately needed by United States planes and those of our allies.

Mr. Jim's high-pressure petroleum factory, in the midst of Hod Hodnett's Lower Jurassic swamp of the pterodactyls, had become a key national asset.

Soon its avgas, just as Cameron Iron's deadly K-guns and Tiny Tim rockets, would be part of the mighty arsenal that smashed the Nazi and Jap war machines. Admiral Hasegawa Kiyoshi, chairman of the Japanese Supreme War Council, summed it all up in a frank statement he made to General Douglas MacArthur after the surrender ceremonies in Tokyo Bay: "American war production doomed the Japanese naval forces, and our nation and its allies." But in mid-March of 1942, as Mr. Jim and Ralph McCullough returned from their high-level conferences in Washington, the final victory in World War II, and capitulation on the battleship *Missouri* by the Japanese, was three-and-a-half years away.

The first thing The Boss asked Ralph to do when they were back in Houston was to set up a meeting with Stanley Gill and Joe Tennant; he wanted their ideas on the Old Ocean refinery as soon as possible. Gill had a classmate from MIT who was an expert on refinery construction; this was Bill Neely, an official with the J. F. Prichard Company, a consulting firm in Kansas City with a growing reputation in planning and building large, complex refineries. About a minute into Gill's summary of Neely's formidable abilities and accomplishments, Mr. Jim spoke up: "You recommend him for Old Ocean, Stanley?" "Absolutely." "Let's get him down here, tomorrow if you can, and get me a little rundown on this firm he's with."

Gill and Neely, with Herb Allen, Tennant and key members of the Prichard organization, made up the technical team which planned the Old Ocean avgas facility and supervised its construction. It was built in record time and went onstream early in 1943 under an operating contract with J. F. Prichard. The Boss, aided constantly by Ralph McCullough, was expediter and liaison to the government agencies and cabinet officers involved; for a time, he was in Washington almost as much as in Houston, accompanied many times by Gill, Neely or other assistants and consultants as required; but President Roosevelt got his avgas, on schedule.

The Old Ocean refinery project paid some important dividends, in addition to strengthening still more Jim Abercrombie's rising reputation in the petroleum industry. Among these dividends were the long-overdue voiding of a 1935 contract with Texaco, and Jim's decision to challenge the entrenched idea (still prevalent as late as World War II) that natural gas was an essentially worthless byproduct, best suited to flaring.

When Old Ocean's wells first came into production, Texaco had the only major pipeline in the area; consequently, H&A was in a weak bargaining posture when Jim and Dan sought a convenient market for their crude. They agreed reluctantly to accept $1.34 a barrel from Texaco, and this contract price was still in effect in 1942. By then, crude was actually worth an average of about $2.75, or more than twice what H&A was getting from Texaco.

Jack Blalock, retained to represent H&A in matters regarding the avgas facility, found that new agreements with federal agencies in effect cancelled the 1935 contract with Texaco. This was great news; Ralph McCullough, forced for years to watch The Boss lose fifty percent of every barrel of Old Ocean crude, was especially pleased to see things righted. He reckoned without Mr. Jim, who was also gratified to see the unrealistic agreement with Texaco abrogated, but refused to charge the government a penny more than the old rate of $1.34 per barrel. "There's a war on," he said. "We'll get market for Old Ocean crude one of these days, but Uncle Sam pays $1.34."

H&A was selling dry gas from the Brazoria County field to Dow Chemical's nearby installations at two cents per one thousand cubic feet. The incredibly low price really concerned The Boss, who was ever more conscious of the real value of natural gas and already predicting that it would sell in time for more than crude, once energy values were equated. He had apparently been thinking about the matter more and more; one day, during a discussion of the Dow contract, Mr. Jim suddenly asked Gill and Neely: "what would it cost to find out—to prove—what natural gas is really worth in relationship to crude? First of all, I guess, how could you prove such a thing?''

Gill answered: ''Take a pilot plant to really prove it. Then you could do exact measurements of the Btus (British thermal units) in differing quantities of natural gas and of crude oil, using many samples and varied procedures.'' Neely nodded, and added: ''It would probably work—but it would cost plenty to do it right.''

''What's 'plenty'?,'' Abercrombie asked. Neely thought for a moment before answering: ''Hard to say, really; probably around a million for the pilot plant; a first-class lab, well equipped; and good investigators working a year or so.'' Mr. Jim was silent, but he was chomping absent-mindedly on a cigar and thinking hard. ''Who could do it,'' he asked Bill Neely, ''and really do it right?'' Neely and Gill replied at the same time: ''Kellogg.''

A few months later, after a tough session with Dan Harrison, Mr. Jim signed a contract with the famed H. W. Kellogg organization. H. W. Kellogg himself had to approve the project, which was to center upon a small but costly pilot plant at Olean, New York, just over the Pennsylvania border. He delayed approval while he considered the project further. It would tie down a couple of his best men, and Kellogg was not certain you could measure with acceptable accuracy, in a procedure other scientists could replicate and verify, the relationship between the Btus in many varying samples and quantities of crude oil and of natural gas.

Another reason he debated acceptance of the proposed contract with Abercrombie was something Kellogg could not discuss at the time: his organization was hard at work on some top secret experiments for the Manhattan District (atomic bomb) project, and might be asked to provide more manpower for General Leslie Groves, the boss at the Manhattan District.

Kellogg realized the significance of the natural gas study, however, and what it could mean both to the petroleum industry and to his own organization, more and more involved with that industry, in future years. He approved the Abercrombie contract and accepted a down payment of $200,000.

Some fifteen months later, Mr. Jim had his scientific proof of the value of natural gas vis-à-vis crude oil. The Btus in an average barrel of crude were found to be present in about twenty-five hundred cubic feet of natural gas. Even valuing the crude oil at a low price of $1.50 per barrel, the Btus in one thousand cubic feet of natural gas would be worth sixty cents ($1.50 divided by 2.5). Sixty cents was a far cry from the two cents per one thousand cubic feet H&A was receiving for natural gas from Dow Chemical.

It was a costly experiment at Olean, but it proved Mr. Jim's case on the true value of natural gas and hastened the time at which the petroleum industry and those it serves would reevaluate gas and its uses. Someone should find a copy of the Dow Chemical contract at two cents per one thousand cubic feet, incidentally, for the petroleum industry archives.

Dan Harrison kept his own counsel.

The quasi-partnership with Jim Abercrombie in H&A, as well as substantial joint ventures in ranching, constituted a profitable and effective relationship which both men prized and respected; yet they had other business and personal interests that remained distinctly isolate. The Harrisons had moved from the handsome old home on Caroline, in a long-established neighborhood near the Will Claytons, to a splendid new residence on Lazy Lane in Homewoods,[6] two minutes from Jim and Miss Lillie at 2221 River Oaks Boulevard; but aside from an infrequent dinner party, sharing the Harrison box at the opening of the symphony season or the traditional Abercrombie party on Christmas night, the two families saw little of one another.

Similarly, Dan had no interest in the Friday night poker games at the Texas State Hotel, where Jim tested his substantial skill against Judge Elkins, W. A. (Bill) Smith, Gus Wortham and other Houstonians of total impact; nor was he a member of the Suite 8-F crowd at the Lamar Hotel, where Abercrombie sat regularly with the ringmasters of high-level politics, or in attendance at the occasional sessions in the even more rarefied atmosphere of Jesse Jones' penthouse and roof garden on the sixteenth floor of the Lamar.

Jim and Harrison owned ranches together, including the Pot Luck near Kerrville (in partnership with Fishback Wheless) and the big fifty-thousand-acre spread at Campbellton; Dan, however, was not among those who went to what was becoming another Abercrombie tradition: the annual quail hunt on the Blackwell Ranch at Cuero. Harrison seemed to have little interest in guns or in the outdoors although Dan, Jr., before leaving for the service in 1942, had been one of the best young trapshooters in the area, competing regularly at the Houston Gun Club with such marksmen as Tommy Lovett and Dan Bullard.

It was not that Dan Harrison failed to have concerns outside the immediate sphere of business, but that they were so markedly divergent from how Mr. Jim invested his own spare time (what little of it there was). Remembering his days as the Longhorn varsity center in 1902 and 1903, Dan was active in the "Texas Exes" organization, which Hines H. Baker of Humble Oil headed for a time. He was chairman of a committee raising funds statewide for the University of Texas football program, which Coach D. X. Bible had departed Nebraska to resuscitate after a dismal season in 1937 left the 'Horns where they have so seldom been, in the conference cellar. In this effort, Harrison served with J. R. Parten, Congressman-to-be Jake Pickle, Ralph Yarborough and James L. Shepherd, Jr., president of the UT Exes branch in Houston.

In contrast to raising funds for the Orange and White, Jesse Jones had Dan Harrison serving with him and Gus Wortham on a regional committee to plan the New York World's Fair of 1939.

Against this background of Dan's differing pursuits and clear history of keeping his own counsel, Jim Abercrombie was greatly surprised when Harrison came into his Gulf Building office one morning in 1942 and asked if he could discuss some matters "in private." Mr. Jim of course nodded agreement, wondering what this was all about; when Dan sat down without saying anything but looked at the open door to Ralph McCullough's office, Abercrombie went over to close it. He and Ralph had kept the door open for years as they conferred throughout the day, sometimes without even leaving their respective desks.

Dan Harrison came right to the point. He was not getting any younger (although he would live another thirty-two years, into his ninth decade) and "wanted to get things in order." The first thing he had in mind was selling Old Ocean. Abercrombie listened with increasing dismay. It would be a bad time to sell, in his judgment: the tide of war was clearly turning in favor of the United States and its allies, but the renascence of a peacetime economy in which Old Ocean's reserves and their true value could be clearly established and appreciated was at best still several years away. As Dan talked, Abercrombie kept thinking how much reserves of natural gas (already calculated in trillions of cubic feet) would be worth as the price moved up from the give-away level of two cents per thousand cubic feet toward the price of sixty cents determined by the pilot plant at Olean. And he thought about the increased income when their Brazoria County crude was no longer being sold to the government at $1.34 a barrel.

Jim realized that Harrison had finished talking, and was looking at him, awaiting a reply. "I think it's the wrong time to sell, Dan," he said. "We went in this deal as partners, though, in every way except a signed partnership agreement. If you're really convinced we should get out of Old Ocean, I feel obliged to look into it. Let me think it over."

As soon as Harrison left, Mr. Jim went in to see McCullough. "You want to come by the house early tomorrow morning?" he asked. "Got something I really need to discuss. Eddie can drive us around for a while." Abercrombie had stopped driving years before, except for piloting pick-ups (and later, Jeeps) on ranch roads. He found that he could become a real traffic hazard in the city when concentrating on a complex problem he was trying to resolve instead of on red lights and stop signs.

"Early," to Mr. Jim really meant early, as Ralph knew so well. Just before sun-up the next day, the black chauffeur Eddie started the Packard sedan and began driving them toward town, although with no specific destination. Abercrombie had learned long ago that being driven rather aimlessly in this fashion kept him from the interruption of telephones and office routine; it also enabled him somehow to reason his way through a problem—either alone or with someone such as McCullough with whose thought processes he was familiar.

Abercrombie quickly summarized the conversation with Dan Harrison. Mr. Jim emphasized that he wanted to be fair with Dan, but extremely cautious of any sale that underestimated the true value of Old Ocean. "We're not talking just about J. S. Abercrombie interests, Ralph," he said, "this involves my brothers and sisters, and you and some other stockholders who've worked with me all the way back to Burkburnett." Abercrombie then showed him some figures that commanded attention:

Of the other half of the total original ownership of Old Ocean (that belonging to H. W. Hodnett, Everette DeGolyer, their Atlatl Royalty Company and J. C. Karcher), fifteen-sixteenths had already been sold for less than $16 million. Hodnett bought out DeGolyer and their joint holding through Atlatl for $6 million, and then sold three-quarters of his entire stake to a syndicate headed by John Hay Whitney for $8.5 million; he kept the remaining sixteenth "for my grandchildren and their grandchildren." Dr. Karcher's one-fourth went to a group of Chicago investors for $7 million.

Jim shook his head, slowly and sadly. "Less than $16 million for almost half of Old Ocean," he said. "A few years' production of gas alone will be worth that one of these days."

As was so often the case in matters dealing with petroleum, Jim Abercrombie was right.[7]

After Eddie had driven them around for an hour or two, Mr. Jim had a firm plan in mind. He would go to Harrison, ask him to get a detailed appraisal on Old Ocean as soon as practicable, and suggest they see if Naurice Cummings would be willing to look around for a major company seeking sizable new reserves. Jim had heard that Magnolia Petroleum might be in the market, and he seemed to recall that Naurice was a good friend of Magnolia's president or chairman.

Harrison agreed to the plan. It turned out that Cummings had known both Alec Little, Magnolia's president, and Alexander Sinclair, chairman of the board of the Dallas-based company (a subsidiary of Socony-Vacuum, John D. Rockefeller's old Standard of New York) since his roughnecking days. And Magnolia was definitely interested; anyone concerned with building up reserves would want to look into a deal that could bring you one-half of Old Ocean's treasure trove of hydrocarbons.

At this point, Dan Harrison came in with an appraisal. When he showed Jim the figure—$66,666,667, Abercrombie for once almost lost his temper. "How did you come up with a price like that?" he exclaimed, "No one will believe all those sixes, absolutely no one." Harrison explained that it was the value of their properties, "plus enough to take care of taxes and so forth." He had apparently added a specific percentage to the appraised value to get his $66,666,667. Mr. Jim thought for a moment: $50 million plus one-third, he calculated quickly in his head, would be exactly $66,666,667.

After further discussions, Abercrombie was able to have the appraisal rounded off at $66 million; that was at least more credible, he thought to himself, but here I am reducing the price another one percent, not moving it up where it belongs. Magnolia thought the price was still peculiar, or too high, or both; at any rate, Naurice reported back to Jim after another trip to Dallas: "No deal; they think it's too high; at least we didn't show Alec that appraisal of $66,666,667.

The situation had evolved into something Jim Abercrombie wished he had never heard of—selling a prize piece of property he really did not want to dispose of for less than it was worth. With Naurice Cummings' negative report, however, he had a way out of the dilemma: he went to Harrison the next morning and told him Magnolia would not pay $66 million. "That's the end of it as far as I'm concerned," he told Dan. "I'm not willing to cut my price a dime, and they won't pay it."

Abercrombie continued: if Harrison could persuade Magnolia to buy his holdings separately, on his own or through Naurice, sell away. There was no mention, however, of another option: just as in any bargaining position, ask the prospective buyer to reconsider the original price tag of $66 million.

The more he thought about having pulled his interest off the market, the more concerned Abercrombie became. He respected Dan Harrison, in spite of their differences of opinion, and felt a sense of obligation toward him.

After a sleepless night, Mr. Jim returned to Naurice Cummings; he asked his friend to tell Magnolia he had little enthusiasm about selling the Abercrombie one-fourth of Old Ocean; but if withdrawing that portion prevented a sale of the Harrison interest, he would allow his portion to be acquired, also. "A deal's a deal," he told Cummings, "even if you choke on it."

Naurice pondered the message he was to take to the Magnolia officials for quite a time. He admired Jim Abercrombie's willingness to subordinate his own strong feelings to what was essentially a point of honor, but still believed that President Little might elect to buy out Harrison separately for $33 million, and get Jim off the hook. He therefore told Little both properties were available, singly or together, at the original asking price, but that Abercrombie was not particularly interested in selling. Nothing was said about Mr. Jim's wish to dispose of his portion of Old Ocean if his retaining it would prevent a sale by Dan Harrison.

To Cummings' surprise, Alec Little decided to buy out both Abercrombie and Harrison for $33 million each. A purchase of this size had to be approved in New York, by Alexander Sinclair, who quickly ratified the agreement by telephone. Before Naurice left Little's office, however, he says that Sinclair rang back from Socony-Vacuum headquarters. Chairman Sinclair had just received an ill-timed call from Harrison. He told the New York executive an important tax deadline was approaching for him, and if Magnolia wanted his part of Old Ocean separately, he would cut the price to $27.5 million. Sinclair settled for an even $27 million, but guaranteed completion of the sale by December 31, 1942; the papers were signed one day before the deadline, on December 30.

Suddenly, Dan Harrison had left $6 million on the table, and Mr. Jim could keep his part of Old Ocean. Harrison had, however, achieved what was to him an important goal after months of frustrating delay, and may well have saved very significant sums in tax dollars.

Jim Abercrombie was much concerned lest Dan find out just how close he had been to receiving $33 million, instead of $27 million, from Magnolia. Cummings agreed never to reveal what happened as long as Harrison was alive, and says today that Dan did not ever know.

Ralph McCullough tells a different story, almost four decades later. In his version, Magnolia countered the original asking price of $66 million with an offer of $50 million for the combined Harrison and Abercrombie holdings at Old Ocean. Mr. Jim described this offer as "peanuts," and Naurice Cummings reportedly told Alec Little that the $50 million proposal "just embarrassed the hell out of Jim, who wouldn't even take it to his stockholders." Magnolia, McCullough recalls, then upped the ante to $55 million, or $27.5 million to each company, with the sale of one company independent of the other being acceptable.

As weeks stretched into months, Ralph says, Harrison asked Mr. Jim at least to present the offer to JSA Company shareholders. This small group included only members of the Abercrombie family, a few other long-time employees of the JSA Company, Judge Fouts and McCullough.

Mr. Jim brought the shareholders together, according to McCullough, and told them of the $27.5 million offer for the Old Ocean properties. Someone spoke up immediately: "Jim, we'll do whatever you recommend." "Appreciate that, but I can't accept it; I have to have your decision." Milo then said: "For $27.5 million? Why, we'd just be giving it away." Bob and Joe Rice made it clear they were in strong agreement, before John added, "Brother, you've brought us a long way; you're making this company more valuable every day. I say, 'pass'."

Jim had already reported to the meeting that Dan Harrison would very probably accept the $27.5 million offer from Magnolia, for his part of Old Ocean. It was quite clear, however, that the Abercrombie interests were not for sale. Mr. Jim adjourned the meeting and reported the results to Harrison. Harrison, according to McCullough, then accepted Magnolia's $27.5 million, and was in Mr. Jim's office waiting to see him the first thing the next day.

Dan Harrison was an unhappy man. He pointed out that since Abercrombie was no longer with him at Old Ocean, he assumed Jim "no longer wanted to go along with me in the Campbellton ranch." Abercrombie told him he saw no connection between Old Ocean and Campbellton, and no problem in continuing to operate the ranch as in the past. Dan did not agree; he wanted to buy Jim out, but was told that neither Abercrombie nor the ranch were for sale.

When Harrison pressed the matter, and clearly did not want to continue the Campbellton operation as a joint venture, Mr. Jim told him: "Dan, you really do want to have that whole ranch. I'll tell you what I'll do." He took a quarter from his pocket. "Heads, the ranch is all yours; tails, it's all mine. OK?" As McCullough watched, Harrison answered. "Not interested," he said, marching back to his office.

Jim Abercrombie and Dan Harrison were both gentlemen, and they patched up matters even though their unique and profitable "partnership" was at an end. The Campbellton ranch was split down the middle, Jim taking the 27,000 unimproved acres to the south; Dan the improved 23,000 to the north. Each man kept a one-eighth interest in the mineral rights on the other's acreage, to simplify and facilitate any future exploration for oil.

As soon as Magnolia Petroleum had formally taken possession of the properties of Harrison Oil Company at Old Ocean, Mr. Jim had a visit from John Brown, chairman of the board of Standard Oil of New York, and members of his staff. Brown quickly stated his policies regarding Old Ocean: "Mr. Abercrombie, we don't believe in disturbing success; we want you to continue running things, without interference; the only time you'll hear from us is when we are seeking your advice. And we know about the Kellogg pilot plant at Olean; it's doing a fine job for you, for us and for the industry. Just bill us for our part, every month."

It was a real tribute to The Whale of Old Ocean, and one richly deserved.

Soon after this, Jim and Naurice took Miss Lillie and Tinsey to the movies, at the old Metropolitan next to the Lamar Hotel. Everyone liked the Met because if the scenes of the ''current attraction'' Al Lever had displayed out front looked too uninteresting, you could always pay your thirty-five cents at the Loew's State next door instead. After the movie, the men were standing together waiting for Naurice's car in the parking garage. ''I guess you've lost your interest in selling your part of Old Ocean,'' Cummings said. Mr. Jim took a long pull on his cigar and thought for a moment. ''Depends,'' he said. ''You can never tell what'll come up. You and I have fired into some fine coveys of quail right at twilight.''

Naurice kept his contacts with Magnolia Petroleum alive, and almost a year later, Alec Little offered $35 million for the JSA Company. By this time, Mr. Jim wanted $40 million; nor would he split the difference at $37.5 million. Cummings drove all the way out to Cameron late one night to suggest the $37.5 million compromise after Alec Little had pressed him for an answer. He found Abercrombie on the shop floor with Gene Long, a highly skilled toolmaker turned shop manager and now, head of purchasing. Long had solved the problem of a high rejection rate on piston rings being made for CIW gun mounts by an outfit in Detroit. Cameron would make their own through a process Long had worked out in his own garage, and Abercrombie was enjoying hearing all about it.

Cummings thought Mr. Jim might well accept the $37.5 million, but he told Naurice, ''I appreciate your trying to work this out, but no dice. $40 million is a fair price now; just tell Little thanks, and the next time they want to buy out the JSA, the price will be $50 million.'' Jim thought for a moment. ''I like that fellow Little,'' he added. ''Told me right to my face I was a hard trader; I told him I just want my money's worth.''

They had a Coke together, and as Naurice started to leave, Abercrombie said, ''By the way, you ever get that matter straightened out with Dan Harrison?'' (Mr. Jim had gone to Harrison to tell him he thought Naurice Cummings deserved something on the $27 million sale to Magnolia—''at least one percent.'' Dan had finally paid almost one percent to Cummings, but had come back with a request that Naurice pay some $75,000 in legal fees out of the commission.) "No," Cummings replied. "I just don't know what to tell him about that $75,000. "Tell him," Mr. Jim advised, "to go to hell."

Abercrombie did ask Naurice Cummings to keep his eyes open for an advantageous sale at the new asking level of $50 million, however. In the first weeks of 1945, a subsidiary of Standard Oil of Indiana came to Mr. Jim, and to his favorite banker and long-time neighbor at the Warwick, Judge Elkins, with a $50 million offer. Judge Elkins enlisted the services of Naurice, and the deal was in the final stages when a new survey reduced the amount of total acreage involved slightly. As a result, the final documents called for a payment of $49.7 million, rather than $50 million. Jim turned down the whole deal.

Judge Elkins asked him to come by his office a day or two later; Naurice was there also, but let Elkins do the talking. "Now, Jim," said his good friend and fellow Huntsvillean, "I'm surprised at you; what in the world is the difference between $50 million and $49.7 million?"

"Judge, I'm surprised at you, too," was the retort. "Fine banker and lawyer like you. The difference is $300,000."

Jim Abercrombie had just illustrated again one of his basic principles. He would never go back on a deal, or change it, after it was agreed upon.

For James Smither Abercrombie, 1946 was to be a watershed year: he would sell the JSA Company; become more and more involved in the Pin Oak Horse Show, and thereby in the construction and financing of the long-term operations of the Texas Children's Hospital; play his usual major role in significant changes at Cameron Iron Works, as the company began an enormous post-war expansion; and spend increasing time at Suite 8-F of the Lamar Hotel, where the "hatchings" were soon to include both Texas' new governor and a future U.S. senator and president.

Mr. Jim, however, would have pointed out two other events of unusual consequence in 1946: his beloved daughter Josephine graduated from Rice Institute; and there was an especially fine quail hunt at the Blackwell Ranch, where he increasingly found the best of friendship and shooting plus the ability to relax completely from the multiplying pressures of business.

As post-World War II expansion plans were unfurled, the JSA Company and its enormous reservoir of hydrocarbons at Old Ocean became the object of growing attention from prospective purchasers. One of the ablest of the skilled analysts already searching out high-level opportunities to acquire significant reserves had been a vice president of the (Morgan) Guaranty Trust Company as early as 1930, assigned to seek good loans for the huge New York City bank among principal independent producers in Texas and Oklahoma.

This was Luther Cleveland, a native of Washington County who had deserted Chappell Hill, Texas for Manhattan—little knowing that he could have made his fortune right at home selling small Washington County farm homes at unbelievably high prices to well-heeled Houstonians whose wives wanted to fill them with expensive antiques and weekend guests. When he became chairman of the board of the Guaranty Trust during World War II, Cleveland decided to continue to use his prior experience in the Oil Patch to turn up a new series of major loans on his own. There were prospective customers, he knew, with oil properties that could be extremely attractive—not only as solid collateral, but to major integrated petroleum companies or substantial investors looking avidly for reserves.

An alert bank might discover a loan, a commission, a series of loans—or all three, back in that Oil Patch. Jim Abercrombie and the JSA Company were to prove this point for Luther Cleveland.

Ralph McCullough had recommended to Mr. Jim early in 1945 a post-war analysis of the JSA Company's financial needs, looking specifically toward a major new source of "on call" funds to prevent annoying and expensive shopping for short-term loans when cash flow took an unexpected dip, or an unforeseen opportunity presented itself. As indicated, Guaranty Trust was well and favorably known in Texas, primarily through Luther Cleveland; McCullough made a telephone call or two, and Cleveland was soon sitting with him, Abercrombie and Stanley Gill, their reservoir analyst, on the twenty-first story of the Gulf Building.

Cleveland had done his home work for the meeting, although on short notice; he even had notes on Mr. Jim's 1924 trip to London, when he was recommended for the drilling project in Colombia through references originating from J. P. Morgan & Company (founders of what would become Morgan Guaranty Trust). Stanley Gill had not been idle, either; he presented a thorough, conservative but eye-opening analysis of Old Ocean that gave Luther Cleveland plenty of food for thought on the return trip to New York.

There would be no difficulty in arranging a line of credit for Abercrombie's JSA Company; what Cleveland was thinking about now were those trillions of cubic feet of natural gas, and millions of barrels of crude, in Mr. Jim's deep, beautifully-engineered reservoir of Old Ocean.

The answer came to the banker the next morning, as he sat trapped in a taxicab two blocks from his office waiting for the usual crosstown traffic jam to clear. Standard of Indiana (Stanolind) was looking for really good, long-term reserves, and they had both cash and plenty of credit. He called their senior vice-president the next day for a leisurely lunch at the Pierre.

Luther Cleveland was a fast, competent worker. He was back in Houston before the last norther and the River Oaks Azalea Trail—not to check on the new loan to the JSA Company but to propose one of the biggest deals in the history of the Oil Patch—for cash on the barrel head, too. Mr. Jim's eyes lit up a bit when he heard that part early on in the discussions with Cleveland. The price, for all of the thinly-held JSA stock, was $54 million.

The Washington County native, whose acquired Yankee accent always faded the moment he set foot in Texas, had worked with Lloyd Noble of Ardmore, one of the leading independent producers and ranchers in Oklahoma, to organize a new Delaware corporation, the Old Ocean Oil Company (OOOC). OOOC, *mirabili dictu*, had arranged a $30 million, ten-year loan from Guaranty Trust and the Chemical Bank; Stanolind would furnish the remaining $24 million directly, through issuance of twenty-year debentures. J. R. Butler, well and favorably known to Mr. Jim, was to operate the new enterprise as vice-president, general manager and a member of the five-man OOOC directorate, which included Luther Cleveland.

Abercrombie was silent after Cleveland had explained the proposal. Finally, he said, "Bigger than Yount-Lee," with some satisfaction. Stanolind had purchased the Yount-Lee[8] holdings, including the great McFaddin #2 discovery that revived Spindletop, in 1935 for $46 million.

Mr. Jim liked Luther Cleveland, and he liked many aspects of the sale the banker was proposing; but there were obviously some complex factors involved. He thanked Cleveland after asking a couple of questions, and told him, "I'll let you know, yes or no, within a week." Then he asked George Sterns,[9] a new but already invaluable member of the Abercrombie inner circle, to take the Guaranty Trust chairman to the airport. As Sterns left, Mr. Jim called him aside for a moment. "I want to drive out to Cinco in the morning, George—early." "Yes sir, Boss, good and early."

Jim Abercrombie was walking the Cinco Ranch, named for its five (cinco) owners, as the sun came up through low-hanging fog; the dense stand of Harris County pine, oak, holly and yaupon around him was barely fifteen minutes from the Houston city limits, but it was thickly overgrown and had seemingly been undisturbed for years. The only sound came from a pair of chattering gray squirrels; a big raccoon, silently fleeing the intruding Abercrombie, had come too close to their nestlings in a moss-hung live oak.

Once again, Mr. Jim had gone alone to walk in isolation while he pondered a convoluted problem. He began to review the pros and cons of the Stanolind proposal.

The $54 million offer was obviously a lot of money, particularly in 1946; the JSA Company would be receiving $11 million more than had been paid earlier for almost three-quarters of Old Ocean. And he thought of the advantages of having more time for being with Miss Lillie and Josephine; of additional hours with Ed Lorehn and Herb Allen, leading a greatly expanded Cameron Iron Works into the opportunities of a peacetime economy; of the many things he wanted to do at the Campbellton Ranch now that he owned his twenty-three thousand acres of it outright.

He tried to recall how long since he and Naurice had been hunting together at Campbellton,[10] and thought how much he wanted to pursue the idea of a children's hospital that his personal physician, Dr. H. J. (Jack) Ehlers, had recently brought to him. He had been neglecting the enjoyable sessions with Herman and George Brown and all their close friends at Suite 8-F, too. The time gained by selling the JSA Company, and its principal holding at Old Ocean, could be used to great advantage.

There were disturbing drawbacks to accepting the Stanolind offer, however: he was still convinced that the remaining one-fourth of Hod Hodnett's ancient swamp might be worth as much as $200 million in time; and there were other negative factors.

Jim had far more than money invested in that corner of Brazoria County; a dozen years of struggle and disappointment, of tremendous mental as well as physical effort, had to be included in the total cost of the high-pressure reservoir. He could go elsewhere in the Oil Patch for new challenges and the fulfilling sense of success, or perhaps discover both in other endeavors; but would these accomplishments be as meaningful? The riddles of Old Ocean, and there would be fresh puzzles there, he was certain, might be truly unique.

He tried to remember how many years he had been in oil and realized almost four decades had passed since Charles Abercrombie hired him as a roustabout on that wildcat at Cypress. For some reason, he recalled that it was six years later when Red Teague hit the rigs, in 1914; he used to kid Red about that, call him a greenhorn. It was Teague, he remembered, who told a field superintendent at Humble that Jim Abercrombie put down twenty sections of fourteen-foot pipe in three hours, while the driller was in town chasing a blond waitress. The twenty sections didn't hurt his promotion to toolpusher, either. Suddenly, his reverie ended, Jim realized that it was approaching mid-morning. He hurried back to the Cinco clubhouse, with its beautiful big fireplace of chimney rock. George had a small, comforting fire of pine knots under split dry oak. It felt good against the morning chill. He noticed that the sun had burned completely through the earlier fog.

"Let's start back," Jim said. He had come to a decision. As usual, the decision was based largely upon consideration for others. His brothers and sisters, and the few other shareholders in the JSA Company, were not getting any younger; their JSA stock, held for many years, now represented by far the principal asset owned by virtually all of them and their families. Mr. Jim also had in mind doing something substantial for JSA employees who had been with the company a minimum number of years. He would recommend to the shareholders the sale of all JSA stock, at $54 million; if they agreed, Stanolind had just made a hell of an investment, and one Jim felt they would never regret.

A few days later, after one of the shortest and most enthusiastic stockholder meetings on record, Mr. Jim had George drive him by Western Union's new office on Prairie; the old office on Franklin, where the cable that sent him and Miss Lillie to Colombia so long ago had been received, was closed. He wrote out Luther Cleveland's name and address at Guaranty Trust carefully, followed by a one-word message: "Yes." The operator pointed out that he was entitled to nine additional words for the same minimum price, but Abercrombie just smiled and paid.

The contract with Stanolind was signed May 23, 1946. In the same pink-sheeted final edition of the old Houston *Press* that headlined the sale of the JSA Company, there was another front-page story. Bill Rhinehart, "manager of the second Pin Oaks horse show," announced a combined advance ticket sale of thirty-two thousand for three evening performances plus the closing matinee on Sunday. Standing room, however, was still available at what the *Press* continued to identify incorrectly as the Pin *Oaks* Stables, site of the Pin *Oaks* Horse Show. (It was Pin *Oak*, just as it would be for a beautiful Abercrombie horse farm in Kentucky.)

The *Press* story, written by Mary Frazer and copy-edited by none other than Tommy Thompson, author-to-be of *Blood and Money* and other sensational best sellers, noted that "Mr. (Jim) Abercrombie, incidentally, is footing the bill for the entire expenses of the show—all proceeds will go to the hospital recreation fund of the Houston Navy League." It was a very generous arrangement that Mr. Jim had initiated in 1945 with Houston Holidays, a welfare organization for veterans.

Jim Abercrombie had embarked upon a new and different life on that twenty-third day of May in 1946—and it was particularly meaningful that there were two separate stories regarding him on the front page of George Carmack's Houston *Press*. Although Old Ocean was sold, Mr. Jim was to be an even more significant figure in the petroleum industry as his multiple achievements were increasingly recognized; but Mary Frazer's story was prophetic. The enterprising lad from Huntsville, now in the prime of life at fifty-four, was also destined for fresh frontiers and widening accomplishments.

Key additions to the *dramatis personae* were gathering again in the wings, along with an established supporting cast. Soon we will meet Leopold Meyer and Freda Bowen, Randolph Wheless, John Connally, LBJ and others whose lives Mr. Jim is to affect substantially, as our final chapter unfolds.

Notes

[1] The box score on World War II production for the Armed Forces at Cameron Iron Works: 14,286 depth charge projectors; 313,050 arbors and 15,667 breech covers for projectors; 2585 three-inch gun barrels; 438 yokes for four-inch guns; 2642 signal flare projectors; 2298 hydraulic mounts for .20-millimeter guns; and "several thousand" of Admiral Bull Halsey's "Tiny Tim" rockets.

[2] In earlier days, as at Goose Creek and Hull, you literally removed stuck or jammed pipe or casing with dynamite, taking your chances on injuries to men, damage to equipment

and where the explosive charge left pipe and casing. Jim Abercrombie devised a lathe-like tool that went downhole with the pipe. You could then cut pipe or casing where you wanted it cut, safely and accurately. The patented procedure was so successful that it led to the organization of the Red Ball Cutting Tool Division within Cameron Iron Works. Milo Abercrombie headed this Division, and very successfully, until it was sold in 1939 when Milo, John and Joe Rice became heavily involved in the expanded drilling program at Old Ocean.

[3] Most of his friends were certain that Fishback Wheless, a close friend of Mr. Jim and his partner in the Pot Luck Ranch, simply had no forename, or had dropped it in favor of a nickname. He was named for his maternal grandfather William Fishback, a very competent governor of Arkansas.

[4] Jim Abercrombie met Bernard Baruch, the distinguished investor and presidential advisor, in Washington and came to have great admiration for him. Chairman of the War Industries Board in World War I, the ''elder statesman'' of Lafayette Square made a significant contribution toward victory in World War II with his brilliantly-devised programs for the allocation and use of scarce materials, some of which had a major effect upon Cameron Iron Works and the overall petroleum industry. In 1946, at seventy-six, Baruch represented the United States at United Nations conferences on the formulation of policies for the international control of atomic energy. He hunted on his South Carolina plantation near Camden until he was well into his eighties and lived to be ninety-five.

[5] William Signius Knudsen, a native of Copenhagen, was an extraordinary man who left the presidency of General Motors to head the Office of Production Management charged with the overall output of World War II armament. He later served as a lieutenant-general.

[6] Homewoods, as those who attempted to prevent Miss Ima Hogg from establishing an affiliate of the Museum of Fine Arts at 2940 Lazy Lane were to discover, is a separate part of River Oaks with its own superbly drawn restrictions. And Bayou Bend now rivals Wilmington, Delaware's Winterthur as America's finest museum of the decorative arts.

[7] Michel T. Halbouty, the world-class geologist the industry and nation should have heeded a generation ago when he was warning against over-dependence on Middle East oil, has estimated that both crude and natural gas reserves at Old Ocean will last well into the next century if current practices initiated there by Jim Abercrombie are maintained.

[8] Frank Yount and T. P. Lee (Glenn McCarthy's future father-in-law) had brought Spindletop back to life with their McFaddin #2, which came in at five thousand barrels a day on a very small choke, on November 13, 1925. The well, announced to enthusiastic Beaumonters on Magnolia Petroleum's experimental radio station, was only a few hundred yards south of the original Spindletop discovery, which had gone dry. The McFaddin #2 was a key factor in further developments which led to Stanolind paying $46 million for the Yount-Lee Oil Company a decade later.

[9] Mr. Jim once told George Brown that George Sterns ''made up many times over for all those political contributions we failed to get from Jim West.'' He was recalling in jest one of his first political fund-raising expeditions, when John Nance Garner was running for the Democratic nomination for president. Down at Suite 8-F, the assessment for Cactus Jack's best friends had been set at $5000, then a handsome sum. Abercrombie went by the usually generous Jim West's office to pick up an expected $5000, but got absolutely nowhere with West. He returned with some additional firepower, namely George Brown and W. A. (Bill) Smith. For some reason, Jim West simply did not want to contribute to the Garner war chest, and he had a simple yet effective technique for such situations. When the trio walked in, he pulled the big Stetson he wore indoors and out over his brow, turned around in his chair and began staring silently out the office window. ''OK, Jim,'' Abercrombie said. ''Is it 'yes' or 'no'?'' There was no answer; West did pull the Stetson down a little further. His callers realized that they had been stonewalled, and left. ''It's

'no','' Mr. Jim told Brown and Smith when they were outside. ''No doubt about it.'' They laughed out loud, and went back to 8-F.

George Sterns had been driving for Jim West for years, and Abercrombie had come to know the intelligent and highly dependable black man, who went along on hunting expeditions to a West ranch in Brooks County, and elsewhere. When Jim West died suddenly late in 1942, Sterns decided he would not work for his son and namesake (aptly called ''Silver Dollar'' because he gave away the cartwheels by the dozen and had thousands of them stored in his River Oaks basement); ''Mr. Jim, Jr.,'' Sterns explained, ''was a good man, but he tended to flare up now and again.''

Instead, Sterns took a wartime job at the San Jacinto Ordnance Depot down on the Ship Channel, where he was the only black on the payroll. After a year or so, he resigned, saying simply that ''things weren't too easy out there,'' even though the pay was good. He had decided to enroll in a school for masseurs at Hot Springs, Arkansas and return to Houston to open a ''health club,'' when he ran into Mr. Jim coming out of the Gulf Building. Abercrombie, the recruiter, had been looking for George; they talked a moment, and he asked for Sterns' telephone number. Several months later, returned from Hot Springs, George had a call from Joe Short, the Abercrombie office manager. ''Mr. Jim wants you to drive for him,'' said Short. Sterns thought that might be a pretty good job for a while until he could get around to opening the health club. It was a fine job and a relationship that was to mean a great deal to Mr. Jim as well as his immediate family, as we will see. The ''for a while'' turned out to be more than thirty years.

[10] The quail hunting picked up considerably at Campbellton after Abercrombie discovered that Dan Harrison had bought some fine adjoining acreage without informing him. When the ranch was divided, Mr. Jim found some hard-working Mexicans who knew a thing or two about attracting quail. They constructed dozens of attractive natural refuges for the nesting birds and scattered large supplies of seeds in the vicinity. New coveys of quail flocked to the area.

Chapter 10

1946–1975

Final Decades of High Achievement

A new master plan unfolds . . . Generous bonuses for JSA employees . . . Of Calgary, Alaska and the Middle East . . . Herb Allen's wondrous forging press, and post-war expansion at Cameron Iron . . . The death of Ed Lorehn . . . Mr. Jim, Dr. Jack Ehlers and Leopold Meyer bring the dream of a children's hospital to reality . . . Pin Oak Stables and a fabulous horse show . . . Randy Wheless and then Freda Bowen join the new organization . . . Mustang Motte, quail and camaraderie . . . Scientific ranching, pinkeye and Rube Goldberg along the Guadalupe . . . 8-F wins the second time around with Landslide Lyndon . . . Jamie and George, the eighth generation of Abercrombies in America . . . Jim and Ralph McCullough come to John Connally's rescue . . . Major new philanthropy and a forty-year trust for TCH . . . Illness, but never a complaint . . . CIW becomes international, and very large . . . "It's so lonely, and I want to be with him."

A new plan was unfolding in James Smither Abercrombie's logical and precise, yet inventive and far-ranging intellect as he watched the phalanx of lawyers crowding the little conference room in the Gulf Building complete the sale of the JSA Company on May 23, 1946. That day, simmering in heat and high humidity in Houston's August-like late spring, would deeply affect the remaining years of his life.

He had a few moments to reflect now, before the endless calls from the news media. Reasonable financial security, he realized, had never meant that much to him personally; it was something he was quite confident of being able to achieve. Yet it had become increasingly important for him in the role of *paterfamilias* (that role he never seemed to escape) to find some degree of security for the extended Abercrombie family. Now $54 million (that vast sum in cash he had really accepted more for others than for himself) was a reality.

Jim knew there was a strong possibility of his seeking new goals and accomplishments now that Old Ocean, a major preoccupation for the past dozen years, was suddenly gone—and only a few months after completion of the final war contracts by Cameron Iron. As he pondered this, he became aware how much he had been thinking of a different pattern of life, a changing master plan, now that he was almost fifty-five.

Such a plan might have been subliminal for months—even years, gathering substance in the rich storehouse of Mr. Jim's memory and in the subconscious of his fertile, creative imagination. As we watch it evolve, his emerging design for the future can be identified as a product of both past and present. Jim's pattern for the years to come reflected all that he had learned since the first 1908 job as a roustabout; it recalled London and Cartagena and the blowout at Hull, as well as untold thousands of hours spent with Harry Cameron and Ed Lorehn and Herb Allen at Cameron Iron; but the altered blueprint now surfacing in consciousness was also strongly influenced by recent experiences, and by goals he had never had time to seek.

Other parts of the emerging plan seem to have been far more deeply buried in Jim Abercrombie's subjacent, innermost mind, and even in the gene bank of the centuries. These more obscure elements hearkened back to the generations of Abercrombies who cherished the good earth, and knew how to make it more productive—to a long tradition of helping one's fellowman, whether by Attorney-General James Abercromby's donation of £10 toward the founding of Charles Town, South Carolina on April 11, 1734; Charles Abercrombie's gift of the courthouse square in Sparta, Georgia; or General Anderson Abercrombie's assistance to Konoyarhika's Upper Creeks, in seed corn made precious by drouth and in protection for the tribe's ancestral burial mounds near Brickyard, Alabama.

Another area of Jim Abercrombie's evolving plan was revealed, also, every time he raised his shotgun at Mustang Motte, or sent his favorite bird dog Polly after a downed quail. The ghost of the Grand Falconer was with him as he tramped the fields at Cuero or Campbellton (relishing the sound of rustling oak leaves underfoot that foretold tomorrow's blustery norther), or trained young pointers much as Alexander Abercromby taught fierce falcons to hunt at Birkenbog.

The first phase of what might be called Mr. Jim's post-Old Ocean plan was based upon almost furious activity, even for a man of his high level of energy. Within six months after the watershed date of May 23, 1946, he had replaced the JSA Company with J. S. Abercrombie Interests, Inc.; set into motion a generous bonus program for former employees; spent countless hours with his key staff members on post-war expansion at the Cameron Iron Works; and begun a study of the feasibility of new exploration and drilling ventures in locations as remote as Calgary, Alaska and the Middle East.

As if his indefatigability required any further proof, Jim also met many times with Dr. Jack Ehlers and Leopold Meyer on a project of tremendous consequence stemming from the highly successful Pin Oak Horse Show; went to Cuero to talk over another major venture with the long-time host of the annual quail hunt, W. A. (Bill) Blackwell; and held strategic political conversations of critical impact with his friends Herman and George Brown up in Suite 8-F. Just to keep things in balance, he spent a long weekend or two shooting ducks with Alfred C. (Pop) Glassell and Charles I. Francis in Louisiana; slipped away to hunt at Campbellton whenever he could; and formed a racing stable. This was backed by a syndicate including Mr. Jim; Josephine; Bob Abercrombie, the Hermann Park jockey of long ago; W. A. (Bill) Smith; and Herman Brown. As promising yearlings were purchased at the Keeneland auctions, there was a need for a horse farm. Mr. Jim and Josephine then acquired Pin Oak Farm at Versailles, Kentucky, just west of Lexington.

He was clearly embarked upon a different pattern of life, embodying elements of the distant past, past, present and future. It would inevitably take Jim Abercrombie into fresh fields of interest and meaningful accomplishment, but would also affect the degree of his continuing participation in areas that had claimed his constant attention for decades.

Even while Joe Moore was completing the incorporation of J. S. Abercrombie Interests, Inc. as a successor to the JSA Company,

Mr. Jim was proceeding at full speed on a matter of profound importance to him. This was the provision of bountiful sums for JSA shareholders and members of the Abercrombie family who had not owned stock in his company, plus substantial bonuses for JSA employees.

There are still in the Abercrombie files dozens of letters attesting to what these bonus payments meant to the recipients, some of whom were former hourly employees unexpectedly receiving $2000 or more.[1] There are letters, for example, from a switchboard operator suddenly able to make a down payment on a home for herself and her invalid mother; a roughneck who could finally buy a small farm he had been saving toward for years; a warehouse supervisor who paid off his residence "free and clear." Plus the instances of "letting a working man catch up with his bills for once," sending a son on to college, "buying the old lady some nice things for the house," or simply adding to the security represented by a savings account.

A frequent theme of these intensely human communications (ranging from pencil scrawls on a dime store tablet to engraved executive stationery) is also gratitude for having worked "for such a fine outfit," or "having known you and your company." Many were touched by the fact that the bonus they received was in the form of a personal check from Jim Abercrombie himself.

Mr. Jim read each of the letters, some of which were from men who had been with the JSA Company since its beginnings; but there were inevitably a few that troubled him. One former employee, on the payroll a grand total of seven weeks, wrote that he had heard of the bonus. He would be particularly awaiting his, since he was "likely to be crippled for life after being in a bomb explosion," and felt he should be given special consideration. Weeks of research by Jim Short, the Abercrombie personnel manager, revealed that the man had not been any closer to bombs than those he saw in a training film. He had been injured, in an automobile accident while AWOL, but was completely recovered although currently residing in a Navy brig. Then there was the ingrate wife of a roustabout with two years' service who wrote not to thank Mr. Jim for a generous and totally unexpected gift to her husband, but to inquire why his check was smaller than one received by an old-time JSA roughneck next door to them.

Abercrombie did not comment on the few atypical letters, much as they disturbed him. He reacted to the other communications, however, in characteristic manner. When Joe Moore came by with the final draft of some key documents regarding the new JSA Interests corporation, he told him, ''Joe, everything we've been able to do comes down to having good people working for us. You have to find 'em, and you have to keep 'em, if you're going to succeed.'' Joe agreed.

Mr. Jim went on: ''I'm sure these papers are fine; you drew them up, and we've been over them before; but I want you to add something.'' ''Yes, sir; what's that? '' Moore responded. ''The best retirement program of any independent exploration and drilling company in the country.'' Joe Moore worked out the details with Joe Short and Ralph McCullough. They came up with a remarkably sound and generous plan that Abercrombie approved several weeks later, and put into immediate effect.

Mr. Jim went to Calgary in 1947 on a passport renewed for the first time since it was first issued in 1924. Asked for five personal references and the length of time he had known them, he listed some fairly reputable Texans in this order: James A. Elkins, thirty years; Jesse H. Jones, thirty years; Ernest O. Thompson, twenty-five years; J. Sayles Leach, twenty-two years; and Herman Brown, fifteen years. The impact was undoubtedly lost on some clerk in the Passport Office, but that was about as formidable a roll call of references as anyone could provide.

In the Canadian oil center, Jim looked into the vast new strike at Leduc, a little dairying town that would spawn Alberta's boom in petroleum. The more he discovered about Canada's governmental and regulatory climate, however, the less he liked the deal. Perhaps even in 1947, Abercrombie had a foreboding of Pierre Trudeau's punitive policies, high taxes and distasteful episodes such as the takeover of Texasgulf. While in Calgary he learned something of the potential for oil and gas in Alaska from an Edmonton geologist. The geologist tried to get him involved in exploration southwest of Anchorage along the Kenai Peninsula. It was an interesting proposition, but even the preliminary costs seemed far out of line. Alaskan prices, he learned quickly, were far above those in the Lower Forty-Eight; but after you found oil and paid a substantial differential to transport it to market, you received Lower Forty-Eight prices for it.

Back in Houston, Mr. Jim met with a group from Dallas on a drilling proposition in the Persian Gulf. Cameron products were in wide use throughout this region of deep, high-pressure wells and had been rushed to waiting ships before and during World War II (sometimes under escort by highway patrolmen) to make a tight sailing schedule to Ras Tanura, Manama or Bushehr. After studying the proposal for a joint venture, he decided to participate for two reasons: further opportunities to test CIW equipment under severe field conditions, and the potential for bringing in some really prolific wells in a region then noted for thick oil-bearing sands and quick profits. This first (and successful) investment in the Middle East would be the forerunner to a much larger deal for Jim Abercrombie, beginning in mid-1948 in the so-called Neutral Zone between Kuwait and Saudi Arabia.

The changeover at CIW from the weapons of war to pieces of iron was expedited enormously by relaxation of what had been harsh controls over the production of equipment for the petroleum industry, and by the traditionally close cooperation between Mr. Jim, Herb Allen and Ed Lorehn.

Soon after Pearl Harbor, draftees were drilling with wooden guns, or at best 1917 Springfield rifles; our production of the newly-adopted carbines, tanks, airplanes, ships and all types of ammunition was a mere fraction of what was needed to meet the challenge of a worldwide conflict. The War Production Board therefore severely limited, and soon prohibited, the manufacture of virtually the entire non-military product line at CIW by stringent controls on metals and other basic materials.

By early 1943, however, the Petroleum Administration for War (PAW) was demanding a higher and higher level of petroleum products for the Armed Forces while initiating gasoline rationing for civilians. After a brief yet fierce struggle among top bureaucrats, the official word went out: wells are running at capacity, and we cannot have more oil without more drilling; the petroleum industry needs equipment if it is to drill, so divert critical materials to Cameron Iron and similar manufacturers. From a low point where inventories were becoming exhausted, CIW began a sizable increase in output for the oil industry by mid-1943, while simultaneously maintaining a high level of production for the military.

Oil tool and equipment volume passed that of armament in the spring of 1945, as Navy contracts were coming to an end, and CIW went smoothly and strongly into the post-war era under the impetus of wise and farsighted recommendations by Herb Allen, approved by The Boss and then brought to reality by the Abercrombie-Allen-Ed Lorehn team.

Herb wanted a major expansion of manufacturing space; innovative and expensive, yet highly efficient equipment; and heavy emphasis upon product development and improvement. He got all three. A two hundred fifty thousand-square foot addition to the Katy Road plant was launched soon after V-J Day, and on December 1, 1946 this installation officially became the headquarters for Cameron Iron. Old 711 Milby, already decrepit when Jim Abercrombie and Harry Cameron opened up for business there twenty-six years earlier, became a warehouse and repair shop; but Mr. Jim would retain a special affection for the original location, jammed up against the railroad tracks with its rusting tin sides, ugly brick facade and shop floor of dirt and sawdust. Nor could Ed Lorehn ever forget the tiny, crowded office where he sat behind a second-hand desk and stand-up telephone with his hat on, trying to draw up a production schedule while Harry straightened out hot iron with a sledge hammer; or Herb Allen his own even smaller office sitting almost in Milby Street, littered late at night with The Boss' empty Coca-Cola bottles.

Herb had a "crow's nest" office at Katy Road; from this vantage point, he could see what was going on everywhere on the production floor. Mr. Jim was out as usual one evening in 1944; Allen watched him talking with a machinist who was running some twelve-inch casing heads. Soon he came up to Herb and pointed down on the floor, shaking his head. "You'll scrap half of those castings;" Mr. Jim said, "maybe more." "That's right, Boss; they drafted three more really good machinists last month; the quality on some shifts is just pathetic. We no more than get 'em trained, and they're gone."

Jim was silent for a long moment. "What could you do," he asked Herb, "to really stop scrappage?" "Simple," Allen replied, "although it's never been done as far as I know. Just build a huge, plenty heavy forging press and forge everything right here." "Look into it," said The Boss.

Herb Allen did look into it, and he found a possible solution—at a plant in Pennsylvania where he saw wheels for railroad freight cars being forged, and at another factory where intricate parts were being fabricated by a similar process. He had an even more complex problem: the parts he wanted to forge were of unusual sizes and shapes and would have to be made with split dies; side rams would be required to operate the dies. Experimenting with a fifty-ton arbor press back on Katy Road, he made a workable set of split dies and began producing various small forgings.

"I think we know how to build a press that'll make our own forgings," he reported to Abercrombie. "How much?" Jim inquired. Herb wrote the figure $700,000 on a note pad and passed it over without comment. "Lot of money," Abercrombie said. After a moment, he added, "but we're wasting a lot of money; and this press might bring in a lot of new business. Let's build it."

Allen, whose strong suit was brilliant, innovative engineering, and not budgeting, had already run up a pretty good tab for The Boss, counting the forge press and related plant plus tool and die shop. There were also the five Warner & Swasey "4-A" installations, capable of extremely fast and accurate machining operations he had convinced Ed Lorehn and Mr. Jim they should order, "before the post-war rush," along with other new equipment and ongoing product research. The entire bill was reckoned at a little over $3 million, which would place a considerable strain on cash flow.

Herb brought the overall package back to Abercrombie in a week or so, along with a related report on cash requirements for fiscal 1945. Mr. Jim looked at the final estimate for a full minute, and then turned to the attached memorandum on cash flow. He made a little pencil mark on this, and told Allen, "I'll see about it." The next afternoon he came to the rescue with a personal loan of $3 million.

Herb and The Boss had taken the first big step toward fully integrating operations at CIW, from scrap iron to finished product, although the cycle would not be complete for almost another decade, in 1954.

Product research and development began to pay off handsomely between 1945 and 1950, with a new generation of interchangeable wellhead equipment, a lift plug valve combining the separate advantages of gate and plug (ball) valves, the revolutionary new "QRC" (Quick Ram Change) blowout preventer and the first ten thousand-pound pressure per square inch Christmas tree. Herb Allen, named a director of Cameron Iron at the October meeting of the board of directors in 1944, had the leading role in all these developments.

The QRC blowout preventer[2] was to have a dramatic effect upon sales, after it was found that the device reduced "down time" while using the preventer from about a half day to less than five minutes for an experienced crew, and to thirty minutes for even an inexperienced group of workers on a rig.

Cameron Iron Works finally got around to celebrating the company's first quarter-century a year late, in 1946. Sales had reached $10.3 million, and profit was also at a new high of $464,000. There would be a post-war "readjustment dip" in the next two years, but in 1949 sales and profit levels were back almost to 1946, and ready to break into new ground.

Perhaps the most important long-range development as CIW completed its first twenty-five years was evolving and publishing a company philosophy covering vital areas such as research, quality control, standards of service, maintenance and replacement of equipment, employee relations and the principal goals of management. An abstract follows:

To offer the best equipment and latest designs.
To replace promptly all worn or obsolete manufacturing equipment with the best available.
To seek constant improvement of products, aiming always at leadership in a given field of equipment.
To place major emphasis on sound management-employee relations, and to give employee welfare first consideration in company planning and policy-making.
To provide plants of the best construction, properly maintained and equipped to assure employee safety, comfort and well-being.
To maintain a continuing interest in every piece of equipment sold, standing back of it and maintaining it at maximum usefulness.

Four decades ago, Dr. David Greer[3] had what seemed to be an impossible dream. As a gifted and dedicated pediatrician of foresight, he wanted his city to have a children's hospital of the first rank, with a staff capable of diagnosing and treating not only the usual young patient, but the growing volume of unusual and even rare diseases, birth defects and ailments that affect neonates, infants and youngsters. Houston in 1944, however, was still years away from the world leadership in medicine it would fortunately attain, and its age of heroic philanthropy was not quite upon us.

Then, during Christmas week of 1944, Hugh Roy Cullen gave $1 million each to Memorial, Methodist and Hermann Hospitals, adding a like sum for the future St. Luke's Episcopal Hospital after his good friend Bishop Clinton S. (Mike) Quin hurriedly located some preliminary plans for this facility in his files.[4]

Dr. Greer had been named chairman of the Children's Hospital Committee of the Houston Pediatric Society a few months earlier, and he read accounts of the munificent Cullen gifts with growing interest. The pediatrician knew that Dr. Jack Ehlers, through his association with Dr. Judson Taylor, had become Mr. Cullen's physician. He went to see Dr. Ehlers to seek his advice, and thereby took the first step toward forming himself, Jack Ehlers, Leopold Meyer and Jim Abercrombie into a quadrumvirate that would bring his dream of the Texas Children's Hospital to reality.

Jack Ehlers was a skilled physician and general surgeon; popular within and without his profession, he had a fine practice that included both Mr. Cullen and Jim Abercrombie among his many patients. A member of a prominent family in La Grange, Dr. Ehlers' parents had known Hugh Roy Cullen as a young cotton broker who courted Lillie Cranz at the impressive Cranz home down the street from them in the prosperous little county seat of Fayette County.

After a year playing football at the University of Texas, an injury relegated Jack to the tennis court and the chemistry and biology laboratories, where a pre-medical student belonged anyhow. A graduate of the Medical Branch at Galveston, Dr. Ehlers interned at Cleveland General Hospital and followed many of his friends and neighbors from La Grange to Houston. There he married Emerence Truyens, a Rice Institute graduate, and began his association with Dr. Judson Taylor.

David Greer may have been hoping that Jack Ehlers would suggest a direct appeal to Mr. Cullen on behalf of a Texas Children's Hospital. This would not have worked; Mr. Cullen was a man of great heart and generosity, but he had just borrowed $3 million against future income from the prolific Thompson field to pay his pledges to Memorial, Methodist and Hermann Hospitals, and then gone back to arrange for the additional $1 million for Bishop Mike Quin.

Dr. Ehlers suggested instead that Dr. Greer enlarge his committee, adding non-medical members including attorneys, officers of the Junior League and other representatives of leading families. And be certain, he counseled, to get Lep Meyer on the committee.

Meyer had established a firm reputation as a gifted fund-raiser, with quick access to the power structure of the city and state. ''Lep will have some good ideas,'' he predicted.

Jack Ehlers agreed to serve himself, and promised to mention the need for a children's hospital to Jim Abercrombie. He did so, while Mr. Jim was in the midst of complex problems including the new avgas facility at Old Ocean, and the probable need to finance much of the expansion for post-war operations at Cameron Iron out of his own pocket; but he kept two groups waiting a while in order to ask Dr. Ehlers a number of questions. He knew that Houston would have to build more hospitals and was tremendously impressed by the Cullen gifts the past Christmas. ''Jack,'' he finally said, ''nothing upsets me more than a sick child. I can't do anything about it just now, but keep me in mind. It's a compliment to be asked to help with something like a children's hospital.''

One of nine children of a prosperous Galveston merchant, Leopold L. Meyer had graduated from Tulane University, shied away from a career in his father's store, worked briefly at the headquarters for the Santa Fe railroad (then in Galveston) and finally opened a successful bank in Houston. There was a hiatus, he claimed, while he was occupied mainly as a high-class pool shark hanging around the billiard parlors in Galveston's Strand.

Lep was fated, however, to be a merchant, and an extremely able one. Called back home by the illness and subsequent death of his father Achille, young Meyer found himself running the family business before accepting a position with Foley Brothers in Houston. He became executive vice-president and a national authority on retail credit (utilizing his banking experience) at Foley's before it was acquired by the Federated chain. He then opened his own Meyer Brothers stores and became even more active in Houston's community life, heading a number of key campaigns including drives for the Community Chest, Holly Hall and the Child Guidance Center.

By the outbreak of World War II, he was a close friend of many of Houston's leading citizens, and prominent in such well-known organizations as the Fat Stock Show, Civic Music Association and The Hundred Club. With his own apartment in the Lamar Hotel, he was virtually a charter member of the Suite 8-F group, and close to Jim Abercrombie through their many mutual friends including Herman and George Brown, Jesse Jones, Gus Wortham, Bill Smith and others in regular attendance at that unique salon.

Josephine Abercrombie was riding horses by the time she was four, and showed her first horse, the polo pony Lomita, only two years later at six. Her father applauded and encouraged this growing interest, and as it continued, Mr. Jim began looking for acreage reasonably close in as the location for a stable. He found a one hundred-acre tract on Post Oak Road just over the northern boundary of the little city of Bellaire with a "For Sale" sign on it, and asked Ralph McCullough to look into the property. It was relatively isolated in the undeveloped western fringe of the city, and $200 an acre on the depressed 1938 real estate market. The owners, who had probably bought it for $50 or less an acre, agreed to take $18,000 for what became Pin Oak Stables.

Josephine quickly became a skilled equestrienne, winning the title of Champion Child Rider at the All-American Show in Fort Worth on Fairy Boots before she was a teenager. Jim must have been concerned when she began riding, yet he realized what this could mean in the development of self-confidence and self-reliance. "When that gate shuts," he told his daughter, "you're on your own." Miss Lillie, however, said not to look for her in the box during Josephine's events; she'd be in the ladies' room, praying.

By 1945, there were two dozen top-caliber horses wearing the blue and gray of Pin Oak Stables, everywhere from the American Royal in Kansas City to Madison Square Garden. That same year, a group of prominent Houstonians became interested in "Houston Holidays," a benefit to bring wounded veterans from McCloskey General Hospital in Temple to Houston for brief vacations.

They asked Mr. Jim if he would allow them to stage a "Houston Horse Show" at Pin Oak Stables. He not only agreed, but stipulated that he be allowed to pay all expenses, with gross receipts going to Houston Holidays. Thus was launched what would be called the Pin Oak Horse Show beginning in 1946, and much of the impetus toward planning, building and financing operations of the future Texas Children's Hospital.

After the 1945 show, Lep Meyer told Abercrombie up in Suite 8-F that he saw real possibilities of expanding the event. Bill Rhinehart, a professional horse show manager who had helped greatly to make a success of the show, was positive it could be upgraded into "the best in the country." Jim laughed. "Everything has to be the best for you, Lep," he said; but he and Meyer were already thinking alike. A Houston Horse Show Association might well become the fund-raising vehicle for David Greer's dream of a pediatric hospital that Abercrombie had thought of more and more since his original discussion with Jack Ehlers.

"Would you run some sort of a horse show organization if we set it up—be the president?" Jim asked. "Yes," Meyer said, "if you believe in it and what we'd really be aiming for, a children's hospital." Lep had told Abercrombie something about Dr. Greer's committee, without any particular response from Mr. Jim, who had already been briefed on the committee by Dr. Ehlers.

"All right," Jim replied. "Why don't you see Ralph about drawing up some papers. We'll need a state charter, but keep it simple."

The small, original Pin Oak Stables were replaced with a handsome new plant including a ten thousand-seat stadium, fireproof stalls, fine arena and additional barns. When this opened to a capacity crowd on May 23, 1946 (the very day on which Mr. Jim sold Old Ocean), Lep Meyer and Bill Rhinehart, with hundreds of volunteer workers, had the Pin Oak Horse Show rolling. The leaders of the town were in their box seats looking at Morrow Cummings' fat and profitable catalog listing many of America's finest exhibitors and competitors.[6]

Abercrombie went back to Jack Ehlers, after some quiet inquiries that revealed how important the modest Dr. Ehlers could be in the field of establishing hospitals. Jack, it turned out, had been instrumental in getting Hugh Roy Cullen to provide the seed money for moving Baylor Medical School from Dallas to Houston.[5] This helped spark Cullen's interest in the marvelous Christmas gifts of 1944, concerning which Dr. Ehlers had been consulted several times. Robert Jolly, a former evangelist turned superintendent of Memorial Hospital who used to belt out a few revival hymns with Mr. H. R. of a convivial midnight, was responsible for part of this splendid Yuletide philanthropy, but Jack's role was also important.

Dr. Ehlers made some vital recommendations to Abercrombie: plan well and realistically, starting with a sound survey by hospital experts; keep the medical community well informed, and seek the active cooperation of existing medical institutions; finally, meet with the trustees of the M. D. Anderson Foundation early on.

The Anderson trustees, headed by Colonel W. B. Bates (Monroe Anderson's personal attorney) had already taken a central role in the Texas Medical Center (TMC), and several of them were working closely with Dr. E. W. Bertner, the TMC president, and his colleagues on the allocation of hospital sites within the Center.

Jack Ehlers arranged for Mr. Jim and Ralph McCullough to appear with him before the M. D. Anderson trustees in the summer of 1946. The key question came up almost immediately: ''How will the operations of this proposed children's hospital be financed, once it is opened?'' Abercrombie replied, ''I will see that the hospital is adequately supported.'' That was good enough. Jim Abercrombie's word was his bond.

The Junior League assumed sponsorship of the show in 1947 (and later relinquished it, after Gloria Lester (Mrs. George A., III) Hill warned her sisters in the beautiful old John Staub-designed headquarters on Smith that they were ''killing the goose that laid the golden egg,'' and giving up an unparalleled opportunity to move on with a vital community project). The League and its individual members, of course, continued their invaluable contributions to Texas Children's by transferring their Outpatient Department there from Hermann Hospital after TCH opened.

Meanwhile, Dr. Greer's original committee had been expanded and incorporated as the Texas Children's Foundation on August 20, 1947 with these charter members: Drs. A. Lane Mitchell, John K. Glenn, George Salmon, H. J. Ehlers, Raymond Cohen and David Greer; and Miss Nina Cullinan, Mrs. H. Malcolm Lovett, George A. Butler and Leopold Meyer. Dr. Greer was named president; Mr. Butler, secretary; and Mr. Meyer, treasurer.

The proceeds of the Pin Oak Horse Show were now transferred to this foundation, with Jim Abercrombie continuing to pay all costs of the event. After the 1947 show, there were enough funds to move ahead with one of Jack Ehlers' fundamental recommendations: a survey in depth as the basis for designing the best and most modern children's hospital possible. Soon thereafter, M. Foy Martin was retained as architect, and he and Dr. Russell J. Blattner (who was to be chief of staff at TCH) toured the leading pediatric hospitals of America looking for the latest and best concepts in diagnosis, treatment and design.

Meanwhile, the Texas Medical Center had provided a 5.75-acre site for the TCH (Block D of Plot 20-G) on June 3, 1948. Mr. Jim could now make a major move forward. He called on a few of his special friends to join with him in organizing and requesting a charter for the Texas Children's Hospital on March 10, 1950. He recruited Herman Brown, Bill Smith and Lep Meyer right in Suite 8-F; and added Lamar Fleming, Jr., the quiet and distinguished head of Anderson & Clayton; Douglas B. Marshall, Mr. Cullen's new son-in-law; Herman Pressler, a prominent attorney who would serve more than four decades in key posts within the Texas Medical Center; W. J. Goldston and James A. Elkins, Jr. Young Jim Elkins and his recent bride Margaret Wiess had been active in the Pin Oak Horse Show since the "Houston Holidays" beginning.

Now, as Lep Meyer told me at his ninetieth birthday party in 8-F, "it was fish or cut bait." He invited Mr. Jim, Ralph McCullough, Morrow Cummings and their wives to join him at the Biltmore Hotel in Phoenix for a weekend, ostensibly for relaxation, golf, gin rummy, bridge and "big talk." There were furious, almost non-stop, sessions of gin rummy, but Meyer also accomplished his real goal. He got Jim alone for a while in the bar on Saturday afternoon, and told him that Architect Foy Martin had a first but probably accurate estimate of the total cost of the TCH. "$2.5 million," Lep announced, taking a long pull at his bourbon on the rocks while he watched for Abercrombie's reaction.

"Lep," Mr. Jim said, "I want you to do something for me." "What's that?" "Stop drinking that bourbon straight; it'll get you sooner or later; much better, and safer, with branch water." Meyer claimed that it was his last time to have whiskey without a mixer.

Abercrombie did not tell Lep that he and Jack Ehlers and Martin had already been over the details of the design for TCH, and cost estimates, at Jack's home on Brentwood. Instead, he asked a very fundamental question: "This hospital, would it be open to every sick or hurt child? No restrictions on religion, color, whether or not you could pay?" "Absolutely," Meyer answered. "We'll have it written in the bylaws."

Jim stared into his own drink for a minute or two before responding. Then he said, "Well, let's build it. I'll put up one (million dollars) in seed money, and you can go out and rustle up the rest. It's a great cause."

''How do we operate the hospital?'' Lep asked, pressing his luck a little. ''Well, the horse show should continue to help,'' Abercrombie said, ''and I would think that there'll be contributions, once we're actually underway. Other than that, you bring me the amount of the deficit every year-end. I'll handle it for five years, anyhow.'' It was an extraordinary offer, and a tremendously generous one—a costly one as well, as we will see.

Now things began to fall in place, even though Mr. Jim found that bringing a specialized hospital into being was still a long and frustrating experience. A unique joint operating agreement with St. Luke's Episcopal Hospital was signed October 18, 1950; ground was broken on Texas Children's May 21, 1951; and the new facility, a landmark in pediatric care, was dedicated May 15, 1953. Lep Meyer, his appeals for funds strengthened mightily by Jim's $1 million in seed money, raised the additional $1.5 million required in a little more than a year. Abercrombie had reports that his friend's fund-raising adrenalin was pumping a little high. ''I admire your determination and persistence,'' he told Meyer, ''but some people just have other interests, Lep. They can't, or won't, give you what you think they should. Take what you can get, thank 'em and move on to the next stop.'' The friendly advice probably came after Meyer tried to get $1 million of his $1.5 million goal out of George Brown, who told him it was a good proposition but that was sure a lot of money.

Jim Abercrombie knew that the TCH would never be self-supporting; this was particularly true since he had insisted that no child be denied admittance because of ''race, creed, color or ability to pay.'' The Pin Oak Horse Show, reinforced by the good and powerful friends he and Lep and others had recruited to support it, would bring in substantial sums. There was magic in the sheer quality of the show, with its trophies of sterling silver, marvelous horses and riders and the debonair ringmaster C. L. (Honey) Craven, performing with the same elegance as Jan Garber's society orchestra seated in white tie and tails on a dais decorated with a thousand red roses. Some prominent Houstonians became sponsors, bought box seats or answered Morrow Cummings' annual plea for program advertising just to attend the fabulous Horse Show parties at the Bayou Club or Sponsors' Club, including the traditional midnight breakfasts.

Yet Jim Abercrombie, realist that he was, saw growing rather than diminishing gaps between income and outgo at Texas Children's. The immediate solution was the current arrangement under which he simply wrote out a check for the deficit at year-end, but Mr. Jim was already seeking a long-range answer to the escalating needs of the TCH and its young patients. In the meantime, he and Miss Lillie and everyone connected with the hospital found fresh satisfaction in the institution's growing accomplishments.

Jim had been studying how best to organize for the future from the moment the sale of the JSA Company was completed. Early in 1947, after many sessions with (and even more questioning of) Bob and his other brothers; Ralph McCullough; the old-timers at Cameron Iron, Ed Lorehn, Herb Allen and Red Teague[7]; and some of his 8-F colleagues; he saw the advantages of some structural changes.

The new offices of the Abercrombie Interests in the Gulf Building, on the twentieth floor since the departure of Harrison Oil, would become more of a command post, without affecting the considerable autonomy Mr. Jim had always allowed his executives and staff. This would permit the centralization of accounting and fiscal control and shift the emphasis in future exploration and production to searching out major deals. Jim also wanted some flexibility to reorganize, and possibly to expand considerably, his ranching interests.

There would be a relatively small staff: accounting, under Ralph McCullough of course; Gene Chambers, in-house attorney; Joe T. Short, as personnel manager; Randolph Wheless,[8] a talented landman and geologist to head up a new land department; Claude Harris, chief accountant; and a few assistants and secretaries. One thing lacking was a bright, likeable and pretty young woman to serve as a receptionist and operate the small PBX; someone absolutely loyal and dependable who could quickly learn the roles and interrelationships of those in the Gulf Building, at CIW, the ranches and in the field; where to find Mr. Jim himself, locate anyone for him from Jesse Jones to a driller on an offshore rig in Louisiana, or track down Lep Meyer through the formidable and efficient Alice Hatcher, Lep's executive assistant.

Luckily, an attractive, highly intelligent young woman, just 24, was looking for a job at just this time. A friend told her of the opening at the Gulf Building. "Fine people, good pay," she said. "You'll like it there." Thus Freda Bowen, whose husband Harley was with Republic Supply, began a career now in its thirty-seventh year with the Abercrombie organization.

Freda still remembers every detail of meeting Mr. Jim, some days after being interviewed and hired by Joe Short and Ralph. To her, he was six feet tall, but seemingly taller, with piercing blue eyes and an "outdoorsy" complexion. The hair was well-cut, and he was impeccably dressed—"always with a cigar." Abercrombie liked Freda, as did everyone in the organization, for her hard work, brightness and unfailing good humor. They learned too of her honesty and dependability—of her naturalness. Jim noticed one day, when he was firing up a cigar standing near her at the switchboard, that Freda was unconsciously frowning. They were alone; she hesitated for a moment and then looked straight at him. "You know, Mr. Jim," she said, "for someone as well off as you are, you must smoke the cheapest, worst-smelling cigars in the world."

Abercrombie was speechless for a minute; then he burst into laughter, told Freda that his imported Coronas cost $20 a box, and began to appreciate her all the more. Freda, detecting much of her own father in The Boss, came to know also the innate kindness of the man in many ways as the months and years added up. She remembers still a bitter cold day, with the rare threat of sleet in a January noon. Abercrombie came out of the elevator, obviously very angry and muttering to himself. "They ran him out of the lobby," he said cryptically. "Who, Mr. Jim?" "Joe, the *Chronicle* newsboy; the skinny one you can hear a block away; he's about to freeze to death out there."

Jim thought a moment. "Get me Mr. Jones," he said. Jesse Jones was in his office at the Bankers' Mortgage Building. Abercrombie explained the situation: the newsboy had to sell his papers, but this was pneumonia weather and he belonged inside, for once. Five minutes later, the leather-lunged Joe was peddling his *Chronicles* in the overheated lobby of the Gulf Building, in direct competition with one of Ben Taub's newsstands.

Freda Bowen became a friend of all the staff, and of the Abercrombie family. She commiserated with Randy Wheless when

The Boss turned down (out of his long experience) a deal with Gulf Oil in Louisiana that looked ideal on the surface; heard Ralph and Joe Short's hopes and problems and latest jokes; was close to Miss Vinnie (who now worked for the Abercrombie Interests) and Miss Annie; and was a friend of Josephine and Miss Lillie as well.

The legendary quail hunts at Mustang Motte, on the Blackwell Ranch near Cuero, were at their height in the late 1940s and early 1950s, with a guest list straight out of *Who's Who*, *Fortune's 500* and the *Congressional Directory*. Mr. Jim and Bill Blackwell even had a school for pointers and setters that was the talk of Cuero in those days, although Naurice Cummings tried to upstage its graduates with an expensive import from Evansville, Indiana.[9] Jim Abercrombie was seldom happier than on these traditional three-day hunts in January, which are better described by several pages of pictures in the photographic section of this book introduced by Ed Cumming's saga of Mustang Motte.

From the moment of arrival at the comfortable, inelegant old Muti Hotel and the opening "bull session" of camaraderie recounting past hunts over toasts of premium whiskey sipped from Lone Star beer cups, through the late poker games and the exhilarating new hunts for fat quail, to breaking camp amid fresh claims of super marksmanship and filling inside straights—Jim loved it all. But when he went to Cuero that September day in 1946, it was not just to plan the upcoming 1947 weekend on Mustang Motte. He wanted primarily to discuss with Bill Blackwell a ranch the older man had shown him earlier.

This was a big cotton plantation of an earlier era, expanded into a ranch by combining "the old Rather place" with adjoining properties; it was six miles east of Gonzales on Highway 90-A, on a farm road two miles south of 90-A. Bordered by the Guadalupe River, the 4650-acre ranch was among the small rolling hills of south central Texas. Most of the land was cleared and improved, but there were many remaining stands of post oak, with tough mesquite trees on the sandier soil. Rich bottom land was found along the Guadalupe and its tributary creeks; thick clumps of beautiful old pecan trees grew in some of these areas.

Jim liked everything about the property, including the neighboring Czech and German farmers and the nearby county seat of Gonzales, Texas, the "Lexington of Texas." In a tiny museum there he saw the famed "Come and Take It" flag.

The flag had been flown in the first battle of the war for independence from Mexico. Texian volunteers defeated the Mexican commander, Colonel Domingo de Ugartechea, who had been sent to Gonzales to demand surrender of a Texian cannon, on October 2, 1835.

What was emerging was a plan, possibly dormant for many years in Jim Abercrombie's subconscious, to invest both time and hard cash in agriculture and animal husbandry. After all, his distant Scots progenitors were growing oats and raising sheep in Fifeshire as early as the fourteenth century; Robert Abercromby, Sr. founded the American branch in the Piedmont on corn and "hoggs"; and succeeding generations owned some of the largest cotton plantations in ante-bellum Georgia, Alabama and Texas. Mr. Jim's own father managed what would become the biggest prison farm system ever organized.

Abercrombie's original idea was to purchase the rundown Gonzales ranch, stock it with Herefords feeding on rotated pastures, and gradually improve the property from earnings. Soon after the ranch was stocked, Jim's Herefords contracted the highly contagious "pinkeye" (conjunctivitis); now he had a real challenge. He brought in experts from Texas A&M's famed school of veterinary medicine, who set up detailed field experiments and in time developed a successful vaccine against pinkeye.

Soon, Mr. Jim was tremendously interested in the new project at Gonzales. He appointed Dr. Francis C. Jackson of Texas A&M ranch veterinarian and nutritionist, and launched a complex program in controlled feeding. Jackson was both a skilled scientist and a highly practical man. He caught Jim's attention by recommending another approach to the pinkeye problem: cross the Herefords with Brahmas, which were immune to the ailment. To the amazement of most of Gonzales County, the new branch of Abercrombie Ranches, Inc. was to include a pellet factory processing homegrown alfalfa and other highly nutritious forage crops, a vast irrigation system pumping five thousand gallons a minute from the Guadalupe, once over-grazed pastures sown with expensive grasses (fertilized with exotic mixtures from both feed lot and factory) and what the German neighbors called "some Rube Goldberg machines that nice Mr. Abercrombie he done invented."

Detailed records were kept on every animal, as the herd increased from twelve hundred to almost two thousand Herefords, Angus, Brahmas and mixtures of these breeds, tended by twenty or thirty cowboys. As the project grew, Mr. Jim and George Sterns spent more time at the ranch, where Abercrombie's normal working day was from six in the morning to nine at night, followed by watching a good prize fight or old movie on that new phenomenon, television. A special antenna brought in programs from San Antonio, only sixty miles away, or from Austin, even closer.

George often drove The Boss directly from the Gulf Building to Gonzales, while Jim thought or read brief reports from his chief lieutenants. He sometimes brought along "Nuisance," an affectionate cat of indeterminate breed who dozed on his lap; after they stopped for the traffic light in Schulenburg, he often had George drive across the railroad tracks to the ancient Von Minden Hotel; there they bought crisp little German cookies that the children of the ranch foreman prized. The cookies looked exactly like those in Herman Stude's coffee bar so long ago; he remembered that his pal Doc Neuhaus had been a child in Schulenburg before moving to Houston, and wondered if Doc had spent his pennies on Von Minden cookies.

Jim Abercrombie arrived just thirty minutes before the small reception in 8-F honoring Beauford Jester, who had just won the Democratic nomination for governor, then tantamount to election, 701,018 to 355,654, in an overwhelming victory over Homer P. Rainey, former president of the University of Texas, on August 26, 1946. Herman and George Brown had asked him to be there "a half hour early, to get your advice on something."

Mr. Jim had quietly made political contributions for many years, leaning heavily toward conservative Democrats. Sam Rayburn and John Garner on the national scene; Ernest O. Thompson, Beauford Jester and Allan Shivers in key state posts—these were the candidates whose policies he endorsed and supported.

One of his keenest disappointments had been the disastrous campaign for the governorship of his close friend Ernest O. Thompson. The youngest full colonel in the U.S. Army during World War I and an outstanding citizen known statewide as an efficient public official of impeccable character, Railroad Commissioner Thompson and two other well-qualified candidates could not even force Wilbert Lee (Pappy) O'Daniel into a runoff in 1938. Unbelievably, Pappy and his Light Crust Doughboys won in the primary. As a losing and ungracious minor candidate put it, "The king of the demagogues is on the loose, selling biscuits and promises."

Now it was eight years and a world war later. As he was shown into one of the bedrooms at 8-F, Jim saw that the Browns had LBJ with them. The congressman and Abercrombie were friends, of course; Mr. Jim had given generously to Johnson's incredible campaign for the U.S. Senate in 1941.[10] They shook hands, and while pounding him on the shoulder until Jim winced a bit, Lyndon said, "I can hear ole Efram singing out that 'Rock of Ages,' still." This was both a demonstration of LBJ's uncanny ability to store pleasant and colorful details for future use and a diplomatic reminder that he could certainly use another invitation to Mustang Motte. (Efram Bolton was a black with a beautiful, haunting voice; one of the fifteen-man crew imported to take care of things on the annual quail hunt at Cuero, he often sang hymns and spirituals of long ago after dinner.)

Herman Brown came right to the point: there was reliable information that W. Lee O'Daniel would not run for reelection as U.S. senator; although it was still almost two years before the Democratic Party primary of 1948, a man aiming at a winning race had better start getting his ducks in a row. What did Abercrombie think about Johnson making another run for the Senate?

The Browns knew that Jim Abercrombie's views could be crucial, from 8-F and outward through the political and fund-raising galaxy. LBJ had his problems in the Oil Patch on occasion, and would be the first to admit this; he had told colleagues in the Congress that he was identified as a "tool of the oil industry" away from home, and as a "wild-eyed liberal" when he sought campaign funds in some quarters in Texas. Mr. Jim could help convert a few possible dissidents in the 8-F crowd, and with the 8-F brand clearly on him, LBJ was a far likelier critter—vote-wise and fund-raising-wise.

As was his wont, Abercrombie sat quietly for a time, saying nothing as he sipped at his drink and steadily demolished a cut-glass dish of peanuts by his chair. Then he asked two pertinent questions: "Where does Mr. Sam stand?" He knew that Johnson had sided with FDR in a furious row involving the president, Rayburn and Mr. Sam's great friend Cactus Jack Garner. "I think I've patched that up," LBJ answered. "Better had." Jim continued: "How about (retiring Governor) Coke (Stevenson)? Mighty popular man; I hear he's already drinking coffee all over West Texas; made a little sashay through here last month." Stevenson, a prime reason Johnson was not already a U.S. senator,[10] was a low-profile yet persistent and formidable campaigner. "Well," LBJ replied, "Coke's probably gearin' up, all right; but he'll have been out of the governor's chair and the newspapers a year and a half come primary time."

Abercrombie was silent again, while the peanut dish was quietly replenished by a barman. "Lyndon," he said, "You know I'll back you if you run; that was a bad deal they pulled on you back there in '41; you should already have five years' seniority in the Senate as it is." LBJ nodded, and grimaced; the memory of the 1941 election was still bitter within him. "Let me think about the race, make a few calls; I'll stay in touch with Herman and George here." The meeting was over; the majordomo of the 8-F staff was whispering to Herman Brown that Governor-to-be Jester had arrived.

Johnson ran and won, of course, with staunch backing from 8-F. One of his best fund-raising sessions was held on the top floor of the Kentucky Hotel in Louisville, as the group gathered for their traditional weekend at the Kentucky Derby,[11] on the first Saturday in May, 1947. They almost saw history made when Jet Pilot won; sandwiched in-between the King Ranch's little Assault (1946) and Citation (1948), the 1947 victor could have been one of three consecutive Triple Crown winners. Judge Elkins (who often had something on every starter) was so pleased to get even in a friendly but serious game of craps after losing most of the night that he gave his winnings on Jet Pilot to Herman Brown for the LBJ war chest, and made a handsome pledge as well. Everyone followed suit.

The story of Box 13 and "Landslide Lyndon's" 87-vote margin over Coke Stevenson has been told so often that it does not need repeating here. The best versions are in Jimmy Banks' *Money,*

Marbles and Chalk (1977), and in Robert A. Caro's monumental *Lyndon Johnson: The Path to Power* (1982).

Out of the penultimate victory[12] in the 1948 Democratic Party runoff, and its aftermath of hearings, investigations, injunctions and decisions all the way to the U.S. Supreme Court, came a lasting friendship between Johnson and Jim Abercrombie. The new senator saw in Mr. Jim qualities that he prized highly, many of them almost totally absent in his own make-up. Among these were true, selfless giving and Abercrombie's extraordinary ability to value correctly the really important things in life.

I observed this at first hand one Saturday in May of 1958. LBJ, by now the powerful majority leader of the Senate and an emerging candidate for the presidency, had agreed to deliver the Commencement address at the University of Houston. In the morning, I went by to check details of the graduation ceremony, to be televised live by KUHT-TV, with Senator Johnson; upon leaving his suite at the Shamrock, I asked if I could do anything for him. "Yes," he said, "drop me by the Texas Children's Hospital." He and Mr. Jim were to visit a black youngster less than six months old who was recovering from what was then a somewhat unusual operation—a "blue baby" procedure by Denton Cooley of world fame-to-be who had learned the technique from the fountainhead, Dr. Helen Taussig of Johns Hopkins.

Shortly before six that evening, I was back at the Shamrock to take LBJ to the Commencement exercise. His secretary, the gorgeous Mary Margaret Valenti in years to come, greeted me at the door. "He's reading the text to his mother, at Johnson City," she said. "Go in and point to your watch," she added. I did, and in a few minutes, we set off for the University.

As we drove along Holcombe Boulevard and then North MacGregor Drive, LBJ told me about the little heart patient at TCH. He had details of the morning visit in a handsome, leather-bound memo case with his signature in gold on the cover, and saw me glancing at it. "FDR gave me that," he said, as he began to read. The patient's name was Oscar Dove, Jr. of Bryan; operation performed six weeks earlier by Dr. Denton Cooley; the special nurse, Mrs. Bernice Holcomb; but what he really wanted to talk about was Jim Abercrombie. "They could hardly get him to go up to see the little fellow; says he can't stand to see youngsters suffering; but Lep Meyer convinced him that little Oscar was almost completely recovered, and it would do the boy good. Then I found out from

Lep that Mr. Jim pays the entire deficit over there, and doesn't want it known. The man's a saint.''

The admiration was mutual. Abercrombie wrote President Johnson on December 5, 1963:

> ''. . .This dastardly crime has thrust an awesome burden of responsibility on you, but I feel our country is fortunate indeed to have a man of your great knowledge and skill in matters of government to take over as our commander-in-chief. Thirty-two years of outstanding service to our nation have proven by every standard of measurement that you are eminently qualified for the presidency. I want you to know that I have the utmost confidence in your ability. . .''

As the 1950s began, Herb Allen noticed that he saw The Boss much less frequently. Mr. Jim was always available on request[13] and continued as he would to make all major policy decisions; but the sessions before and after midnight were no more, and there were weeks when The Boss was not seen at the new Katy Road headquarters; he maintained contact by telephone and memo.

Cameron Iron was soon a far larger and more complex operation; Allen was increasingly responsible for it after Ed Lorehn suffered a heart attack late in 1950 from which he was never to recover fully. Lorehn was made executive vice-president in order to isolate him from details, but died on July 13, 1954 after a second heart attack. It had been almost thirty-five years since Mr. Jim tracked him down on a dirt road to offer him a job helping to run a tiny machine shop. Abercrombie was deeply grieved; he prized loyalty, long tenure and accomplishment, and Ed Lorehn exemplified them all. Herb Allen, already operating head as vice-president and general manager, would become president and chief executive officer as a new era opened.

In the crucial decade from 1950 to 1960, CIW saw annual sales climb from $10 million to $40 million, with a tripling of the work force from less than seven hundred to almost two thousand. Other developments were of even more consequence: Cameron became an international company, with plants first in England and Canada, and next in Mexico; licensing agreements in France then allowed entry into North Africa, the Middle East and far-flung areas of the world under French control or protection.

Herb Allen's concept of split-die forging, which The Boss had predicted would bring in new business, was providing almost fifty percent of all sales by 1960. The addition of internal steel-making capacity and much larger, more intricate equipment (including a phenomenal twenty-thousand-ton press that Herb designed and Jim had to finance by selling down inventory) gave the company a significant foothold in Korean War armament, power generation (including equipment for the nascent nuclear industry) and the manufacture of jet engines and parts for the aircraft industry. Cameron engineers and field service experts, with innovative developments from Herb himself, maintained company leadership in both new and established "pieces of iron."

From 1951 through 1960, cumulative sales for the decade zoomed to $263,064,000 and profits to $16,897,000; the comparable figures for 1961 through 1970 were $832,975,000 and $46,235,000. At these levels, with seldom-interrupted expansion of work force, plant and equipment both in the Houston area and abroad, the corporate structure of Cameron Iron Works was changed substantially, the company "went public" with eventual listing on the New York Stock Exchange, and a series of reorganizations evolved into what is essentially today's operating divisions.

Herb Allen was correct about Mr. Jim not spending nearly so much time at CIW after 1950, although The Boss was still there for key decisions, and for understanding and support that Allen always said he could have found nowhere else. There were reasons for Jim's lessened appearances, however.

First of all, although he would never admit it, Abercrombie was in almost constant pain for months in late 1950 and 1951 after suffering a slipped disc in his back. George Sterns remembered just when it happened: Mr. Jim and Miss Lillie had been in Phoenix with Lep Meyer, and as soon as possible after their return, he and The Boss went to Gonzales to check on some new Angus-Brahma calves. As Jim bent over to pull on his boots, there was an audible "pop" in his back and immediate, recurring pain. Weeks later, there had to be a spinal fusion. Abercrombie regained much of his energy and drive, but was never the same again physically.

After the opening of Texas Children's Hospital, there was another claim on his time, as chairman of the board of the institution; plus constant interaction with the peripatetic Randy Wheless and his land department; a major drilling venture in the Middle East; and new political projects at 8-F. To complicate things further, an old injury to Mr. Jim's leg dating back to the early days on the rigs became aggravated; he had to undergo another operation that was only partly successful. The old fire returned in time, but he walked often with a sturdy blackthorn cane and hunted quail from a jeep, instead of tramping the fields for hours at a pace that left companions struggling to keep up.

Jim took great satisfaction from Texas Children's, and the close interaction and ever-deepening friendship with Lep Meyer that it involved; yet he saw that there must be some answer to growing deficits at the hospital, and began to study a long-range solution. Meanwhile, Abercrombie Interests, Inc. was reorganized in 1959 as the J. S. Abercrombie Mineral Company, Inc. while production from wells in Texas and Louisiana increased steadily and the Middle East project grew in scope. Mr. Jim's original interest in the Arabian "Neutral Zone" was expanded substantially in 1953 after he and nine partners including Phillips Petroleum and Signal Oil hit a big strike (the Wafra #4) on a concession obtained from Sheikh Ahmad ibn Jabir as-Subah, ruler of Kuwait; and King Ibn Saud of Saudia Arabia. Discovery wells drilled by their American Independent Oil Company (Aminoil) were flowing more than five thousand barrels a day.

The 1950s and 1960s were stirring days in politics, with Mr. Jim often involved in marathon sessions at Suite 8-F. He had always liked John B. Connally (JBC), from first meeting him in 1938. Connally was an assistant in Ernest Thompson's ill-fated campaign for governor while student body president at the University of Texas; he noticed immediately how well Abercrombie treated everyone and the great respect in which his opinions were held. Years later, JBC would be invited to have dinner with Mr. Jim, LBJ and Sam Rayburn when the oilman was in Washington. JBC told Mr. Sam that Abercrombie reminded him of something Sid Richardson had told him: "You ain't learning nothing when you're talking." Jim was a good listener, and when he did say something, people listened, especially in 8-F.

In 1962, Connally returned from service as JFK's secretary of the navy to run a surprisingly strong race for governor; now he was in the runoff for the Democratic nomination with Don Yarborough, and the entire campaign might well hinge on the ability to raise $50,000 to reserve time for statewide radio broadcasts. Reluctantly, he called Mr. Jim, who had already made generous contributions. He was not in the office, but Ralph McCullough said he would ask the Captain (a term he often used when speaking of Mr. Jim to long-term friends) as soon as he could locate him. The strategy meeting at the Driskill Hotel in Austin was about to break up without a solution when McCullough called back. He was in his car on the way to the airport; the Captain said he would guarantee up to $75,000 and asked Ralph to go to Austin immediately to announce the good news to Connally's principal backers in person.

JBC was of course delighted over the $75,000 but explained that he could not hold the meeting long enough for McCullough to get to Austin. "Be there in twenty minutes," Ralph said. "I'm already pulling into the airport and we have a new jet." Connally won the election, became perhaps the most able governor Texas has ever had, for three terms, and never forgot what Jim Abercrombie and Ralph McCullough did for him.

It was also in the 1950s and 1960s that Mr. Jim, with the reluctance born of his innate modesty, began to receive recognition and honors, as from the Houston Pediatric Society (for both him and Miss Lillie), Texas Children's Hospital, Baylor College of Medicine, the Texas Mid-Continent Oil & Gas Association, the Sons of the American Revolution, the National Conference of Christians and Jews and the Houston Fat Stock Show. He was named Houston's Man of the Year, and accorded wide editorial acclaim.

What Jim and Lillie Abercrombie would never forget about the 1950s and 1960s, however, was the joy of having Josephine's two sons, Jamie and George, born in 1957 and 1959 respectively, and of becoming accustomed to the role of doting grandparents as the two healthy, handsome boys began to grow up between frequent visits to 2221 River Oaks Boulevard.

In late 1967, Mr. Jim and Miss Lillie made their greatest contribution, again as quietly as possible. Jim had wanted to celebrate his seventy-fifth birthday, on July 7, 1966, with this splendid philanthropy, but it was almost 1968 before all the arrangements could be completed. The financial plight of TCH had been of growing concern to the Abercrombies for many years; the situation had become more acute since a decision to undertake the necessary expansion of the combined capacity of the interlocked Texas Children's Hospital and Texas Heart Institute of St. Luke's Episcopal Hospital from four hundred to one thousand sixty-three beds, at a cost overall of $33.5 million. The first phase was budgeted at $15 million.

Mr. Jim and Miss Lillie had announced:

> "In furtherance of our desire to ensure the success of the current fund drive and to provide support over a number of years to the Texas Children's

Hospital, we have given to a trust all of the stock in the J. S. Abercrombie Securities Corporation, which company is the owner of a substantial block of the stock of the Cameron Iron Works. Substantially all of the income from this trust is to be paid to the hospital for a period of forty years.''

''The trust'' was the J. S. Abercrombie Foundation, which has since expanded its scope to include special grants and annual gifts to educational, artistic, scientific and other medical institutions in Houston and over the state.

As the 1970s began, Mr. Jim was nearing his eightieth birthday. There were good days and bad days for him physically, but never a complaint. Lillie and Josephine were closer than ever, within the inner family. George Sterns, loyal and helpful George, was always with him, although they could go only infrequently now to Gonzales, and the great hunts at Cuero were over. (He had a favorite new bird dog, given him at an office party on his seventy-fifth birthday, with him often, the two of them looking up instinctively from the garden when migrating flocks flew over against the cloudless sky of a cool perfect day in November.)

He saw Herb and Ralph and Freda, who would soon celebrate her twenty-fifth year with the Abercrombie organization; she could get him to take the bitter medicine that he hated, ''opening my beak like a bird,'' and raise his spirits by coming by in a pretty new frock to have lunch with him and Josephine and Miss Lillie. Naurice was by often to talk of bygone hunts, and the old days at Goose Creek and Lake Charles; Lep kept him up on everything at TCH, and his neighbor Bill Smith talked of new Derby favorites, as well as of Roman Patrol.[11] He went occasionally still to 8-F, to talk politics with Herman and George, until Herman died suddenly in 1972, the same year that he lost Miss Annie and Miss Vinnie within months of one another. Now he had only Bob and John and Joe Rice of his many siblings.

The end came for James Smither Abercrombie on January 7, 1975; he died at home, exactly half-way through his eighty-fourth year. Another of Houston's giants, the like of which we have not yet seen in the new generation of leadership, was gone.

George Sterns drove Miss Lillie often to Glenwood Cemetery, to tend Mr. Jim's grave and to remember his bountiful life, so rich in the love between them, the giving, the high accomplishment. They left old Glenwood near the end of a dark and dismal day, with long-threatening rain just beginning to fall like a filmy curtain obscuring the gravestones.

Miss Lillie said, "It's so lonely; I need to be with him."

Six months after Mr. Jim's funeral, almost to the day, Lillie Frank Abercrombie died and was buried next to her beloved husband.

Notes

[1] Some brief excerpts: "Words cannot express my sincere thanks for the personnell check I received as a present . . . It has been a pleasure to have been employed by a company so generous and thoughtful . . . May I also thank you for the three months' salary I received when I enlisted in the Navy . . . I have never worked for a company that treated its people so well . . . Mr. Jim, your gift was a godsend . . . It makes us proud we fought for a country where we have men like Jim Abercrombie in it."

[2] Ed Lorehn began wondering, as the QRC quickly dominated the field of blowout preventers, whatever happened to the original "Type MO," the prototype for Patent #1,569,247. He asked Bill Upchurch to keep his eye open, especially in long-established fields such as Hull. Upchurch soon noticed a rotting old warehouse near Hull-Daisetta on a tiny pumping lease. Peering inside, he saw a collection of rusting equipment that seemed to go back to Spindletop. The owner was soon located. "Nope, didn't sell nothing out of there." "Them's my keepsakes," he explained. Upchurch told him what he was looking for, and the owner took him inside the warehouse and started poking around. He soon found three or four ancient blowout preventers, and reached over and patted one. "That's Jim Abercrombie's first 'un; my boy and I taken it off an old rig over at Hull." "What'll you take for it?," Upchurch asked. "Oh, you can have it; I knowed Jim before he made it big over there in Houston." When Upchurch persisted, the oldtimer said, "Well, a quart of whiskey 'ud come in handy." Upchurch hauled the MO off in his pickup, and it was soon sent on to the Smithsonian Institution in Washington, D.C. He came back the next day with a quart of Jack Daniels black label and a check for $100.

[3] Dr. David Greer, then the guru of Houston pediatricians, had written a lucid article for one of the medical journals, tracing the history of his specialty back to the fifth century BC but emphasizing that the first children's hospital (L'Hospital des Enfants Malades) was not established until 1802, in Paris. Philadelphia had the first such institution in the United States, beginning in 1855.

[4] The author has vivid memories of the dedication of St. Luke's Episcopal Hospital, after Hugh Roy Cullen asked me to "go out there and help Ike Arnold get that thing open." Arnold, his son-in-law, had a key role in raising the additional funds required for the hospital. Two days before the dedication, the cornerstone had not arrived from the stonecutter, who was encising a most appropriate quotation from St. Luke, the apostle-physician, selected by an august committee of bishops headed by Clinton S. Quin. I was present when the cornerstone was finally delivered; Bishop Quin took a close look at it the moment it was off the truck, and then looked quite disturbed. The stonecutter had studied the text, and decided to edit Scripture: "I am come SO that they might have life." We somehow managed to have the stone recut in an all-night session.

Hugh Roy Cullen also enlivened the proceedings of the dedicatory ceremony for St. Luke's Episcopal Hospital, held on an unbearably hot and humid afternoon late in May under a big tent, with monster thunderstorms brewing to the north and west. After an interminable wait having to do with the procession of bishops and several retakes of a film for the St. Luke's archives under torrid Kleig-type lights, Mr. Hugh Roy was finally introduced for his speech in handsome white suit and heavy beads of perspiration. "Reverend gentlemen," he began, looking straight at the imposing array of bishops, "you don't have to preach that hellfire and brimstone at me anymore. I've been there."

[5] Mr. Cullen also provided, as did Earl Hankamer, a substantial part of the funds to keep Baylor Medical School operating in temporary quarters in the old Sears & Roebuck warehouse on Buffalo Drive (Allen Parkway) until it could be moved to the Texas Medical Center, again with major gifts from Mr. and Mrs. Cullen and the Cullen Foundation.

[6] Morrow Cummings, Naurice's younger brother, is a remarkable man who had attended Rice Institute and Sewanee before taking a job in Houston that paid him less than two hundred dollars a month. After saving five hundred dollars, he invested it on margin in the pyrotechnic stock market of 1928 and 1929. When Black Monday (October 24, 1929) was over, Morrow was not only wiped out but owed seven thousand dollars. A few years later, he was working his way to the top of Houston's strongest insurance agency, and paying back every dime of Black Monday's reverses. Jim Abercrombie, a good friend and bridge partner of the nattily-dressed "Knobby," asked him to become chairman of first the Program Committee, then the overall Advertising Committee for the Pin Oak Horse Show. He filled the post with distinction for more than twenty-five years.

[7] J. M. (Red) Teague, surely one of the most colorful men ever to enter the Oil Patch, joined the CIW sales staff in 1937 after many years on the rigs, and became a phenomenally successful salesman. Some said that Red made the change after he tangled with a giant roughneck while enforcing rig discipline the only way he knew how—with his fists. The roughneck finally got an unbreakable hold on Red and kept excitedly yelling, "I'm gonna kill you; I'm gonna kill you, for sure." "Just lemme loose," Teague finally blurted out, "and I'll drop dead right here."

Jim Abercrombie told Ed Lorehn once, "If we get a contract to drill in Hell, Red'll be two hundred feet into brimstone before Satan knows he's spudded in." They both welcomed him on the Cameron sales force because he had so many friends everywhere. Teague was even expert at fire-fighting and had been called in on the infamous Vermilion Bay blowout where H. L. Patton lost his right arm and two best men. Myron Kinley, as skilled as Patton in taming wild wells, also valued Red's opinion. He had saved Kinley and his crew once by pointing out an unseen hazard in another Louisiana blowout. "That well," he pronounced, "will eat your lunch if you try to cap it that way."

Teague would bring in one of the largest orders ever received by Cameron up to that time, within a year after becoming a CIW salesman. He worked for weeks on a Texaco problem well at Avery Island, helping to design special equipment before the dangerous blowout was finally sealed off. Texas Company officials gave him a purchase order that included fifty-two blowout preventers and came to more than $200,000. He then had a pint of Crab Orchard with Coke and collapsed in total exhaustion to sleep twenty-four hours in a New Iberia hotel.

[8] Randolph Wheless, Fishback's younger brother, was once described by Mr. Jim as a "feisty little runt, good friend and damn good geologist and land man." Trained at the University of Texas, he had impressed Abercrombie while working for Sun Oil out of Kerrville and living there with his parents to help look out for his father, convalescing from tuberculosis in the Hill Country. Randy was quite helpful in an unusual crisis involving Josephine, and the family never forgot it. Josephine had become quite ill while at the Pot Luck Ranch near Kerrville with her mother, just as the Guadalupe River went into one of its unexpected and highly dangerous floods. Randy helped get her safely to his parents' home, and she and Miss Lillie stayed there until young Jo recovered. Randy joined the JSA Company in 1941, and headed up the land department for the new J. S. Abercrombie Interests, Inc. for the dozen years this corporation was in existence. He then continued with J. S. Abercrombie Mineral Company, and is still a consultant for the latter firm.

Fishback Wheless once asked his little brother what he thought about his new boss soon after Randy had joined the JSA Company. "I'd fight a buzz saw for him," the younger Wheless replied. And he would have.

[9] Characteristically, Jim Abercrombie arranged for Naurice Cummings to have a handsome bonus after the $54 million sale of the JSA Company in 1946. Naurice claimed that he had nothing to do with the final negotiations, but this did not deter the generous Mr. Jim. A few weeks later, Cummings heard of a fabulous bird dog in a kennel in Evansville, Indiana. "This dog had a nose like a vacuum cleaner, huge feet, great point," he still recalls, "—best-looking thing you'd ever want to see."

Naurice paid a large sum for this apparently prodigious animal, had it flown to Houston and presented it to Jim. Abercrombie, most appreciative, was very touched; and like Cummings, he could not wait to try the new phenomenon in the field. Cuero was a hundred miles away, but there were still a few late coveys around nearby Cinco Ranch, feeding off the remnants of the rice harvest; the next day, he and his long-time hunting buddy headed out with the new dog for Cinco, looking for quail. They found them, and the huge hound pointed out the birds like a champion. "Look at that," Mr. Jim said. "Tail like an arrow, leg cocked just right." The quail whirred up, they fired almost simultaneously, and two went down. "Fetch," Abercrombie told his splendid new dog.

"Dog looks to have a gentle mouth, too," Jim said with some satisfaction; but when the pointer failed to come back after a minute or two, he and Naurice went over to the little clump of brush where the birds had fallen, thinking they were only wounded. Their big champion from Indiana had eaten one quail, leaving some feathers, the feet and the entrails; he was starting in on the second. Mr. Jim was never able to dissuade the dog from this disastrous habit. "That fine-looking animal was retired to stud after the best trainers couldn't do a thing with him," Naurice remembers. "Produced some of the finest pups you'd ever want to see; that blood line's still around, and the grandsons fetch quail instead of eating 'em."

[10] In the spring of 1941, Lyndon Baines Johnson was 32 years old and a two-time congressman from the Tenth District of central Texas; he became a surprise candidate for the U.S. Senate seat of Morris Sheppard, who had died April 9, 1941 after twenty-nine years in office. There were to be twenty-eight other candidates, chief among them Gerald Mann, attorney-general and "Red Arrow" of SMU football fame; Martin Dies, the crusading anti-Communist congressman; and the deliberately late filer, W. Lee O'Daniel. Largely unknown, LBJ had some powerful and marketable assets: the support of Herman and George Brown; a picture of him shaking hands with FDR at Port Aransas during a presidential vacation that included tarpon fishing; key friends over the state, some in the highest echelons of politics, publishing and business; and perhaps most important, enormous ambition.

The Browns would provide themselves, and solicit from others, very large sums of money to underwrite a new type of political campaign in Texas: repeated statewide radio broadcasts; blanket advertising in weekly and daily newspapers alike; tremendous and continuing support from the White House; a traveling vaudeville show; and a brain trust with such political stars of the future as Roy Hofheinz and John B. Connally. When crowds failed to appear at LBJ's rallies, Judge Hofheinz counseled cash lotteries, the addition of chorus girls to the vaudeville show, hundreds of billboards showing the FDR-LBJ handshake, and more sound trucks and advance men. John Connally provided organizational genius, his own expanding contacts and dependable follow-through.

From a beginning four percent in Joe Belden's then-new political poll, LBJ was leading the pack on election eve; he was five points ahead of O'Daniel, and Mann and Dies (Hofheinz called him "Old Liver Lips") had faded. I stood in the office of George Cottingham, editor of the Houston *Chronicle*, at midnight on election night, and watched Cottingham himself write the headline about LBJ's election; with ninety-six percent of the vote in, and clear trends established in late-reporting counties, Johnson was assumed to have an insurmountable lead. But LBJ and Connally still had to learn hardball politics; and they failed to realize the strength of the beer lobby in Austin, the Texas Brewers Institute.

When Connally very properly allowed vote totals to be officially announced from counties LBJ had won soon after the polls had closed, he permitted the opposition to discover exactly how much slack they would have to take up in order to win a close election. The Brewer's Institute, fearing Governor O'Daniel's increasingly Prohibitionist speeches and appointments, decided that it was vital to replace him with Lieutenant-Governor Coke Stevenson, who would automatically move up if O'Daniel became senator. There is substantial evidence that once "Pappy's" shortfall was known with some accuracy, enough "late returns" and "adjusted totals" were discovered to defeat LBJ. Some say that the word was out in some sophisticated Austin quarters as early as Sunday evening: "Pappy's" margin on Tuesday would be "somewhere safely over a thousand votes;" Coke Stevenson was the next governor and O'Daniel was enroute to Washington, D.C. The certified difference was thirteen hundred and eleven votes. LBJ and JBC had learned a bitter but invaluable lesson, and one they would remember.

[11] One of the major disappointments of Jim Abercrombie's life was an injury to Roman Patrol, the champion three-year-old that he, Josephine, his brother Bob, Herman and George Brown and Bill Smith owned. A leading candidate for the Kentucky Derby, Roman Patrol was sired by the great Nasrullah. He injured an ankle after winning the Louisiana Derby and other major tests, and had to be retired to stud. Roman Patrol was a beautiful and spirited animal of unusual promise and potential, but there were other Abercrombie-Brown-Smith horses, such as Intercepted, in the winner's circle on leading tracks.

[12] LBJ, after winning the sensational 1946 Democratic Party runoff from Coke Stevenson, still had to withstand a surprisingly strong challenge from H. J. (Jack) Porter, an independent oilman, great friend of H. R. Cullen and Republican leader, in the general election.

[13] Mr. Jim hurried out to Cameron Iron on an unusual mission late one night in 1946, when an independent union was threatening to strike at midnight unless its members received increases ranging from seventy-five cents an hour for machinists to thirty-five cents an hour for floor sweepers. Abercrombie was characteristically sympathetic to the working man; he could remember a 1917 strike in Houston to enforce a minimum wage of four dollars a day. After some protracted but peaceful discussion, Jim announced that he had come to a decision. "We'll pay the increases," he said, "but you've got things a little turned around. The floor sweepers get the six bits an hour, and the machinists the thirty-five cents. Sweepers need a raise more." There was some further brief discussion, and then Abercrombie pulled out his watch. "It's almost two in the morning," he said. "I'm going home. That's my offer, and it's final. A strike out here, I figure, might last a long time." The offer was accepted.

Epilogue

Now it was the summer of 1983.

Mr. Jim and Miss Lillie had been gone almost a decade, and 1991 would mark both the centennial of Jim's birth and the arrival of his great-great-great-grandfather Robert Abercromby, Sr. in the Piedmont of North Carolina to-be, exactly two hundred and fifty years before in 1741.

Josephine was president of Abercrombie Mineral Company, vice-chairman of the board of trustees of Rice University, and one of the eight directors of Cameron Iron. CIW's chairman and chief executive officer was among the most able and experienced men in the petroleum industry, M. A. (Mike) Wright, chairman of Exxon during one of that corporation's periods of remarkably strong and solid growth.

The other six directors were Herb Allen (chairman until his retirement from that post at Cameron, and former chairman of the governing board at Rice); Dr. Thomas D. Barrow, native Houstonian and son of an Humble Oil chairman, a brilliant geophysicist now vice-chairman of Standard of Ohio; Frank Borman, the former astronaut who heads Eastern Air Lines; Philip Burguieres, CIW's president; Charles W. Duncan, Jr., third-generation Houstonian, former head of Coca-Cola and currently president of the Warren-King Companies; and James A. Elkins, Jr., son and namesake of Mr. Jim's friend of so many years, who has brought First City Bancorporation to the top of the banking industry.

There were seventeen Cameron plants now, located at Houston, Cypress, Odessa and Sealy in Texas; Oklahoma City; Patterson, Louisiana; Compton, California; Edmonton, Canada; Livingston, Scotland; Singapore; Leeds, England; Melbourne, Australia; Celle, West Germany; Beziers, France; Mexico City; Buenos Aires; and Maracaibo, Venezuela. Results for fiscal 1982, just announced, showed Cameron Iron surpassing the $1 billion mark in sales for the first time, at $1,147,255,000; with net profits of $153,582,000. This was light years away from the beginning in 1920, when sales were $27,741.94 and profits $4,609.13—and a tribute to CIW's strength and stability in a time of severe recession within the Oil Patch.

Ralph McCullough, so close to The Boss for so many years, was retired now; and Freda Bowen, an executive secretary beginning her thirty-eighth year with the organization, was the senior employee in terms of current active service. She had retained her attractiveness, vivacity and good humor as her responsibilities steadily increased. Joe Moore, defender of Old Ocean and many another Abercrombie interest, was crusty, active and able in his eighties. The old Abercrombie Mineral offices in the Gulf Building, headquarters for predecessor companies also, had been moved in 1974 to Post Oak Road. Another move came in 1977, to 5005 Riverway, in a handsome glass building in the booming new area just off Woodway Drive and the West Loop.

Texas Children's Hospital was expected to admit more than sixty thousand patients in 1983, treating youngsters ever more skillfully and effectively under Mr. Jim's policy of admittance for all, regardless of race, color, creed or ability to pay. The Hospital remains the principal beneficiary of the Abercrombie Foundation, although the Foundation's philanthropy continues to include other worthwhile institutions and causes.

John was the lone survivor now, of Jim Abercrombie's brothers and sisters. Only Naurice Cummings and Bill Smith remained of his closest friends—of Suite 8-F and Mustang Motte and hundreds of good hunts and horse races and political campaigns and friendly arguments over a drink or a bowl of Lamar Hotel chili. Leopold Meyer and George Brown had died within months of one another in late 1982 and early 1983, and 8-F was closed along with the entire Lamar Hotel (the ghosts of the politicians of four decades slipping in and out of the storied old suite of a dark midnight). Lep's ninetieth, and final, birthday party, given by George Brown and Bill Smith, had filled 8-F with his friends on June 21, 1982.

The Pin Oak Horse Show, removed in 1974 to the Jim and Lillie Abercrombie Arena at the Astrodome, had left the honeysuckle and charm of the old site on Post Oak forever. There the distinguished Italian architect and dean of Yale's School of Architecture, Cesar Pelli, was drawing up a master plan for Pin Oak Center, a major Abercrombie development of the future. At Gonzales, the Abercrombie Ranch of controlled experiments and wondrous gadgetry was producing the best of beef for the consumer market, just as the Campbellton property, under the trade name 74 Ranch. Nor were Mr. Jim's strong interests in politics and horse racing forgotten. Josephine was a substantial supporter of selected conservative candidates, not only in Texas but in key contests over the nation. At Versailles, Kentucky, she maintained a showplace horse farm and stables. The Abercrombie silks of blue and gray had been victorious recently in France, where Grease, a filly with great speed and fine prospects, won the Prix de Mallaret, Prix Chloe and Prix de la Nonette along with victories in England and in Italy.

The grandsons Jamie and George, the eighth generation of Abercrombies in America, were preparing to take their place within the Abercrombie organization. Jamie was graduated from Rice University on May 7, 1983 after interrupting his training for experience as a jet pilot. George, having already formed his own small company, was preparing for studies in computer science and business at St. Thomas University.

As the thirtieth anniversary of Texas Children's neared, in May of 1983, I went by the hospital trying to recapture that day three decades earlier when TCH began its marvelous mission of mercy. In the lobby, I studied Mr. Jim's portrait for a minute and looked down to see a child of four or five standing beside me and also absorbed in the picture. Her mother was sitting nearby with a tiny night case, waiting to have the little girl admitted. ''Mama,'' the child said, pointing to Abercrombie's portrait, ''who's that man with the cigar? The mother studied the picture for a moment and replied, ''I don't know, baby; but he looks like a good man—a kind man.''

Index